D1614437

The Voice of Virtue

The Voice of Virtue

Moral Song and the Practice of French Stoicism, 1574–1652

MELINDA LATOUR

OXFORD
UNIVERSITY PRESS

OXFORD
UNIVERSITY PRESS

Oxford University Press is a department of the University of Oxford. It furthers
the University's objective of excellence in research, scholarship, and education
by publishing worldwide. Oxford is a registered trade mark of Oxford University
Press in the UK and certain other countries.

Published in the United States of America by Oxford University Press
198 Madison Avenue, New York, NY 10016, United States of America.

Library of Congress Control Number: 2022918950
ISBN 978–0–19–752974–4

DOI: 10.1093/oso/9780197529744.001.0001

1 3 5 7 9 8 6 4 2

Printed by Integrated Books International, United States of America

To Patrick, for everything

Contents

Contents

List of Illustrations

Plates

*All the illustrations mentioned above are available at the center of the book as vivid
color plates*

Tables

Examples

List of Web Materials

I.1.   Title page of Philippe Duplessis-Mornay, *Excellent discours de la vie et de la mort* ([Geneva]: Jean Durant, 1576). Bibliothèque de Genève. https://doi.org/10.3931/e-rara-6320

I.2.   Recording of Paschal de L'Estocart, *Pour mourir bien heureux*, by Ludus Modalis https://open.spotify.com/track/62PjlgMsFHkjxR6r8zmobD?si=65466b05922f4a9b

I.3.   Albrecht Dürer, *Saint Jerome in His Study* (1514). The Metropolitan Museum of Art, NY https://www.metmuseum.org/art/collection/search/336229

1.1.   Symphorien Champier, *Symphonia Platonis cum Aristotele: et Galeni cum Hippocrate* (Paris: Josse Bade, 1516). BnF, Gallica ark:/12148/bpt6k523307

1.2.   *King Henry IV, as Hercules, Vanquishing the Lernaean Hydra*, circle of Toussaint Dubreuil (c. 1600). The Louvre, Paris https://collections.louvre.fr/en/ark:/53355/cl010066625

2.1.   *Quatrains du sieur de Pybrac en musique*, in *Nouveau recueil et élite de plusieurs belles chansons joyeuses, honnestes, et amoureuses* (Rouen: Richard l'Allemand, 1581). D-W, 5 Musica http://diglib.hab.de/drucke/5-mus/start.htm?image=00159

2.2.   Thomas Smith, *Self-Portrait* (c. 1680). Artstor DP1694. https://library.artstor.org/#/asset/AWSS35953_35953_31187477

2.3.   *Sur le mespris de la mort par Mr Mathieu*, in Jean Rousson, *Recueil de chansons spirituelles* (La Fleche: Louis Hebert, 1621). BnF, Gallica ark:/12148/bpt6k319736s

2.4.   *De la vie, et de la mort, par Mr Mathieu*, in Jean Rousson, *Recueil de chansons spirituelles* (La Fleche: Louis Hebert, 1621). BnF, Gallica ark:/12148/bpt6k319736s

2.5.   *Portrait de Mathieu Molé, en pied, la main posée sur une table*, engraved by Michel Lasne (1590–1667). BnF, Gallica ark:/12148/btv1b8404345x

3.1.   Orlande de Lassus, *L'homme se plaint de sa trop courte vie*, in *Vingtdeuxième livre de chansons* (Paris: Le Roy and Ballard, 1583), Superius. BnF, Gallica ark:/12148/btv1b52502955r

3.2.   Jean Planson, *A bien parler*, in *Les Quatrains du Sieur de Pybrac* (Paris: Le Roy and Ballard, 1583), Superius and Tenor. BnF, Gallica ark:/12148/btv1b52502833n

4.13. Recording of Paschal de L'Estocart, *Tu me seras tesmoin*, by Chant 1450. https://open.spotify.com/track/5afYcLLmBvi5jZ1Ebhz2UG?si=f0a3f480e8ef4b87

4.14. Paschal de L'Estocart, *Mondain, si tu le sçais*, in *Premier livre des Octonaires de la vanité du monde*, ed. Henry Expert (Paris: Salabert, 1929), 7–11. Measure numbers added. IMSLP / Public domain

4.15. Recording of Paschal de L'Estocart, *Mondain, si tu le sçais*, by Ensemble Clément Janequin. https://open.spotify.com/track/5pMk9ddmHJKWLEz eR74paN?si=2a11b82265004472

5.1. Paschal de L'Estocart, *L'eau va viste*, in *Premier livre des Octonaires de la vanité du monde*, ed. Henry Expert (Paris: Salabert, 1929), 1–2. Measure numbers added. IMSLP / Public domain

5.2. Recording of Paschal de L'Estocart, *L'eau va viste*, by Ensemble Clément Janequin https://open.spotify.com/track/4h11pYpH8oa99D2BPryesg?si= df550d1bc1ad45b7

5.3. Recording of Paschal de L'Estocart, *Le beau du monde s'efface*, by Anne Quentin https://open.spotify.com/track/2vKBOyUFrOOaT9hm93l jj7?si=f8a144ae0e184e59

5.4. Paschal de L'Estocart, *Orfevre, taille moy une boule bien ronde*, in *Premier livre des Octonaires de la vanité du monde*, ed. Henry Expert (Paris: Salabert, 1929), 20–24. Measure numbers added. IMSLP / Public domain

5.5. Paschal de L'Estocart, *Peintre, si tu tires le monde*, in *Seconde livre des Octonaires de la vanité du monde*, ed. Jacques Chailley and Marc Honegger (Paris: Salabert, 1958), 82–85. https://imslp.org/wiki/File:PMLP480255-lestocart_octonaires_de_lavanite_liv2.pdf

5.6. Jean Jacques Boissard, *Il y a Vicissitude, et Variation en toutes choses*, in *Emblematum liber / Emblemes latins* (Metz: Jean Aubry and Abraham Faber, 1588), 28–29 https://www.emblems.arts.gla.ac.uk/french/emblem. php?id=FBOa010

5.7. Paschal de L'Estocart, *Le monde est un jardin*, in *Premier livre des Octonaires de la vanité du monde*, ed. Henry Expert (Paris: Salabert, 1929), 38–41. Measure numbers added. IMSLP / Public domain

5.8. Étienne Delaune, Emblem L, *Le monde est un jardin*. F-Pneph, Ed. 4.a. Rés, in-folio. Photo: author. Courtesy of the BnF

5.9. Esther Inglis, *L'eau va viste*, in *Octonaries upon the Vanity and Inconstancy of the World* (1600), 25v–26r. US-Ws, MS V.a.91 https://luna.folger.edu/ luna/servlet/detail/FOLGERCM1~6~6~243953~116271:Octonaries-upon-the-vanitie-and-inc

8.1. Marin Le Roy Gomberville, *La guerizon de l'ame est la plus necessaire*, in *Doctrine des mœurs, tirée de la philosophie des Stoiques* (Paris: Louys Sevestre for Pierre Daret, 1646). BnF, Gallica ark:/12148/btv1b85625076

8.2. Hendrick Goltzius, *Homo bulla* (Haarlem, 1594). Rijksmuseum. Public domain http://hdl.handle.net/10934/RM0001.COLLECT.367035

8.3. Paschal de L'Estocart, *J'apperceus un enfant*, in *Seconde livre des Octonaires de la vanité du monde*, ed. Jacques Chailley and Marc Honegger (Paris: Salabert, 1958), 18–23. https://imslp.org/wiki/File:PMLP480255-lestocart_octonaires_de_lavanite_liv2.pdf

8.4. Recording of Paschal de L'Estocart, *J'apperceus un enfant*, by Ensemble Clément Janequin https://open.spotify.com/track/1pUf6883WdMqflC GsheBYB?si=02e328f42aac4163

8.5. Marin Le Roy Gomberville, *Tout se pert avec le temps*, in *Doctrine des mœurs, tirée de la philosophie des Stoiques* (Paris: Louys Sevestre for Pierre Daret, 1646). BnF, Gallica ark:/12148/btv1b85625076

8.6. Paschal de L'Estocart, *Quel monstre voy-je là*, in *Premier livre des Octonaires de la vanité du monde*, ed. Henry Expert (Paris: Salabert, 1929), 76–80. Measure numbers added. IMSLP / Public domain

8.7. Recording of Paschal de L'Estocart, *Quel monstre voy-je là*, by Ensemble Clément Janequin https://open.spotify.com/track/0cliVRRSimGeAdg c7WYzox?si=f4d18d1dcec64804

8.8. Recording of Claude Le Jeune, *Quel monstre voy-je là*, by Anne Quentin https://open.spotify.com/track/5fbbkMs6DjYiLt7HecVcXU?si=45b61 d4c64824c6f

8.9. Jacques de Gheyn II, *Vanitas Still Life* (1621). Yale University Art Gallery. Public domain https://artgallery.yale.edu/collections/objects/52114

8.10. Recording of Claude Le Jeune, *Quand la Terre au Printemps*, by Ensemble Jacques Feuillie https://open.spotify.com/track/4pZcfup3sqK7wiDSMEz pDK?si=8251931cce374eb3

8.11. Recording of Claude Le Jeune, *L'eau va vite en s'écoulant*, by Ensemble Jacques Feuillie https://open.spotify.com/track/4gUSFQC96kgd83H RhQ9Zp5?si=78cf65a719fd4521

8.12. Recording of Claude Le Jeune, *Mon ame, où sont les grand discours*, by Ensemble Jacques Feuillie https://open.spotify.com/track/2qljI1r7SpE 2avo477kxzy?si=9140002d5e884fcf

8.13. Jacques de Gheyn II, *Allegory on the Equality of all Mankind in Death* (1599) https://www.britishmuseum.org/collection/object/P_1895-0915-1031

8.14. Hendrick Goltzius, *Fame and History* (1586). The Metropolitan Museum of Art, NY. Public domain https://www.metmuseum.org/art/collection/ search/343578

Preface

"Some things are within our power, while others are not. Within our power are opinion, motivation, desire, aversion, and, in a word, whatever is of our own doing; not within our power are our body, our property, reputation, office, and, in a word, whatever is not of our own doing."[2] So begins the *Handbook* of the great Roman Stoic Epictetus, a work that has exerted an enduring influence well beyond the boundaries of any formal philosophical school. Epictetus's core teachings have been so influential, in fact, that they still circulate widely, even among those who do not know anything about Stoicism. While I was in the process of drafting this manuscript in 2020, COVID-19 struck the globe, isolating individuals and families and provoking widespread uncertainty and anxiety about our collective and personal futures. What was in our control, and what was out of it? My social media accounts saw a dramatic uptick in memes, diagrams, and advice that paraphrase Epictetus's paradigm for finding tranquility in difficult times, almost always without any acknowledgment of the ancient source.

Meanwhile, Stoicism has been experiencing a powerful revival. It has gained popular appeal through blogs like the *Daily Stoic* and a wide range of books and podcasts aimed at a popular audience with accessible paraphrases and commentary on the teachings of Seneca, Marcus Aurelius, and Epictetus in particular. The focus of this revival, unsurprisingly, is on the power of Stoicism to control and regulate negative, unwanted, debilitating emotional states (such as anxiety, depression, addiction, and anger). Our modern-day

---

[1] Antoine de Chandieu, *Octonaires sur la vanité et inconstance du monde*, ed. Françoise Bonali-Fiquet (Geneva: Droz, 1979), 91.

[2] Epictetus, *Discourses, Fragments, Handbook*, trans. Robin Hard, ed. Christopher Gill (Oxford: Oxford University Press, 2014), 287.

Stoic revival is not so different from the sixteenth-century revival of Stoicism, whose adherents, as we will see, were less interested in debating the unity of the soul or converting wholesale to an ancient philosophy than in using this philosophy in strategic and sometimes partial ways to cultivate happiness, inner freedom, and peace of mind.

I began the research that inspired this book in 2013. As I wrote my dissertation on moral song collections, I highlighted the eclecticism of these settings, reading certain topics, exercises, and questions through humanist, Platonist, and Aristotelian streams, with only a brief mention of Stoicism. In the early stages of turning the dissertation into a book, I decided to add a single chapter focused on the Stoic accent of these collections to round out my philosophical approach. Diving headlong into the corpus of ancient and early modern Stoic philosophy, however, I realized that Stoicism was not merely an accent, but arguably the most important source that had guided the production and use of these collections. Not only were certain unique doctrines and teachings from Stoicism evident in these works, but the specific topics and questions from the Aristotelian and Platonic lineages that I had been recognizing in moral song texts and the attendant musical practices were precisely the parts of those traditions that had been extensively developed within Stoicism. What can legitimately be seen as an eclectic assortment of themes drawn from Heraclitus, Pythagoras, Plato, and Aristotle finds an appealing order and unity by late Roman Stoicism.

As William Bouwsma observed, Stoicism is surely one of the most important philosophical influences on the entire tradition of European thought, and yet paradoxically, it has remained the least recognized.[3] Like much of the popular Stoic therapeutic advice circulating within social media, sixteenth- and seventeenth-century humanism was influenced by a Stoicism that quickly became so pervasive as to become practically invisible, so pragmatic as to be accepted as mere common sense. Long dismissed by modern scholarship as a paltry synthesis of earlier Hellenic thought, this compatibility of Stoicism with other ancient traditions made it more attractive to early modern readers, who were typically intellectual omnivores, interested in multiple streams of ancient and contemporary philosophy. The French humanist and rhetorician Omer Talon (d. 1562) explains his own approach as a merchant perusing a marketplace of wisdom:

---

[3] William Bouwsma, *A Usable Past: Essays in European Cultural History* (Berkeley, CA: University of California Press, 1990), 21–22.

> If there is anything in the writings of Plato that suits and is useful to me, I accept it; if there is anything good in the gardens of Epicurus, I do not despise it; if Aristotle purveys something better, I accept it; if the merchandise of Zeno is more vendable than that of Aristotle, I abandon Aristotle to give myself to Zeno; if everything sold in the shops of the philosophers is vain and useless, I buy nothing at all.[4]

The ancient Stoics openly encouraged this kind of individual thinking over doctrinal purity. Chrysippus specifically acknowledged that one did not need to subscribe to the complete Stoic system to benefit from its psychological therapeutics.[5] Seneca urged his readers not to slavishly imitate any philosophical system, but to make it their own. In Letter 84, he used the analogy of a bee collecting honey from different flowers, and even more compellingly, the example of a choir where each voice retains its distinctiveness within the context of a harmonious whole.

Keeping this broader philosophical polyphony ever in mind, my own study attends most closely to the Stoic voice resounding across this era through moral poets and composers, singers and listeners. What you will read in the following pages is an account of this period that is carefully grounded in historical evidence yet far from definitive or complete. Like Plato's Timaeus, I advise the reader that what follows is only a "likely account" (*eikôs logos*) or "likely story" (*eikôs muthos*) of the Stoic voice of virtue interwoven through this richly textured and multivalent sonic landscape.

---

[4] Talon, quoted in Ramus, *Praefationes*, 96; cited in William Bouwsma, *The Waning of the Renaissance, 1550–1640* (New Haven, CT: Yale University Press, 2000), 50.
[5] Richard Sorabji, *Emotion and Peace of Mind: From Stoic Agitation to Christian Temptation* (Oxford: Oxford University Press, 2010), 2.

Acknowledgments

The research for this book was generously supported by an American Council of Learned Societies Fellowship (2019–20), a summer stipend from the National Endowment for the Humanities (2018), several Tufts Faculty Research Awards (2016–21), and additional research funds associated with the Rumsey Family Junior Professorship, graciously established by Celia and Ian Rumsey. Publication costs were defrayed by a subvention from the Kenneth Levy Fund and Martin Picker Fund of the American Musicological Society, supported in part by the National Endowment for the Humanities and the Andrew W. Mellon Foundation.

The portions of this research conducted during my three years of doctoral research in Paris (2013–16) were supported by a Bourse Jeanne Marandon from the Société des Professeurs Français et Francophones d'Amérique, a Eugene Wolf Travel Award from the American Musicological Society, and a Lynn and Maude White Fellowship in Renaissance Studies from the UCLA Center for Medieval and Renaissance Studies. An exchange fellowship from the Newberry Library allowed me the extraordinary privilege of taking courses in print culture and paleography at the renowned École nationale des chartes, and an ACLS/Mellon Dissertation Year Fellowship allowed me to spend 2015–16 in residency at the vibrant Centre d'études supérieures de la Renaissance at Tours.

This book would not have been possible without the encouragement of numerous colleagues, mentors, and friends. I received crucial feedback on the completed manuscript from Jeanice Brooks, Anthony Long, and Jean-Claude Carron as part of a book workshop funded by the Center for the Humanities at Tufts, and from the expert insights of the anonymous reviewers for the press. Among those who read earlier versions of my work and offered advice that shaped this project, I wish to thank Isabelle His, Julien Gœury, Laurent Guillo, Loris Petris, Théodora Psychoyou, Tim Carter, Jane Bernstein, Richard Freedman, Kate van Orden, and my unparalleled doctoral advisor, Olivia Bloechl. I owe Ghislain Dibie special mention for sharing drafts of his transcriptions of L'Estocart's *Quatrains* along with his many insights into the collection. I deeply appreciate the assistance and erudition of librarians around the world, particularly those at the Bibliothèque nationale de France, who have facilitated both in-person and virtual access to their collections over the course of this project.

During my research leave in California in 2019–20, I benefitted from the warm scholarly communities and resources at UC Santa Cruz and UC Berkeley. My fantastic colleagues in the Department of Music at Tufts University, my former professors and classmates at UCLA, and a host of friends both old and new have been vital sources of camaraderie and motivation, especially Andrea Moore, Catherine Deutsch, Zachary Wallmark, Nathan Myrick, Erika Honisch, Ireri Chávez-Bárcenas, Cesar Favila, Emily Pollock, and Lester Hu. Several Tufts students, Brad DeMatteo, Matt Estabrook, and Cooper Nesmith, offered helpful research assistance and transcriptions, and Aaron Kirschner engraved the final music examples. Allison van Deventer and Josh Rutner offered editorial assistance as I prepared my first full draft during the most difficult period of the pandemic, and Bonnie Blackburn's sharp eye improved the final manuscript. I am grateful to Norman Hirschy, Suzanne Ryan, Sean Decker, Hinduja Dhanasegaran, and the team at Oxford University Press for their work in bringing this book to publication. Finally, I would like to thank my entire Latour and O'Brien family for filling my life with laughter, food, and love. Most of all, I thank my husband Patrick, who has been my closest companion and deepest listener throughout this long labor of scholarly passion.

Editorial Principles

Unless otherwise indicated, all classical translations are from the Loeb Classical Library, all Neo-Latin poetic translations are by David Butterfield (Queens' College, University of Cambridge), and all translations from French sources are my own.

When quoting from primary sources, I have remained as close to the original text as possible, generally retaining the original spelling, punctuation, and diacritical marks. However, to improve the readability of these citations, I have regularized certain printing conventions—such as *u/v* and *i/j* interchangeability, the use of the long *s*, and other special characters such as the eszett—according to standard use. I have expanded the contractions signaled by macrons, tildes, and ampersands. I have accentuated the first of two "ee" in feminine adjectives/past participles, but I have not supplied accents elsewhere unless needed to clarify the meaning. Finally, I have corrected minor printing errors. Citations drawn from critical editions and other secondary sources are quoted as they appear in these published sources. Latin titles will be presented in English translation in the text; however, I retain the French titles of primary sources. Due to space constraints, I do not offer transcriptions of prose citations that have been translated in the text; however, I include them for all poetic citations.

My musical examples retain the note values of the original sources. However, I have added barlines and modernized the key signatures and cleffing. The original clefs (G2, C1, etc.) are indicated at the head of each example. On rare occasions, I have rectified obvious pitch or rhythmic errors.

A select bibliography of printed primary sources concludes the book. All secondary sources are cited in full at first mention and fully indexed. Lastly, I have included dates for all pre-modern figures in the index.

Abbreviations

BHR	*Bibliothèque d'Humanisme et Renaissance*
BnF	Bibliothèque nationale de France, Paris
B-Br	Bibliothèque royale de Belgique (KBR), Bruxelles
FB	*French Vernacular Books: Books Published in the French Language before 1601*. Edited by Andrew Pettegree, Malcolm Walsby, and Alexander Wilkinson. Leiden: Brill, 2007
F-Pneph	Bibliothèque nationale de France, Département des Estampes et de la photographie, Paris
F-Psg	Bibliothèque Sainte-Geneviève, Paris
GLN	GLN 15-16. Bibliography of 15th- and 16th-century prints from Geneva, Lausanne, and Neuchâtel. http://www.ville-ge.ch/musinfo/bd/bge/gln/index.php
Guillo–B	Laurent Guillo, *Pierre I Ballard et Robert III Ballard. Imprimeurs du roy pour la musique, 1599–1673*, 2 vols. Sprimont: Mardaga, 2003
Guillo–L	Laurent Guillo, *Les Éditions musicales de la renaissance*. Paris: Klincksieck, 1991
D-W	Herzog August Bibliothek, Wolfenbüttel
IMSLP	International Music Score Library Project. https://imslp.org/wiki/Main_Page
JAMS	*Journal of the American Musicological Society*
Lesure	François Lesure and Geneviève Thibault, *Bibliographie des éditions d'Adrian Le Roy et Robert Ballard, 1551–1598*. Paris: Heugel, 1955
RISM	Répertoire international des sources musicales https://rism.info/index.html
Sylvester, *Works*	Josuah Sylvester, *Du Bartas, His Divine Weekes and Workes, with a Complete Collection of all the other Most Delightfull Workes*. London: Humphray Lownes, 1621
USTC	Universal Short Title Catalogue. https://www.ustc.ac.uk
US-Ws	Folger Shakespeare Library, Washington, DC

About the Companion Website

www.oup.com/us/thevoiceofvirtue

Oxford has created a Web site to accompany *The Voice of Virtue*. Material that cannot be made available in a book is provided here. We encourage you to consult this resource in conjunction with the chapters. Examples available online are indicated in the text as Web 1.1, Web 1.2, ... and so on.

Introduction

Singing Stoicism

Musicians were the cheefest professours of philosophie.[1]

"Paschal, your pleasant sounds bring the World back to life, in these rich tombs now buried."[2] This laudatory verse for Paschal de L'Estocart's polyphonic settings of the *Quatrains de Pibrac* (1582) proposes the collection as a means of regeneration for a world in decay. Likewise, a poem praising L'Estocart's first collection of *Octonaires de la vanité du monde* (1582) recommends his music as a tonic for the "funereal grief" overwhelming the land, celebrating the power of these settings to "bind the senses with a new art, so that they can dispel the dark clouds of sadness, and bring the light of humor," and closing with the potent query, "Is this not a fitting cure for its diseases?"[3]

Composed after decades of bloody religious war, L'Estocart's music prints emphasize the therapeutic power of song to address the mounting moral crisis. A verse prefacing the contratenor part for L'Estocart's *Quatrains* of 1582 decries the widespread death of virtue:

> En ce papier je voy la vertu painte.
>
> Morte vertu! Le temps te veut ainsi.

---

[1] *The Praise of Musick, 1586: An Edition with Commentary*, ed. Hyun-Ah Kim (London: Routledge, 2018), 111.

[2] "Paschal, tes plaisans sons resuscitent le Monde / En ces riches tombeaux maintenant enterré." Although prefacing the tenor part of L'Estocart's *Premier livre des Octonaires de la vanité du monde* (Lyon: Barthélemy Vincent [Geneva: Jean I de Laon], 1582), the third and fourth lines make it clear that the poem was praising L'Estocart's *Cent vingt et six quatrains du Sieur de Pibrac* (Lyon: Barthélemy Vincent [Geneva: Jean I de Laon], 1582).

[3] "Cùm sint funereo dolore mersa, / Dudum tempora nostra, . . . arte noua ligantque sensus, / Atras tristitiae ut fugare possint / Nubes, atque ioci referre lucem. / Non haec apta suis medela morbis?" L'Estocart, *Premier livre des Octonaires*, bassus only.

The Voice of Virtue. Melinda Latour, Oxford University Press. © Oxford University Press 2023.
DOI: 10.1093/oso/9780197529744.003.0001

> Mais si les cœurs n'ont plus de toy souci
> En vers et sons demeure au moins emprainte.

[On this paper, I see virtue painted. / Virtue dead! The times wish you so. /
But even if hearts are no longer concerned with you, / in verse and sound at
least remain imprinted.]

This laudatory verse may have been devised by Jean I de Laon, the Genevan
printer of wisdom literature who did the presswork for L'Estocart's beautiful moral song collections.[4] The writer wittily praises the significance of the
book arts by invoking a double process of music printing—the physical production of the book copy and a mental impression upon the minds of the
singers and hearers of these settings.

It was Zeno, the founder of Stoicism, who apparently invented this
striking metaphor, describing a process of mental imprinting as the kind
of impression left by a signet ring in wax.[5] Sixteenth-century readers
were familiar with the Stoic roots of this analogy, for Zeno was frequently cited in emblems and other popular moral prints, marketed to
an audience of virtue-lovers. Thus, L'Estocart's laudatory quatrain offers
the perfect introduction to this book, which will take as its core themes
the production and use of polyphonic moral song collections and the
sympathetic union of Stoic philosophy and music as a remedy for public
discord.

What Is Moral Song?

Although the practice of setting moral texts to music has a longer history
and broader geographical scope, this study centers on three popular sets of
moral poetry and their numerous musical settings: Guy du Faur de Pibrac's
Quatrains (1574); the *Octonaires de la vanité du monde* (c. 1574) by Antoine

---

[4] For this attribution, see Eugénie Droz, "Jean de Sponde et Pascal de L'Estocart," *BHR* 13, no. 3
(1951): 317. There were two Genevan printers known by this name: the elder Jean I and his nephew
Jean II. Although the presswork for L'Estocart's prints has long been attributed to Jean II, recent
scholarship concludes that they were the work of the master printer Jean I, who remained active
until 1599. See Christophe Chazalon, "Théodore de Bèze et les ateliers de Laon," in *Théodore de Bèze
(1519–1605)*, ed. Irena Backus (Geneva: Droz, 2007), 69–87.
[5] Margaret Graver, *Stoicism and Emotion* (Chicago, IL: University of Chicago Press, 2009), 24–25;
and Håvard Løkke, *Knowledge and Virtue in Early Stoicism* (Dordrecht: Springer, 2015), 15.

de Chandieu, Simon Goulart, and Joseph Du Chesne; and Pierre Mathieu's *Tablettes ou Quatrains de la vie et de la mort* (1610).[6] Texts from these moral collections inspired polyphonic settings by the most important composers of the day, such as Orlande de Lassus, Paschal de L'Estocart, Guillaume Boni, Claude Le Jeune, and Artus Aux-Cousteaux. This printed corpus of moral song defines the period of this study—from the first printing of Pibrac's *Quatrains* (1574) to the printing of Aux-Cousteaux's final musical edition of Mathieu's *Tablettes* (1652).

The dramatic success of vernacular moral song across the fragmented religious landscape was driven by the capacity of these prints to offer practical tools for repair and renewal in the aftermath of violent and prolonged unrest—a point emphasized throughout the prefaces and contents of these collections. Poets, composers, and singers explored the artistic possibilities of these ethical and reparative aims, as they cultivated a vibrant communal therapeutic practice formed not upon religious belief, but through a shared search for wisdom. In her magisterial work on French religious music, Denise Launay noted this nonpartisan use of moral song collections in a brief paragraph that served as the first inspiration for this study:

> It is in this same spirit of tolerance, or neutrality, that short poems of a moralizing nature were conceived and realized, collections that were often set to music and which became very fashionable at the end of the sixteenth century until the middle of the seventeenth century. I mean the *Quatrains moraux*, the *Octonaires de la vanité du monde*, the *Tablettes de la vie et de la mort*, and other versified adages, imprinted at the same time with a Christian morality and pagan wisdom.[7]

As Launay recognized, these moral texts offered ethical teachings of ancient philosophy that were compatible with Christian morality. Grouping them under the umbrella of religious music, she crucially notes that the contents of these moral collections do not fit neatly into the sacred category. Moral

---

[6] The critical editions consulted for this study are Antoine de Chandieu, *Octonaires sur la vanité et inconstance du monde*, ed. Françoise Bonali-Fiquet (Geneva: Droz, 1979); Joseph Du Chesne, *La Morocosmie ou De la folie, vanité, et inconstance du Monde, avec deux chants Doriques, De l'Amour céleste et du Souverain bien (1583)*, ed. Lucile Gibert (Geneva: Droz, 2009); Guy du Faur de Pibrac, *Les Quatrains; Les Plaisirs de la vie rustique et autres poésies*, ed. Loris Petris (Geneva: Droz, 2004); Pierre Mathieu, *Tablettes de la vie et de la mort*, ed. C. N. Smith (Exeter: University of Exeter, 1981); and *Quatrains moraux: XVIᵉ et XVIIᵉ siècles*, ed. Éric Tourrette (Grenoble: J. Millon, 2008).

[7] Denise Launay, *La Musique religieuse en France du Concile de Trente à 1804* (Paris: Société Française de Musicologie, 1993), 103.

collections certainly did not fit any better within the corpus of the secular *chanson*, whose diverse topics of love and longing offered popular (and sometimes bawdy) entertainment. Musical settings of moral poetry, clearly aimed at edification, were more serious and purposeful in their tone, and they were consistently approved of and promoted by religious leadership across the conflicted confessions, even when these groups disagreed vehemently on other musical questions. This generic discomfort that troubles the boundary of the religious and secular corpuses is precisely what allowed moral poetry and its musical settings to flourish across the confessional divide at a time of overwhelming uncertainty and religious conflict.

Scholars have long noted the odd presence of moral or moralizing texts in the late sixteenth-century vernacular music repertoire.[8] Protestant *chanson spirituelle* prints often contained a moral song or two, in collections mostly populated with devotional or theological texts. The discussion of these settings, however, has remained at the margins, even though the presence of moral song became more overt in the late sixteenth century with the publication of large-scale polyphonic collections of moral poetry.[9]

Scholars of French literature, by contrast, have devoted significant attention to moral poetry as a literary category that gained prominence in the second half of the sixteenth century.[10] Building upon a tradition of writing, collecting, and memorizing snippets of moral poetry that goes back to antiquity, the genre of moral poetry and its musical settings began to take discernible shape as a printed genre in the mid-sixteenth century. In terms of format, vernacular French moral poetry developed in the sixteenth century as a *forme brève*—poetry composed of short stanzas (typically *quatrains*, *sixaines*, or *huitains*) that have an independent meaning and unite loosely across a

---

[8] See Édith Weber, *La Musique protestante de langue française* (Paris: Champion, 1979), 15; Howard Mayer Brown, "The 'Chanson Spirituelle,' Jacques Buus, and Parody Technique," *JAMS* 15, no. 2 (1962): 145–73; Anne Ullberg, *Au chemin de salvation: La chanson spirituelle réformée (1533–1678)* (Uppsala: Uppsala University, 2005), 285–88; and Frank Dobbins, *Music in Renaissance Lyons* (Oxford: Clarendon Press, 1992), 264.

[9] For foundational work on isolated collections, see Marie-Alexis Colin, "Les *Quatrains* de Guy du Faur de Pibrac en musique," in *L'Humanisme à Toulouse (1480–1596)*, ed. Nathalie Dauvois (Paris: H. Champion, 2006), 535–54; Kate van Orden, *Materialities: Books, Readers, and the Chanson in Sixteenth-Century Europe* (New York: Oxford University Press, 2015), 228–65; Annie Cœurdevey, *Roland de Lassus* (Paris: Fayard, 2003), 310–13; Jane Bernstein, "Lassus in English Sources: Two Chansons Recovered," *JAMS* (1974): 315–25; and Isabelle His, *Claude Le Jeune (v. 1530–1600): Un compositeur entre renaissance et baroque* (Arles: Actes sud, 2000), 95–99.

[10] For an introduction to this corpus, see Jean Vignes, "Pour une gnomologie: Enquête sur le succès de la littérature gnomique à la Renaissance," *Seizième Siècle* 1 (2005): 175–211; and Jean Lafond, "Des formes brèves de la littérature morale aux XVIe et XVIIe s.," in *Les Formes brèves de la prose et le discours discontinu: XVIe–XVIIe siècles*, ed. Jean Lafond (Paris: Vrin, 1984), 101–22.

collection through their shared themes, tone, and/or ethical contents. Even with this basic definition in hand, the detailed work of circumscribing the moral repertoire proves challenging, as Jean Vignes has noted, especially if one attempts to trace the outer limits of the genre. For just as the boundaries of moral philosophy in this period blur into the domains of theology, natural law, metaphysics, and politics, so too do the poetic, visual, and musical expressions of moral philosophy frequently overlap with devotional and religious interests.[11]

This porousness of the boundaries of the moral genre, however, did not discourage Guillaume Colletet, a French poet and founding member of the Académie française in 1634, from writing the first treatise and catalogue dedicated to the genre of moral poetry. His *Traité de la poésie morale, et sententieuse* (1658) offers the first attempt to document the flourishing sixteenth-century interest in moral poetry, which he catalogues according to specific criteria and justifies by commentary. According to Colletet, moral poetry is a genre "that hates nothing as much as the ineptitudes and the vanities of the world, [and] is that which treats morals, which gives good precepts for living well and is truly the veritable science of man."[12] Colletet emphasizes a crucial distinction between the categories of moral poetry (*poésie morale*), natural poetry (*poésie naturelle*), and sacred poetry (*poésie divine*), making it clear in both his treatise and accompanying catalogue that moral poetry should be considered distinct from sacred or devotional poetry, which does not give moral precepts but rather "sings the praises of the Gods, treats different modes of worship, sacrifices, and the mysteries of Religion."[13] An essential feature of moral poetry, in Colletet's view, is the expression of ethical precepts in a neutral philosophical tone, thus avoiding the polemical or zealous tone inflecting religious texts of the period. By contrast, moral poetry gently inspires readers to rise above human nature, tame their passions, and learn to govern themselves.

Colletet's treatise and catalogue define the moral genre as including texts centered on the vanities of the world; morals and conduct; principles for living well; and the science of human nature and behavior. Current scholarship on Renaissance moral philosophy upholds Colletet's early definition, fleshing out his basic categories in more detail. According to David Lines, the

---

[11] Vignes, "Pour une gnomologie," 177.
[12] Guillaume Colletet, *Traité de la poésie morale et sententieuse* (Paris: Sommaville et Chamhoudry, 1658), 44–45.
[13] Ibid., 27.

primary topics of moral philosophy developed in the Renaissance were the role of the will and intellect in virtue cultivation; the nature of happiness; the virtues; the practice of moral education; definitions of justice; debates about the nature and composition of the soul; and the relationship of the passions to a virtuous life.[14]

Based on this literary and philosophical foundation, I consider moral song to be a category of vocal music that includes the full range of topics and questions recognized under the banner of moral philosophy, or ethics. Whereas "moralizing" suggests a narrower interest in prescribing codes of conduct based on an established ethical framework, we can see from the definitions above that an engagement with moral philosophy or ethics as a system includes a deliberately open-ended process of inquiry that attends to the larger structural questions and overarching value system that ultimately shape these moral guidelines. This more dynamic mode of philosophical engagement calls attention to the enduring controversies over what elements and streams of the pagan classical heritage could be suitably borrowed, modified, or cited for Christian use, for the boundary between licit and illicit ethical positions remained constantly in flux and needed to be shored up through regular cultural construction and maintenance. Tracing the rise of interest in moral song in early modern France thus recognizes musical performance as a surprisingly effective philosophical participant in this long and nuanced process of forging a culturally and religiously recognizable moral practice.

What this study offers, therefore, is a fresh understanding of early modern song as a source for the cultural history of philosophy. David Lines has emphasized the value of such a cultural approach to Renaissance ethics, arguing that it was primarily in the informal realm that philosophical work was accomplished.[15] Whereas medieval ethics mainly developed through highly specialized work (such as treatises and commentaries), the period from around 1400 to 1600 saw an explosion of informal interest in moral philosophy created by and for non-specialists via a broader range of formats— from emblem books to poetry. These informal, mostly vernacular, materials circulated alongside an increased production of formal and academic philosophical work both in Latin and in vernacular languages. Pitched at a musical level perfect for learned amateur recreation, moral song gave voice to these

---

[14] David Lines, Introduction to *Rethinking Virtue, Reforming Society: New Directions in Renaissance Ethics, c.1350–c.1650*, ed. David Lines and Sabrina Ebbersmeyer (Turnhout: Brepols, 2013), 13–14.
[15] Ibid., 19.

interests and encouraged a broad community of performers to contemplate ethical questions through a dynamic process of part-singing. This attention to the philosophical work of moral song, in turn, unlocks new dimensions for understanding the ethical initiatives embedded in early music composition and practice. My study thus follows a rich musicological tradition—modeled elegantly in the work of Martha Feldman, Jeanice Brooks, and Kate van Orden—that illuminates the composition of a musical corpus through attention to its critical and intellectual contexts of use.

Singing Stoicism

Considering that Stoicism was the ancient philosophy most dramatically on the rise in the late sixteenth century, it should not be a surprise to find a sustained interest in Neostoic philosophical remedies across the moral song collections produced between 1574 to 1652. Historians of philosophy generally mark the beginning of Neostoicism with the publication of Justus Lipsius's *On Constancy* (1584) and Guillaume Du Vair's *Philosophie morale des Stoiques* (1585), and the traditional disciplinary preference for "great man" authors of formal treatises has caused these two figures to become the only two widely recognized Neostoics.[16] This narrow focus has long obscured the incredible cultural power of the Stoic revival, which had been gaining ground since the mid-fifteenth century through a mounting wave of printed editions of the Roman Stoics: Seneca, Epictetus, and the emperor Marcus Aurelius. Reliable information about the earlier Greek Stoics (Zeno, Cleanthes, Chrysippus, Posidonius) was also increasingly available in the sixteenth century through abundant editions of the writings of Cicero, Diogenes Laertius, Plutarch, and Galen, whose accounts of Stoic philosophy gave early moderns a broad view of the diversity of thought within the Stoic tradition. These sources inspired direct and, in some cases, systematic engagement with Stoic thought by a stunning array of sixteenth- and seventeenth-century intellectuals across early modern Europe. Spanning the major currents of intellectual activity, Stoicism offered a philosophical thread that could be traced through the

---

[16] Justus Lipsius, *De constantia libri duo, qui alloquium praecipue continent in publicis malis* (Leiden: Christophe Plantin, 1584); Guillaume Du Vair, *La Philosophie morale des Stoiques* (Paris: [Abel l'Angelier], 1585).

Protestant and Catholic reforms of education and worship—all the way to the development of the new science.[17]

The composer Paschal de L'Estocart presents a fascinating—and until now completely unrecognized—model of musical engagement with this building wave of Neostoicism. Although overshadowed musically in his own time by his more successful contemporaries Orlande de Lassus and Claude Le Jeune, L'Estocart displayed the most overt interest in producing musical settings of Neostoic moral poetry, offering two polyphonic collections of settings of *Octonaires* by Antoine de Chandieu, Simon Goulart, and Joseph Du Chesne, as well as a full set of polyphonic arrangements of Pibrac's *Quatrains* in 1582. Furthermore, L'Estocart's *Sacred Songs* (1582) reveals that his taste for setting Stoic thought went beyond his *Octonaires* and *Quatrains* collections.[18] In fact, this *mélange* of vernacular and Latin texts includes a fascinating pair of polyphonic settings inspired by Seneca's famous observation in his essay *On the Brevity of Life*: "It takes the whole of life to learn how to live, and—what will perhaps make you wonder more—it takes the whole of life to learn how to die."[19]

The Latin version, arranged by L'Estocart for six voices, reads:

Ut tibi mors foelix contingat, vivere disce.
Ut foelix possis vivere, disce mori.

The French version, set by L'Estocart for five voices, reads:

Pour mourir bien heureux, à vivre faut aprendre.
Pour vivre bien heureux, à mourir faut entendre."

[To die happily, learn to live. To live happily, one must learn to die.]

---

[17] See John Sellars, *Stoicism* (Berkeley, CA: University of California Press, 2006), 4–30 and 135–50; John Sellars, ed., *The Routledge Handbook of the Stoic Tradition* (London: Routledge, 2016); Pierre-François Moreau, ed., *Le Stoïcisme au XVIᵉ et au XVIIᵉ siècle: Le retour des philosophies antiques à l'âge classique* (Paris: Albin Michel, 1999); Margaret J. Osler, ed., *Atoms, Pneuma, and Tranquillity: Epicurean and Stoic Themes in European Thought* (Cambridge: Cambridge University Press, 2005); and Jacqueline Lagrée, *Le Néostoïcism: Une philosophie par gros temps* (Paris: Vrin, 2010), 16–21.

[18] Paschal de L'Estocart, *Sacrae cantiones, quatuor, quinque, sex et septem vocum* (Lyon: Barthélemy Vincent, [Geneva: Jean I de Laon], 1582).

[19] Seneca, *De brevitate vitae* 7; Seneca, *Dialogues and Essays*, trans. John Davie (Oxford: Oxford University Press, 2007), 146.

Seneca's paradoxical advice—that to learn the art of living, one must learn the art of dying—became the heart of Neostoicism, appearing in condensed and creative forms across the printed and manuscript wisdom genres (from emblems to friendship albums), and reverberating through polyphonic song. Although the Latin text for *Ut tibi mors foelix* can be found in printed *florilegia* of moral sayings,[20] L'Estocart probably took the French text for *Pour mourir bien heureux* from the *Excellent discours de la vie et de la mort* (1576) by the Protestant diplomat, pastor, and scholar Philippe de Mornay, lord of Plessy-Marly (1549–1623)—better known as Duplessis-Mornay—where this exact French rendition of the maxim is featured on the title page.[21] [Web I.1] Duplessis-Mornay's *Excellent discours* was a landmark work of Neostoicism that was published simultaneously in Geneva and Paris, as well as in English translation. In the ensuing decades, the work circulated through numerous editions and translations and remained an influential source of Senecan thought throughout the period of this study.

The *Excellent discours* opens with an original treatise summarizing Stoic teachings on death. In typical Neostoic fashion, Duplessis-Mornay remarks upon the general compatibility of Stoicism with Christianity, while also noting specific points of divergence. Guided by his dual role as pastor and scholar, Duplessis-Mornay reminds his Christian readers of the hope of everlasting life—not present in Stoicism—and recommends a balance between the Stoic emphasis on self-reliance and fortitude and a humble dependence on the power of God for achieving the Stoic aims of constancy, endurance, and wisdom. The second half of the print offers a large selection of translations of Seneca's moral writings on death and dying, systematically working its way through the epistles, consolations, and essays—including, of course, a translation of the famous passage cited above on learning to die. Duplessis-Mornay concludes his treatise with a condensed restatement of the paradoxical advice that was his guiding light for the entire work: "Mourir pour vivre, et vivre pour mourir." Die in order to live; and live in order to die.[22]

L'Estocart's musical arrangements of Seneca's maxim reflect the broader humanist interests of the period. His compositional approach developed as an extension of the polyphonic madrigal and chanson writing that was

[20] Celio Calcagnini, *Caelii Calcagnini ferrariensis, protonotarii apostolici, opera aliquot* (Basel: [Frobenius], 1544), 647.
[21] Philippe Duplessis-Mornay, *Excellent discours de la vie et de la mort* ([Geneva]: Jean Durant, 1576).
[22] Ibid., 70.

popularized earlier in the sixteenth century by composers such as Jacques Arcadelt, Cipriano de Rore, Clément Janequin, and Orlande de Lassus. These vernacular genres were known for their expressive text setting, featuring frequent text painting (in which specific words, actions, or concepts were musically illustrated through sound and sometimes visual correspondence) and justifying an increased use of dissonance and chromaticism in the service of the text. L'Estocart's five-voice arrangement of the French version of the text—*Pour mourir bien heureux*—accents the uncomfortable theme of death in the opening phrase through pointed chromaticism in the upper voices before deliberately moving to the sweeter flat realm for the admonition "learn to live." [Web I.2][23] After the charming shift to a rhythmically lively homophony on the phrase "to live well," there is a return to slow, imitative polyphony for the remainder of the setting, with the final phrase—"it is necessary to learn to die"—repeated again and again in long, overlapping lines. Learning to die takes not a day, but a lifetime, as L'Estocart's compelling setting sonically reminds the singers and listeners.

Christian Stoics

Perfectly suited for a Christian audience long directed to contemplate death, L'Estocart's polyphonic arrangements of Seneca's maxim were included in his collection of *Sacred Songs* with no citation of their Stoic inspiration. Even Cœurdevey and Besson's recent critical edition of the collection makes no mention of the Stoic roots of these texts, despite the fact that Seneca's *On the Brevity of Life* was one of the most circulated texts in L'Estocart's time, and this particular lesson on learning to die was one of Seneca's most frequently cited maxims. This example underscores the challenge of circumscribing moral song as a genre, as well as moral song's critical importance for understanding the influence of specific streams of ancient thought on Christian practices.

The theme of the contemplation of death, inconstancy, and vanity was widespread across the ancient world. Indeed, the Stoics frequently acknowledged their debts to the pre-Socratics (Pythagoras, Heraclitus) and Plato as the originators of their most foundational doctrines. The Stoic tradition,

---

[23] Paschal de L'Estocart, *Sacrae cantiones* (1582), ed. Annie Cœurdevey and Vincent Besson (Turnhout: Brepols, 2004), 100.

however, brought these themes together in a particularly influential way that synthesized and ultimately transformed these earlier ideas into their own distinct philosophical system and therapeutic practice. Seneca notes this in his Letter 58, questioning how reading the Platonic "technicality" or "idea" of inconstancy does anything to help us understand how to live well. It was the Stoics, he subtly reminds us, who transformed these abstract pre-Socratic and Platonic topics into a full-fledged program aimed at helping us live well. Early moderns like Duplessis-Mornay likewise recognized this practical benefit of Stoicism. *Excellent discours* explains that Stoic philosophy offers useful therapeutic tools even for devout Christians, for despite their theological confidence in their eternal destiny, they still struggle to overcome fear in this life:

> We are Christians, we say to ourselves. We believe in eternal life after this mortal one. We believe that death is only a separation of the body from the soul, that the soul returns to its blessed rest, [etc.]. . . . We fill all our books with these beautiful statements, and yet when we come to the point, the solitary name of death, as the most horrible thing in the world, we tremble and shiver.[24]

Duplessis-Mornay's translation of Seneca's 30th letter goes on to give these Christians astonishing advice: "Would you like to never again fear death? Then think about it always." Seneca's 26th letter offers them an even more radical proposal, claiming that "the one who exhorts us to meditate on death, exhorts us to meditate on freedom. Whoever has learned how to die, has unlearned how to be a slave."

The pursuit of human freedom thus emerges as the driving logic behind the Stoics' and Neostoics' strategy of detachment from "externals" like health, wealth, and reputation, and it motivated their pervasive focus on mortality. They held, counterintuitively, that happiness and freedom could only be obtained by giving up the relentless pursuit of worldly pleasures, desires, and sources of security. It was this therapeutic efficacy of Stoicism that attracted sustained Christian interest, and that continued to reinvigorate an interest in reading ancient Stoic writings and borrowing their exercises for use in tandem with devotional practices.

[24] Duplessis-Mornay, *Excellent discours*, 61.

In contrast to Stoic physics, which was problematic for its materialism and its nuanced theology that fell somewhere between theism and pantheism, Stoic moral philosophy was extremely compatible with Christianity and for the most part could be borrowed and translated directly for Christian use with little to no revision. This was in part because Stoicism was the dominant philosophy in the Roman empire at the time of the New Testament, and it exerted a clear influence on the development of early Christian ethics.[25] It thus comes as no surprise that Stoicism was never entirely forgotten in the Christian tradition, with its long practice of selectively borrowing from ancient philosophy to invigorate religious thought. In his revised address to the reader of *On Constancy*, Lipsius acknowledged this appropriating impulse: "I know that the counsel of St. Augustine is that it is necessary to gather what the Philosophers have written, *and having taken it away from these unjust possessors, appropriate it to our usage.*"[26] In the case of Stoicism, this strategy went beyond appropriation from "unjust possessors" and took the even more potent form of bringing high-profile moral teachers such as Seneca into the Christian fold.[27]

Despite these borrowings—or perhaps because of them—Stoicism remained a thorny pagan presence in the Christian tradition. In Denise Carabin's words, "Stoicism worried and reassured religion."[28] Lipsius's revised address to the readers of *On Constancy* defends his work against his religious critics: "If I intended to do Theology, I failed: and if it is Philosophy, why are they blaming me? . . . I will do Philosophy, but Christian."[29] Unlike Plato, who remained a citational authority long after his views had been largely displaced, Stoicism was used and borrowed far more consistently than it was ever acknowledged or cited, even at the pinnacle of its early modern revival. This broader ambivalence toward Stoicism—which attracted open hostility in theory, yet pervasive approval in practice—became the most common mode of engagement with the sect across the Christian confessions

---

[25] See Runar Thorsteinsson, *Roman Christianity and Roman Stoicism: A Comparative Study of Ancient Morality* (Oxford: Oxford University Press, 2013); and Tuomas Rasimus et al., eds., *Stoicism in Early Christianity* (Grand Rapids, MI: Baker Academic, 2010).

[26] Emphasis in the original. Justus Lipsius, *Deux livres de la constance de Just. Lipsius: Esquels en forme de devis familier est discouru des afflictions, et principalement des publiques, et comme il se faut resoudre à les supporter* (Tours: Jamet Mettayer, 1592), unpaginated preface.

[27] Chiara Torre, "Seneca and the Christian Tradition," and Roland Mayer, "Seneca *Redivivus*: Seneca in the Medieval and Renaissance World," in *The Cambridge Companion to Seneca*, ed. Shadi Bartsch and Alessandro Schiesaro (Cambridge: Cambridge University Press, 2015), 266–88.

[28] Denise Carabin, *Les Idées stoïciennes dans la littérature morale des 16e et 17e siècles (1575–1642)* (Paris: Champion, 2004), 47.

[29] Lipsius, *Deux livres de la constance*, fols. iiir–ivr.

in the early modern period. Jean Calvin launched his intellectual career by publishing a commentary on Seneca's *On Mercy* (1532), defending him in the preface with the claim that, in ethics, "he reigns supreme." Calvin went on to boast that "our Seneca was second only to Cicero, a veritable pillar of Roman philosophy."[30] Yet on other occasions Calvin went to great lengths to distance himself from Stoicism. Scholars suggest that he may have coined the term "Neostoic" in a polemical passage within his *Institutes of the Christian Religion* (1536), attacking these "new Stoics" (*novi Stoici*) for their ideal of eliminating the passions (*apatheia*), rather than valiantly accepting suffering as ordained by God.[31] Calvin's attack on Stoicism ultimately concerned semantics, not substantive difference, suggesting that his anti-Stoic posturing was crucial precisely because his teachings proved difficult to distinguish from theirs. Calvin's colleagues and opponents certainly saw it this way, for they repeatedly warned him that his own doctrine of predestination seemed dangerously like Stoic fatalism. Fellow reformer Philip Melanchthon even called Calvin "Zeno" in a letter expressing frustration with his colleague's dogmatic stance on predestination that embroiled Geneva in controversy in the early 1550s.[32]

The Christian investment in the *memento mori* tradition—which came down into the Renaissance alongside the *contemptus mundi* and *ars moriendi* traditions—testifies to the intimacy of Stoic and Christian therapeutics. St. Jerome became a figurehead for this Stoicized Christianity.[33] The custom of depicting him with a skull, which began around 1500, reflected his explicit promotion of the Stoic methods for Christian contemplative practice that were recommended by influencers like Erasmus and captured by the brush of Albrecht Dürer. In Dürer's *Saint Jerome in His Study* (1514), the Stoic

---

[30] John Calvin, *Calvin's Commentary on Seneca's De Clementia*, ed. Ford Lewis Battles and André Malan Hugo (Leiden: Brill, 1969), 9.

[31] Calvin, *Institutes* 3.8.9. See Justus Lipsius, *On Constancy*, trans. John Stradling, ed. John Sellars (Exeter: Bristol Phoenix Press, 2009), 2n10.

[32] Referencing Calvin's infamous imprisonment of Jerome Bolsec for challenging his views on predestination the year before, Melanchthon lamented in correspondence from 1552: "But see the madness of this age! The Genevan battles over Stoic necessity are such that a certain person who disagreed with Zeno was thrown into prison." Cited in Barbara Pitkin, "The Protestant Zeno: Calvin and the Development of Melanchthon's Anthropology," *The Journal of Religion* 84, no. 3 (2004): 346. See also Pierre-François Moreau, "Calvin: Fascination et critique du stoïcisme," in *Le Stoïcisme au XVIᵉ et au XVIIe siècle*, ed. Moreau, 51–64; Barbara Pitkin, "Erasmus, Calvin, and the Two Faces of Stoicism," in *The Routledge Handbook of the Stoic Tradition*, ed. Sellars, 153; and Elizabeth Agnew Cochran, *Protestant Virtue and Stoic Ethics* (London: Bloomsbury, 2018), 25–26.

[33] Marcia Colish, *The Stoic Tradition from Antiquity to the Early Middle Ages* (Leiden: Brill, 1985), 2:70–91; and Leopoldine Prosperetti, *Landscape and Philosophy in the Art of Jan Brueghel the Elder (1568–1625)* (Aldershot: Ashgate, 2009), 39–40.

symbols of the skull, the candle, and the hourglass anchor the painting. As Jerome turns his head toward the skull, meditating on death, he sees the crucifix mounted on his desk in his direct line of sight. It is through Christ, and a remembrance of not only death but also the hope of eternal life, that this meditation can ultimately be accomplished [Web I.3]. Neostoic publications frequently cite St. Jerome in support of the suitability of Stoicism for Christian use, as we see in Thomas James's dedicatory epistle to his 1598 English translation of Du Vair's *Philosophie morale des Stoiques*:

> Let it not seeme strange unto us that Philosophie should be a meanes to help Divinitie, or that Christians may profit by the Stoicks. . . Philosophie in generall is profitable unto a Christian man, if it be well and rightly used: but no kinde of philosophie is more profitable and neerer approching unto Christianitie (as S. Hierome saith) than the philosophie of the Stoicks. Let us then that are Christians follow them as farre foorth as they have followed the trueth.[34]

This was well-established advice in the age of Lipsius, encouraging a surprisingly rich yet critical approach to Stoic philosophy and practice.

Cultural Neostoicism

With this complex relationship of Stoicism with both Christianity and other philosophical schools always in mind, I will use "Neostoic" and "Neostoicism" throughout this book in the broadest cultural sense of the terms—following John Sellars in applying these terms to any early modern author "whose works display the influence of Stoic ideas."[35] When used in this cultural sense, it should be clear that these terms do not demand philosophical purity, a systematic approach to philosophy, or a personal conversion to the sect. As Jacqueline Lagrée clarifies, Neostoicism never became a formal school, and is best understood as a "stream of thought" that infused certain Stoic concepts—like the notion of providence, an interest in constancy, and ethical directives to follow nature—into radically new contexts.[36]

---

[34] Guillaume Du Vair, *The Moral Philosophie of the Stoicks*, ed. Rudolf Kirk (New Brunswick, NJ: Rutgers University Press, 1951), 45.
[35] Lipsius, *On Constancy*, ed. Sellars, 9; Carabin, *Les Idées stoïciennes*, 28–30.
[36] Lagrée, *Le Néostoïcism*, 11.

Cultural Neostoicism illuminates a rich field of mostly informal, poetic, and artistic philosophical activity nourished by Stoic thought that worked alongside other ancient philosophies and religious perspectives. This expansive lens allows for different levels of knowledge and participation, takes account of the Christian tendencies to read Stoicism in particular ways, and acknowledges the contributions of women intellectuals like Madeleine de L'Aubespine, Marie Le Jars de Gournay, and Esther Inglis; poets and artists working in informal philosophical media; and children who learned their first Stoic lessons through wisdom prints such as poems, songs, and emblem books. It is only by broadening our definition of these terms that we can properly recognize the vast influence of Stoicism in the early modern period and evaluate the degree to which it permeates the intellectual and cultural output of the sixteenth and seventeenth centuries.

There remains a deep lacuna with regard to the influence of Stoicism on music production and practices in sixteenth- and seventeenth-century Europe. Even in scholarship focused on contexts known to be hotbeds of Neostoicism—and sometimes even when citing the work of established Neostoics—musicologists have almost exclusively favored Platonist or Aristotelian readings, taking little heed of William Bouwsma's famous warning in 1975 against that "quaint but durable" view of the Renaissance as limited to a choice between Plato and Aristotle.[37] Several earlier musicological studies have at least begun to broach a possible Stoic influence on musical thought and practices, though neither in the time period nor in contexts known to be the center of Neostoicism. Jamie Kassler, for example, has illuminated the Stoic influence on the scientific and musical writings of later seventeenth-century England and France.[38] Musicologists have also afforded some attention to Neostoicism within seventeenth-century Italian opera, particularly in regard to Monteverdi's *L'incoronazione di Poppea* and numerous other operatic works that feature Seneca and other Stoics in leading roles.[39] What these accounts lack is an awareness of the longer tradition of singing Seneca *off the stage* (and in predominantly Protestant lands, no less), which could give a critical context for these staged portrayals.

---

[37] Bouwsma, *A Usable Past*, 20–21.

[38] Jamie Kassler, *Inner Music: Hobbes, Hooke and North on Internal Character* (London: Athlone, 1995); and Jamie Kassler, *Music, Science, Philosophy: Models in the Universe of Thought* (Aldershot: Ashgate, 2001).

[39] For example, Wendy Heller, "Tacitus Incognito: Opera as History in 'L'incoronazione di Poppea,'" *JAMS* 52, no. 1 (1999): 39–96; and Ellen Rosand, "Il Ritorno a Seneca," *Cambridge Opera Journal* 21, no. 2 (2010): 119–37.

Furthermore, the uneven grasp of Stoicism and Neostoicism in this literature has troubled the analysis of these later Italian works. For example, several of the most central assertions about Neostoicism in Iain Fenlon and Peter Miller's *The Song of the Soul* are based on an outdated perspective of the movement, such as their claim that the Stoics demanded a withdrawal from the world and discouraged their followers from engaging in political life.[40] Exactly the opposite was the case in both theory and practice, as we will see in the following chapters. Ancient Stoics like Seneca and Marcus Aurelius and their Neostoic admirers overwhelmingly saw it as their duty to engage in civic life when given the opportunity, though always with the caveat that public service should be pursued only for the common good and not for self-indulgence, personal glory, or ambition—and that public office should be given up without complaint if derailed by the whims of fortune. Stoic withdrawal to the "inner citadel" was a periodic therapeutic exercise designed to cultivate internal peace of mind; it was not a justification for political avoidance or hermitry.[41]

Up to this point, the most significant work on the riches of cultural Neostoicism has come from art history, for the prominent early modern genre of still-life *vanitas* paintings—with their characteristic skulls, rotting fruit, dying flowers, and other overtly Stoic images of the inconstancy and ephemerality of the world—has more often been recognized as a philosophically driven mode of artistic production and viewing.[42] As if the Stoicism of the genre needed to be even more obvious, some *vanitas* images included a bust of Seneca or verses of moral poetry, explicitly reminding viewers that the visual was linked to an elaborate intellectual culture and its associated regulatory meditative practices. Musical instruments and partbooks often appear in these paintings—presented at first blush as one of the pleasurable and prestige-oriented "vanities" of the world. However, as scholars have noted, these images of music frequently invite contradictory interpretations

---

[40] Iain Fenlon and Peter Miller, *The Song of the Soul: Understanding "Poppea"* (London: Royal Musical Association, 1992), 21–44. Peter Miller offered a fuller philosophical context in his "Stoics who Sing: Lessons in Citizenship from Early Modern Lucca," *The Historical Journal* 44, no. 2 (2001): 313–39.

[41] Diogenes Laertius summarizes the Stoic position in *Lives* 7.121–23. For a broader view of withdrawal in the period, see Robert A. Schneider, *Dignified Retreat: Writers and Intellectuals in the Age of Richelieu* (New York: Oxford University Press, 2019), 2–4.

[42] See Thijs Weststeijn, *The Visible World: Samuel Van Hoogstraten's Art Theory and the Legitimation of Painting in the Dutch Golden Age*, trans. Beverley Jackson and Lynne Richards (Amsterdam: Amsterdam University Press, 2008), 83–119; and Alain Tapié, "Petite archéologie du vain," in *Les Vanités dans la peinture au XVIIe siècle*, ed. Alain Tapié (Caen: Albin Michel, 1990), 69–77.

bolstered by music's ambiguous position at the boundary of nature and artifice, perception and reality, moral virtue and worldly vanity.

The moral song collections inspired by this Stoic framework explicitly heighten the fundamental tension between music's nature and function in the art of living, and they reveal song as an equally sensitive means of engaging Stoicism in early modern France and beyond. At the most basic level, these moral settings enlarged interest in Stoic moral philosophy by circulating their fundamental tenets to a wider audience through attractive paraphrases set to music. Although a complete analysis of Stoic and Neostoic views on music is beyond the scope of this study, the polyphonic collections that set Neostoic moral poetry to music offer a fruitful starting point. Aside from the very basic yet noteworthy fact that these philosophical themes and doctrines were chosen by a range of composers and printers for polyphonic collections, the laudatory poetry and other liminal materials that preface the prints by L'Estocart, Boni, Le Jeune, and Aux-Cousteaux offer insights into how these moral songs were produced and used within this broad therapeutic movement.

In Chapter 1 ("Neostoic Remedies"), I introduce the moral crisis posed by the French religious wars and document the rising interest in the reparative powers of both music and philosophy. Although Platonism had been the favored philosophy in French court circles of the mid-sixteenth century, the 1570s and 1580s saw a shift toward Stoicism as a resource for understanding and controlling the passions. During the reign of Henri IV, Stoicism grew to become the dominant stream of thought as Catholics and Protestants across the francophone world developed contemplative and musical strategies of Stoic consolation capable of soothing individual and communal strife.

Chapter 2 ("Imprinting Virtue") introduces the three moral song collections at the center of this study. The poets, composers, and first audience for the *Quatrains*, *Octonaires*, and *Tablettes* were active participants in the Neostoic resurgence spearheaded by the Catholic magistracy associated with the Palais de Justice in Paris and Reformed Protestant pastor-scholars based in Geneva. Although exhibiting stylistic differences, these three collections were linked through their shared Stoic borrowings, print histories, and musical settings.

Chapter 3 ("The Exercise of Harmony") considers the influence of Stoic educational theory and epistemology on the composition and use of Pibrac's *Quatrains*. Memorized widely in early modern education and set in abundant musical arrangements, the *Quatrains* embody the brevity and stylistic

restraint so prized in Stoic rhetoric. The repetitions at the heart of this didactic repertoire suggest a mode of moral progress rooted in both intellectual knowledge and lived experience—daily practices capable of forging an
invisible community of virtue-lovers united not by religious affiliation but
through a shared pursuit of wisdom.

Chapter 4 ("Musical Paradoxes") unpacks the themes of paradox and contradiction within the Stoic-inflected moral song corpus, from the pithy paraphrase settings of the *Paradoxa Stoicorum* included in Boni's and L'Estocart's
Quatrains to the rhetoric of contradiction structuring the poetic, visual, and
musical *Octonaires*. These sonic and emblematic expressions offer sophisticated engagement with the Stoic consolatory techniques recommended for
eliminating destructive emotions and finding inner freedom and constancy.

Chapter 5 ("Sensing Beauty") takes on the problem of beauty and pleasure
in the moral repertoire through an examination of the exquisitely illustrative
Octonaires corpus. Although the Stoic tradition frequently warned against
the links between beauty, pleasure, and immoderate desire, they displayed a
profound courage in embracing the risks of aesthetic and sensory experience
as an essential pathway to fully rational moral formation. When the prefaces
and content are considered, the *Octonaires* offer a window into an ethics of
musical beauty through what may be for some an unlikely place: musical text
painting. There, in a musical domain often devalued for its childish literalism
or its amateur accessibility, we find a script for bringing thought and feeling
into counterpoint through a richly multi-sensory musical experience.

Chapter 6 ("Sound Judgment") explores the crisis of musical knowledge provoked by the revival of Skepticism—a movement closely tied to
Neostoicism. Although Stoicism played the most pivotal role in shaping early
modern theories of the emotions, it was Skepticism that drove the conversation on epistemology, marshaling detailed arguments against an uncritical
trust in sensory knowledge. The role of musical hearing, and its relationship to folly or wisdom, attracted significant attention in these Skeptic and
Neostoic discussions, driving stylistic reforms that prioritized clarity and
comprehension of the musical text over virtuosic compositional pyrotech-
nics. As the producers of moral song collections grappled with these critical
sensory concerns in a period of increased global expansion, they revealed the
gendered and racialized stakes of both musical knowledge and virtue.

Chapter 7 ("Moral Ordering") outlines the philosophical implications of
the broad impulse toward modal organization displayed by Claude Le Jeune's
Octonaires. Grounded in Stoic views of universal harmony and sympatheia,

these musical practices of modal ordering served as a means of *moral* ordering, modeled by the ensemble of singers and working outward to a harmonious regulation of the civil sphere.

Chapter 8 ("Rehearsing Death") returns to the most central exercise of Stoic therapeutics and its invitation to daily meditate on human transience. The rich expression of the *memento mori* theme in moral song collections, emblems, and *vanitas* paintings called for an aesthetic contemplation of mortality, the excruciating reality of decay, and the glory of ruins. Drawing attention to the problems of time and duration, these skillful artistic compositions therapeutically naturalize the instability of temporal experience through a heightened appreciation of the present.

The conclusion, "Suspensions of Desire," comes back to the counterintuitive role of pleasure, ambition, and riches in the multidisciplinary moral corpus, revealing striking musical encounters of desire that rival those in the love corpus. The Neostoic exercise of self-mastery turns out to be surprisingly fleshly and cleverly balanced at the precarious juncture between teaching and temptation. Virtue, as a sung practice, thus proves to be both rational and fully invested in the corporeal processes of the singing body.

As we will see throughout this study, Stoics and Neostoics were fond of paradoxes, and their nuanced appreciation for the expressive effects of music and poetry, while ultimately retaining an emphasis on emotional regulation, serves as a prime example of their ability to artfully negotiate the tension between opposing positions. We see this skill in many aspects of Stoic philosophy: their radical individualism was held in tension with their understanding of the complete interconnectedness of the universe; their call for detachment from the world was balance by their demonstrated commitment to remaining involved in civic life and serving in political office. This careful negotiation between detachment/participation in worldly affairs was modeled by Seneca and Marcus Aurelius and continued to resonate in the early modern period, as the Neostoic movement was powered by those serving prominently in law and governance. Even in terms of worldly benefits, the Stoics found a middle position between the asceticism of the Cynics and the Aristotelian view of wealth and health as Goods, allowing for the possession of great wealth and power so long as one retained a state of mind that was not attached to these ephemeral and unstable comforts.

The same holds true for our understanding of Neostoicism, which I believe can only be understood in all of its paradoxical richness through the dynamic inflections of this philosophy that were sung and heard with great

pleasure and moral understanding. The presence of such a musical corpus—
singing Stoicism—offers a previously unknown source of evidence for the
extent to which this moral philosophy stimulated the mainstream lettered
culture of the period. More importantly, this corpus of bold, evocative,
and sensory music—which emerged from Neostoicism and circulated its
themes to a broader public—demands a reappraisal of Neostoicism itself.
In circumscribing moral song as a printed genre and considering its ana-
lytical and performative use, we can see its true potential. This analysis not
only illuminates the influence of Stoicism on music, but it also shows that we
cannot fully understand Neostoicism as an intellectual or cultural movement
without accounting for its vibrant musical practices.

1

Neostoic Remedies

All is troubled in this Kingdom and everyone
seeks a remedy for the public calamity.[1]

The bloody French Wars of Religion, which pitted Catholics against the emerging Protestant sect in a series of civil conflicts between 1562 and 1598, provoked a moral crisis that differed significantly from those encountered in many other situations of large-scale violence. The parties involved were not only neighbors and compatriots but also identified as Christians—a fact that severely weakened the moral foundations of the Christian Church. In his *Discours politiques et militaires* of 1587, the Huguenot leader François de La Noue admitted the shared responsibility for the damage caused by the wars, lamenting the loss of life and the Church's moral authority: "it is our wars over religion that have caused us to forget religion."[2]

This chapter considers the nature of this moral crisis and the range of subsequent efforts aimed at cross-confessional repair. Although early efforts focused unsuccessfully on religious rites, the final decades of the sixteenth century saw a rise in more neutral, philosophical sources for restoring public and private tranquility. Joined through richly interlocking therapeutic traditions, both music and Stoicism emerged as attractive resources for cross-confessional collaboration. They were harnessed together in moral song collections, offering a practical mode of Stoic psychotherapy that reached from the French magistracy all the way to Geneva.

---

[1] Lipsius, *Deux livres de la constance*, printer's dedication.
[2] François de La Noüe, *Discours politiques et militaires* (Basle: François Forest, 1587), 6.

The Voice of Virtue. Melinda Latour, Oxford University Press. © Oxford University Press 2023.
DOI: 10.1093/oso/9780197529744.003.0002

Rupture and Repair

Natalie Zemon Davis, Denis Crouzet, Barbara Diefendorf, and other cultural historians of early modern France have emphasized religious zeal as the fundamental motivation behind the local violence—revising an earlier historiography that saw religion as a pretext for civil or political maneuvering.[3] Catholics and Protestants shared a view of community predicated on the link between the sacred and the civic. Religious division posed a clear threat to public life and the medieval link between kingly and religious authority. By this logic, the more radical factions splintering Catholics and Protestants justified bloodshed, rioting, and other public disorder as a necessary—and acceptable—means of restoring the social body by purging the corrupting elements that were defiling it.

During and just after the First War of Religion (1562–63), the divide between Catholics and Protestants continued to widen. Beyond their shared ideal of community and their mutual justification of violence in defense of it, the warring confessions diverged dramatically in their sense of how best to restore their community and rebuild the kingdom. Catholics sought to purge heresy, restore the sacred and venerated spaces in the city, and return to Christian unity, while Protestants sought a godly society where their right to worship on their own terms would be accommodated. Although both camps made early efforts to reestablish friendship and civil harmony, these initial strategies had little grounding in any adequate moral authority that could cross the confessional gulf and thus did little to unite the fractured populace.[4]

The bloody St. Bartholomew's Day Massacre of 1572 shocked both sides of the conflict with the intensity and cruelty of its religious violence. Prompted by rumors about a Huguenot plot against the Crown, Parisian Catholics murdered several thousand Protestants in a wave of mass carnage that rippled across the French kingdom. In the long aftermath of this bloodshed, many Catholics and Protestants began to express a loss of faith in the moral compass of their governing religious and political institutions, turning

---

[3] See Denis Crouzet, *Les Guerriers de Dieu: La violence au temps des troubles de religion (vers 1525–vers 1610)*; Denis Crouzet, *Dieu en ses royaumes: Une histoire des guerres de religion* (Paris: Champ Vallon, 2008); Barbara Diefendorf, *Beneath the Cross: Catholics and Huguenots in Sixteenth-Century Paris* (New York: Oxford University Press, 1991); and Natalie Zemon Davis, *Society and Culture in Early Modern France: Eight Essays* (Stanford, CA: Stanford University Press, 1975).

[4] Barbara Diefendorf, "Rites of Repair: Restoring Community in the French Religious Wars," *Past and Present* 214, no. 7 (2012): 30–51.

instead toward a more moderate position, which disavowed the pretext of religion as a justification for violence.

As Pierre Charron later clarified in his influential *De la sagesse* [*On Wisdom*] (1601), the French religious wars proved that religious piety does not ensure excellence in moral character. For Charron, the problem was that when morality was subsumed in religion, the former became only a tool in the service of religion. This allowed religious zealots to condone horrifying immorality, from treason to gross violence. He lamented that these evil acts were "not only lawful and permitted, colored by the zeal and care of religion: but even praiseworthy, meritorious, and canonizable, if it serves in the progress and advancement of religion, and the pushing back of its adversaries."[5] Although Charron was clearly not arguing against religion per se (despite contemporary charges that he promoted atheism and libertinism), he identified the danger of religious zeal unchecked by a robust ethical system. Drawing upon ancient views of wisdom—"especially Seneca and Plutarch," as he explains in the preface—Charron proposed a rationalized ethical system that would temper devotion with reason, moderate the passions, and ensure that any proposed act of religious piety also followed the law and order shared commonly in nature. An admirer of Michel de Montaigne, Charron was a lawyer at the court of the Parlement of Paris before leaving his legal career for theological work. He secured the post of *prédicateur ordinaire* to Marguerite of Valois, Queen of Navarre at the court at Nérac, which was frequented by Philippe Duplessis-Mornay, Guy du Faur de Pibrac, and other figures associated with Neostoicism. He had the ear of Henri de Navarre—the future Henri IV—who attended his sermons and reportedly greatly enjoyed his preaching. Though published several years later, Charron's *Sagesse* was penned between 1597 to 1599, during the preparation of Henri IV's Edict of Nantes, and was marked by similar interests in cross-confessional healing after the horrors of the Massacre.[6]

Although there had been a faction calling for reconciliation from the start of the Wars, an increasing number of Catholics and Protestants responded to the Massacre by actively seeking modes of repairing the damage wrought by the continued conflict. The nascent traces of non-violence, tolerance, and cross-confessional dialogue that had been present from the beginnings of

---

[5] Pierre Charron, *De la sagesse* (Bordeaux: Simon Millanges, 1601), 2:5, 370–71.

[6] Lagrée, *Le Néostoïcisme*, 130–34; Renée Kogel, *Pierre Charron* (Geneva: Droz, 1972), 30–36 and 703; and Natasha Constantinidou, *Responses to Religious Division, c. 1580–1620: Public and Private, Divine and Temporal* (Leiden: Brill, 2017), 22–31 and 71–112.

the conflict blossomed in the final decades of the century into a widespread virtue movement whose aim was individual and corporate moral repair. Scholars have recognized aspects of this late sixteenth-century impulse toward moral improvement in a variety of contexts and modalities, including court activities, political legislation, community rituals, devotional practices, and artistic performance.[7]

Two distinct centers of virtue reform emerged over this period: a predominantly Catholic movement fueled by the *parlementaire* circle connected to the Palais de Justice in Paris, and a Protestant movement based in Geneva that was closely linked to the Low Countries and England. Although the two remained distinct in their confessional and political orientations, there was abundant overlap between them, as prints and people flowed from one center to the other through artistic, intellectual, legal, and diplomatic networks. What developed in this nexus between the confessions was a movement that looked to both music and philosophy as therapeutic resources that could be exploited in the work of recovering virtue, restabilizing the land, and moderating the passions. This movement was fed by twin reparative traditions coming down from ancient Greek and Roman thought: one dedicated to the recovery of philosophy as a remedy, the other ascribing special reparative powers to musical sound and harmony. These humanist lineages were often intertwined—as we see explicitly illustrated in Symphorien Champier's *Symphonia Platonis cum Aristotele: et Galeni cum Hippocrate* (1516), whose title page positions the four featured philosopher-doctors as a viol consort. [Web 1.1]

Harmonious Treatments

Although the scope and significance of the ailments varied greatly, the application of musical sound as a remedy for physical and mental suffering was a through line in the European cultural tradition. Tales of music's ethical power—offering miraculous as well as mundane treatments for everything

---

[7] See, for example, Mark Greengrass, *Governing Passions: Peace and Reform in the French Kingdom, 1576–1585* (Oxford: Oxford University Press, 2007), 1–5; Benjamin J. Kaplan, *Divided by Faith: Religious Conflict and the Practice of Toleration in Early Modern Europe* (Cambridge, MA: Harvard University Press, 2009); Margaret M. McGowan, *Dance in the Renaissance: European Fashion, French Obsession* (New Haven, CT: Yale University Press, 2008), 41–60; and Kate van Orden, *Music, Discipline, and Arms in Early Modern France* (Chicago, IL: University of Chicago Press, 2005), 81–124.

from civil discord to lovesickness—were still widespread, if subject to rational critique in the late sixteenth century.[8] Both mental illness and moral erosion were framed as disorders that spanned the psychophysical spectrum, suggesting an interlocking combination of musical, spiritual, and medicinal treatments. The source of these views was the Pythagorean/Platonic lineage, which forged a connection between the vibrational harmony of the spheres and the proper working of bodies and souls here in the earthly realm. Marked by the work of Marsilio Ficino, the Neoplatonism revived in the Renaissance highlighted the mystical, therapeutic, and moral powers of music—a vein of thought that profoundly shaped the sixteenth-century reforms of sacred music and inspired new directions in amateur and elite artistic activities.[9]

The landmark music treatises of Pontus de Tyard, *Solitaire premier* (1551) and *Solitaire second* (1552), reflect this growing synergy between the reparative union of music and philosophy in the influential poetic program spearheaded by Pierre de Ronsard and the other members of the Pléiade working within the milieu of the French court.[10] As Howard Mayer Brown notes in his seminal article, Tyard's two *Solitaires* reveal the poles of French musical thought under construction in the late sixteenth century—the cosmic and the rhetorical.[11] These poles were brought into productive tension with the creation of the Académie de poésie et de musique, formed by the Catholic poet Jean-Antoine de Baïf (a core member of the Pléiade) and the composer Joachim Thibault de Courville by 1567, but finally given official authorization in November of 1570. Boasting an elite roster, including Guy du Faur de Pibrac and Claude Le Jeune, the Académie brought together a cross-confessional group of composers, poets, and listeners at the court of Charles IX to explore nuanced strategies of conciliation for the divided

[8] See Peregrine Horden, ed., *Music as Medicine: The History of Music Therapy since Antiquity* (Aldershot: Ashgate, 2014); Carla Zecher, *Sounding Objects: Musical Instruments, Poetry, and Art in Renaissance France* (Toronto: University of Toronto Press, 2007), 94–103; Linda Phyllis Austern, *Both from the Ears and Mind: Thinking about Music in Early Modern England* (Chicago, IL: University of Chicago Press, 2020), 217–67; and Remi Chiu, *Plague and Music in the Renaissance* (Cambridge: Cambridge University Press, 2020), 13.

[9] See Jacomien Prins, *Echoes of an Invisible World: Marsilio Ficino and Francesco Patrizi on Cosmic Order and Music Theory* (Leiden: Brill, 2014), 25–207; Gary Tomlinson, *Music in Renaissance Magic: Toward a Historiography of Others* (Chicago, IL: University of Chicago Press, 1993), 110–42; and Hyun-Ah Kim, *The Renaissance Ethics of Music: Singing, Contemplation and Musica Humana* (London: Pickering and Chatto, 2015), 53–101.

[10] Greengrass, *Governing Passions*, 13–53; van Orden, *Music, Discipline, and Arms*, 62–83; and Jean-Eudes Girot and Alice Tacaille, *"Que me servent mes vers?" La musique chez Ronsard, avec un supplément vocal de 22 chansons* (Paris: Classiques Garnier, 2020), 115–78.

[11] Howard Mayer Brown, "'Ut musica poesis': Music and Poetry in France in the Late Sixteenth Century," *Early Music History* 13 (1994): 4–6.

kingdom through musical and artistic means. Guided by a belief in the link between musical regulation and moral order, the Académie sought to recuperate the ancient patterns of literary meter for vernacular poetry, binding musical sound to measured verse. The innovative style of *musique mésurée à l'antique* codified in these Académie experiments ensured the closest union of music to the text, including strict homorhythm and the quantitative application of longs and breves that would correspond to the natural accents of the prosody.[12]

The most venerated Protestant composer of moral song, Claude Le Jeune, played a key role in the Académie and became the most influential proponent of *musique mesurée* as a resource for polyphonic composition.[13] Composed several decades after these academic experiments, Le Jeune's *Octonaires* demonstrate the composer's full power to synthesize the quantitative principles of *musique mesurée* within the context of contrapuntal chansons setting non-measured verse. Le Jeune's counterpoint often follows the Académie's rules for prosody in the individual lines. This subtle attention to prosody gives the text a surprising intelligibility—even in the more complicated contrapuntal passages—and underscores a shared complex of moral and epistemological issues that I will discuss in more detail later in this study. Le Jeune also had a hand in mounting Balthasar de Beaujoyeulx's extravagant court spectacle of 1581, the *Balet comique de la Royne*, where these musico-ethical activities reached their zenith. Lavishly dramatizing the victory of the King's Justice and the Moral Virtues over Circe's vicious disorder, the printed score (1582) offered prefatory material that elucidates its Neoplatonist framework and reparative objectives.[14]

Although Neoplatonism was the philosophy that most overtly underpinned the musico-ethical activities of the French court at mid-century, by the 1570s and 1580s the philosophical emphasis was shifting toward Stoicism. Guy du Faur de Pibrac, the magistrate and author of the *Quatrains*, was a key figure in this transition, both in his founding role in the establishment of the Académie in the early 1570s and through his participation in the later Académie du Palais, sponsored by Henri III. Among the

---

[12] See Frances Yates, *The French Academies of the Sixteenth Century* (London: Warburg Institute, 1947), 14–27, 36–76, and 199–235; D. P. Walker, *Music, Spirit, and Language in the Renaissance*, ed. Penelope Gouk (London: Variorum Reprints, 1985), 91–100 and 151–86; and Marc Deramaix et al., eds., *Les Académies dans l'Europe humaniste: Idéaux et pratiques. Actes du colloque international de Paris (juin 2003)* (Geneva: Droz, 2008).

[13] His, *Claude Le Jeune*, 239–366.

[14] Balthasar de Beaujoyeulx, *Balet comique de la Royne* (Paris: Le Roy et Ballard, 1582), fol. 5v.

distinguished group of participants in the latter were Jean Dorat, Pierre de Ronsard, Philippe Desportes, and "even some ladies who had studied," including Marguerite de Valois, Madame de Nevers, la Maréchale de Retz, and Madame de Lignerolles, who gave speeches admired by the group.[15] Stoic moral philosophy was one of the moral philosophies under discussion in these Académie sessions, held either in the king's cabinet at the Louvre (after his meal), or in one of his residences in Blois, Fontainebleau, or Olinville.[16] Although the lectures represented a broad diversity of thought, Stoicism emerged as a point of interest for its emphasis on controlling the passions— particularly debilitating and destructive ones, like anger and grief. Several publications circulated the content of these philosophical discussions to a wider readership. The four-volume *Academie françoise*—published in parts between 1577 and 1608 by the Protestant Pierre de La Primaudaye, *gentilhomme de la chambre* for François, the duke of Anjou in the early 1580s—outlines the discourse of a small private academy in Anjou, which may or may not have been based in fact. In any case, the account resonates with the known content of Henri III's palace lectures and their inflections of Neostoicism.[17] A smaller—but very highly regarded—treatise also linked to these discussions was published by Marie Le Gendre, dame de Rivery, who, like La Primaudaye, may have been a participant in the Palace Academy. Her publication, the *Cabinet des saines affections* [Cabinet of Healthy Passions] (1595), which also appeared under the title *L'Exercice de l'âme verteuse* [Exercise of the Virtuous Soul] (1596/1597), was a significant expansion of an earlier Neostoic treatise, published anonymously as *Des saines affections* (1584). Although the attribution of this 1584 treatise remains complicated, scholars agree that it was probably the work of Madeleine de L'Aubespine, a woman with connections through birth and marriage to the highest *parlementaire* circles in Paris, which had fomented the Stoic revival.[18]

---

[15] Cited in Marie Le Gendre, *L'Exercise de l'âme vertueuse*, ed. Colette Winn (Paris: H. Champion, 2001), 15. See also Robert Sealy, *The Palace Academy of Henry* III (Geneva: Droz, 1981), 177–79.

[16] Alexandre Tarrête, "Stoïcisme et anti-stoïcisme à l'Académie du Palais," in *Les Académies dans l'Europe humaniste*, ed. Deramaix, 643–62; Anthony Levi, *French Moralists: The Theory of the Passions, 1585 to 1649* (Oxford: Clarendon Press, 1964), 9; and Loris Petris, "Le Magistrat gallican et l'Académie du Palais: Le Discours de l'ire, et comme il la faut moderer de Guy Du Faur de Pibrac (étude et édition)," *Nouvelle revue du XVIe siècle* 22, no. 2 (2004): 57–82.

[17] See Yates, *French Academies*, 122–27.

[18] On the problems of attribution, see Madeleine de L'Aubespine, *Cabinet des saines affections*, ed. Colette H. Winn (Paris: H. Champion, 2001), 12–15. To complicate matters further, some editions of the *Cabinet des saines affections* were attributed to Marie Le Jars de Gournay, another well-known author of Neostoic works.

Considering that Stoicism was one of the ancient philosophical schools to come out of the Socratic lineage, this late sixteenth-century shift in emphasis from Neoplatonism to Neostoicism offered a natural transition between long-enmeshed philosophical systems.[19] As Isaac Casaubon, Professor of Greek at the Academy of Geneva, put it, "Even the Stoics came from the school of Socrates, as if from the Trojan horse."[20] The influence also cut in the opposite direction, for just as the early Stoics borrowed key elements from the Platonic tradition, the later Neoplatonist school explicitly spliced aspects of Stoicism into its moral outlook. Thus, in some ethical concerns— such as the therapeutic view of philosophy, the vanity and inconstancy of the world, and the powerful notion of universal harmony—Neostoicism and Neoplatonism developed as two entangled limbs of a single tradition. Their distinction as unique philosophical schools can be seen in their different priorities, methods, and deployments of these themes within their divergent traditions, which I will outline at the end of this chapter.

Stoic Remedies

It was during Henri IV's reign that France saw the full blossoming of Neostoicism as a cross-confessional movement that offered a sympathetic philosophical harmony in an otherwise discordant landscape. As a former Protestant who retained many of his longstanding connections and alliances to the Genevan intellectual elite, Henri IV bridged the two major centers of French Neostoicism, bringing the Protestant movement anchored in Geneva into much closer contact with the Catholic movement propelled by the members of the Parlement of Paris and the activities of the court. Grounded in a cool, rational stability, Stoicism offered an appealing doctrine of order— a "désangoissement," according to Denis Crouzet—that promised to counter the religious extremism of the League, who were the enemies of the Paris magistrates and the Protestants.[21] Henri IV, praised for his fortitude, moderation, clemency, and justice, was frequently portrayed in painting and song

---

[19] See Levi, *French Moralists*, 46–52; Mauro Bonazzi and Christoph Helmig, eds., *Platonic Stoicism, Stoic Platonism: The Dialogue between Platonism and Stoicism in Antiquity* (Leuven: Leuven University Press, 2017); and A. G. Long, ed., *Plato and the Stoics* (Cambridge: Cambridge University Press, 2013).

[20] Cited in Mark Morford, *Stoics and Neostoics* (Princeton, NJ: Princeton University Press, 1991), 18n17.

[21] Crouzet, *Dieu en ses royaumes*, 448–52; and Crouzet, *Les Guerriers de Dieu*, 2:554–84.

as a modern-day Hercules, a key model of virtue in the Stoic tradition, and the "roi de raison" (King of reason), subject to the same universal laws of rationality as his subjects.[22] [Web 1.2] This Stoic emphasis on regulating destructive emotions through the power of constancy and reason gained broad appeal across the warring confessions. Although both camps continued to rigidly defend an entrenched position on theological and ecclesiastical matters, they found common ground in their appreciation of the therapeutic potential of Stoicisim to mend the damage to personal tranquility and communal virtue.

Stoicism offered early modern practitioners a method for eliminating the passions (*pathē*)—extreme emotions that they described as diseases of the mind that could be cured. Because the Stoic tradition regarded the passions cognitively, as errors of judgment regarding the nature and value of external things, they developed a specific therapeutic method, called consolation, to expose and reshape these structural beliefs. At the heart of the consolatory program was a focus on the paradox of control: it is only by recognizing and accepting what is beyond individual control (all externals) that a person can understand and exert maximal control over what *is* in their power (virtue alone). Worldly comforts, intense relational attachments, and other common sources of security and pleasure were strategically dismissed as "indifferents" (*adiaphora*) because they could be so easily swept away by the whims of fortune. Inner virtue, on the other hand, was held to be the only good, for virtue alone can be cultivated and maintained regardless of external circumstances and offers the only guaranteed route to true happiness, inner peace, and lasting contentment.

In this way, Stoicism offered a philosophy of life capable of grappling with the most agonizing troubles of human existence, not a mode of abstract speculation or mental showmanship. As classicist Martha Nussbaum has demonstrated, Stoicism and its rival Hellenistic schools, Skepticism and Epicureanism, were philosophies explicitly construed to deal with devastating, chaotic, and anxiety-producing circumstances.[23] The leading figures of late sixteenth-century Neostoicism from across the confessional divide repeatedly emphasized this therapeutic purpose of Stoic thought, which they recognized as a "living philosophy" that offered a practical remedy

---

[22] Edmund H. Dickerman and Anita M. Walker, "The Choice of Hercules: Henry IV as Hero," *The Historical Journal* 39 (1996): 315–37.

[23] Martha Nussbaum, *The Therapy of Desire: Theory and Practice in Hellenistic Ethics* (Princeton, NJ: Princeton University Press, 1994), 316–401.

for contemporary troubles.[24] In Justus Lipsius's preface to the reader for
On Constancy, he criticizes those who miss the reparative aim of philosophy: "They use it as a divertissement, not as a remedy, and turn the most
serious instrument of life into a sportage with trifles."[25] Simon Goulart,
a leading pastor and scholar based in Geneva, persistently underscores
the reparative possibilities of Stoicism in his *Œuvres morales et meslées de
Senecque* (Paris, 1595), a three-volume collection of translations of Seneca
and Epictetus, complemented by fragments of other Stoic authors and
abundant explanatory essays devoted to Stoicism. One of Goulart's original
contributions was his dialogue based on Senecan therapeutics, the *Discours
en forme de devis entre le sens et la raison*, which, the subtitle explains,
will offer "remedies against diverse accidents of this life."[26] Furthermore,
Goulart's extensive Neostoic treatise, *Ample discours sur la doctrine des
Stoiques*, recommended the "beautiful sentences of the Stoics" for their
ability to regulate both thoughts and external actions, and promote stability
in the domestic and civil state.[27]

Guillaume Du Vair, counselor of the Parlement of Paris, became the most
prominent French Neostoic of his time. In his address to the reader for his
1591 edition of Epictetus's *Handbook*, he acknowledges that his interest in
Stoicism as a remedy was inspired by the woman-authored treatise *Cabinet
des saines affections*. Du Vair wrote that reading this treatise "full of beautiful and grave sentences for strengthening our minds in such a time as this
one" made him "wish to return to the writings of the Stoics and, there, search
for some consolation."[28] Du Vair went on to publish a famous dialogue in
1594 with an explicitly reparative thrust that pays homage to Lipsius with the
title *De la constance et consolation ès calamitez publiques* [On Constancy and
Consolation in Public Calamities].[29]

The Stoic method for achieving external constancy through inner
consolation—long known in the European tradition through such works as
Seneca's three consolatory letters and Cicero's *Tusculan Disputations*—proved,

[24] Léontine Zanta, *La Renaissance du stoïcism au xvie siècle* (Paris: H. Champion, 1914); Lagrée, *Le
Néostoïcisme*, 15, 120–29; and Constantinidou, *Responses to Religious Division*, 116–53.

[25] Lipsius, *On Constancy*, ed. Sellars, 28–29.

[26] Seneca, *Œuvres morales et meslées de Senecque*, trans. Simon Goulart (Paris: Jean Houzé, 1595).
All citations will be drawn from the 4th ed. (Geneva: Jean Arnaud, 1606), 1:210–17.

[27] Ibid., 3:327.

[28] Cited in Guillaume Du Vair, *Traictez philosophiques*, ed. Alexandre Tarrête (Paris: H. Champion,
2016), 23. See n18 above.

[29] Guillaume Du Vair, *De la constance et consolation ès calamitez publiques* (Paris: [Mamert
Patisson] Abel L'Angelier, 1594).

1595 attractive to those working in law and governance.[30] Diogenes Laertius had even reported in *Lives* 7.26 that Zeno of Citium, the founder of Stoicism, was the first to coin the word "duty" and write a treatise about it. Recall that the first printed classical text in Europe in 1465, Cicero's *On Duties*, was a key source of Stoic thought, and it was bound together with another influential source of Stoicism, Cicero's *Paradoxa Stoicorum*. The growing circulation of Seneca's consolatory works by and for the magistracy made their therapeutic aim of restoring personal and public constancy explicit, as we see in the jurist Ange Cappel's *De la consolation de la mort* (1584), a translation of Seneca's *Consolation to Marcia*. Dedicated to the Queen mother Catherine de' Medici and signed in Paris on 25 June 1584—just fifteen days after the death of her youngest son, François (duke of Anjou and Alençon)—this work expresses Cappel's desire "to bring by my writings some remedy for your misfortune." After having done extensive research into the consolatory tradition, he explains that he found Seneca's writings unparalleled for their ability to penetrate, resonate, and heal misfortune.[31] In a similar vein, Geoffroy de La Chassaigne, souldan de Pressac, also from a powerful *parlementaire* family, opened his dedicatory epistle for his French edition of Seneca's *Epistles* (1582) with the oft-cited story of Philippe, King of Macedonia and his son Alexander as an illustration for why kings should study philosophy: "it engenders in the soul a firm and absolute resolve against death and fortune."[32] Like Cappel, La Chassaigne proposes Seneca as the best choice for learning constancy in the face of unstable forces.

Du Vair's union of these Stoic themes in *Constance et consolation* was powered by this reparative wave, and his treatise is notable for the subtle musical element he includes in his philosophical exercise. Du Vair stages Orpheus, Musaeus, and Linus as his three interlocutors and comforters. This trio was well known through sources like Diogenes Laertius's *Lives* 1.2–4 (which describes them as contemporaries just before the Trojan wars): Orpheus's musical powers are famous; Linus is credited with inventing music in Greece and teaching Hercules the harp; and Musaeus is cited as a composer of ethical verses, hymns, and odes. Du Vair's legendary trio offers just a hint of what turns out to be a surprisingly extensive interest in music

---

[30] Carabin, *Les Idées stoïciennes*, 664–71; and Graver, *Stoicism and Emotion*, 196–211.

[31] Seneca, *De la consolation de la mort*, trans. Ange Cappel (Paris: Felix le Magnier, 1584).

[32] Seneca, *Epistres de L. Annœe Seneque, philosophe tres-excellent*, trans. Geoffroy de La Chassaigne, souldan de Pressac (Paris: Guillaume Chaudière, 1582).

and the arts displayed by the Neostoic magistracy and their intellectual interlocutors in Reformed Geneva.

The Problem of Stoic Music

Stoicism—with its famous hostility to emotion and disregard for pleasure—would seem an odd place to find a sustained appreciation of music as a sonic practice. Wouldn't Stoics be precisely the sort to ban music—that dangerous, vain, or licentious pursuit—entirely? Even if they were to allow music, wouldn't a Stoic approach to musical practices be rather dull? Wouldn't their concern to moderate, rather than heighten, emotional experience necessarily dampen the most compelling aspects of music—in particular, the arousal of sensory pleasure? In other words, wouldn't Stoics aim to produce music that would leave you *un*ravished and *un*moved?

Surprisingly, based on the evidence from early modern Neostoics and their ancient models, the answer is a resounding no. However, the presumption of an anti-music stance has long shadowed the tradition. Antoine de La Faye raises this idea in his laudatory contribution prefacing the bassus part for Paschal de L'Estocart's first collection of *Octonaires*.[33] The poem goes on the defensive against those "Catos" who disapprove of singing and all other happy pursuits. Both Cato the Elder and Cato the Younger were associated with Stoicism and were even proposed as candidates for the ideal Stoic sage. The figure of the dour Stoic who disapproved of music has been accepted in the standard historical accounts of the French magistracy. Historians like Nancy Roelker have agreed upon the centrality of Stoicism as a defining feature of the "mainstream parlementaire mentalité"; they have assumed, however, that a commitment to Stoicism left no room for "frivolous" activities like music, taking the narrow recommendations for *parlementaire* education as codified by Bernard de La Roche-Flavin's *Treize livres des Parlements de France* (1617) as standard practice for the magistracy.[34]

We should not take La Roche-Flavin's proscriptions against music, poetry, non-essential travel, and even the pleasure of study as accepted *parlementaire* practice, given the clear historical evidence, for example, that leading

---

[33] On this attribution, see Melinda Latour, "The Performance of Friendship: Paschal de L'Estocart and his Circle at the University of Basel, 1581–1583," *Music and Letters*, 102 (2021), 411–41.

[34] Nancy Lyman Roelker, *One King, One Faith: The Parlement of Paris and the Religious Reformations of the Sixteenth Century* (Berkeley, CA: University of California Press, 1996), 98–105.

magistrates like Pibrac, Du Vair, and Mathieu Molé, who were praised for their austerity, not only were interested in "honneste" music, poetry, and art, but were often involved in the production and patronage of these practices. The same holds for the famed asceticism and austerity of Protestant Geneva, also unfairly stereotyped as maintaining a rigidly anti-music stance. Even the earlier critiques of the marble, music-hating Stoic—as described in La Faye's laudatory verse—take on a new light when examined more closely. La Faye, a medical doctor by training and Professor of Philosophy and Theology at the Academy of Geneva, displayed an overt personal interest in Stoicism. His inscription for George Paul Nützel's album, signed in Geneva, offers Seneca's famous maxim from Letter 101, "What matters is how well you live, not how long."[35] His philosophically complex laudatory offering for L'Estocart ulti- mately concludes with a Stoic justification of music's curative power to regu- late and manage negative emotional states. As we will see, Neostoic writings were often the first to bring up the negative stereotypes of Stoicism as a way to assert their own moderated approach to Stoicism. This more flexible and humane Stoicism turns out to be a fair and sensitive reading of what scholars today generally agree the ancient school may have taught and practiced all along regarding music, poetry, and other affective artistic activities.

Classicists have demonstrated that the ancient Stoic position on music— with and without text—was far more positive than one might assume. Although the Stoics agreed with Plato's *Republic* about the potential dangers of poetry and music (such as communicating false opinions and values), they did not approve of Plato's recommendation that poets be banned from the city. Moreover, they vehemently disagreed with their competing Hellenistic school, the Epicureans, whose ethics of withdrawal from civic life led them to reject poetry and culture altogether. In fact, the Stoics proved to be some of the most zealous defenders of poetry and music, which they saw as essential elements of their ethical, pedagogical, and therapeutic program.[36]

In the eyes of the Stoics, the concision and clarity of the *forme brève* that defines moral poetry as a genre would have easily justified the texts of di- dactic collections, such as the *Quatrains* by Pibrac and the *Tablettes* by Mathieu. Moreover, the prevailing emphasis on the close union of music and text emphasized in the polyphonic settings would have further supported a

---

[35] British Library, Egerton MS 1213, fol. 148r.
[36] Martha Nussbaum, "Poetry and the Passions: Two Stoic Views," in *Passions and Perceptions: Studies in Hellenistic Philosophy of Mind*, ed. Jacques Brunschwig and Martha Nussbaum (Cambridge: Cambridge University Press, 1993), 97–149.

general Stoic outlook, for whom *logos* ("word" or "speech") was the driving, rational force of the divine universe. But what of the purely musical art and its aesthetic possibilities? Did Stoics find any value in music as sound, feeling, and sensation, or foster an appreciation for what musical experience offers that cannot be put into words or translated into propositional content? Both the ancient and early modern versions of Stoicism would answer in the affirmative.

Paul Scade reveals that the Stoics agreed with Plato and Aristotle on a number of fundamental musical questions, proposing that music could arouse or calm the emotions, discipline impulses and influence actions, produce proportion in the soul, bring health to the body through regular practice (like diet and exercise), and serve the establishment and maintenance of justice and order in a state.[37] Even more importantly, A. A. Long's work on Stoic *harmonia* shows that the principles of Greek music theory acted as a sonic framework onto which the Stoics mapped the ordered rationality of the universe.[38] Following Plato, the Stoic geographer Strabo described the universe as "constituted in accordance with harmony."[39] The Stoics saw Voice as the foundation of Dialectic, or Logic, and they regarded all musical activity as embedded in *logos* regardless of whether it was paired with text. As Zeno wrote, "Come, let us observe what harmony and voice, gut and sinew, wood and bone, send forth when they partake of logos, proportion, and order."[40]

Two speeches delivered before the Parlement of Paris—one by Pibrac in 1572 and the other by Du Vair at the important opening session of 1601— reveal an interest in the therapeutic application of music in Stoicism and its philosophical forbears, both as a multidimensional metaphor and as a lived practice that could be applicable to the governance and repair of the state. While drawn from a range of classical sources in the music encyclopedia tradition, both accounts borrow heavily from Plutarch, one of the favorite authors of the French robe. Recounting the Herald's opening cry at the Olympic games, "Chante, mais chante justement" (Sing, but sing in tune), Pibrac explains that "these words have often ravished me with admiration . . . and they can be accommodated to our exercises of Justice, for so we ought all to sing, justly and in legitimate measure, both those who plead and

[37] Paul Scade, "Music and the Soul in Stoicism," in *Selfhood and the Soul: Essays on Ancient Thought and Literature in Honour of Christopher Gill*, ed. Richard Seaford et al. (Oxford: Oxford University Press, 2017), 197–218.

[38] A. A. Long, *Stoic Studies* (Cambridge: Cambridge University Press, 1996), 202–21.

[39] *Geography* I.10, ch. 468. 10.

[40] Plutarch, *De virtute morali* 443A.

those who defend."[41] Pibrac goes on to describe the proportions of music as an analogy for justice, rooted in the richly numerical Pythagorean account offered in Plato's *Timaeus*, and leading to a Senecan ethical conclusion that civil discord is rooted in this opposition between *mine* and *yours*. Pibrac then paraphrases Zeno's famous admiration of the ordering power of music, taking the proportions of universal harmony into practical, legal territory.

We see this subtly Stoicized take on the broad musico-therapeutic tradition in Guillaume Du Vair's discourse dedicated entirely to the subject of music and justice upon his opening of Parlement in 1601, published in his *Œuvres* (1619). After rehearsing a long and well-known litany of examples across the ancient and biblical traditions of music's therapeutic powers, Du Vair proposes a pragmatic consideration of how these musical practices can model an ordered administration of justice. He demonstrates through his examples that music offers more than a temporary emotional change: it promises a method for shaping a more justly balanced and stable practice of life, in harmony with the fundamental principles of Nature and the rational order of the cosmos. He cites as an example the Thebans who held Harmony as their goddess and by her principles created Athens upon a musical foundation: "justice and music are the same art, for the same proportions render things harmonious, firm, and durable."[42] He cites too Strabo's story of Thales, who was both a good musician and celebrated jurist, adding that another Athenian jurisconsult, Masurius Sabinus, was also a practicing musician. After comparing the workings of justice to a harmonious choir and the strings of a lyre, Du Vair then offers his own account of Zeno encountering the lyre player, awed by the power of animal guts and bone to govern the human soul when played "justement par les nombres," adhering to the proper ratios of musical proportion.

Music as Psychotherapy

The large-scale moral song collections that I will outline in the next chapter grew directly out of this fertile musico-philosophical ground, as the poets, composers, and primary audiences of these collections were directly

---

[41] Guy du Faur de Pibrac, *Harangues et actions publiques des plus rares esprits de notre temps* . . . (Paris: Gilles Robinot, 1609), 777.

[42] Guillaume Du Vair, *Œuvres* (Paris: Pierre Billaine au Palais, 1619), 183.

connected to the Neostoic centers and clearly recognized their therapeutic potential. With their union of moral texts with musical harmony, these collections offered a unique, multi-sensory therapeutic experience suitable for the daily contemplative practices recommended for individuals and communities suffering from prolonged religious and civil conflict.

Du Vair's opening speech to the Parlement of Paris lays the groundwork for this Stoicized approach to music therapy with a discussion of the Platonic harmony of the spheres, a doctrine that circulated widely through Cicero's "Dream of Scipio." After mentioning Pythagoras and Plato on universal harmony, Du Vair goes on to quote Cicero's account more thoroughly, citing "ce grand Scipion," whose flight to the heavens allows him to actually hear the harmony of the spheres ("ceste harmonie celeste"), caused by the sound of the seven planets that by the hand of eternal Providence govern the lower world. He wants to consider the practical effects of these lofty theories and "this mundane music, that is in usage among us," which is a shadow of this celestial harmony and which offers a model for just human relations on earth.[43]

Cicero's "Dream of Scipio" (*Somnium Scipionis*) is a short but famous section of *De re publica* (composed between 54 and 51 BCE). Although Cicero was clearly inspired by Plato's "Myth of Er" and *Timaeus*, his account in the "Dream of Scipio" offered a distinctly Stoic take on these subjects. "Dream of Scipio" rehearses a dialogue between Scipio Aemilianus (185–129 BCE) and his adoptive grandfather Scipio Africanus the Elder. After the younger Scipio falls asleep following a long night of excess, his grandfather's spirit brings him to the heavens where they view the entire cosmos and hear the harmony of the spheres, which he describes as the sound produced by the movements of the planets and their fixed intervals.

Arguably the most influential account of cosmic harmony, the "Dream of Scipio" became an important text throughout both the Stoic and Platonic lineages, and the work offers insight into their intimacy and distinctiveness as schools. It was read through a Neoplatonic lens by Macrobius, whose *Commentary upon Scipio's Dream* was influential in the earlier European reception of the work and was cited by Boethius and Gioseffo Zarlino, among others. We know from Macrobius's *Commentary* what the Neoplatonic interest in the work was: the focus on lofty questions of the immortality of the soul and the stages of ascent and descent of the soul. These were the primary issues in Plato's cosmological treatises such as the *Timaeus* and the

43 Ibid., 181–82.

Phaedo, and they remained the subjects most interesting to early modern Neoplatonists like Ficino and Pontus de Tyard.

Cicero's "Dream of Scipio" secured an equally enduring place in the Stoic lineage. Both of the Scipios featured in the narrative were iconic Stoic figures. Scipio the Elder appeared in Cicero's *On Duties*, where he is praised for his artful balance between service and self-care. Book III opens: "Scipio used to say that he was never less idle than when he had nothing to do and never less lonely than when he was alone." This sentence presents the paradoxical tension balancing *otium* and *negotium*—leisure and duty—which became an important construct in the Stoic guide to inner self-care and the fulfillment of social and communal obligations, including active public service.[44] The younger Scipio Aemilianus was also a Stoic icon admired for his model of wise friendship, his constancy, and his commitment to duty. Scipio Aemilianus was the junior interlocutor with Marcus Porcius Cato in Cicero's *On Old Age*, and he was a friend of the Stoic philosopher Panaetius of Rhodes, the student of Diogenes of Babylon who became the head of the Stoa in Athens in the second century BCE. Neostoics like Lipsius looked to Scipio and his circle as models of the cultivation of a socially rigorous Stoic way of life. Lipsius particularly admired Panaetius as "one of the greatest" Stoics.[45] And in Goulart's *Œuvres morales et meslées de Senecque*, in a section recounting the sentences of Panaetius, he emphasized this friendship between Scipio the Younger and Panaetius, citing Cicero's *On Duties*, book 1, as his source.[46] Particularly as the "Dream of Scipio" began to be bound and read in Latin and vernacular editions alongside Cicero's more overtly Stoic works with the same interlocutors, the practical and therapeutic aspects of the narrative gained clarity.[47] Although beginning from the same cosmological starting point as *Timaeus*, Cicero's "Dream" brings the discussion down into eminently practical terrain guided by core Stoic priorities. Here, the contemplation of the universe is a way to understand the human place within the divine order (insignificant yet also integral to the whole); to recommend against human ambition and the pursuit of worldly fame (which will end in crumbling ruins); and to cultivate a commitment to public service guided by an unshakeable inner constancy.

[44] Gretchen Reydams-Schils, *The Roman Stoics: Self, Responsibility, and Affection* (Chicago, IL: University of Chicago Press, 2006), 93–113.
[45] Morford, *Stoics and Neostoics*, 15.
[46] Seneca, *Œuvres morales et meslées de Senecque*, trans. Goulart, 3:307.
[47] For a list of French editions, see Andrew Pettegree et al., *French Vernacular Books* (Leiden: Brill, 2007), 1:394–99.

The enduring legacy of the Stoic "Dream of Scipio" within the musical tradition can still be seen in the eighteenth century, as the fifteen-year-old Mozart composed (with a libretto by Pietro Metastasio) a dramatic serenade called *Il sogno di Scipione* (K. 126), based on Cicero's work. Mozart and Metastasio's musical rendition takes the Ciceronian plot in an even more overtly Stoic direction. Instead of representing the Elder Scipio guiding his grandson through an altered perspective of his own life based on a viewing of the cosmos, this dramatic serenade introduces the female pillars of Stoicism—Fortune and Constancy— who visit the dreaming Scipio and require him to choose between them. Calling upon Cicero's original, Constancy here solicits the ghosts of Scipio's father and grandfather to aid her in pleading her case. Of course, true to Scipio's Stoic ideals, he chooses to be guided by the voice of Constancy rather than rely on unpredictable Fortune.[48]

Musicologists have left Stoicism almost entirely out of this long conversation on music therapy and universal harmony. A recent example of this broader lacuna in the literature on music philosophy can be found in *Sing Aloud Harmonious Spheres*, edited by Jacomien Prins and Maude Vanhaelen. Although this volume greatly enriches our understanding of the Pythagorean and Platonic lineages of universal harmony, there is no recognition of the Stoic contribution to this early modern soundscape. Especially considering that several scholars included in the collection were writing about work associated with the Stoic tradition—such as Cicero's "Dream"—or writing about the later sixteenth and seventeenth centuries—the heart of the Stoic revival—the absence of Stoicism is particularly striking. Most telling, however, is that accounts of these later traces of the Neoplatonic lineage—like so many other examples in the scholarly literature—note that the questions, methods, and priorities no longer retain the hermeticism, mysticism, and concern with the immortality of the soul that dominated earlier Ficinian Neoplatonism, having shifted by the later sixteenth century to a rationalized, empirical, mechanical, materialist, and/or scientific approach to musical and ethical phenomena.[49] These descriptors form the standard definition of ancient Stoicism in relationship to its Platonic foundations.

---

[48] The work has been largely dismissed for the "essentially undramatic, allegorical nature" of the libretto. See E. T. Glasow, "Il Sogno di Scipione: Wolfgang Amadeus Mozart," *Opera Quarterly* 17, no. 4 (2001): 740.

[49] Jacomien Prins and Maude Vanhaelen, eds. *Sing Aloud Harmonious Spheres: Renaissance Conceptions of Cosmic Harmony* (London: Routledge, 2017), 1–9; Penelope Gouk, "The Role of Harmonics in the Scientific Revolution," in *The Cambridge History of Western Music Theory*, ed. Thomas Christensen (Cambridge: Cambridge University Press, 2002), 223–45; and Suzanne Clark

Scholars of ancient philosophy widely agree that Platonism and Neoplatonism dwelt on the ideal and the immaterial. By contrast, the Stoics were famously rational empiricists who brought core Platonic themes down to earth with a radically materialist, causal, and pragmatic approach that was supported by their mature philosophy of mind and moral psychology.[50] Thus when reading conservative late sixteenth- and early seventeenth-century writings still explicitly engaging Neoplatonism, it remains crucial to consider the role of Neostoicism in propelling these broader intellectual and interpretive shifts toward scientific rather than magical musical thinking on cosmic harmony and its therapeutic power. The Stoic approach to the therapeutic power of music did not center on the mystical, occult, or theurgic approach to sound that best characterizes the Neoplatonic interest in these subjects. Stoicism offered a more psychological and cognitive approach to music therapy no longer reliant upon an enchanted worldview for its efficacy (although Stoicism explicitly supported a belief in the divine), and its use of music as a remedy went beyond the commonplace medicinal recommendations to enjoy music for health, relaxation, or bodily refreshment. Stoic therapy was undergirded by a richly detailed philosophy of mind and moral psychology. In fact, the founder of modern-day cognitive behavioral therapy (one of the most used methods of psychotherapy today) explicitly borrowed from the Stoic tradition.[51]

In emphasizing the psychological, rational, and cognitive thrust of Stoic therapy, it is essential to understand that although the Stoics inherited the Platonic dualism of mind versus body, their consistent strategy of finding unity within contradictions allowed them to overcome the extreme intellectualism of the Platonic mind/body split. Although the Stoics borrowed extensively from the Platonic tradition, this pragmatic rationalism and subsequent denial of Plato's forms marked their first major departure from that heritage and led them to seek relational causation through physical phenomena and empirically observable experiences. In contrast to the rather lofty and mystical approach to the interconnected World Soul found in Plato's *Timaeus*,

---

and Alex Rehding, eds., *Music Theory and Natural Order from the Renaissance to the Early Twentieth Century* (Cambridge: Cambridge University Press, 2005), 6.

[50] Brad Inwood, *Stoicism: A Very Short Introduction* (Oxford: Oxford University Press, 2018), 27–34; A. A. Long, *Epictetus: A Stoic and Socratic Guide to Life* (Oxford: Oxford University Press, 2002), 16–33; and Sellars, Introduction to *The Routledge Handbook of the Stoic Tradition*, ed. Sellars, 1–3.

[51] Donald Robertson, *The Philosophy of Cognitive-Behavioural Therapy (CBT): Stoic Philosophy as Rational and Cognitive Psychotherapy*, 2nd ed. (London: Routledge, 2020), 15–119.

the Stoics brought these concepts down to earth through the empirical observation of Nature. They understood the soul (including but not limited
to our concept of mind) in a more tangible way, arguing that both the flesh
and soul were corporeal and governed by the physical laws of the universe.
Following Plato to some extent, the Stoics developed a certain dualism between these two types of bodies and worried about the tendency of the fleshly
part to block or diminish the reasoning faculties. However, they avoided the
pitfalls of Platonic metaphysical dualism by developing an ultimately unified
and holistic account of critical sense processes that harmonized the physical
sensorium with a process of evaluative judgment that remained grounded in
Aristotelian sensory theory.

In this way, Stoicism strategically synthesized the two most important
disagreements between the Platonic and Aristotelian traditions—a maneuver that provided a ready-made Hellenistic template for the oft-touted
reconciling tendencies of the Renaissance. The solitary sentence that Thomas
Mathiesen's summary of music philosophy from antiquity to the Middle Ages
affords to Stoicism—as merely "a synthesis of Pythagorean, Platonic, and
Aristotelian viewpoints"—turns out to be significant, even in its dismissal.[52]
The musical lineage of Platonism and Neoplatonism, theoretically, had only
a begrudging access to the physical senses—recall that Plato's *Phaedo* 65e
had positively fantasized about a pure and unfettered knowledge, "rid, as
much as possible, of eyes and ears and, broadly speaking, of the body altogether."[53] This places the musician in an awkward position, and compounds
the theoretical impasse that has plagued so much Neoplatonist work: that
their mystical universal harmony, while powerful on a cosmic level, had no
clear physical correlation to music as practiced, sung, or heard by human
bodies on earth. Aristotle offered little help in resolving this problem, as
he had roundly mocked the notion of cosmic harmony altogether.[54] It was
Stoicism that negotiated this divide by uniting the ordering power of universal harmony drawn from the Platonic tradition with a richly sensory concept of cognition following Aristotle though further developed through their
systematic union of ethics, logic, and physics. Stoic psychotherapy, though

[52] Thomas J. Mathiesen, "Antiquity and the Middle Ages," in *The Routledge Companion to Philosophy and Music*, ed. Theodore Cracyk and Andrew Kania (London: Routledge, 2011), 261.
[53] Of course, this quote is hyperbolic, as Plato does ultimately resign himself to the practical necessity of the bodily senses. The point remains, however, that the pure life of the mind remained the Platonic ideal. See A. A. Long, *Greek Models of Mind and Self* (Cambridge, MA: Harvard University Press, 2015), 119–22.
[54] Aristotle, *De caelo* 2.9.

predicated on rationality, did not lead to a dismissal of the body, its sensations and feelings, or the physical world. Stoic cognition, in fact, remained deeply materialist and cautiously prized the sensory practices and perceptions of the body—a point that opens fascinating lines of inquiry into the musical practices influenced by the Stoic therapeutic tradition.

From this vantage point, we can begin to see how and why the famously austere Stoics and Neostoics cultivated a sustained interest in musical practice as one of the "habitudes of the wise." According to the Stobaeus *Anthology* 2.5–12, the Stoics understood the habitudes of the wise as crafts or artistic practices that "lead to what is in accord with virtue." "They are not knowledge; but they leave them in the class of virtuous conditions, and consistently they say that only the wise man is a music lover."[55] Quintilian also remarked upon the surprising Stoic emphasis on music as foundational for sagehood: "the leaders of that sect which appears sternest and harshest to others were of this opinion, that they thought it the task of the wise man to devote some attention to these studies."[56] Early moderns picked up on this stream of thought, as we see in the Ode that prefaces Jean de Bournonville's 1622 collection of settings for Pibrac's *Quatrains*, published when Stoicism was at its most fashionable and recognizable. The laudatory writer, Roch de Beaulieu, narrates the example of Socrates learning music in his old age in explicitly Stoic terms. Ignoring the criticism of others for his interest in music lessons, Socrates pursued musical training in the belief that he "could not merit the high title of sage without knowledge of this beautiful art" (*Tu ne crois meriter le haut tiltre de Sage / Sans sçavoir ce bel Art*).[57] De Beaulieu goes on to state that Greece therefore honors musical practice and the appreciation of musical beauty as essential for self-knowledge and wisdom. In cherishing music, the poet concludes, "the Greek is recognized to the furthest East as a perfect sage" (*Le Grec est recognu jusqu'au lit de l'Aurore, / Pour un Sage parfait*). The image of an ideal sage who cherishes beautiful music adds desperately needed dimension to the rigid cardboard cutout of Stoic sagehood, demanding a therapeutic experience predicated on a warm and unflinchingly human engagement with sound.

---

[55] Brad Inwood and L. P. Gerson, eds., *Hellenistic Philosophy: Introductory Readings* (Indianapolis, IN: Hackett, 1988), 203–7.

[56] Ralph Doty, "Chrysippus' Theory of Education," *Journal of Thought* 20, no. 2 (1985): 75.

[57] Jean de Bournonville, *Cinquante Quatrains du Sieur de Pybrac* (Paris: Pierre Ballard, 1622).

2

Imprinting Virtue

Lo, heer in Paper is poor Vertue painted:
Alas, dead Vertue! Thus these Times doo use-thee:
Yet, if all hands, yet if all hearts refuse-thee,
Remain Thou ever in these Songs imprinted.[1]

In her 1606 preface to her deceased brother Claude Le Jeune's *Octonaires de la vanité et inconstance du monde*, Cecile Le Jeune describes the collection as "a work small in appearance but large in effect" (*œuvre petit en aparence, mais grand en effect*). The same could be said for moral song as a genre. This seemingly marginal domain of musical and poetic activity in the decades around 1600 offers a history of production and use that sheds new light on the way the growing "cult of Seneca" harnessed the joint power of song and Stoicism in its work of reordering the divided landscape. From Paris to Geneva, large-scale collections of vernacular moral poetry—such as the *Quatrains de Pibrac*, the *Octonaires de la vanité du monde*, and Mathieu's *Tablettes de la vie et de la mort*—and their plentiful musical settings repackaged these therapeutic initiatives for use in educational, domestic, and recreational practice.

The *Quatrains de Pibrac*

The late sixteenth-century flourishing of moral song is nowhere more evident than in the extraordinary fortune of the *Quatrains* by Guy du Faur de Pibrac. Shortly after its first printing of fifty poems in 1574, the *Quatrains* became a classic text. Reprinted and gradually expanded, the

[1] L'Estocart, *Quatrains*, contratenor part, translated by Josuah Sylvester and printed in *Du Bartas His Divine Weekes and Workes, with a Complete Collection of all the other Most Delightfull Workes* (London: Humphray Lownes, 1621), 1195 (henceforth cited as Sylvester, *Works*).

collection reached its definitive form of 126 poems by 1576.[2] Although much of Pibrac's didactic sampler transmits commonly accepted ancient and popular wisdom, several texts directly summarize Stoic philosophy, paraphrasing the famous Stoic paradoxes and translating other key teachings of Seneca and Epictetus on the unity of virtue, the idea of worldly goods as "indifferents," the need to understand what is in our control and what is not, and the value of self-knowledge and self-governance. Among his Senecan texts, Pibrac's Quatrain 117 paraphrases the opening of Seneca's *On the Brevity of Life*:

> L'homme se plaint de sa trop courte vie,
> Et ce pendant n'employe où il devroit.
> Le temps qu'il a, qui suffir luy pourroit,
> Si pour bien vivre avoit de vivre envie.

[Man complains that his life is too short, / and yet does not employ it as he should. / The time that he has, might be sufficient for him, / if, to live well, he did desire.]

The Stoicism of Pibrac's *Quatrains* goes beyond his reworking of commonly known Stoic teachings—it inflects the overarching poetic style of the collection. As Loris Petris has shown, the consistent *abba* form of each decasyllabic four-line poem models constancy; the terse delivery offers proverbial weight; and the borrowed and newly devised moral content repeatedly drives home a commitment to stability in the soul and the state as the highest objectives.[3] Pibrac's first biographer, Charles Paschal, noted in his *Vie de Pibrac* (1584) that Pibrac regarded Seneca as a kind of soul mate (*l'amy du cœur*) and viewed his writings as a philosophical remedy for the troubled times.[4]

Pibrac was born in Toulouse into a noble family of *parlementaires*—one of the leading political families in the kingdom and longstanding supporters of humanist learning. Toulouse was the source of a new, humanist approach

---

[2] Guy du Faur de Pibrac, *Cinquante Quatrains, contenans préceptes et enseignemens utiles pour la vie de l'homme, composez à l'imitation de Phocylidees, d'Epicharmus et autres anciens poëtes grécs* (Paris: Gilles Gorbin, 1574). The full 126 poems appeared in *Les Quatrains du seigneur de Pybrac... de nouveau mis en leur ordre, et augmentez par ledict seigneur* (Paris: Frédéric Morel, 1576).

[3] Pibrac, *Les Quatrains*, ed. Petris, 10–11, 50, 62–63; and Loris Petris, "L'Hospital, Pibrac et Montaigne: Trois magistrats-écrivains face au néostoicisme chrétien," in *Stoïcisme et christianisme à la Renaissance*, ed. Alexandre Tarrête (Paris: Rue d'Ulm, 2006), 71–91.

[4] Charles Paschal, *La Vie et moeurs de messire Guy du Faur, seigneur de Pybrac*, trans. Guy du Faur, seigneur d'Hermay (Paris: Thibault Du Val, 1617), 246.

to law—*mos gallicus*—founded in the early sixteenth century by Guillaume Budé and the jurist Andrea Alciato, whose landmark emblem book, *Emblematum libellus* (1534), frequently draws upon Stoicism in its depictions of virtue and vice. In the 1540s, Pibrac studied in Italy with Alciato, and back in Toulouse, in 1548, he studied with another famous legal humanist, Jacques Cujas. Thus his collection of *Quatrains* was birthed from this lineage, often treating the same moral themes and aims as emblem books, and writing them for the same general audience.[5]

As a magistrate whose illustrious career gave him a position of influence in both the Paris Parlement and the royal court, Pibrac was well-positioned to spearhead a program of moral reform in the wake of the St. Bartholomew's Day Massacre. The *Quatrains de Pibrac* were written first for the future ruler and magistrate to learn the principles of character needed for just governance. They were thus inscribed in the "mirror of princes" literature—a long pedagogical tradition inspired by Seneca's *On Mercy*. Following this model, Pibrac's collection consistently emphasizes the importance of inner self-restraint and self-knowledge as a critical foundation for those serving in positions of power, delivering quips like "To overcome oneself is the great victory" (Quatrain 47) and "Whoever wishes to make the most of his achievements / He should control his anger" (Quatrain 46).[6] Simon Goulart's *Ample discours sur la doctrine des Stoiques* describes Stoic political theory according to these aims, in a passage based on Seneca's *On Anger* (1.5) arguing that the health of the public body depends upon the moral formation of the Prince who must learn to resist the lust for power, achieve self-mastery, overcome his passions, and despise the pomp and delights of the world. For "the one who cannot master himself by reason cannot properly govern others."[7] While Pibrac's *Quatrains* remained associated with the education of the robe, the *Quatrains* reached beyond the edification of *parlementaire* families and became standard material for domestic and formal education, appearing in quotation in a range of printed texts, inspiring musical settings, and resounding in recitation and song throughout the French-speaking world well into the next century.

[5] Pibrac, *Les Quatrains*, ed. Petris, 3–6; Carabin, *Les Idées stoïciennes*, 52–53, 69–70; Bouwsma, *A Usable Past*, 129–54; and Karl Enenkel, *The Invention of the Emblem Book and the Transmission of Knowledge, ca. 1510–1610* (Leiden: Brill, 2019), 3–124 and 179–230.

[6] Quatrain 47, "Vaincre soymesme est la grande victoire," and Quatrain 46, "Qui a desir d'exploiter sa proüesse / Dompte son ire." See Pibrac, *Les Quatrains*, ed. Petris, 163n65; and Levi, *French Moralists*, 52–53.

[7] Seneca, *Œuvres morales et meslées de Senecque*, trans. Goulart, 3:381.

Pibrac's *Quatrains en musique*

The impressive publishing history of Pibrac's *Quatrains* was enriched by a number of musical settings of the poetic text (see Appendix 1, Table A1.1). Between 1580 and 1622, well over three hundred printed musical settings of texts from the *Quatrains* were produced by a range of celebrated composers and editors, some of whom had close ties to Pibrac's circle.[8] The earliest settings appeared in the *Nouveau recueil et élite de plusieurs belles chansons joyeuses, honnestes, et amoureuses*, first printed in 1580 by Thomas Mallard and then in 1581 by Richard l'Allemand. [Web 2.1] The simple melody was clearly meant to be used for all 126 of the *Quatrains*, but we do not know where it originated. Perhaps it was newly printed in the first monophonic edition, or it may have already been in widespread oral use.

Appearing shortly after these humble monophonic editions, Guillaume Boni's ambitious *Quatrains du Sieur de Pybrac* (1582) marks the only attempt to offer unique polyphonic settings for each of the 126 texts. Boni may very well have known Pibrac personally, if Yates is correct in speculating that Boni was a participant in Baïf's Académie.[9] Indeed, the pair may also have connected when Boni was serving as the choirmaster at the Toulouse Cathedral, around 1565.[10] Boni dedicated his *Quatrains* settings to Henri III's younger brother, François, duke of Anjou, who probably already appreciated the poetry, considering that Pibrac was serving as his chancellor at the time.

Paschal de L'Estocart's *Cent vingt et six quatrains du Sieur de Pibrac* (1582) was the only collection of Pibrac settings to rival Boni's in sheer size and musical interest. A known associate and friend of highly-placed Protestant scholars and pastors with a documented interest in Neostoicism, L'Estocart offered 117 unique polyphonic arrangements of Pibrac's texts in an edition that was financed and published by printers and booksellers in Lyon and Geneva. He dedicated his collection to Charles III, duke of Lorraine, praising him for practicing "the wise warnings that the learned Pibrac gives to kings

---

[8] See Marie-Alexis Colin, "Les *Quatrains* de Guy du Faur de Pibrac en musique," 535–36; van Orden, *Materialities*, 231–47; and Melinda Latour, "Les *Quatrains* de Pibrac en musique: Supplément bibliographique," *Revue de musicologie* 102, no. 1 (2016): 143–52.

[9] Guillaume Boni, *Les Quatrains du Sieur de Pybrac mis en musique a 3. 4. 5. et 6. parties* (Paris: Le Roy et Ballard, 1582, repr. 1583); ed. Marie-Alexis Colin (Tours: Centre de musique ancienne, Musica Gallica, 2000); Yates, *French Academies*, 106.

[10] See Greengrass, *Governing Passions*, 260; and Jeanice Brooks, "Music and Devotion in Renaissance Toulouse: The Motets of Guillaume Boni," in *"La Musique de tous les passetemps le plus beau": Hommage à Jean-Michel Vaccaro*, ed. François Lesure and Henri Vanhulst (Paris: Klincksieck, 1998), 18–24.

and princes" and expressing his hope that the musical settings would assist his progress on this virtuous path.

The success of these earlier collections may have inspired the involvement of the most famous contributor to Pibrac's musical corpus, Orlande de Lassus, who was widely acknowledged as the finest composer of his time and was afforded the status and perks of an international superstar. The royal music printers Le Roy and Ballard opened their *Vingtdeuxième livre de chansons* (1583) with seven settings of the "Quatrains de Monsieur de Pybrac" set for four voices by Lassus. According to Annie Cœurdevey, this attribution to a literary author in Le Roy and Ballard's *chanson* series was exceptional, and it signaled the immense importance of the magistrate Pibrac as the author of the poetic collection as well as the market appeal of the polyphonic settings already in circulation.[11]

Additional polyphonic settings for selected *Quatrains* continued to appear in the years that followed, though none of these later collections survive with all parts extant. In 1622, the final known collection of Pibrac arrangements appeared, this time by Jean de Bournonville, whose *Cinquante Quatrains du Sieur de Pybrac* (1622) supplied fifty polyphonic settings in two to four voices. The title page names Bournonville as the *maître de musique* for the choir school at Amiens Cathedral, a position he had already held at Saint Quentin and Abbeville. By the end of 1631, he was established as director of the choir school of the Sainte Chapelle in Paris, where he stayed for a short time until his death.[12] Among Bournonville's students was the young Artus Aux-Cousteaux, who went on to compose the final moral song collections considered in this study.

The *Octonaires de la vanité et inconstance du monde*

Around the time that Pibrac's *Quatrains* exploded onto the print market in 1574, the first nineteen of Antoine de Chandieu's *Octonaires de la vanité et inconstance du monde* began circulating in manuscript.[13] The *Octonaires* are

[11] Cœurdevey, *Roland de Lassus*, 310.

[12] Denise Launay and James R. Anthony, "Bournonville family," *Grove Music Online*. https://www.oxfordmusiconline.com/.

[13] The earliest manuscript sources of the *Octonaires* are found in BnF, f. lat. 8143; Rasse des Noeux, BnF, f. fr. 22565; and Rime Françoise, Harvard, Houghton Library, F MS Fr 337. On the sources and earlier dating of the *Octonaires*, see Julien Goeury, *La Muse du Consistoire: Une histoire des pasteurs poètes des origines de la Réforme jusqu'à la révocation de l'édit de Nantes* (Geneva: Droz, 2016), 336–43.

short moral poems written in *huitains* (eight lines). Like other examples of the *forme brève*, each stanza in the *Octonaires* has a self-contained meaning, yet the collection finds a loose unity through recourse to a consistent tone and recurring moral imagery reflecting the rising Neostoicism of Chandieu's intellectual sphere.

Chandieu was a wealthy noble, venerated Reformed pastor, active diplomat, talented polemicist, and esteemed scholar, recognized by his contemporaries as the "silver horn" of Geneva, positioned in the Protestant hierarchy between Jean Calvin's gold and Theodore Beza's bronze. Although Chandieu's later career as a prominent Reformed pastor and theologian tied him closely to Genevan circles, his early education placed him firmly in Pibrac's sphere of legal humanism. In fact, Chandieu may have studied with Pibrac himself, for Chandieu studied law as a teenager at the illustrious University of Toulouse while Pibrac was still on the faculty. It was sometime between 1552 and 1555 that he left for Geneva to meet Calvin and embraced the Reform. This encounter eventually convinced him to leave behind his law career in Paris and take a post as a Protestant pastor there. When Chandieu's Paris congregation was devastated by the 1572 Massacre, he fled to Geneva and received a post as a professor of theology at the Lausanne Académie.[14]

It was during Chandieu's early years in Swiss lands as a refugee of the Massacre that he penned his *Octonaires*, which exemplify a shift from his strident earlier polemic works toward the therapeutic tone that characterizes what many agree was his finest work. Whereas Pibrac's *Quatrains* mostly involves direct paraphrases of Stoic teachings, Chandieu's *Octonaires* move beyond direct paraphrases and offer what might be best characterized as an original therapeutic response to Neostoicism by imaginatively developing its key moral themes and aims in a way that would be legible for his Christian readership.

Chandieu's interest in Stoicism may have been encouraged by his close personal relationship with Philippe Duplessis-Mornay, whose *Excellent discours de la vie et de la mort* (1576) furnished the French version of the Stoic maxim on learning to die. Chandieu lived with Philippe and his wife Charlotte Arbaleste in 1586, and their relationship was so intimate that the couple named Chandieu the godfather of their newborn daughter. Both

---

[14] For Chandieu's biography, see Theodore van Raalte, *Antoine de Chandieu: The Silver Horn of Geneva's Reformed Triumvirate* (Oxford: Oxford University Press, 2018), 14–15 and 31–47; and Sarah Barker, *Protestantism, Poetry and Protest: The Vernacular Writings of Antoine de Chandieu, c. 1534–1591* (Farnham, UK: Ashgate, 2009), 16–48.

personally and in terms of translations of his work, Duplessis-Mornay's influence reached beyond France, becoming an important conduit of French Neostoicism to the Anglophone world due to his diplomatic missions to England on behalf of Henri de Navarre beginning in 1577. During these visits, Philippe and Charlotte developed a friendship with Sir Philip Sidney and Mary Sidney Herbert, the Countess of Pembroke, who produced an important English translation of Duplessis-Mornay's *Excellent discours*.[15]

Like the *Excellent discours*, the *Octonaires* corpus follows the central teachings and aims of Stoicism by urging a therapeutic meditation on death and the inconstancy of the world—by portraying Nature as a mirror of life; by critiquing false opinions; by warning of the danger of attachment to externals, which fade quickly and do not satisfy; by presenting the Stoic trio of vices—ambition, avarice, and luxury—as sicknesses of the mind; by suggesting that fear is linked to both irrational pleasure and desire; by calling for the regulation of disturbing passions; and by valorizing the work of the senses while warning that they can be deceived.

More surprising from a literary perspective, the poignant *Octonaires* corpus also resonated directly with Pibrac's strictly disciplined *Quatrains*. Although the *Octonaires* corpus borrows from the same Stoic sources, and in some cases treats the same moral topics as Pibrac's *Quatrains*, it exhibits a marked difference in style, with the *Octonaires* penned in a deliberately inconstant heterometric verse, evoking the fundamental instability of the world. Thus these collections developed as two sides of the same moral coin: the staid regularity of Pibrac's *Quatrains* models the constancy and austerity of Stoic virtue, whereas the *Octonaires* poetry offers an evocative experience of inconstancy meant to guide the reader in a contemplative practice toward greater tranquility and stability.

The shared moral and therapeutic underpinnings of Pibrac's *Quatrains* and Chandieu's *Octonaires* were apparently well-recognized in the period, for despite their clear stylistic differences and the fact that the authors came from opposing sides of the religious conflict, the collections were frequently bound together in printed and manuscript collections of moral poetry throughout the period. They circulated together in Valagre and Maisonfleur's *Cantiques du sieur de Maisonfleur*

[15] See Philippe Duplessis-Mornay, *Il "Discours de la vie et de la mort"*, ed. Mario Richter (Milan: Vita e pensiero, 1964), 1–33; and Elizabeth Pentland, "Philippe Mornay, Mary Sidney, and the Politics of Translation," *Early Modern Studies Journal* 6 (2014): 66–99.

after 1586 and in numerous other cross-confessional moral and spiritual collections over the following decades.[16] Several of Pibrac's Stoic *Quatrains* have direct corollaries in Chandieu's *Octonaires*. For example, both Quatrain 25 (*Les biens du corps*) and Octonaire 37 (*Antiquité, pourquoy as-tu donné*) express the Stoic challenge to Aristotle's view of wealth as a good. Quatrain 117 (*L'homme se plaint de sa trop courte vie*), inspired by Seneca's *On the Brevity of Life*, seems to have been the source for several *Octonaires*. Consider Chandieu's *Quand on arrestera*, which became the opening text in the standard ordering after the first complete prose edition of 1583:[17]

> Quand on arrestera la course coutumiere
> Du grand Courrier des cieux qui porte la lumiere,
> Quand on arrestera l'an qui roule toujours
> Sur un char attelé de mois, d'heures, de jours,
> Quand on arrestera l'armée vagabonde
> Qui va courant la nuict par le vuide des cieux,
> Descochant contre nous les longs traicts de ses yeux,
> Lors on arrestera l'inconstance du Monde.

[When we can stop the customary course / Of the great Messenger of the heavens who brings the light: / When we can halt the year, which rolls always on a winged chariot, drawn by months, hours, days: / When we can halt the wandering army, / Which runs through the night across the void of the heavens, / Shooting long arrows at us from its eyes, / Then we can halt the world's inconstancy.]

Seneca's *On the Brevity of Life* is particularly salient in its similar recourse to the imagery of the constant cycle of the heavens as a way of making an ethical argument about how to understand the ephemerality and fragility of our lives (and pleasures) on earth:

---

[16] These include Theodore Beza's *Tragédie françoise du sacrifice d'Abraham* (Geneva: Jacob Stoer, 1598), the *Poèmes chrestiens et moraux* [Geneva: Jean II de Tournes] [c. 1600], and the multi-lingual *Viri clarissimi et amplissimi Vidi Fabri Pibracii . . .* (Lyon [Geneva]: François Le Fèvre, 1598). On these collections, see Goeury, *La Muse du Consistoire*, 344–45.

[17] Antoine de Chandieu, *Meditations sur le psalme XXXII . . . Ont esté aussi adjoustez cinquante octonaires sur la vanité du monde* (Geneva: G. Laimarie, 1583).

Present time is very short, so short, indeed, that some people think there is none; for it is constantly on the move, like a rushing river; it ceases to exist before it has arrived, and no more tolerates delay than the heavens or the stars, whose ever-restless motion never lets them remain in the same track. Accordingly, those busy with other things concern themselves only with present time, which is so short that it cannot be seized, and even this is stolen from them.[18]

In other words, reading Seneca's text reveals that Chandieu's *Quand on arrestera* develops the same lesson presented in Pibrac's Quatrain 117—that life is fleeting and should be used well—though it does so more subtly, through recourse to the natural imagery depicted in this later passage of Seneca's essay.

Chandieu's fifth Octonaire also harnesses the imagery of water as a picture of the brevity of life and a caution against attachment to the world:

> Vous, Fleuves et Ruisseaux, et vous, claires Fonteines,
> > De qui le glissant pas
> > Se roule roule en bas,
> Dites-moi la raison de vos tant longues peines.
> C'est pour monstrer au doigt que ta vie en ce Monde
> > S'enfuit ainsi que l'onde,
> > Et ta felicité
> Ne s'arreste icy-bas où rien n'est arresté.

[You, Rivers and Streams, and you, clear Fountains, / whose slippery pace / rolls, rolls on down, / tell me the reason for your long troubles. / It is to point out that your life in this World / flees from you like the wave, / and your happiness / does not stay here below where nothing is halted.]

Although Seneca offers the river analogy in the passage above, Chandieu could also have drawn inspiration from the great Stoic emperor Marcus Aurelius, who penned something very similar in his *Meditations*, a work that was available in a 1570 French translation by Pardoux Du Prat.[19] "We

---

[18] Seneca, *De brevitate vitae* 10; Seneca, *Dialogues and Essays*, trans. Davie, 150.
[19] Marcus Aurelius, *Institution de la vie humaine, dressée par Marc Antonin*, trans. Pardoux Du Prat (Lyon: Vve G. Cotier, 1570). On the early modern circulation of the *Meditations*, see Jill Kraye, "'Ethnicorum omnium sanctissimus': Marcus Aurelius and his Meditations from Xylander

find ourselves in a river," he notes to himself. "Which of the things around us should we value when none of them can offer a firm foothold?"[20] The Stoic view of the inconstancy of the heavens and the ever-changing cosmos was meant to provoke reflection on each person's value system. It asks people to consider whether they have assigned improper value to fleeting externals (false opinions), or whether they have cultivated a value system guided by reason and with attention to what is enduring and what is entirely in their control—and thus is the only constant foundation for happiness and virtue.

Although Chandieu's philosophical borrowings are often subtle, on several occasions he is more direct in pointing to his Stoic sources, as seen in Octonaire 22:

> Si le ciel est un cercle et son poinct est la terre,
> Comme le Philosophe enseigne et nous fait voir,
> Pourquoy, povres Mondains, vous faictes-vous la guerre,
> A qui pourra le plus de ceste terre avoir?
> Pourquoy, povres Mondains, prenez-vous tant de peine,
> Trompez du fol espoir d'une ambition vaine?
> O dangereux erreur! de ne cognoistre point
> Qu'en vain on se travaille à mespartir un poinct.

[If heaven is a circle and its point is the earth, / as the Philosopher teaches us to see, / why, poor Worldly Ones, do you make war / over who can have more of this earth? / Why, poor Worldly Ones, do you take such trouble, / tricked by the crazy hope of a vain ambition? / O dangerous error! to not understand / that in vain we toil to divide a point.]

The philosopher referenced in this passage would easily have been recognized as Seneca. Mornay's "Avertissement au Lecteur" for the *Excellent discours* notes that Seneca was known to his circle as "The Philosopher," an honor that had typically been reserved for Aristotle. More importantly, Seneca had made precisely this moral point, using the scale of the universe as an analogy

to Diderot," in *Humanism and Early Modern Philosophy*, ed. Jill Kraye and M. W. F. Stone (London: Routledge, 2000), 107–34.

[20] Marcus Aurelius, *Meditations* 6.15; trans. and ed. Gregory Hays (New York: Modern Library, 2003), 71.

in his *Natural Questions* (I, Preface, 7–9), recommending a zoomed-out view of the cosmos as a way to demonstrate the futility of militaristic conquest and empire-building: "Is this that pinpoint which is divided by sword and fire among so many nations? How ridiculous are the boundaries of mortals!"

This exercise in perspective, identified by Pierre Hadot as the "View from Above," was modeled on Cicero's *Dream of Scipio* (introduced in the previous chapter) and appears across the Stoic and Neostoic corpus, from Seneca to Lipsius.[21] Marcus Aurelius referenced this rational technique in his *Meditations*. On several occasions in these reflections, the Roman Stoic described the whole earth as only a point (4.3; 8.21), as just such a reminder to resist the ambition and greed that fuels conflict and war. The entry in Book IV is longer than most of his quips and situates this perspective of the earth as a mere point within his related advice to see the world as a city of rational beings who exist for one another (4.3). This argument of universal harmony underpinning Chandieu's Octonaire 22 thus adds dimension to Pibrac's Quatrain 6 (*Tout l'univers n'est qu'une cité ronde*) on the world city as comprised of diverse yet rationally interconnected beings with an inherent capacity for mutual understanding and sympathy.

Despite this clear evidence of a critical engagement with the rising tide of Neostoicism in the 1570s and 1580s, the philosophical and moral aspects of the *Octonaires* have gone almost entirely unmentioned by scholars of French literature in favor of religious and devotional readings of this poetry. In fact, the voice that calls out across the collection, warning against worldly attachment, has long been read as the voice of a preacher who is seeking to convert his congregation from sin. Several scholars have at least briefly noted the moral character of the poetry.[22] Françoise Bonali-Fiquet located Chandieu's *Octonaires* within a "moralizing and meditative tradition"; Launay described them as "imbued simultaneously with Christian morality and pagan wisdom"; and Isabelle His importantly categorized the *Octonaires*

---

[21] Lipsius, *On Constancy*; ed. Sellars, 127–28; Pierre Hadot, *Philosophy as a Way of Life: Spiritual Exercises from Socrates to Foucault*, ed. and with an introduction by Arnold I. Davidson, trans. Michael Chase (Malden, MA: Blackwell Publishing, 2017), 238–50; and Robertson, *The Philosophy of Cognitive-Behavioural Therapy*, 210–18.

[22] See, for example, Bonali-Fiquet's commentary for Octonaire 47: "Les exhortations du prédicateur visent à amener le pécheur à se repentir et à confesser sa faute." Chandieu, *Octonaires*, ed. Bonali-Fiquet, 91. Classic spiritual readings are offered in Terence Cave, *Devotional Poetry in France, c. 1570–1613* (New York: Cambridge University Press, 1969), 146–71; and Françoise Bonali-Fiquet, *Engagement spirituel et procédés stylistiques dans les Octonaires sur l'inconstance et vanité du monde d'Antoine de la Roche-Chandieu* (Paris: Presses de l'École Normale Supérieure, 1995).

settings as "chansons morales."[23] A series of emblems that Etienne Delaune created for Chandieu's *Octonaires*, published with the poetry (Strasbourg, 1580), support this philosophical reading, for they depict an image of the male teaching voice as an ancient sage (like the philosopher in Octonaire 22), not a Reformed preacher.[24] Employed at the royal mint in Paris by 1552, Delaune may have been privy to the musico-philosophical activities of Baïf's Académie; the teaching figure in the *Octonaires* certainly foregrounds the philosophical orientation of those court experiments.[25] Delaune's sage wears a toga and is usually pictured within an iconic copse of trees seen in numerous other portrayals of antiquity from the period (see Plate 1). Harmonized by the feminine voice of Virtue—whom Delaune represents as Minerva—the sage calls out to the worldly person to let go of vain passions and the lust for power, pleasure, and wealth, which create violence and conflict, and instead find wisdom and virtue in living and dying well.

Harmonizing the *Octonaires*

The depth and sensitivity of the *Octonaires* corpus offered particularly rich inspiration for musical exploration. The musical settings of the *Octonaires* comprised just three polyphonic collections in total—two by L'Estocart and one by Claude Le Jeune—and they are among the most daring, imaginative, and compelling musical compositions of the entire period (see Appendix 1, Table A1.2).

The first printed link between Pibrac's and Chandieu's collections was a musical one, for L'Estocart's double volume of *Octonaires* (1582) went to press in Jean I de Laon's atelier in Geneva a few months before his settings of Pibrac's *Quatrains* (1582).[26] L'Estocart's *Premier livre des Octonaires de la vanité du monde* (1582) sets twenty-six texts by Chandieu for three to six

---

[23] Chandieu, *Octonaires*, ed. Bonali-Fiquet, 23; Launay, *La Musique religieuse*, 103; and His, *Claude Le Jeune*, 95–99. Lucile Gibert has also noted the Neostoicism of Du Chesne's *Octonaires*; see Du Chesne, *La Morocosmie*, ed. Gibert, 34–35, 80–87.

[24] Antoine de Chandieu, *Octonaires sur la vanité et inconstance du monde* (Strasbourg: Bernard Jobin, 1580). See Florence Mauger, "Antoine de Chandieu et Etienne Delaune: Les *Octonaires sur la vanité et inconstance du monde*, un recueil d'emblèmes?," *BHR* 58, no. 3 (1996): 611–29. Though designed by Etienne Delaune, the emblems were engraved by his son Jean.

[25] Per Bjurström, "Etienne Delaune and the Academy of Poetry and Music," *Master Drawings* 34, no. 4 (1996): 351–64.

[26] These three prints were quickly followed by L'Estocart's final two collections, the *Sacrae cantiones* (1582) and *Cent cinquante pseaumes de David* (1583), a speed that suggests a post-hoc publication packaging.

voices, while his *Second livre des Octonaires de la vanité du monde* (1582) arranges two more sets of twelve *Octonaires* by another pair of Protestant notables involved in the sixteenth-century Neostoic resurgence, Simon Goulart and Joseph Du Chesne, sieur de la Violette.[27] While the composer may have only known Pibrac through his poetry, L'Estocart had close ties to all three poets of his *Octonaires*, who were high-profile members of his elite Protestant network linking the University of Basel to the Academy of Geneva.[28]

Goulart began his education by studying civil law in Paris and becoming active in the Parlement of Paris, before changing course for Geneva in 1566. He soon joined Chandieu as one of the most highly regarded pastors and scholars at the head of the Reformed church. An active editor of music, Goulart was also one of L'Estocart's closest friends, and in the preface to his second collection of *Octonaires*, the composer credits Goulart with inspiring him to set Chandieu's poetry and to devote his musical talents to "grave and holy things" (*choses graves et saintes*).[29] In addition to providing half of the poetic texts for L'Estocart's second collection of *Octonaires*, Goulart contributed numerous laudatory poems to L'Estocart's prefaces that framed the philosophical and musical contributions of his prints. While his intellectual interests were broad, Goulart's prodigious publishing career included an impressive output of essays, editions, and translations dedicated to bringing Stoicism to a broader, vernacular readership. After reediting Jacques Amyot's pioneering translation of Plutarch (*Œuvres morales et meslées de Plutarque*, 1581), he went on to produce a massive, three-volume translation of Seneca's complete works (*Œuvres morales et meslées de Senecque*, 1595), to which he appended translations of other Stoic writings, such as Epictetus's *Handbook*, as well as his original

[27] Of the twelve Octonaires composed by Goulart for L'Estocart, three were later reprinted among a group of "Treize Octonaires de la vanité du monde," included in Pierre Poupo's *La Muse chrestienne* (Paris: Jeremie des Planches, 1585), 83–87. Du Chesne's twelve Octonaires set by L'Estocart had been composed earlier as part of *La Morocosmie*, for which Du Chesne had received a privilege in January of 1574. However, that print did not appear until 1583, after selected poems had been published in L'Estocart's arrangements. See Du Chesne, *La Morocosmie*, ed. Gibert, 29.

[28] For L'Estocart's biography, see L'Estocart, *Sacrae cantiones*, ed. Cœurdevey and Besson, vii–xiii; and Laurent Guillo, *Les Éditions musicales de la Renaissance lyonnaise* (Paris: Klincksieck, 1991), 101–3. The scant evidence of his later years (1584–87) places him in an ultra-Catholic milieu in what appears to be a turn from his Protestant past. For L'Estocart's social network and confessional affiliation, see Latour, "The Performance of Friendship," 411–41.

[29] See Scott Manetsch, *Calvin's Company of Pastors: Pastoral Care and the Emerging Reformed Church, 1536–1609* (Oxford: Oxford University Press, 2015), 54–55; Richard Freedman, "Listening to the Psalms among the Huguenots: Simon Goulart as Music Editor," in *Psalms in the Early Modern World*, ed. Linda Phyllis Austern et al. (Farnham, UK: Ashgate, 2011), 37–60; and Annie Cœurdevey, "Simon Goulart, mélomane et contrefacteur," in *Simon Goulart: Un pasteur aux intérêts vastes comme le monde*, ed. Olivier Pot (Geneva: Droz, 2013), 345–416.

treatise, the *Ample discours sur la doctrine des Stoiques*, which offers a detailed and helpfully sourced outline of all three branches of Stoic philosophy. He also translated and edited Neostoic works by Justus Lipsius and others.[30]

Joseph Du Chesne began his medical studies at the University of Basel in 1572, ultimately obtaining his doctorate in medicine. By 1573, he had settled primarily in Geneva. There, in 1574, he married Anne de Trye, the grand-daughter of Guillaume Budé, the founder of French humanism at Toulouse; he not only inherited the family's considerable wealth and titles, but gained influence through their prestigious social and intellectual connections. In 1576, Du Chesne became the physician for François, the duke of Anjou, and undertook diplomatic missions on his behalf. He eventually established a thriving medical practice in Geneva, where he became close friends with Goulart and Theodore Beza, who promoted his career and even became the godfather for Du Chesne's daughter. After the crowning of Henri IV, Du Chesne returned to Paris and became one of the king's personal physicians (*médecin ordinaire du roi*), remaining in that city until his death in 1609.[31]

Claude Le Jeune, the second composer of polyphonic *Octonaires*, also bridged the Protestant and Catholic spheres. As a Protestant long associated with the French court (who by 1596 was serving as *compositeur de la chambre* for Henri IV), Le Jeune was well-positioned between the major currents of Neostoicism—the Protestant stream linking Huguenot France with Geneva, the Low Countries, and the British Isles, and the Catholic stream centered in Paris and nourished by the French court. In 1606, Le Jeune's collection of *Octonaires de la vanité et inconstance du monde* appeared posthumously under the direction of his sister Cecile. His polyphonic collection sets twenty-nine texts by Chandieu, four by Goulart, and three by Du Chesne. The composer set three pieces in each of the twelve modes, with each modal group realized for three to four voices. In her preface to the collection, Cecile notes that her brother had intended to expand his collection of musical settings for the *Octonaires* by devising an additional three settings for each modal group, this time for five to six voices. His plans, however, were cut short by his death.

Le Jeune's *Octonaires* became one of his most beloved collections, as evidenced by their repeated publication and later testimonials. In marked contrast to the problematic reception of his earlier *Dodecacorde*, the

---

[30] Carabin, *Les Idées stoïciennes*, 680–90; and Amy Graves, "Les Épreuves du Huguenot et la vulgarisation du stoicisme: Simon Goulart, Jean de L'Espine et Sénèque," in *Stoïcisme et christianisme à la Renaissance*, ed. Tarrête, 123–25.

[31] Du Chesne, *La Morocosmie*, ed. Gibert, 7–33.

Octonaires found immediate and lasting acceptance among both Protestants and Catholics.[32] Building upon reprints of the collection produced by his firm in 1611 and 1631, Robert III Ballard reissued Le Jeune's *Octonaires* again in 1641—with a new dedication to the French chancellor, Pierre Séguier, and new prefatory material—signaling a continued appreciation of this collection by the generations of Paris magistrates following Pibrac.

In verse and song, the *Octonaires* had an unusual afterlife that extended from the British Isles all the way to the Americas. A famous seventeenth-century *vanitas* painting, Thomas Smith's *Self-Portrait* (c. 1680), takes us full circle from death's visual depiction, its expression in moral verse, its resounding power in music, and back again. [Web 2.2] It features a sheet of legible poetry underneath the skull in the artist's right hand, headed by the incipit, "Why why should I the World be minding"—an English version of Goulart's Octonaire *Mais que feroy-je plus au monde*, translated by Josuah Sylvester.

Sylvester was a key conduit of French Neostoic moral poetry for English audiences. He produced full translations of Pibrac's *Quatrains*, the *Octonaires* by Chandieu, Goulart, and Du Chesne, and Mathieu's *Tablettes* over the course of his career, all of which were published together in his complete works beginning in 1621.[33] Sylvester's two sections of *Octonaires* carried no attribution in these later prints, only the titles *Spectacles* and *Mottoes*. *Spectacles* offered an English-only translation of Chandieu's fifty Octonaire texts. By contrast, *Mottoes* offered twenty-four dual-language Octonaires—twelve by Goulart and twelve by Du Chesne—and the selection of texts and ordering clearly suggests that L'Estocart's second collection of musical settings was Sylvester's source for the translations, as Peter Auger has recognized.[34] If this were not already sufficient evidence of his musical source, *Mottoes* offers an Appendix of five poems, one referencing "Paschal and Pibrac."[35] Auger goes astray, however, in assuming that this Appendix was newly composed by Sylvester. I have found these poems to be translations of laudatory verses printed in the prefaces to L'Estocart's *Quatrains* and *Octonaires*. Sylvester's

[32] His, *Claude Le Jeune*, 379–81.

[33] Sylvester, *Works*, 557–84, 1034–56, and 1176–95.

[34] Peter Auger, "The Octonaire in Thomas Smith's *Self-Portrait*," *Huntington Library Quarterly* 80, no. 1 (2017): 10–12.

[35] Sylvester, *Works*, 1195. Appendix poem (1) Although thou canst not write so rare a Ditty (from L'Estocart, *Quatrains*, superius); (2) The Vertuous, reading and recording sweet (from L'Estocart, *Quatrains*, bassus); (3) Surcease thy Musick, lay aside thy Muses (from L'Estocart, *Quatrains*, tenor); (4) Lo, heer in Paper is poor Vertue painted (from L'Estocart, *Quatrains*, contratenor); (5) As fiercest Lion, fretting in his Cage (from L'Estocart, *Second livre des Octonaires*, bassus).

print, therefore, offers tantalizing evidence that L'Estocart's reputation extended much further than anyone had assumed, despite the absence of any reprints of his collections. More importantly, this case reveals that polyphonic musical settings served as textual sources in the circulation, copying, and translation of moral poetry, further solidifying the symbolic (if not also practical) link between the diverse modalities of wisdom prints circulating throughout the age of Neostoicism.

The *Tablettes* of Pierre Mathieu

Pierre Mathieu produced a third major collection of moral poetry that inspired polyphonic arrangements: the *Tablettes ou Quatrains de la vie et de la mort*. Composed entirely in twelve-syllable alexandrines in consistent *rimes croisées* (*abab*), the first two *centaines* of one hundred quatrains apiece appeared by 1610, followed by a third *centaine* that was published posthumously by the author's son Jean-Baptiste in 1628.[36] All three hundred poems offer a consistent therapeutic approach to death and loss as groundwork for living well, which C. N. Smith recognized as infused with a Stoicism that continued to fascinate those living in early seventeenth-century France.[37] Like the earlier *Quatrains de Pibrac* and *Octonaires*, Mathieu's *Tablettes* emerged as a poetic response to a large-scale crisis in the kingdom, appearing as it did just after the shocking murder of Henri IV, which once again plunged the kingdom into instability and a series of power struggles as the crown passed to the young Louis XIII and his regent mother Marie de' Médici.[38]

Mathieu, too, began his career in law and jurisprudence, serving as a lawyer in Lyon before joining the court as royal historiographer around 1610.[39] Considering that he was writing his collection at the height of the Neostoic movement at the French court, it is unsurprising that this collection offers the most consistent and overt reliance on Stoicism, with the majority of the collection borrowing explicitly from Epictetus and Seneca and offering a poetic counterpart to Du Vair's *Philosophie morale des Stoiques*. Written in line with the program of Stoic consolation summarized by Du Vair, Mathieu's

---

[36] Pierre Mathieu, *Tablettes de la vie et de la mort* (Lyon: Pierre Rigaud, 1611); and Mathieu, *Tablettes ou Quatrains de la vie et de la mort* (Rouen: Jacques Cailloüe, 1628).

[37] Mathieu, *Tablettes de la vie et de la mort*, ed. Smith, v.

[38] Mack P. Holt, *The French Wars of Religion, 1562–1629*. Cambridge: Cambridge University Press, 2005), 173–89.

[39] Mathieu, *Tablettes*, ed. Smith, vi–vii.

Tablette I.2 asserts that "Birth and death are daughters of Nature, / Who has nothing foreign, frightful, or imperfect."[40] Developing this point extensively through creative imagery and a host of historical examples, Mathieu's collection seeks to alter incorrect opinions of death that are at the root of fear and grief.

Although the terse regularity of Mathieu's style harks back to Pibrac's earlier collection, the more consistently Stoic moral content and imagery— e.g., comparing human life to a candle in the wind, a wilting flower, a comedy with an unknown number of acts, smoke, dust, a shadow, and a dream—also links the work directly to the *Octonaires* corpus.[41] On a number of occasions, Mathieu's collection offers texts that clearly resonate with both the *Quatrains* and *Octonaires*, such as Tablette III.55, which criticizes the Aristotelian position on wealth as a good and cautions against the danger of mishandled wealth in a line of reasoning rooted in the Stoic position on worldly goods as an indifferent:

> Ceux qui se sont meslez donner les noms aux choses
> Nous ont trompez nommant les richesses du bien,
> Ce sont biens comme sont les espines des roses,
> Et causent de grands maux a qui n'en use bien.

[Those who involve themselves in giving names to things / Have deceived us in naming riches a good, / These are goods like the thorns on roses, / And cause great misfortune to those who mishandle them.]

Likewise, Tablette II.4 utilizes the Senecan river imagery and ties it to a related passage in Seneca's *On the Brevity of Life*—where he reminds us that we are dying every day of our lives:

> Le temps va comme un vent, comme un torrent il coule,
> Il passe, et rien ne peut l'empescher de courir:
> Qui sçait combien de maux en un moment il roule,
> Croit que cesser de vivre, est cesser de mourir.

---

[40] "La Naissance et la Mort sont filles de Nature, / Qui n'a rien d'estranger, d'affreux ny d'imparfait." *Quatrains moraux*, ed. Tourrette, 157.

[41] Like the *Octonaires*, Mathieu's *Tablettes* have been compared to Duplessis-Mornay's Senecan project in the *Excellent discours*. See Carabin, *Les Idées stoïciennes*, 71–73; and Chandieu, *Octonaires*, ed. Bonali-Fiquet, 23.

[Time flies like the wind, like a stream it flows. / It passes, and nothing can stop its course: / Whoever knows how many troubles it can crowd into a moment, / Believes that to cease living, is to cease dying.]

The shared themes and images invited a fruitful pairing of Mathieu's *Tablettes* with these earlier moral collections. It circulated frequently with Pibrac's *Quatrains* in abundant editions, and occasionally also with the *Octonaires*— as we have already noted in collections of Sylvester's English works. In addition, all three moral collections were united in the pocket-sized edition published by Jacques Caillöue (Rouen, 1628), the first to feature all three *centaines* of Mathieu's *Tablettes*, as well as Pibrac's *Quatrains* and twenty-six of Chandieu's *Octonaires*.

The Musical *Tablettes*

The musical settings for these major works of moral poetry also offered numerous points of resonance between the three collections (see Appendix 1, Table A1.3). Like Pibrac's *Quatrains*, Mathieu's *Tablettes de la vie et de la mort* saw its first musical publication appear in a monophonic edition: Jean Rousson's *Recueil de chansons spirituelles* (1621). Rousson's print includes two separate monophonic settings for Mathieu's moral poetry, the first titled "On the contempt of death by Mr Mathieu" and the second named "On life and death, by Mr Mathieu."[42] [Web 2.3 and 2.4]

In 1636, Pierre Ballard published a collection of fifty three-voice polyphonic settings of Mathieu's *Tablettes* by the composer Artus Aux-Cousteaux, titled *Les Quatrains de Mr Mathieu, mis en musique à trois parties selon l'ordre des douze modes*. The concision of the polyphonic settings recalled the large *Quatrains* collections by Boni and L'Estocart, while the systematic approach to mode signaled a clear link to Le Jeune's *Octonaires*. Although Aux-Cousteaux notes in his preface that Mathieu composed the collection for the instruction of his choirboys, the choice to publish the settings for a larger audience in 1636 appears to have been a success, for Robert III Ballard reprinted the collection in 1643 with identical musical and prefatory material. Then, in 1652, the firm published Aux-Cousteaux's sequel, the *Suite de*

---

[42] Jean Rousson, *Recueil de chansons spirituelles, avec les airs nottez sur chacune d'icelles* (La Fleche: Louys Hebert, 1621), 28 and 86.

la première partie des Quatrains de Mr Mathieu, mis en musique à trois voix, selon l'ordre des douze modes.

Aux-Cousteaux received his musical education at Saint-Quentin, under the tutelage of Jean de Bournonville (introduced earlier for his collection of Pibrac *Quatrains* settings). After Aux-Cousteaux's training at Saint-Quentin, he went on to serve as *haute-contre* for the chapel of Louis XIII from 1613 to 1627. He succeeded Bournonville at Saint-Quentin, then succeeded him again as chapel master at Amiens for two years. In June 1634, he left Amiens to become a "clerc haute-contre" (singing again under the direction of Bournonville) at the Sainte Chapelle du Palais, where he spent the rest of his career. Given the longstanding relationship between Aux-Cousteaux and Bournonville, it seems reasonable that Bournonville's 1622 collection of *Quatrains de Pibrac* might have been the inspiration for Aux-Cousteaux's initial interest in composing his own moral music settings.

Although Aux-Cousteaux experienced regular difficulty in his professional relationships, he benefited from the patronage and protection of highly placed magistrates.[43] He dedicated his first collection of musical *Tablettes* to Nicolas Le Jay (c. 1574–1640), who was a royal councilor, Premier Président of the Parlement of Paris, and Keeper of the Seals (*garde des Sçeaux*). The composer then dedicated his 1652 *Suite* to another important magistrate, Mathieu Molé (1584–1656), who followed in these positions of Premier Président of Parlement and Keeper of the Seals.

Considering that Aux-Cousteaux was listed as still occupying a post in Paris until 1651—as a member of the Sainte Chapelle—he would probably have seen firsthand the rioting and violence that ravaged the city. It is striking to note the difference in the tone of the prefaces for Aux-Cousteaux's 1636/ 43 musical settings and his *Suite* in 1652, the year that marked the conclusion of the Fronde. The first collection focuses primarily on praising the dedicatee (Le Jay) and lauding the beauty of the musical settings. Aux-Cousteaux's *Suite*, however, specifically notes the violence and instability of the recent political conflict, referencing "these times of misery where a million people languish" and pointing toward his patron Molé's role in the reestablishment of tranquility. As Premier Président, Molé became a popular hero for his courageous negotiations with the crown on behalf of Parlement at the outset of the Fronde. Like generations of magistrates before him, Molé displayed

[43] René Reboud, "Messire Arthus Aux Cousteaux, Maître de Musique de la Sainte-Chapelle du Palais, 1590–1654," *XVIIᵉ Siècle* (1964): 403–17.

a continued interest in Stoic constancy. His portrait shows him standing next to a painting of a rock in a stormy sea, where his device is printed: *Stat mole immotus*. The verse ornamenting the base of the portrait praises him in overtly Stoic terms, as intrepid in the face of danger and having a constant heart and face: "Il ne change jamais de cœur ny de visage." [Web 2.5]

In setting Mathieu's Neostoic poetry, Aux-Cousteaux's polyphonic *Tablettes* served the philosophical interests of his longstanding patron Molé and earlier *parlementaires* like Pibrac, who remained deeply committed to civil order and justice. Their emphasis on order and self-restraint should not, however, be regarded as a promotion of militarism, top-down state control, or absolutism.[44] Lipsius's anti-tolerance and militarism in his later political work diverged from the therapeutic aims of his own far more popular *On Constancy* as well as the broader Neostoic movement, which was not only focused on reconciliation and tolerance but deeply distrustful of the ambition that leads to empire-building and war. Stoicism and Neostoicism clearly advocated independent thinking, rigorous personal freedom, and self-directed (not state-controlled) moral restraint. The *parlementaire* promotion of Neostoicism was rooted in this delicate commitment to both inner freedom and civil stability. The Ancien Régime was governed by a constitutional process, where the crown and the court both exercised power in negotiating royal policies. The Parlement remained staunchly independent of the crown and offered a resistance to monarchal power by vigorously defending its own rights to check and modify outcomes to retain this delicate balance of power. However, as Nancy Roelker has clarified, this resistance was in no way an attack on the monarchy, for the mainstream *parlementaire* position supported the monarchy in its constitutional form.[45] In this view, the monarchy needed to be stabilized and regulated, but not done away with. Like Seneca offering calm wisdom to the volatile emperor Nero, the Palais de Justice took a particular interest in shaping just and measured rulers, well in control of their own passions and able to work toward a consistent and fair exercise of justice for the entire populace.

[44] Gerhard Oestreich launched this problematic yet enduringly influential theory of Neostoicism as the ideology underpinning absolutism and the disciplinary state. For a summary of his views, see Gerhard Oestreich, *Neostoicism and the Early Modern State*, ed. Brigitta Oestreich and H. G. Koenigsberger, trans. David McLintock (Cambridge: Cambridge University Press, 1982), 6. However, Peter Miller has brilliantly demonstrated that Oestreich's interpretation grossly misinterprets Neostoicism to serve his idiosyncratic attempt to justify National Socialism. See Peter Miller, "Nazis and Neo-Stoics: Otto Brunner and Gerhard Oestreich before and after the Second World War," *Past and Present* 176 (2002): 144–86.

[45] Roelker, *One King, One Faith*, 319.

We can see this mapped out in the consistent promotion of Neostoicism on the part of *parlementaires* for the moral education of the Prince and the court. Attention to Aux-Cousteaux's laudatory contributions suggests that his moral collections attracted the admiration of an elite group of painters, intellectuals, and literary figures at the forefront of Parisian Neostoicism. I will discuss Aux-Cousteaux's laudatory contributors in more detail in Chapter 9; for now, however, I will close this chapter by pointing out that the liminal materials offered for Aux-Cousteaux's *Tablettes* link the project to the social world suggested in the preface and dedication of Ballard's 1641 edition of Le Jeune's *Octonaires*. This Parisian circle included several figures associated with Cardinal Richelieu and the nascent Académie française, such as Guillaume Colletet—the author of the first treatise on moral poetry—and his son François. (One of these Colletets signed their family name to a laudatory verse for Ballard's 1641 *Octonaires* in praise of the chancellor Pierre Séguier.) Marin le Roy de Gomberville, another founding member of the Académie française, composed a Neostoic emblem book, *Doctrine des mœurs, tirée de la philosophie des Stoiques* [Doctrine of Morals, Drawn from the Philosophy of the Stoics] (1646), which had a long afterlife in both France and England.[46] Pierre Daret borrowed the engravings for Gomberville's *Doctrine des mœurs* from Otto van Veen's *Emblemata Horatiana* (1607), another work with clear personal and philosophical links to Neostoicism.[47] Gomberville's print was dedicated to the Queen Mother of France, Anne of Austria, with the intention that it would be used for the education of the young Louis XIV. In a substantial second dedication to Cardinal Mazarin, Gomberville situates the work within the longer Stoic "mirror of princes" tradition, and the preface offers a rich discussion of the importance of the visual arts in the Stoic moral tradition. One of Aux-Cousteaux's laudatory contributors, the royal painter and syndic of the Académie Royale de Peinture et Sculpture, Nicolas Bellot, also wrote an original Neostoic treatise, *Le Stoïque chrestien, ou la Victoire de la joye innocente et vertueuse sur la tristesse* [The Stoic Christian, or the

---

[46] Marin le Roy de Gomberville, *Doctrine des mœurs, tirée de la philosophie des Stoiques* (Paris: Pierre Daret, 1646). Among the numerous later editions were Penelope Aubin's two English editions of the work, *The Doctrine of Morality, or A View of Human Life, According to the Stoick Philosophy*, trans. Gibbs, ed. Aubin (London: E. Bell, 1721) and *Moral Virtue Delineated, In One Hundred and Three Short Lectures, Both in French and English, on the Most Important Points of Morality*, trans. Gibbs, ed. Aubin (London: J. Darby, 1726).

[47] Otto van Veen, *Quinti Horatii Flacci emblemata* (Antwerp: Hieronymus Verdussen, 1607). Otto van Veen was a member of Justus Lipsius's circle, and he was the Neostoic painter Peter Paul Rubens's teacher. See Catherine Lusheck, *Rubens and the Eloquence of Drawing* (London: Routledge, 2017), 4.

Victory of innocent and virtuous joy over sadness] (1655).[48] These works elaborated the artistic, musical, and poetic exercise of Stoicism, linking the musical *Tablettes* of Aux-Cousteaux to the production and collection of some of the most important *vanitas* paintings, treatises, and emblem books inspired by Neostoicism and bringing the full range of artistic modalities into philosophical counterpoint.

[48] Nicolas Bellot, *Le Stoïque chrestien, ou la Victoire de la joye innocente et vertueuse sur la tristesse* (Paris: Jean Paslé, 1655).

3

The Exercise of Harmony

What is any of this but training—
training for your *logos*, in life observed accurately, scientifically.[1]

What is virtue, and how can one cultivate it? This question, long at the heart of moral philosophy, took on special urgency during the chaos of civil war, and it found a particularly clear expression in the wave of moral prints that offered attractive training to both young and old across the fractured kingdom and beyond. In a speech delivered before the Parlement of Paris in 1569—several years before the publication of his famous *Quatrains*—Guy du Faur de Pibrac argued that "moral virtue consists not in speculation and intelligence, but in action and execution, and that it is necessary to apply one's hand to the work, if we wish to be and become virtuous."[2] This emphasis on the action and execution of virtue as a practice that must be cultivated through daily exercise would ultimately drive the composition and widespread application of his poetic collection. Although Aristotle's *habitus* has been the most widely recognized source of this view, we can see that Pibrac's notion of moral progress rooted in practical action was influenced, at least in part, by Stoicism, for Pibrac supports his call for daily practice in virtue with citations from Cato, Chryssipus, and Zeno. Most importantly, Pibrac cites Epictetus, whose *Discourses* (2.9) crystalized the Stoic approach: "That is why philosophers recommend that we shouldn't be contented merely to learn, but should add practice too, and then training."

By some accounts, the Stoics denied the possibility of moral progress in keeping with their doctrine of virtue and vice as without gradations.

---

[1] Marcus Aurelius, *Meditations* 10.31; trans. Hays, 139.
[2] Guy du Faur de Pibrac, *Recueil des poincts principaux de la remonstrance faicte en la Cour de Parlement de Paris, à l'ouverture des plaidoiries aprés la feste de Pasques 1569* (s.l., 1570), 7–8.

The Voice of Virtue. Melinda Latour, Oxford University Press. © Oxford University Press 2023.
DOI: 10.1093/oso/9780197529744.003.0004

As Zeno put it, a stick is either crooked or straight. However, according to Diogenes Laertius in *Lives* 7.26, Zeno also said that "well-being is attained little by little, yet it is no little thing itself."[3] This early Stoic notion of moral progress was embedded in their foundational epistemology, which was optimistic in asserting that it was possible to acquire the knowledge we need to live well from our everyday surroundings and experiences.[4] The Roman Stoics later developed a full-fledged notion of virtue cultivation rooted in practical, habitual action designed for everyday people to make progress according to their strength and capacity. They demonstrated that progress was made through contemplation and daily exercise, which could be united to reshape our value system in a way that afforded consistency in our behaviors, emotions, and relationships.

Perhaps more than any other publication of this era, Pibrac's *Quatrains* reveal the subtle influence of Stoic educational theory and epistemology on the artistic style and practices at the core of early modern moral formation. The poetic and musical *Quatrains* repertoire models the values of Stoic didacticism, where simplicity, brevity, and restraint offer stylistic guideposts for training and exercise toward virtue. These "anti-rhetorical" stylistic priorities not only offered a common-sense form of persuasion, but also had accrued practical value since ancient times as being ideal for memorization. Stoic didacticism developed as the project of shaping children into rational beings and creating a storehouse of knowledge that could serve as the building blocks for moral reasoning. The repeated cultural practice of learning the *Quatrains* formed the basis of an imagined community of virtue lovers; in addition, it afforded an important role to music as an agent in cognition and virtue acquisition. By examining the pedagogical and recreational uses of Pibrac's *Quatrains*, which were recited, sung, and committed to memory, we can begin to see how this poetry and music as experienced in daily exercise bridged the gap between knowledge and behavior—transforming abstract theory into a philosophy of living.

[3] Diogenes Laertius, *Lives of the Eminent Philosophers*, trans. Pamela Mensch, ed. James Miller (Oxford: Oxford University Press, 2020), 323.
[4] Løkke, *Knowledge and Virtue in Early Stoicism*, 5–6.

Bien Dire, Bien Faire

In editions of the *Quatrains* after 1576, Pibrac included a single prefatory poem advising the reader of his didactic priorities. "I have not attempted to fashion this work in a sweet style in order for it to please," he warned, "because I intend to give it only to those whose sole concern is good conduct."[5] This stress on moral function over surface style underpins Kate van Orden's assessment of Pibrac's collection as "a disciplinary medium" for those seeking guidance in upright living, in what initially seems to be a hedge against the momentum toward poetic charm stimulated by Ronsard and the Pléiade decades earlier.[6] Closer attention to Pibrac's documented interest in eloquence offers a hint against taking this preface as an excuse for poor artistry. Although certainly not a professional poet, Pibrac was revered for his oratorical skill. He was a longstanding friend of the Pléiade, particularly Ronsard, and he was a joint participant in Henry III's Palace Academy, with its attention to eloquence as a partner to moral philosophy.

The question of artistic style becomes more acute as we remember that the most celebrated composers and printers in the francophone world published high-quality polyphonic collections of Pibrac's poetry. Paschal de L'Estocart's 1582 polyphonic collection of *Quatrains de Pibrac* (1582) offers an impressive display of artistic craft, yet the preface still follows Pibrac's lead in emphasizing moral edification over artistic concerns. The superius part includes a liminal verse ("To poets and musicians") by Simon Goulart, which links the art of singing well to that of speaking well:

> Si tu ne sais si doctement escrire,
> Si tu ne peux si doucement chanter,
> Sois vertueux: c'est pour te contenter.
> Car faire bien est trop plus que bien dire.

[If you do not know how to write in such a learned way, / If you cannot sing so sweetly, / Be virtuous: it is what will make you happy. / Because living well is infinitely better than speaking well.]

---

[5] "Je n'ay tasché cest oeuvre façonner / D'un stile doux, à fin qu'il puisse plaire: / Car aussi bien n'entens-je le donner, / Qu'à ceulx qui n'ont soucy que de bien faire." Pibrac, *Les Quatrains*, ed. Petris, 146.

[6] Van Orden, *Materialities*, 239–45.

In the same spirit as Pibrac's introductory poem, Goulart advises that even if you are not the most learned person or the best singer, you should be virtuous, because it is better to live well (*faire bien*) than to speak well (*bien dire*).

Goulart's laudatory verse was clearly shaped by a Stoic approach to eloquence and education. André de Rivaudaux's 1567 edition of Epictetus's *Handbook* used similar language in his summary of Chapter 56, "Il ne se faut amuser a bien dire, mais a bien faire."[7] Later on, Goulart's own treatise on Stoic philosophy (*Ample discours sur la doctrine des Stoiques*) attributed exactly this sentiment to the school of Seneca: "The Stoics have in no way despised eloquence, although they have been more conscientious about instructing their disciples to live well than to speak elegantly."[8] The urgency of learning how to live well, and not to waste creative energy by developing surface appeal devoid of moral purpose, was behind the Stoic preference for vocal restraint.[9]

Brevity was the hallmark of the Stoic style. Diogenes Laertius quotes Zeno as having responded to comments on the concision of his maxims with, "You are right. And their syllables should be shortened as well, if possible."[10] Cicero's introduction to the *Paradoxa Stoicorum* describes the Stoics as a sect "that does not aim at oratorical ornament at all or employ a copious mode of exposition, but proves its case by means of tiny little interrogatory pin-pricks."[11] The compact Stoic style (also known as the Attic style) gained traction precisely because of this renunciation of flowery language. Goulart's *Ample discours* finds a unique sort of eloquence in "the brusque and dry style of Seneca" that may not be appreciated by those accustomed to Cicero, and yet it proves unparalleled in its ability to stimulate and persuade his readers.[12] Seneca's terse sentences thus offered a fresh rhetorical model in the late sixteenth century, overtaking the earlier penchant for Cicero's longwinded

---

[7] André de Rivaudeau, *La Doctrine d'Epictete stoicien* (Poitiers: E. de Marnef, 1567), 28.

[8] In Seneca, *Œuvres morales et meslées de Senecque*, trans. Goulart, 3:335.

[9] See Seneca, *Epistles* 45 and 52; Seneca, *De brevitate vitae* 12; Epictetus, *Discourses* 2.1–4.

[10] *Lives* 7.20; trans. Mensch, 320. Goulart circulated this sentence in his *Apophthegmes de Zenon* in Seneca, *Œuvres morales et meslées de Senecque*, 3:296.

[11] Cicero, *Paradoxa Stoicorum* 2–3. See also Diogenes Laertius, *Lives* 7.20 and Henri Estienne, *Introduction à la lecture de Sénèque (1586)*, ed. Denise Carabin (Paris: H. Champion, 2007), 255.

[12] In Seneca, *Œuvres morales et meslées de Senecque*, trans. Goulart, 3:327. On Senecan rhetoric, see Marcus Wilson, "Rhetoric and the Younger Seneca," in *A Companion to Roman Rhetoric*, ed. William J. Dominik and Jon Hall (Malden, MA: Wiley-Blackwell, 2007), 425–38; Shadi Bartsch, "Rhetoric and Stoic Philosophy," in *The Oxford Handbook of Rhetorical Studies*, ed. Michael J. MacDonald (Oxford: Oxford University Press, 2017), 215–21; and Gareth Williams, "Style and Form in Seneca's Writing," in *The Cambridge Companion to Seneca*, ed. Bartsch and Schiesaro, 135–49.

symmetries.[13] Stylistic restraint appealed to early moderns partly on moral grounds, due to its perceived transparency. Echoing Seneca's advice in Letter 40.4 that "speech which applies itself to the truth should be unaffected and plain," Pibrac quipped in his Quatrain 74, "le parler brief convient à verité"— brief speech belongs to truth.

Performing Brevity

The Stoic rhetorical values of brevity and simplicity guided the composition of the polyphonic settings of Pibrac's texts, modeling the affective and ethical dimensions that could be built into a compact musical form. In general, the polyphonic *Quatrains* offer models of economy and clarity, featuring short musical phrases, frequent and predictable cadences, and a restricted range in all voice parts. This restraint guides L'Estocart's first setting, *Dieu tout premier, puis pere et mere honore*, which takes approximately 45 seconds to sing from start to finish (see Example 3.1). After a sober homophonic opening on "Honor God first" (mm. 1–3), the line becomes more flexible when moving to the earthly realm, "then your father and mother" (mm. 3–8). The treatment of the second line, "Be just and upright, and in all seasons," suggests the primacy of internal constancy through a placid homophony (*Sois juste et droit, et en toute saison*, mm. 9–15), which is repeated almost identically in the third line, "Give justice to the innocent" (*De l'innocent prends en main la raison*, mm. 16–22), for the exercise of public justice comes from internal morality. The fourth line presents the climax of the quatrain, both textually and musically, as the superius, contratenor, and bassus leap dramatically upward to illustrate that "one day God most high will be your judge" (*Car Dieu te doit là haut juger encore*, mm. 23–32). The entire fourth line then returns in an identical repetition in all voices to bring the setting to a confident close (mm. 33–42). The imperfect repetition of lines 2 and 3, where the text exhorts humans to be just and upright in their dealings, contrasts with the exact repetition of the final line, where God is the one who judges from on high in divine perfection.

---

[13] See Morford, *Stoics and Neostoics*, 77. On musical Ciceronianism, see Martha Feldman, *City Culture and the Madrigal at Venice* (Berkeley, CA: University of California Press, 1995). For a comparison of Senecan vs. Ciceronian rhetoric, see Christian Mouchel, *Cicéron et Sénèque dans la rhétorique de la Renaissance* (Marburg: Hitzeroth, 1990), 120–22 and 158–63.

Example 3.1 Paschal de L'Estocart, *Dieu tout premier, puis père et mère honore,*
in *Cent vingt et six quatrains du Sieur de Pibrac* (Lyon: Barthélemy Vincent
[Geneva: Jean I de Laon], 1582)

Example 3.1 Continued

Example 3.1 Continued

Prioritizing clarity and comprehension of the moral text, L'Estocart's settings reflect a broader concern with the careful union of music and poetry. This primacy of the word—which increased throughout the sixteenth century and birthed innovative genres like monody by the turn of the century in Italy—has long been recognized as one of the musical consequences of humanism. What musicologists have only rarely taken into account in their analysis of this word-centered musical period is that humanism was fundamentally inflected by Stoicism. It was incubated in the earlier work of the Florentine Platonists and even more overtly drove the development of the particular brand of French legal humanism that supported musical activities associated with city, court, and university life in the time of Pibrac and Du Vair, as outlined in the previous chapters of this book.

The interpretive possibilities of this Stoicized humanism were worked out more clearly in the settings devised for Pibrac's paraphrase of Seneca's *On the Brevity of Life* (Quatrain 117, *L'homme se plaint de sa trop courte vie*). Although the contratenor part for Lassus's 1583 four-voice setting of *L'homme se plaint* did not survive, the extant parts suggest a simple gravity of style unfolding in Lassus's typical freely imitative counterpoint, with few melismas and almost no repeated text until the close of the setting.[14] [Web 3.1] After the straightforward syllabic opening for "Man complains that his life is too short, / and yet does not employ it as he should," the arrival of the first melisma—in the opening of the third line "The time that he has" (*Le temps qu'il a*)—emphasizes and aesthetizes Seneca's concern with temporality by drawing out the passing time as the text lingers in a decorative expansion of notes extending the life of a single syllable.

In the passage that inspired Pibrac's text—*On the Brevity of Life* (1)—Seneca likewise urges his readers to pay careful attention to the moment by moment passage of time as a daily measure to ensure purposeful living:

> It is not that we have a short space of time, but that we waste much of it. Life is long enough, and it has been given in sufficiently generous measure to allow the accomplishment of the very greatest things if the whole of it is well invested. But when it is squandered in luxury and carelessness, when it is devoted to no good end, forced at last by the ultimate necessity we perceive that it has passed away before we were aware that it was passing.

---

[14] Lassus, *Vingtdeuxieme livre de chansons*, fol. 3v; ed. Jane Bernstein in *The Sixteenth-Century Chanson*, 14 (New York: Garland, 1987), 176–77.

This episode and the many similar examples across the Stoic corpus reveal that the preference for simplicity and brevity in the rhetorical arts had a double moral underpinning: it mirrored the austerity and voluntary restraint that were advocated by the Stoics and also served as a moral analogy for their call to remember the brevity of our lifespan and live fully attuned to the present moment.

L'Estocart's setting for *L'homme se plaint* also creatively illustrates this moral attention to time (see Example 3.2). After an avalanche of complaining that sweeps across the voices in the opening points of imitation, L'Estocart dramatically rushes into the cadence at "life is too short" in a sudden musical realization of life's precarity (*trop courte vie*, mm. 7–8). This unexpected reduction of the musical phrase, which might take a singer or listener by surprise, thus models Seneca's warning from the opposite direction as Lassus's treatment. The remainder of the setting plays further with duration, as in the longer note values given to the repetition of "the time he has" (*Le temps qu'il a*, mm. 10–12), and the decorative melismas extending the desire to live (*vivre envie*, mm. 16–17 and 20–22).

Guillaume Boni displayed a particular sensitivity to the formal constraints posed by Pibrac's poetry, informed no doubt by his involvement in the humanist-rich *parlementaire* circles in Toulouse. Across his collection, Boni establishes a relatively simple polyphonic texture, typically set in note-against-note counterpoint, as a means of preparing striking shifts to homophony that emphasize salient words or passages in the text. His setting of *L'homme se plaint* (X.8) offers the most sophisticated union of the moral and stylistic elements contained in the poetry. The use of repeated text goes beyond conventional breaks at the poetic caesura—in some cases setting smaller, uneven blocks of the poetic line in increasing increments that build to the cadence. After Boni opens with the cacophony of jubilant polyphonic complaining, he abruptly cuts the phrase short in m. 6, with a break after "de sa trop courte," before finishing the poetic line in the following measure with the full phrase "de sa trop courte vie" (see Example 3.3).

Seneca was famous for precisely this technique of lopping off the ends of phrases and gradually building up from smaller, incomplete units to finally unveil the full meaning or significance of what came before.[15] Boni gives musical expression to Seneca's clipped and sententious rhetorical style in the opening of another of Pibrac's texts emphasizing brevity,

---

[15] See Estienne, *Introduction à la lecture de Sénèque* (1586), ed. Carabin, Bk. 2, Chapters 1–2, 154–201. For the visual expression of this choppy rhetorical style, see Lusheck, *Rubens and the Eloquence of Drawing*, 142–43.

Example 3.2 Paschal de L'Estocart, *L'homme se plaint de sa trop courte vie*, in *Cent vingt et six quatrains du Sieur de Pibrac* (Lyon: Barthélemy Vincent [Geneva: Jean I de Laon], 1582)

Example 3.2 Continued

Example 3.3 Guillaume Boni, *L'homme se plaint de sa trop courte vie*, mm.
1–11, in *Les Quatrains du Sieur de Pybrac* (Paris: Adrian Le Roy and Robert
Ballard, 1582). Based on the edition by Marie-Alexis Colin, with original note
values restored

Example 3.3 Continued

Quatrain 19, *Bref, ce qui est* (II.6). He opens by pausing immediately after the "fleeting" first word before repeating it again with the same vertical harmony immediately afterward (*Bref . . . bref ce qui est*, mm. 1–3). He utilizes a similar technique in the third line: *Si tost . . . si tost que Dieu l'a voulu pour le mieux* (mm. 12–15 and 19–22).[16] Boni's settings thus demonstrate that Stoic stylistic restraint and repetition, when approached sensitively, should lead neither to rigidity nor narrow thinking. Their surface

---

[16] Boni, *Les Quatrains*, ed. Colin, 33. Boni uses a similar approach in *Le malheur est commun* (V.9) and *Le sage est libre* (V.10), which will be discussed further in Chapter 4.

austerity yields subtle yet significant contemplative possibilities for those engaged in the long-term pursuit of virtue.

Rational Impressions

Virtue, for Stoics and Neostoics, was predicated on rationality, which went far beyond knowledge or mere thinking to connect all mental and physical processes through the divine spark of the *logos* embedded in every human being. Importantly, they developed a craft analogy that relied on music and other arts to emphasize the embodied practices and skills required to build this mature human capacity. Pibrac made this connection in his Quatrain 13, *A bien parler, ce que l'homme on appelle*, which draws in part on Seneca's Letter 41.[17]

The Parisian organist Jean Planson's setting of *A bien parler* gives a compelling musical take on this link between the human voice, rationality, and the divine.[18] Breaking away from the restrained, generally syllabic polyphony typical of the Pibrac musical corpus, Planson unleashes a rising melisma on the opening "To speak well" that underscores this Stoic notion of voice as an essential marker of humanity. After clarifying that speaking well is "a ray of divinity" and "an atom birthed from unity," he closes with a mirroring melisma spun out as a vocal "emanation from the eternal source" [Web 3.2]. Planson's setting offers a musical template for the connection between eloquence and divine *logos*, described by Guillaume Du Vair in his *On Eloquence* as "an exquisite communication of discourse and reason." In an extension of the concerns raised by his older colleagues in the Académie du Palais (like Pibrac), Du Vair argued for this divinely-furnished eloquence to direct the passions like a ship's rudder (*le gouvernail des ames*), and inscribes his comments within the Platonic tradition of the harmony of the spheres, as "shaping morals and affections like certain tones, and tempering them in such a fashion that they in fact birth infinitely melodious harmonies."[19]

Voice (*phonē*) was central to the Stoic notion of "right reason" (*recta ratio*). The language arts were thus placed among the skills or crafts

---

[17] "A bien parler, ce que l'homme on appelle, / C'est un rayon de la divinité: / C'est un atome esclos de l'unité: / C'est un degout de la source eternelle." See Pibrac, *Les Quatrains*, ed. Petris, 152n22, and Seneca, *Epistles* 41.1, 5–6. Mathieu makes a similar point in Tablette I.74.

[18] Jean Planson, *Les Quatrains du Sieur de Pybrac, ensemble quelques Sonetz, et Motetz, mis en Musique à 3. 4. 5. et 7. parties* (Paris: Le Roy and Ballard, 1583), superius, fol. 8v; tenor, fol. 8r.

[19] Guillaume Du Vair, *De l'eloquence françoise*, fol. 12r; ed. René Radouant (Paris: Société française d'imprimerie et de librairie, 1908), 142.

deemed essential for following nature (*logos*), making sound judgements, and building constancy and temperance. It was due to this view of language at the heart of reason that some Stoics argued for beginning with logic before moving on to ethics and physics. Though they found no agreement on the order of priority, Stoic teachers generally agreed that these fields were interconnected and should be taught in combination.[20]

L'Estocart's careful compositional choices reflect a deeper logic that bridges these philosophical domains through his strategies of text organization and internal text painting. L'Estocart chose to create individual settings for just 117 of the 126 *Quatrains de Pibrac*. On eight occasions in the collection, the composer repeated a musical setting, and in one case he used the same setting for three quatrains, linking together several texts on the same topic (see Table 3.1). This repetition of musical settings in L'Estocart's collection, as Marie-Alexis Colin notes, offers further evidence of the composer's "primary concern to appropriate the text."[21] It also serves a clear rhetorical function, musically opening up a sophisticated interpretive relationship between the two or three linked verses. For example, the first pairing—Quatrains 16 and 17—ties together two texts asserting a Stoic and Christian understanding of the solitary will of God at the center of creation, in opposition to the Platonic notion of infinite "ideas" proposed in the *Parmenides* (142c–143a) and read through Ficino.[22]

The second pairing—Quatrains 20 and 21—unites two texts written against Epicureanism, criticizing them (unfairly) for their denial of God and suggesting that their pursuit of pleasure leads humans to act as mere beasts. In all but one of the eight pairs, the quatrains with the same musical setting appeared side by side in the 1576 poetic collection, and the topical relationship between them, when followed in sequence, would have been clear to an educated reader. In one case, however, L'Estocart altered the standard order of Pibrac's collection, offering Quatrain 86 (*Le nombre sainct*) with the same setting as Quatrain 87 (*Vouloir ne faut*), which had originally appeared as Quatrain 91 in the 1576 edition. Both texts explore the topic of justice, and together they reinforce the notions of equality, balance, and inner restraint that foster stability both in the self and the civil sphere.

In general, strophic settings, where the same music is used for multiple texts, are viewed as less sensitive to the words, given that both the nuance

[20] Diogenes Laertius, *Lives* 7.39–40.
[21] Colin, "Les *Quatrains* de Guy du Faur de Pibrac en musique," 544.
[22] Plato, *Parmenides* 142c–143a; and Ficino, *Theol. Platonica*, 2.12. See Pibrac, *Les Quatrains*, ed. Petris, 153n25.

Table 3.1 Repeated musical settings in Paschal de L'Estocart, *Cent vingt et six quatrains du Sieur de Pibrac* (Lyon: Barthélemy Vincent [Geneva: Jean I de Laon], 1582).

No. in L'Estocart	No. in Pibrac	Incipit	Notes
16	16	*Au ciel il n'y a nombre infiny d'Idees*	Against the Platonic
17	17	*Il veult, c'est faict: sans travail et sans peine*	Idea in favor of the unified will of God (Stoic physics/ Christian).
20	20	*Ne va suivant le troupeau d'Epicure*	Against Epicureanism
21	21	*Et ce-pendant il se veautre et patouille*	for supposedly denying the existence of God, debasing humanity by positing sensual (beastly pleasure) as the goal.
55	55	*Làs! que te sert tant d'or dedans la bourse*	On poverty and social
56	56	*Si ce-pendant le pauvre nud frissonne*	responsibility.
57	57	*As-tu, cruel, le cœur de telle sorte*	
59	59	*Le sage est libre enserré de cent chaines*	On the constancy of
60	60	*Le menasser du Tyran ne l'estonne*	the sage.
77	77	*Ainsi deslors que l'homme qui medite*	On the universality of
78	78	*On dict soudain, voila qui fut de Grece*	knowledge.
81	81	*Pour bien au vif peindre la Calomnie*	On slander.
82	82	*Elle ne faict en l'air sa residence*	
86	86	*Le nombre sainct se juge par sa preuve*	On justice and the
87	91	*Vouloir ne fault chose que l'on ne puisse*	need for self-restraint.
113	113	*L'estat moyen est l'estat plus durable*	On constancy and
114	114	*De peu de biens nature se contente*	moderation.

of accent and the special effect of any musical illustrations are presumably weakened or sacrificed altogether. L'Estocart's careful use of repeated settings, however, enhances the music/text relationships. We can see this in his pairing of the Stoic paradox, Quatrain 59 (*Le sage est libre*), with Quatrain 60 (*Le menasser du Tyran*) (see Plate 2). It would have been more obvious, perhaps, to link *Le sage est libre* with its previous text, *Le malheur est commun*—which was also drawn from the *Paradoxa Stoicorum*—but the musical link between *Le sage est libre* and *Le menasser du Tyran* reinforces the shared Stoic theme of the constancy of the sage, who is invulnerable to exterior circumstances.

Furthermore, L'Estocart's compositional choices for these paired settings skillfully express both texts through subtle musical strategies that amplify and interpret each against the other at key moments. These repetitions double their logical power across the settings, offering something beyond rote duplication to become an expansive moral exercise. For example, in the climactic third line of each text—"Alone assured / He alone knows" (*Seul asseuré / Il connoit seul*)—the sage's solitary self-assurance finds a shared emphasis in the slow, weighty delivery. The conclusion of the line, which dramatically ascends to the top of the soprano range, links the hazardous circumstances confronting the sage—"in the middle of danger" (*au milieu du danger*)—with the confident knowledge of "what he has earned" (*ce qu'il a merité*), in a subtle reminder of the radical Stoic promise that true contentment remains invulnerable to both worldly trouble and the lure of ambition that could so easily corrupt princes and kings.

Repetitions of Virtue

The impressive publication history of the *Quatrains de Pibrac*, both read alone and *en musique*, attests to the collection's success at the supple boundary between moral pedagogy and pleasurable recreation. The *Quatrains* were not only repeatedly reissued and reprinted over the course of a century, but were also regularly included in general education primers after sections offering basic instruction on reading and arithmetic. In the seventeenth century, the *Quatrains* were also frequently included in civility manuals (widely disseminated prints focused on proper comportment and etiquette). In both the general education texts and the later civility prints, Pibrac's *Quatrains* were often the only poetic text included, and had a special use that the other contents did not: they were specifically meant to be committed to memory as a foundation for mature moral reasoning.

Jean Héroard's *De l'institution du prince* (Paris, 1609) recommends that the prince who would one day become "good and gentle, wise, prudent and courageous" be given the *Quatrains* "to read, and then to recite by heart."[23] The expression to learn something "by heart" (*apprendre par cœur*) had a deeper meaning shaped

---

[23] Jean Héroard, *De l'institution du prince* (Paris: J. Jannon, 1609), 5, 12.

by the Stoic tradition of locating the soul (and cognition) in the heart.[24] Touted
by numerous other educational theorists, Pibrac's collection was widely accepted
as the cornerstone of early childhood moral education, and it was memorized by
girls and boys from leading families across the Catholic and Protestant divide.
For example, in 1606, the seven-year-old Charlotte de La Trémoille, from a high-
ranking Protestant family, wrote a letter to her mother, Charlotte-Brabantine
d'Orange-Nassau, at the court of Henri IV, in which she mentioned that she had
already learned all of the *Quatrains de Pibrac* by heart: "Mother, since you left,
I became wise, thanks to God; you will find me fully learned; I know seventeen
Psalms, all the *Quatrains de Pibrac*, all the *huitains* of Zamariel [the *Octonaires*
of Chandieu], and what is more, I speak Latin."[25] Louis XIII (b. 1601) underwent
this process of moral formation between 1605 to 1607 as he gradually memorized
Pibrac's *Quatrains* under the guidance of doctor Héroard himself.[26] Héroard's
account offers intriguing insight into the role of music as a corollary, or aid to
this process, as the entry for September 17, 1607 notes: "He said his quatrains de
Pibrac in music." Thus, Héroard's journal suggests that the pedagogical use of the
Quatrains may have included singing, as well as memorizing and reciting them.

The earliest known printed musical settings of Pibrac's *Quatrains*, and
Mathieu's closely linked *Tablettes* (which were often memorized alongside it)
marshal further evidence of the use of music in these didactic practices. The
Pibrac monophonic editions printed by Thomas Mallard (1580) and Richard
l'Allemand (1581) utilize a limited vocal range, almost entirely stepwise motion (punctuated with occasional small skips), and rhythmic values limited to
breves and semibreves [see Web 2.1]. Offering slightly more challenging melodic contours, the two triple-meter airs that Jean Rousson printed for Mathieu's
Tablettes were already well-known. Rousson noted that he chose airs "as popular
as possible, in order that children and all kinds of people could learn them."[27] [see
Web 2.3 and 2.4] With each tune recommended for at least one hundred texts,
these simple melodies were presented as a pedagogical hook, especially appealing
to young children slowly learning the entirety of these collections by heart. Even
as a mnemonic device, using these simple melodies to sing all the *Quatrains* from

[24] See the section "Apprendre, ou dire quelque chose par cœur," in Étienne Pasquier, *Les Recherches de la France d'Estienne Pasquier* (Paris: Laurens Sonnius, 1621), VIII. 8, 697–98. For the Stoic implications, see Christopher Gill, "Galen and the Stoics: Mortal Enemies or Blood Brothers?" *Phronesis* 52, no. 1 (2007): 105–7.

[25] Transcribed in Henriette de Witt-Guizot, *Charlotte de La Trémoille, comtesse de Derby, d'après des lettres inédites conservées dans les archives des ducs de La Trémoille, 1601–1664* (Paris: Didier, 1870), 12.

[26] Pibrac, *Les Quatrains*, ed. Petris, 26.

[27] Rousson, *Recueil de chansons spirituelles*, unpaginated preface.

either collection presents a dramatic case of strophic repetition. Van Orden has foregrounded the ethical work embedded in such repetitions, read through the notion of Aristotelian *habitus*, which regarded repeated action as the means for building moral virtue. By this logic, the efficacy of short moral poems like the *Quatrains de Pibrac* lay not only in the wisdom contained in the text but also in the mechanisms by which they were learned, used, and remembered—that is, in the everyday practice of learning to recite and sing them.

Pibrac's Quatrain 61 spotlights this habitual action in the long process of virtue-formation:

> Vertu és mœurs ne s'acquiert par l'estude,
> Ny par argent, ny par faveur des Roys,
> Ny par un acte, ou par deux, ou par trois,
> Ains par constante et par longue habitude.

[Virtue in our habits is not acquired by study, / Neither by money, nor by the favor of Kings, / Neither by one act, or by two, or by three, / But by constant and long practice.]

It is significant that this verse on repetition and *habitus* arrives in the middle of a series of texts devoted overtly to Stoicism. As mentioned earlier, Quatrains 58–60 (*Le malheur est commun*; *Le sage est libre*; and *Le manasser du Tyran*) focused on the Stoic constancy of the sage, and Quatrains 62–63 were clearly based on Seneca's theory of education.[28] These texts contextualize the "constant and long practice" advocated in Quatrain 61, with the call for meditation and absorption of a limited number of quality texts in Quatrain 62 (*Qui lit beaucoup*) and followed by a craft analogy in Quatrain 63 (*Maint un pouvoit*) that progressing in wisdom takes commitment and practice—for "what artisan becomes a perfect master on the first day of their apprenticeship?"[29]

Whether vocalized in speech or rehearsed through song, the repetitions embedded in the process of memorization moved away from the rote learning embedded in the Scholastic paradigm and instead pointed toward a more thoroughly humanist project that encouraged the focused contemplation of a smaller quantity of worthwhile sources that were explicitly designed to evolve

---

[28] See Seneca, *Epistles* 2, 45, and 84.
[29] "Maint un pouvoit par temps devenir sage, / S'il n'eust cuidé l'estre ja tout à faict; / Quel artisant fut onc maistre parfaict, / Du premier jour de son apprentissage?" Pibrac, *Les Quatrains*, ed. Petris, 168–69.

from a knowledge of speaking well to living well. The Stoic process of repetition was not a static drill, but an exercise serving moral progress: in every return to the same maxim in poetry or song, the meaning could be enlarged and pushed to new contemplative horizons. The moral practice and training involved in learning maxims was thus an active means of achieving a union of knowledge, action, and experience—a virtous state that was not only knowledgeable (*savant*) but, more importantly, wise (*sage*).

Musical practice modeled the critical union between disciplinary theory and lived practice, as we see in the words of the Stoic Musonius Rufus, included by Simon Goulart in his *Fragmens des Stoiques* (translated from the Stobaeus anthology): "Virtue is not only a contemplative science, but active also, as are medicine and music." Just as these disciplines are exercised according to theoretical principles, the path toward virtue must unite principled teaching with daily action.[30] Guillaume Boni's five-voice setting of *Vertu és mœurs* (V.12) offers a musical experience of this continual moral progression. Opening with staid homophony for the first line, Boni immediately repeats the opening text ("Virtue and morals"), using the same stately rhythm but varying the harmony. He continues in this severe style until the third line, where he sets the text "Neither by one act, or by two or by three" with an exposed, repeating melismatic figure in the contratenor (*par deux ou par trois*, mm. 18–20). The final line recasts the solemnity of the earlier text into a determined melodic repeating in each voice part (mm. 21–39), evoking the persistence needed to make progress in virtue. Boni then reprises the third and fourth lines (mm. 28–39), folding in multiple short structural repetitions of both text and music along the way that drill home the deeper message of the quatrain—that making progress in virtue always takes place in the plural. Virtue will not be acquired in a day, but requires persistence and constant exercise over a lifetime.

Making Progress

Interest in singing the *Quatrains* as a mode of lifelong moral improvement continued into the seventeenth century, in both print and manuscript sources. Evidence of the cultural importance of singing Pibrac's moral poetry in the decades around 1600 appears indirectly in several references to the *Quatrains de Pibrac* as a *timbre*—a popular tune used to sing newly devised texts. A single-sheet print from 1594, the "Chanson nouvelle de

---

[30] Seneca, *Œuvres morales et meslées de Senecque*, trans. Goulart, 3:232.

la Prinse du Visconte de Chamois," indicates in the heading that the text should be sung to the tune *Dieu tout premier, puis père et mère honnore*—clearly referencing the opening text of Pibrac's *Quatrains*.[31] Considering that no musical notation was given, which was standard for this sort of ephemeral print, we can only speculate on the musical contours of this *timbre*. It is possible that it refers to the melody printed in the monophonic editions from 1580–1581, which could suggest that those earlier prints had succeeded in entering the popular repertoire. The important point, however, is that this 1594 *chanson* print suggests that a melody for the *Quatrains de Pibrac* was in wide enough circulation by the end of the sixteenth century to be useful as a *timbre*, and able to be recalled by only a title and no accompanying musical notation.

The interest in composing new settings of the *Quatrains* fell dramatically after Jean de Bournonville's polyphonic publication of 1622, as this style of poetry fell further out of fashion. The moral contents, however, continued to find admirers, as we see in Jacques Langois's late seventeenth-century edition of Pibrac's *Quatrains*, updated for modern-day tastes.[32] The address to the reader closes with the following choice recommendation: "Those who would like to sing them, will easily find some airs on similar sixains; The Lord Raphaël, living in the Cloister of the Sepulchre, ruë S. Denis, seems to have created some expressly for this purpose." Information on the identity of the mysterious noble who composed the sixains and of "Lord Raphaël" is elusive. But Langois's advice for those who wish to sing the collection—either to use preexisting airs composed for *sixains* or to use Lord Raphaël's newly composed settings for the updated Pibrac collection—supports the idea that engaging the *Quatrains* through song was a widespread practice.

At the beginning of the next century, Christophe Ballard published a new musical setting of the *Quatrains* in his collection *Chants des Noels anciens et nouveaux de la grande Bible, notez avec des basses* (1703).[33] His print included as its closing entry the *Quatrains de Pibrac*, presented as an air in triple meter with basso continuo [Web 3.3]. The words for the first quatrain appear with the music, followed by the next nine quatrains. The Ballard print thus

---

[31] Antoine Le Roux de Lincy, *Recueil de chants historiques français depuis le XIIe jusqu'au XVIIIe siècle* (Paris: Charles Gosselin, 1842), 2:554.

[32] *Les Quatrains de Mr de Pybrac changez en sixains, a la maniere dont on parle aujourd'huy. Avec des annotations qui expliquent les entroits les plus difficiles, pour l'instruction des enfans* (Paris: Jacques Langois, 1687).

[33] *Chants des Noels anciens et nouveaux de la grande Bible, notez avec des basses, imprimez pour la première fois* (Paris: Christophe Ballard, 1703).

bookends the musical settings of Pibrac's *Quatrains* by reviving the strophic format of the early monophonic editions.

In the years following the Ballard noël collection, music for the *Quatrains de Pibrac* appeared again in Simon-Joseph Pellegrin's collection *Airs notez des cantiques sur les points les plus importans de la religion et de la morale chrétienne. Noels nouveaux et chansons spirituelles* (Paris: Le Clerc, 1705). Pellegrin suggests the tune "Quatrains de Pibrac" for singing his newly composed chanson texts. In his index of timbres, he lists the "Quatrains de Pibrac" tune as an anonymous "vaudeville." The binder's volume of this print, held at the Bibliothèque nationale, includes two copies of the same notated melody for Pellegrin's "Quatrains de Pibrac," one printed by Christophe Ballard and the other a manuscript copy. Comparing the Pellegrin timbre in these two sources with the 1703 air printed in Ballard's *Chants des noëls*, we see that they are different versions of the same basic melody, thus suggesting the expected melodic variation that characterizes orally circulating tunes (see Example 3.4).

The inclusion of a musical setting for the *Quatrains de Pibrac* in these collections of noëls may seem odd, since these moral texts make no reference

Example 3.4 Comparison of the Ballard and Pellegrin timbres for the *Quatrains de Pibrac*

to the themes or characters of the Christmas story. However, a survey of noël prints from the sixteenth century and beyond shows that it was common for noël collections to conclude with text or two on a moral theme, given the association of moral projects with the new year.[34] A common new year's resolution was to commit to memorize a moral collection, such as the *Quatrains de Pibrac.* For example, in a letter to his mother dated from the beginning of 1604, Henry, Prince of Wales, declared his resolution to memorize the *Quatrains de Pibrac* during that year.[35] Encouraging these resolutions, some offered collections of moral poetry as gifts at the new year. Many of Esther Inglis's virtuosically scripted copies of Pibrac's *Quatrains* and Chandieu's *Octonaires* were designed and presented according to these moral practices. Among her extant calligraphic books were a New Year's gift of the *Octonaires* to Prince Henry and a magnificent manuscript copy of the *Quatrains* that was a New Year's gift to Sir Thomas Hayes at the start of 1607.[36]

This association of moral poetry with an active notion of making progress that was rooted in the yearly calendar stretches all the way back to the earliest polyphonic collections of the *Quatrains.* In the backmatter for the bassus part of L'Estocart's *Quatrains*, the printer Jean I de Laon frames the project as an example of making progress in musical and moral terms. De Laon's reference to the composer's advancement in his craft "de bien en mieux" recalls one of Andrea Alciato's famous emblems bearing the title *In dies meliora / Toujours de bien en mieux,* which appeared across many versions and iterations of Alciato's emblem book[37] [Web 3.4]. The 1584 illustrated edition with both Latin and French makes it clear that this emblem, focused on the idea of getting better every day—i.e., making moral progress—was associated with the New Year. This is a call to moral progress and an encouragement to persevere through a long and difficult enterprise, perfecting it little by little. Pibrac himself used similar language in his 1569 speech before the Parlement of Paris that elaborated on the necessity of daily moral growth ("tousjour croissant et augmentant de bien en mieux").[38] Goulart's *Ample discours* also harnessed this language in his call for a Stoic-guided moral progress: "Those who have in their souls the seeds of true piety, of sincere

[34] Pierre Rézeau, *Les Noëls en France aux xvᵉ et xviᵉ siècles* (Strasbourg: ELIPHI, 2013), 3–5.
[35] Guillaume Du Bartas, *The Divine Weeks and Works of Guillaume de Saluste, Sieur Du Bartas, Translated by Josuah Sylvester,* ed. Susan Snyder (Oxford: Clarendon Press, 1979), 1:20–21.
[36] A. H. Scott-Elliot and Elspeth Yeo, "Calligraphic Manuscripts of Esther Inglis (1571–1624): A Catalogue," *The Papers of the Bibliographical Society of America* 84, no. 1 (1990), nos. 32, 41, 43, 45.
[37] Andrea Alciato, *Emblemata / Les emblemes,* trans. Claude Mignault (Paris: Jean Richter, 1584), fols. 67v–68r.
[38] Pibrac, *Recueil des poincts principaux,* 43.

uprightness, of gentleness and prudence, will recognize our Stoics in man-
ifold places, and in the cry of these foreign witnesses encourage themselves
(as I hope and desire) to run better and better [*de bien en mieux*] towards the
bailey of virtue."[39]

Moral improvement was not a guaranteed result of reading and singing
these texts, as Goulart's laudatory verse for the bassus part of L'Estocart's
Quatrains warns:

> Le vertueux, lisant, chantant ces vers,
> De meilleur cœur à son devoir se range.
> Le vicieux, ici jugé, ne change,
> Ains chante, lit, et demeure pervers.

[The virtuous person reading, singing these verses / With a better heart
governs himself to live uprightly / The vicious, here judged, change not /
And thus sing, read, and remain perverse.]

Although the action of reading and singing these musical settings would certainly propel a virtuous person, it was not automatic: even the most skillfully composed, avidly repeated setting would have no influence on a vicious
person. The perceived ethical efficacy, as expressed here, was contingent on
the willingness of the singer to internalize (and not merely sing and read) the
moral instruction. Here we can see a practical working out of the Stoic theory
of virtue and vice as being without gradation, in a circularity that encouraged
moral progress—though it was possible only for the virtuous.

Conclusion: Amateurs de vertu

This community of virtuous users served as the presumed audience for Boni's
Quatrains—a point made clear in the printer Adrian Le Roy's preface to the
collection:

> Among all the subjects that concern Christian piety as much as human gov-
> ernment, I hold the Quatrains of Pibrac as most praiseworthy for the good
> teaching that they contain, as admirable for their sententious brevity and
> sweet-flowing style [*la sentencieuse brieveté, et dous-coulante veine*] that one

---

[39] Seneca, *Œuvres morales et meslées de Senecque*, trans. Goulart, 3:327–28.

notices in them. And in truth, seeing them rightly received and treasured, I have thought that a musical setting appropriate to such a subject would provide no less profit to good morals, than to provide pleasure in the honest recreation of those who are lovers of virtue [*amateurs de vertu*].[40]

This address to the "amateurs de vertu," which appears across a range of moral prints, asserts a shared identity for a community of buyers and users of these prints. Art historian Leopoldine Prosperetti has illuminated the importance of emblem books and other Stoic-inflected genres of early modern art in cultivating an intelligent lay public equipped to unravel the subtle ethical codes embedded in these materials. She inscribes the *amateurs de vertu* in a long lineage of wisdom-lovers stretching through the Stoics all the way back to Plato and Pythagoras, who forged communal bonds through the pursuit of virtue.[41] Prosperetti's work joins a large interdisciplinary body of work focused on the growth of such invisible communities—sometimes envisioned as a broader "republic of letters"—whose members were attracted to a non-confessional mode of piety and edification that could unite them during this long period of religious conflict in the age of the Protestant and Catholic Reforms. Guided by the Neostoic interest in civility and friendship as a reparative force that could operate across the boundaries of personal difference and opinion, Pibrac's *Quatrains* embodied this neutral mode of philosophical piety and generated a practical mode of making progress toward virtue as an interconnected community rather than in isolation.

A fundamental tenet of Stoicism was that the entire universe is a world-city, a community of sages, as Pibrac's Quatrain 6 (*Tout l'universe n'est q'une cité ronde*) summarizes:

> Tout l'univers n'est qu'une cité ronde,
> Chacun a droict de s'en dire bourgeois,
> Le Scythe et More autant que le Gregois,
> Le plus petit que le plus grand du monde.

[All the universe is only a round city, / Where each person has the right to citizenship: / The Scythe and Moor as much as the Greek, / The smallest as well as the most powerful in the world.]

---

[40] Facsimile reproduced in Boni, *Les Quatrains*, ed. Colin, xliv.
[41] Prosperetti, *Landscape and Philosophy*, 46.

The Stoics viewed humans as naturally and fundamentally social beings, designed to live in community and called to participation in civic life. Marcus Aurelius, after all, reminded himself that "rational beings exist for one another."[42] A surprising feature of Stoicism is that it was quite inclusive in its views, proposing for example—quite radically for the pre-modern world—that women possessed the same rationality as men and were thus just as equipped for philosophical work. They furthermore theorized a community of sages that extended this equal human rationality to every human being on earth—regardless of religion, culture, or class—envisioning everyone as joined by the same *logos* and capacity for virtue that connected all living things together in mutual sympathy. This doctrine of profound interconnectedness balanced out the potential isolation of the perfect sage, tempering it within a pragmatic mode of making progress together toward virtue.

Werner van den Valckert's *An Allegory of Music* (1625) offers a fascinating visual representation of this inclusive Stoic doctrine of universal harmony that extends beyond boundaries of gender, age, religion, or cultural origin (see Plate 3).[43] Painted at the height of the Neostoic movement in the Dutch Republic, Valckert offers what appears to be a simple scene of polyphonic singing. Depicted open-mouthed and singing in harmony from printed notation, the exoticized quartet features a princely Moor, a bare-breasted woman in the guise of a Muse, an old man squinting through his spectacles, and a cherubic child, who are brought into harmonious counterpoint through the intertwining of their voices.[44]

Singers had abundant opportunity to model this idea of a symphony of virtue-lovers as they made their way through the rich and varied corpus of musical settings for Pibrac's *Quatrains*. Through these layers of recitation, repetition, and reflection, the *Quatrains de Pibrac* took on an aura of universality, as though they came from the anonymous collective voice of wisdom, rather than from the pen of one author. Éric Tourrette has attributed some of the overwhelming and enduring popularity of the *Quatrains de Pibrac* to this

---

[42] *Meditations* 4.3; trans. Hays, 38.

[43] The work was long misattributed, first to Otto van Veen and then to Jan Lievens. It was Bernhard Schnakenburg who rejected the authorship of Lievens and suggested Werner van den Valckert—an attribution which has since been confirmed with a signature and date. Bernhard Schnackenburg, *Jan Lievens*, no. R4. See http://www.steigrad.com/van-der.

[44] I will consider the racial and gendered composition of this painting and the musical settings for Pibrac's *Tout l'universe* in Chapter 6.

perception of universal collective wisdom, a phenomenon that he calls "the proverb effect." Although it was well known that Pibrac wrote these moral verses, the focus on practical advice and the simple style of the *Quatrains* launched it into the realm of widely accepted proverbial wisdom. "The proverb effect," according to Tourrette, "is the exquisitely breathtaking experience of a voice that is both single and multiple."[45]

As Pibrac's *Quatrains* were learned and recited by countless voices across generations in the personal and communal work of making moral progress, these repetitions fueled the moral authority of the poetic content, generating collective precepts that were normalized into broader use. As moral song became a common educational and recreational interest across the confessions, it brought Catholics and Protestants from across the political and religious spectrum into a virtuous community of users formed through print. By sharing and using these same poetic and musical tools for virtue repair, such as the *Quatrains de Pibrac*, they created a cultural storehouse of Stoic-inflected ethical precepts that would become recognizable and influential across the confessions, into the next century and beyond.

---

[45] Éric Tourrette, "L'Effet de proverbe dans les *Quatrains* de Pibrac," *Seizième Siècle* 1 (2005): 158–59.

4

Musical Paradoxes

> To follow the *logos* in all things
> is to be relaxed and energetic,
> joyful and serious at once.[1]

Cherished by their admirers and scorned by their critics, the Stoics' penchant for paradoxes went beyond their counterintuitive maxims to underpin much of their philosophical system and moral psychology. This fascination with paradox left an indelible imprint on the wisdom literature of the period, which circulated its quirky and astute proposals through emblem books, moral poetry, and musical settings. In this chapter, I consider the layers of paradox that guided the composition and practice of Stoic musical settings. Not only were the Stoic paradoxes paraphrased in moral poetry and sung in polyphonic arrangements, but the prevailing compositional language of the time offered a colorful palette for experimenting with contradiction, enigma, and ambiguity. The three popular moral song collections that are at the heart of this book offer nuanced poetic and musical strategies of engagement with the joint artistic and philosophical dilemmas developed within the Stoic paradox tradition.

Paradoxia Epidemica

Small in form, yet packing a surprising blow to common assumptions, the paradox grew to epic proportions in early modern Europe. According to Rosalie Colie's *Paradoxia Epidemica*, the world of early modern paradox encompassed a diverse cluster of related rhetorical and moral devices,

---

[1] Marcus Aurelius, *Meditations* 10.12; trans. Hays, 136.

The Voice of Virtue. Melinda Latour, Oxford University Press. © Oxford University Press 2023.
DOI: 10.1093/oso/9780197529744.003.0005

ranging from formal utterances built on self-contradiction to less-structured arguments and *exempla* relying more subtly on ambiguity, ambivalence, and counterintuition for their effect.[2] What binds these various expressive forms under the umbrella of "paradox" is their shared strategy of subverting common opinion. In Pierre Coustel's notes for his French translation of the *Paradoxa Stoicorum* (1666), he hazards that "Paradoxes are maxims that appear new and surprising, because they do not conform to the sentiments of the people and shock some of their presumptions; however, they are often supported by very strong and very convincing reasons."[3] Although the Stoics developed counterintuitive maxims in abundance, Cicero's *Paradoxa Stoicorum* canonized the six deemed most central to their philosophical system: (1) Virtue is the only good; (2) Virtue is sufficient for happiness; (3) All the vices and virtues are equal; (4) All fools are mad; (5) The sage alone is free; and (6) Only the wise person is rich. The *Paradoxa* became one of the most beloved texts of the late fifteenth century. After its first printing in 1465 (together with Cicero's *On Duties*) the work circulated in sixty-nine editions before 1500, and many more afterward. Its popularity in the humanist tradition was ensured in part by Petrarch's promotion of the text as one of his favorite books.[4] After 1574, the Pibrac paraphrases of these Stoic texts were regularly sung and memorized via simple *timbres* passed down through oral tradition and in print. By 1582, music enthusiasts could look to Guillaume Boni's and Paschal de L'Estocart's large polyphonic collections of Pibrac's *Quatrains* for brief but vibrant musical settings of these maxims.

For example, Pibrac's Quatrains 58–59 are based on the most famous of Stoic paradoxes (V and VI), which assert the freedom of the sage regardless of social or political position:

> Le malheur est commun à tous les hommes,
> Et mesmement aux Princes et aux Roys:
> Le sage seul est exempt de ces loix:
> Mais où est-il, làs, au siecle où nous sommes?

[2] Rosalie Colie, *Paradoxia Epidemica: The Renaissance Tradition of Paradox* (Princeton, NJ: Princeton University Press, 1967), 3–9.

[3] Cicero, *Traduction des Paradoxes de Cicéron, avec des notes*, trans. Pierre Coustel (Paris: Charles Savreux, 1666), 121.

[4] On these Renaissance editions, see *Cicero's "Paradoxa Stoicorum": A Commentary, an Interpretation and a Study of its Influence*, ed. Michele Ronnick (Frankfurt: Peter Lang, 1991), 216–19.

[Misfortune is common to all humans, / And even to princes and kings. / The sage alone is exempt from these laws. / But where is he, alas, in our time?]

> Le sage est libre enserré de cent chaines,
> Il est seul riche, et jamais estranger:
> Seul asseuré au milieu du danger,
> Et le vray Roy des fortunes humaines.

[The sage is free bound by one hundred chains. / He alone is rich and never a stranger. / Alone assured in the midst of danger, / And the true king of human fortune.]

This Stoic paradox of the invulnerable sage circulated in a range of emblem prints, such as Otto van Veen's *Emblemata Horatiana*, and it circulated in polyphonic settings by Guillaume Boni and Paschal de L'Estocart.[5] [Web 4.1]

Boni set these paradoxes—*Le malheur est commun* and *Le sage est libre*— as a pair of simple trios that would have offered an ideal starting place for the beginners in any ensemble. In the context of the paradox, they accrue an important moral valence by challenging the common assumption that simplicity of language implies shallowness of content, or that less complicated music indicates less social prestige. Stoic adages were themselves paradoxically both elementary—often the first lesson to be learned—and exceptionally challenging to comprehend fully, demanding prolonged contemplation by even the wisest of adherents. Likewise, Boni's restrained musical style, while certainly helpful for amateurs, also resonated with the values driving the highest levels of professional music production, as witnessed in the cultivated simplicity of the mid-century *voix de ville* and fashion for strophic airs that took court circles by storm in the decades around 1600.[6] Considering the heightened influence of Stoicism at court during this period, this broader aesthetic shift toward simplicity and clarity even in pleasure-oriented settings on love and desire was probably not a coincidence. This paradoxical tension between simple and profound,

---

[5] Otto van Veen, *Quinti Horatii Flacci emblemata* (Antwerp: Philip Lisaert, 1612), 82–83.

[6] Jeanice Brooks, *Courtly Song in Late Sixteenth-Century France* (Chicago, IL: University of Chicago Press, 2000), 13–29, and Kate van Orden, *Music, Authorship, and the Book in the First Century of Print* (Berkeley, CA: University of California Press, 2014), 150–53.

popular and learned, elite and common, which troubles any simplistic understanding of late sixteenth-century musical genres, also marks the materiality of Boni's collection. As Kate van Orden has noted, the quarto format and elegant typesetting signaled the importance of Boni's print in the Le Roy and Ballard catalogue. However, the extremely rare and rather luxurious scoring for three to six voices would have made the print accessible to singers of a wide range of musical competencies, perhaps also inviting novice singers to progress incrementally from basic trios to more advanced settings.[7]

In Boni's pair of trios on the paradox of the sage, the overarching simplicity increases the effect of his Senecan rhetoric of clipped sententiousness and semantic build (introduced in the previous chapter). *Le malheur est commun* opens with the superius singing, "misfortune is . . ." (*Le malheur est . . .*), taking a dramatic breath in measure 2 before explaining that "misfortune is common" (*Le malheur est commun*, mm. 3–4), and after another suspenseful breath, adding the most critical point of this adage that misfortune is "common to all humans" (*commun à tous les hommes*, mm. 4–6). Later in the setting, Boni takes a similar approach when raising the classic Stoic question of whether the perfect sage can ever be found. From measures 17 to 21, he builds incrementally toward the climax of the question—"But where is he . . . but where is he, now . . . now, in our age?" (*Mais où est-il . . . mais où est-il, làs, . . . làs, au siècle où nous sommes?*)—capped off by a repeat of that entire line to close the setting in measures 21–26 (see Example 4.1). *Le sage est libre* employs a similar Senecan build that excites immediate anticipation for the full unveiling of the well-known paradox: "The sage . . . The sage is free . . . The sage is free bound by one hundred chains" (*Le sage . . . Le sage est libre . . . Le sage est libre enserré de cent chaines*, mm. 1–6). The self-reliance of the sage is then reinforced musically in the courageous upper voice that opens with the third line exposed and completely "alone" (*seul*) at measure 12 (see Example 4.2).

These frequent false starts and unexpected phrase lengths make Boni's collection of polyphonic *Quatrains* settings quite engaging to sing. He often adds a layer of musical irony or satire to Pibrac's straightforward pronouncements that subtly undermines the strict tone of the adage—very much in the style of Horace, whose own satirical packaging of Stoic adages required individual contemplation by leaving the poet's relationship to this

---

[7] Van Orden, *Materialities*, 250–57.

Example 4.1 Guillaume Boni, *Le malheur est commun*, mm. 17–21, in *Les Quatrains du Sieur de Pybrac* (Paris: Adrian Le Roy and Robert Ballard, 1582). Based on the edition by Marie-Alexis Colin, with original note values restored

moralizing in deliberate ambiguity. Boni's settings, which never give way to the extremes of either silliness or gloominess, thus dynamically model a productive Stoic tension. They call for a confrontation with the most difficult and serious questions of human existence, all while maintaining a sense of humor and effortless composure.

The "Géladacryse": Laughing-Crying

The inaugural French-language emblem book, *Le Theatre des bons engins* (Paris, 1540), composed by the jurist Guillaume de La Perrière, opens its dedication to Marguerite de Navarre with an explanation of the paradoxical Stoic approach that undergirds the collection:

Example 4.2 Guillaume Boni, *Le sage est libre*, mm. 1–14, in *Les Quatrains du Sieur de Pybrac* (Paris: Adrian Le Roy and Robert Ballard, 1582). Based on the edition by Marie-Alexis Colin, with original note values restored

Madame, the Stoic Philosopher Seneca (to whom without controversy, the learned assign among the Latin philosophers the principal place of Moral Philosophy) says in humble words full of great substance: that Fortune is never at rest, and more, that she does not customarily give joy without sadness, sweetness without bitterness, rest without work, renown without desire, and generally no happiness without misfortune, which I perceive in myself presently verified.[8]

Although La Perrière's attention to these Senecan contradictions was widely emulated in cultural practice, the Stoic manipulation of paradox also drew persistent critique as the impossible formulations of a lunatic fringe. Indeed, the Stoics were known to early moderns as much through their critics as they were through their proponents. A famed example is Plutarch's *On Stoic Self-Contradiction*, wherein the author mockingly points out the many impossible contradictions embedded in Stoic doctrine. Of course, Plutarch's writings against the Stoics eventually circulated with key Stoic writings in *promotion* of the sect, such as Hieronymus Wolf's important editions of Epictetus's works from 1560 on, thus offering a more balanced understanding of the problem of Stoic self-contradiction.[9]

Pibrac's dramatic close to his 58th Quatrain—asking, "Where is the sage, here in our time?"—pointed out one of the underlying contradictions built into Stoic philosophy: the nearly impossible qualifications for sagehood. While it certainly resonated with Neostoics living in the particularly chaotic and violent period of civil war, this signature rhetorical question of the Stoics transcended any particular historical context. The Stoics openly acknowledged that their bar for sagehood—demanding complete *apatheia* (freedom from all passions, and in the most extreme reading of the Stoics, perhaps even all emotion)—was so high as to be humanly unattainable. This radical idealism disconcerted early moderns; as Pierre Ronsard pointed out in one of his Palace Academy lectures, so long as we have our vital organs (where the passions were said to reside), we will have emotional disturbances

<hr>

[8] Guillaume de La Perrière, *Le Theatre des bons engins, auquel sont contenus cent emblemes* (Paris: Denis Janot, 1540, sig. A3r–v). See Alison Saunders, *The Sixteenth-Century Emblem Book: A Decorative and Useful Genre* (Geneva: Droz, 1988), 62–70.

[9] *Epicteti Enchiridion, hoc est pugio, sive ars humanae vitae correctrix . . .* (Basel: Johannes Oporinus, 1560).

("Tant que nous aurons foye et cœur, veines, artères et sang, nous aurons des perturbations").[10] One of the only candidates agreed upon by Stoics as a potential sage was their beloved Socrates, with early moderns like Henri Estienne agreeing on a small slate of other nominees, including Cato the Younger, Ulysses, and Hercules.[11] But even here, it was clearly the distant mythical ideal of these philosophical figures—rather than their messy historical and human selves—that qualified for sagehood. Although early moderns like Ronsard doubted the possibility of eliminating disturbing emotions, they recognized that Stoicism across its long history offered the most profound and widely effective method for managing unwanted emotions and promoting emotional and social constancy. In Erasmus's mocking assessment in *Praise of Folly* (1511), the ideal Stoic sage must be "a marble statue of a man, utterly unfeeling and quite impervious to all human emotion."[12] The very impossibility of sagehood revealed an underlying moral quandary: in accomplishing the inhuman (complete *apatheia*), the Stoic sage loses his own humanity.

Madeleine de L'Aubespine's *Cabinets des saines affections* offers a typical Neostoic concern with moderating the supposed extreme of ancient Stoic *apatheia*. She argues that the passions are not "fundamentally bad, as the Stoics maintain, but they must be contained within strict limits. It is necessary, according to Plutarch, to restrain them (not to eliminate them completely as the Stoics wish), to preserve and cultivate what is good in them."[13] This stated preference for the Plutarchan aim of moderating rather than eliminating the passions was a typical feature of Neostoic writings seeking to distance themselves from the charges of rigid extremism that tarnished the reputation of the sect. This moderate (Plutarchan) position, however, was not far off from the Stoic position all along, for the ancient Stoa recognized the danger of eliminating all emotion. As Diogenes Laertius reported in *Lives* 7.117, the Stoics say that "the wise man is passionless, because he is not prone to fall into such infirmity. But they add that in another sense the term apathy is applied to the bad man, when, that is, it means that he is callous and relentless." Abundant Stoic writings confirm that ancient Stoics across the school

[10] Édouard Fremy, *L'Académie des derniers Valois, 1570–1585* (Paris: Leroux, 1887), 227.
[11] Estienne, *Introduction à la lecture de Sénèque (1586)*, ed. Carabin, 43.
[12] Erasmus, *The Praise of Folly*, trans. C. H. Miller (New Haven, CT: Yale University Press, 1979), 45.
[13] L'Aubespine, *Cabinet des saines affections*, ed. Winn, 22.

not only acknowledged emotion and feeling, but also viewed them positively within certain, rational parameters.

The Stoics' realistic acceptance of human emotion was illustrated in their approach to a pair of Greek philosophers, Democritus and Heraclitus, who were a well-known topic in the ancient and early modern world. When confronted with the instability and folly of the world, Democritus was reduced to laughter, whereas Heraclitus wept. Pibrac's Quatrain 98 offers a standard account of this episode:

> Ri si tu veux un ris de Democrite
> Puis que le monde est pure vanité
> Mais quelque fois touché d'humanité
> Pleure nos maux des larmes d'Heraclite.

[Laugh, if you wish, a laugh of Democritus, / Since the world is pure vanity. / But sometimes, touched with humanity, / Cry over our misfortune with the tears of Heraclitus.]

Alciato represented this philosophical duo in his emblem *On human life*.[14] [Web 4.2] The verse and commentary emphasize that the Democritus/ Heraclitus provocation was more urgent than ever, inspiring Heraclitus's tears over the evil of the world or inspiring even more mockery from Democritus over its heightened folly. While religious discord was already troubling Europe at the time of the earliest French version of 1536, the later sixteenth-century editions of this emblem appeared in the wake of the most violent period of the conflict. These later readers certainly resonated with the question of how to respond to the instability and folly of the world around them. The standard version of the French emblem concludes: Considering the times, it is difficult to know "whether I should laugh, or cry" (*si je devray rire, ou plorer*).

Although these two pre-Socratic philosophers became widely known through multiple ancient lineages, the Stoic tradition in particular featured them in its ethical writings. Seneca discussed the pair in several of his most famous works as symbolic of the problem of human emotion in the face of the world. In *On Anger*, Seneca uses them as a double-sided hedge against anger, asking "What room is there here for anger, if everything calls either

---

[14] Andrea Alciato, *Livret des emblemes* (Paris: Chrestien Wechel, 1536), sig. N7v–8r.

for laughter or tears?" (2.10.5). *On Tranquility* also discusses the problem, at first arguing in favor of mild laughter over weeping. Seneca advises the careful contemplation of the causes that give rise to joy and sadness, ultimately concluding that "it is better to accept calmly the ways of the public and the vices of man, and be thrown neither into laughter nor into tears" (15.1–5). This delicate tension between extremes became the way this pair most influenced the Stoic tradition.

Boni's four-voice setting of *Ri si tu veux* (IX.1) takes this balanced approach to the affective duo. Beginning with his typical semantic build, Boni animates laughter ("Ri") with a brief upward melisma that falls off into a rest before picking up again with the full opening hemistich ("Ri si tu veux") and offering renewed bubbles of melismatic mirth until the close of line 1.[15] The justification for Democritus' laughter, which arrives in the second line—"that the world is pure vanity"—receives aptly brief notice, rushing through this line of verse in a few bars that first destabilizes the sense of the tactus before reaching a clear cadence and return to rhythmic homophony at measures 8–9. Boni devotes the rest of the setting to the tears of Heraclitus. In the third line, when setting the text for being touched by "humanity," Boni allows an augmented second to occur, nonsimultaneously, as the B-flat in the contratenor passes to a C-sharp in the superius and back to a B-flat again in the bassus in measure 11. This returns even more awkwardly in measure 12, as the weak cadence that closes the third line includes a trailing C-sharp in the superius that falls immediately into the cliché of lamenting B-flats at "weep" (*pleure*) to open the fourth line. These expressive devices echo Boni's more dramatic use of dissonance earlier in *Ne va suivant* (II.7)—jumping onto an augmented sonority (B♭-D-F♯) when warning against the pull of following the Epicurean gaggle of pleasure-seekers.[16]

On the surface, Boni employs some of the expected contrasts between musically laughing and crying in *Ri si tu veux*—namely, flowing melismas in hard or natural hexachords for Democritus in the first half followed by augmented note values, the introduction of flats and the soft hexachord, and descending melodic lines for the tears of Heraclitus. Boni, however, subtly undercuts the sonic power of these affective extremes. Particularly when we compare this setting to the rest of his *Quatrains*, we can see that Boni's text

---

[15] Boni, *Les Quatrains*, ed. Colin, 194–95.
[16] Ibid., 35, m. 10.

painting for the laughing Democritus is quite gentle in comparison to the wildly ebullient melismas unleashed for the wandering traveler in *Le voyageur* (III.7) and the bird call of *L'oyseleur caut* (IV.3). Even the second half of *Ri si tu veux*, with its flatted, falling figures, comes across as less melancholic than tranquil, through bassus motion that mostly emphasizes the stabilizing B-flat to F cadence points. In other words, Boni's setting structurally illustrates the Democritus/Heraclitus opposition, even as his restrained expressive choices push toward affective unification. Somehow, he manages to create a musical setting that expresses a rather calm laughter and a somewhat hopeful weeping.

The Neostoic painter Peter Paul Rubens offered precisely this Stoic moderating take on the dilemma in visual form in his 1603 painting *Democritus and Heraclitus*, where Democritus is not laughing, and Heraclitus is not weeping. Rather than underscoring the traditional emotional contrast between the pair, Rubens offers contradictions in his portrayal of each philosopher. John Lepage has aptly noted that Rubens gives Democritus a rather serious, even saintly demeanor, with his hand on the giant globe in the foreground, while Heraclitus looks more mischievous than pious, even though his hands are folded as though in prayer.[17] [Web 4.3] In this way, Stoics and Neostoics rationalized the Democritus/Heraclitus opposition into a paradoxical unity that fully acknowledged the reality of human emotion when confronted with the world, while curbing its perilous extremes.

L'Estocart deploys this complex expressive strategy in his trio setting of *As-tu mis en oubliance* (II.5), an Octonaire penned by Goulart. Also built upon the opposition between the laughing/weeping of Democritus and Heraclitus, Goulart's text situates the dilemma as emblematic of the broader contradictions of life/death and youth/old age:

> As tu mis en oubliance,
> Homme, ta brutale enfance?
> Riant, oses tu chanter
> Les erreurs de ta jeunesse?
> En courant vers la vieillesse,
> Voudrois tu bien plaisanter?

---

[17] John Lepage, *The Revival of Antique Philosophy in the Renaissance* (New York: Palgrave Macmillan, 2012), 11n14.

> Pleure donc, puis que ta vie,
> Est à tous maux asservie.

[Have you forgotten, / O Man, your brutal childhood? / Laughing, do you
dare sing about / The errors of your youth? / In running towards old age, /
Would you like to joke around? / Weep then, because your life / Is enslaved
to misfortune.]

In his setting for Goulart's Octonaire, L'Estocart displays a far more sophisticated approach to this philosophical pair than he did in his straightforward
treatment of Pibrac's *Ri si tu veux* on the same theme. In L'Estocart's *As tu
mis en oubliance*, the youthful laughter is the closest any of these settings
comes to the exuberant silliness of worldly chanson writing, with the quick
repetitions of "laughing" (*riant*, mm. 16–24) that are "running" (*courant*)
toward old age (mm. 30–39). [Web 4.4] Yet he goes on to subvert the expected shift in tone. Following Goulart's poetic subversion that frames the
sorrow as a joke, L'Estocart sets the "weeping" in ternary proportions (mm.
44–46), one of the composer's favorite sonic illustrations of worldly pleasure.
By this point in the second book of *Octonaires*, the message could not be
clearer: the lilting dance of worldly desire is the root cause of sorrow. The musical warning accelerates in the final line—"Is enslaved to misfortune" (*Est
à tous maux asservie*)—as a long chain of suspensions seductively lures the
singers to the closing cadence (mm. 52–57 and 63–68).[18]

The Democritus/Heraclitus problem thus models the Stoic treatment of a
paradox, which offers a pair of extremes, an opposition, or a binary, but then
moves toward a space of unifying or holding in some balanced tension this
contradiction. Taken together, the pair rationalized the problem of human
emotion and its potentially contradictory impulses with the reminder that
falling into either extreme is unhealthy, and that the wisest response to the
reality of the world is a posture of detachment—one that acknowledges
the problem of emotion while refraining from an undue investment in its
claims.[19] Jacques Grévin's *La Gélodacrye* (1560) suggests precisely this rhetorical maneuvering by creating an ironic unity out of the Greek words for
laughter (*gelos*) and tears (*dacrya*), where one paradoxically laughs and cries

---

[18] Paschal de L'Estocart, *Second livre des Octonaires de la vanité du monde*, ed. Jacques Chailley and
Marc Honneger (Paris: Salabert, 1958), 15–17.
[19] See Loris Petris, "Rire ou pleurer?: L'homme face au monde, de Rabelais à Montaigne,"
L'Information littéraire 58, no. 2 (2006): 12–21.

at the same time. Michel de Montaigne, too, capitalized on the theme of simultaneous crying/laughing in his essay I.38 (*Comme nous pleurons et rions d'une même chose*) where he reveals the embedded contradictions inherent in our emotional responses to our circumstances.[20]

We see this balanced approach developed further in the groundbreaking *Vanitas Still Life* (1603) by Jacques de Gheyn II, which inscribes Democritus and Heraclitus into a Stoicized mode of artistic contemplation. [Web 4.5] The panel features a human skull with a cut flower on one side and smoke from an urn on the other. Above the skull hangs a bubble, with a barely visible wheel and leper's rattle floating within it. On the arch at the top of the panel, the motto *Humana Vana* appears, flanked by Democritus and Heraclitus on either side, laughing and weeping at the inconstancy and vanity of the world. Rather than falling in with either Democritus or Heraclitus, the Stoic tradition preferred to keep them bound together as a paradoxical symbol of the problem of human emotion. The wheel (a symbol of Fortune and, in this depiction, a torture device), serves as a double warning through the skull and coins scattered on the ledge below—cautioning that human life, material security, and wealth can vanish through just a simple turn on that axis of privilege or pain.

Goods of the Body and Soul

"All that is mine I carry with me." According to Cicero's account in the *Paradoxa Stoicorum* and Seneca's *On the Constancy of the Sage*, these were the words spoken by the philosophers Bias and Stilbo upon realizing that they had lost everything.[21] French and Latin versions of Alciato's emblem with this motto developed the paradox of the sage's invulnerability to misfortune. [Web 4.6] Even when faced with utter loss and devastation, "he makes everything for the best" (*il faict tout pour le mieux*). The sage fears neither theft nor violence from man or beast, "and in high and low finds himself assured" (*Et de hault et d'embas il se trouve asseuré.*)[22]

The sage could remain secure—as well as free and rich—even when faced with complete loss of material and bodily benefits because, as the Stoics

---

[20] Michel de Montaigne, *Essais* (Bourdeaux: Simon Millanges, 1580).
[21] Cicero, *Paradoxa Stoicorum* 1.8; Seneca, *De constantia sapientis* 6.3 and *Epistles* 9.19.
[22] Alciato, *Emblemata / Les emblemes* (1584), fols. 55r–56r.

reasoned, these externals were never essential for happiness or virtue anyway. Pibrac's Quatrain 25 (*Les biens du corps*) summarizes the message of the first Stoic paradox on the ontology of virtue. Opposing the commonly accepted Aristotelian position on material benefits as being "goods," the Stoics held that virtue alone can remain steadfast regardless of outer circumstances, and thus it is the only true and constant good in the life of the ideal and impervious sage.

> Les biens du corps et ceux de la fortune,
> Ne sont pas biens, à parler proprement,
> Ils sont sujects au moindre changement:
> Mais la vertu demeure tousjours une.

[The goods of the body and those of fortune, / are not goods, to speak properly. / They are subject to the least bit of change: / But virtue remains always one.]

Boni's five-voice setting for *Les biens du corps* (II.12) illustrates the inconstancy of worldly goods through the use of an uncharacteristic amount of chromaticism for the collection, with melodic lines vacillating between natural/hard hexachords and fictive hexachords (see Example 4.3). These tonal inconstancies begin from the outset, when the text is still neutrally unfolding in imitative polyphony, with the first line—"The goods of the body, and those of fortune." This musical hint reveals its negative message in the second line, explaining that these material benefits "are not goods, to speak properly." By the third line, the faster rhythm adds to this accusation of their inconstancy with a quick rocking that illustrates that these false goods "are subject to the least bit of change" (mm. 16–17). The closing line of verse—"But virtue remains always one" (*Mais la vertu demeure tousjours une*)—suggests a rich double entendre, as the final "one" both refers to virtue being a "good" and also asserts that virtue is *one*, a unity, following the Stoic doctrine. Boni's setting illustrates this unified constancy of virtue with augmented note values and elongated, overlapping lines that are suddenly free of the slippery chromaticism that had destabilized the unfolding of the first three lines of the quatrain (mm. 18–23 and 28–33).

Stoic paraphrases like Pibrac's *Les biens du corps* remind us why the sect has so often appealed to those living in troubled times. The Stoic position on

Example 4.3 Guillaume Boni, *Les biens du corps*, mm.1–23, in *Les Quatrains du Sieur de Pybrac* (Paris: Adrian Le Roy and Robert Ballard, 1582). Based on the edition by Marie-Alexis Colin, with original note values restored

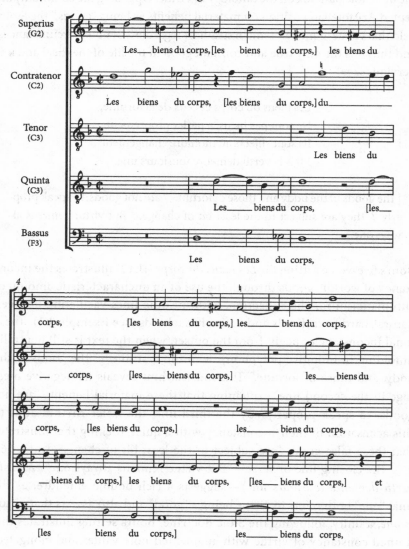

Example 4.3 Continued

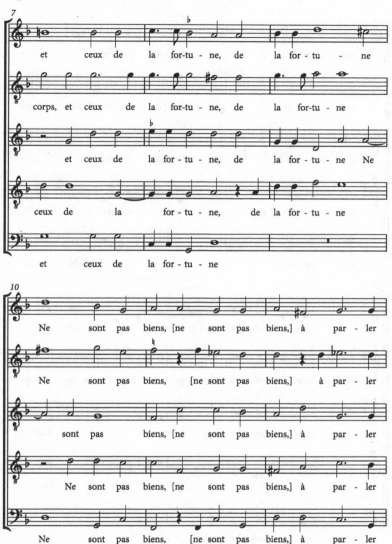

Example 4.3 Continued

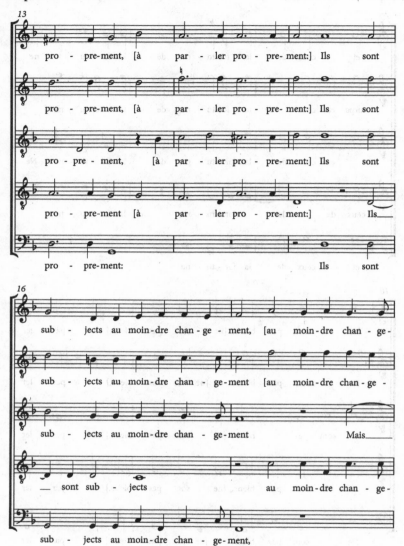

Example 4.3 Continued

virtue offered a clear pathway to emotional stability and tranquility even amid precarity and uncertainty. Rather than living in fear of sudden poverty or loss of position, Stoics urged a focus on what is always within our control—that is, the sage-like ability to cultivate virtue regardless of the inconstancy of our worldly fortunes. As Coustel summed it up in the preface to his French edition of the *Paradoxa Stoicorum* (1666), the Stoics "apply themselves to exhort people to virtue alone, to animate them to constancy, and to assure more and more their minds against the upheavals and diverse accidents of fortune."[23]

In Goulart's substantive introductory essay for Seneca's *On Providence*, which he alternatively titled, "Why Good People are Afflicted when there is a divine providence which governs the world," he frames Seneca's treatise as a remedy for the age-old question of why bad things happen to good people. He points out that in times of plenty, people are quick to acknowledge the wisdom and goodness of God, but in catastrophic times, they audaciously doubt and question. For French Protestants, who had lived under persistent persecution and violence for decades, this was a pressing concern: If God was on their side, wouldn't that divine favor translate into good health, wealth, protection, and prosperity for their community? Why were their enemies flourishing while the faithful were suffering? Goulart explains that "Such confusions of judgment have given occasion to the most learned Stoics to think about remedies that one can apply to this problem."[24] Seneca and the Stoics resolved this question brilliantly by responding that none of those externals (like wealth, health, and prosperity) are really "goods" anyway, but mere "indifferents," which come and go for all people and have no bearing on one's favor in the eyes of God.

Goulart's original work, the *Six Paradoxes chrestiens* (1593), takes this paradoxical position on worldly benefits in a more overtly Christian direction with his set of reformulated maxims supported by biblical and theological writings.[25] The second and third paradoxes explicitly valorize suffering, building upon Seneca's argument throughout *On Providence* that it is potentially good to experience trials, as these tribulations can bolster moral character.[26] Odet de La Noue (who had close ties to Goulart, Joseph Du Chesne, and the composer Claude Le Jeune) also promoted this paradoxical view of the potential benefit of suffering in his *Paradoxe, que les adversitez sont plus necessaires que les prosperitez* [Paradox, that adversity is more needed than prosperity] (1588), where he argues for the role of trials in building

[23] Cicero, *Traduction des Paradoxes de Cicéron*, trans. Coustel, unpaginated preface.
[24] Seneca, *Œuvres morales et meslées de Senecque*, trans. Goulart, 1:185–86.
[25] Simon Goulart, *Six Paradoxes chrestiens* ([Geneva: Gabriel Cartier]: Jacob Stoer, 1593).
[26] Seneca, *On Providence* 2.7, 3.1, 3.3, 4.1, 5.9. See Inwood, *Stoicism*, 58–59.

the fortitude and resolve of the faithful church. La Noue's *Paradoxe* was translated into English by Josuah Sylvester (along with Pibrac's *Quatrains*, the *Octonaires*, and the *Tablettes*). Sylvester's prefatory verse for La Noue's treatise depicts this Stoic contrast between the fickle face of Fortune against the unassailable constancy of Virtue: "Chameleons change their colour: Guile her game: / But (in both Fortunes) Vertue's still the same."[27]

The ancient goddess Fortuna, frequently depicted as blindfolded and turning her famous wheel, serves as a key figure in Stoic thought, for it is only by fully understanding the inconstancy and fickleness of the world that humans can protect themselves from being utterly devastated by tragedy and loss, or the anxiety and fear of potential loss that can destroy the mental health of even a person living in plenty.[28] When not shown turning her wheel, Lady Fortune was most often portrayed as standing on a ball in turbulent water, as in Gilles Corrozet's emblem *L'image de la Fortune*, where her other foot rests on a dolphin while her hand holds a broken mast.[29] [Web 4.7] Alciato's emblem *Art assisting Nature* offers a similar image of Fortune on her round ball with her toe dipping into the water, this time facing Mercury at rest on a stable cube. [Web 4.8] The sea—known for its ability to turn from tranquil into terrifying in mere moments—offered a ship-faring culture an enduring analogy for the unpredictability of placing our happiness in the hands of Fortune, whose blindfolded eyes warn that life's inconstancies strike all humans without respect to power or privilege. Seek out goods that cannot be lost in a shipwreck, the Stoicized commentary for the 1615 edition advises, for "there is no figure more mobile or less firm than the sphere, but the cube remains firm."[30]

The Shape of Constancy

Constancy was the core of Stoic virtue, as Du Vair and other Neostoics repeatedly emphasized, for it was here that the true hope of remedy for the instability of public chaos and inner turmoil was to be found. As Justus

[27] Sylvester, *Works*, 621.
[28] Reydams-Schils, *The Roman Stoics*, 68.
[29] Gilles Corrozet, *Hécatomgraphie* (Paris: Denis Janot, 1540), sig. F7v–8r.
[30] Alciato, *Emblemata / Les emblemes* (1584), fol. 136r; and Andrea Alciato, *Les Emblemes* [Part Two], trans. Jean Lefevre and Jean II de Tournes (Geneva/Cologny: Jean II de Tournes, 1615), 235–36.

Lipsius influentially explained in *On Constancy*: 'Constancy' is a right and immovable strength of the mind, neither lifted up nor pressed down with external or casual accidents. By 'strength' I understand a steadfastness not from Opinion, but from judgement and sound Reason."[31] This unshakeable internal fortitude that leads to civil stability was the desired outcome of the musical exercises embedded in Stoicized educational initiatives like the *Quatrains de Pibrac*.

Composed in an unchanging four-line square form, Pibrac's *Quatrains* modeled a poetic experience of constancy. The evenness of the decasyllabic line offers the balance of a binary divisibility, and the consistent *rimes embrassées* (*abba*) utilized by Pibrac further demarcate the outer corners of this box. Pibrac explained the moral symbolism of the square shape in his Quatrain 39:

> La Verité d'un Cube droict se forme
> Cube contraire au leger mouvement:
> Son plan quarré jamais ne se dément,
> Et en tout sens a tousjours mesme forme.

[The truth of a cube stands it upright / A cube resists wobbling: / Its square form never dissembles; / And in all senses always keeps the same form.]

The Cube thus represented the unmoving solidity of truth and became a powerful representation of the constancy that was the aim of Stoic exercise.

Boni's four-voice setting for *La verité d'un cube* (IV.2) shapes a sonic impression of this square constancy. The setting opens with a bold homophonic opening that lets "The truth" of the opening words sink in, before pausing and restarting the entire line in measure 4.[32] The reduced note values in Colin's modern score obscure the visual effect that Boni offers the singers here. The shape of the opening breve in all voices is a big square, and its length adds a feeling of sonic weight to the claim for both constancy and truth. Free of the wobbling of rounder shapes expressed in the flash of quick rocking at "au leger mouvement" (mm. 8–9), the solid cube does not easily move. If singers have not quite picked up the imagery

---

[31] Lipsius, *On Constancy*, I, 4; ed. Sellars, 37.
[32] Boni, *Les Quatrains*, ed. Colin, 74–75.

of the long opening breves, the third line makes the visual correspondence unmistakable, as Boni completely arrests the motion of the line with two large breves, sung in all voices, on the text describing the "square form" (*son plan quarré*) of the upright cube (mm. 12–13 and 14–16). The concept of shape again finds clever illustration in the final line, where the ornament in the superius on the text for "same form" is repeated at measures 24 and 27.

In contrast to the square cube's physical and moral stability, the sphere became associated with instability, not only because the globe was the image of the terrestrial world with its constant cyclical changes, but also because of the physical properties of the sphere, which moves and rolls easily. Catherine Hofmann's survey of early modern emblems reveals that while positive images of the globe as representing the elegant perfection and order of the divine cosmos were possible, it became much more common for the round sphere to represent the changing whims of Fortune and pattern of human folly that characterized life on earth.[33] Georgette de Montenay's *Emblemes, ou Devises chrestiennes* (1567/1571) features a sphere in twelve of her innovative moral illustrations. Among the numerous emblems featuring an iron ball as an image of the base and inconstant world, Montenay's emblem *This is the Victory that Overcomes* features a large tripartite ball representing the material world in the foreground, in opposition to a sturdy square-winged pillar, symbolizing the constancy and reason of faith.[34] [Web 4.9]

For Pibrac and his *parlementaire* circle, the archenemy of square constancy was the polished courtier, whose actions and speech were driven by ever-evolving fashion and overblown vanity rather than based in the solidity of virtue. Like abundant emblems crafted in this exact vein, Pibrac's Quatrain 105, *Ne voise au bal*, warns against the duplicity of those at court, who use their capacity for beautiful speech to dissimulate:

> Ne voise au bal, qui n'aymera la danse,
> Ny au banquet qui ne voudra manger,
> Ny sur la mer qui craindra le danger,
> Ny à la Cour qui dira ce qu'il pense.

[33] Catherine Hofmann, "The Globe as Symbol in Emblem Books in the West, Sixteenth and Seventeenth Centuries," *Globe Studies* 49/50 (2002): 81–120.

[34] Georgette de Montenay, *Emblemes, ou Devises chrestiennes* (Lyon: Jean Marcorelle, 1567/1571), fol. 6r.

[Let nobody go to a ball who doesn't like to dance; / Nor to a banquet anyone who doesn't wish to eat; / Nor put out to sea if they are scared of danger; / Nor go to court, if they want to say what they think.]

The mechanical allure of this quatrain, with its chains of negation, represents the artificiality of courtiers bound by their need to follow the crowd.[35] Although Pibrac's poetic treatment of this courtly artifice retains the solidity of his regular *abba* form, the moral warning takes an alternate form— inconstancy—in the musical settings by Boni and L'Estocart. Both composers used a cut C as their standard time signature across their collections, generally only shifting to ternary groupings for textual emphasis or to illustrate a specific passage of text. However, for Pibrac's *Ne voise au bal*, Boni and L'Estocart chose to strategically depart from the straightforward pulse of duple meter by offering the entire setting in triple.

Whereas Boni breaks into ternary rhythm only six times in the collection of 126 settings, L'Estocart's *Quatrains* frequently exploits the contrast between duple and triple groupings, although often the metrical shift serves to merely emphasize an important section of text, rather than illustrating, amplifying, or commenting upon it. An example of triple as emphasis comes in L'Estocart's *Le malheur est commun* (Quatrain 58), which shifts to ternary for lines 2–4 in the text (discussing the significance of princes and kings and the exemption of the sage), before returning to standard duple for the closing half of the final line and its return to the contemporary age. However, in other examples from the *Quatrains*, L'Estocart utilizes the shift to triple as a physical, visual, or conceptual illustration or amplification of the textual content. We can see this more interesting application of triple in his setting of *La verité d'un cube* (Quatrain 39): here the composer deploys duple meter as the musical analogy for the truthful and stable cube, contrasting it with the round shape of ternary groupings, with their rolling, unstable motion.

Confusion abounded throughout this period over the appropriate notation, terminology, and performance of ternary passages, which could be signaled through either black notation or a 3 before the passage. Known as *triple*, *sesquialtera*, or *hemiola*, among other possible names, these passages signaled an opposition between duple and ternary groupings that could occur in the same line sequentially or between two different voice parts simultaneously. As Ruth DeFord has shown, the persistent conflicts in

---

[35] Pibrac, *Les Quatrains*, ed. Petris, 185n134.

notational practices and terminology for these passages left theorists in a twist, and performers had to cobble together their own strategy for resolving these rhythmic ambiguities in practice.[36] What was unanimous, however, was that a ternary passage (whether notated in semibreves or minims) that appeared in all voices would be sung to one *tactus*. Scholars and editors today, therefore, generally recommend a relationship between duple and ternary that maintains a constant tactus at the level of the bar that gives the same total duration for the duple and triple groupings (i.e., two semibreves in cut C equals three semibreves in 3).[37]

One of the debates in this period was whether a ternary passage in three equal semibreves should be sung unequally, as a "proportionate" *tactus* where the first two-thirds of the *tactus* fall on the downstroke, while the remaining third comes on the upstroke. Boni's setting of Pibrac's *Donner beaucoup* (VIII.11) nods to this practice of an unequal *tactus* by shifting to a ternary passage on the text "par proportion" (mm. 19–23), which he notates unequally, as a breve plus semibreve to avoid any confusion.

Ternary passages, particularly when realized with an unequal *tactus*, offered a strong metrical feel, and invoked the sensual motion of dancing. This physical quality of the dance was certainly an inspiration for both Boni's and L'Estocart's choice to set Pibrac's *Ne voise au bal* entirely in triple. Both composers retain their standard cut C as the time signature, adding a 3 next to it. This was one of the standard methods for signaling ternary meter; however, when used for this text about the duplicity of courtly speech, it also offers a subtle moral image: the duple meter norm of constancy or virtue is here overlaid with triple as a clear type of elegance, artifice, or excess. In the image of the courtier, aesthetic variability was negatively linked to inconstancy and signaled by the excess movement of the triple grouping.

The moral repertoire regularly targets courtiers as examples of how the highly polished social arts serve a fashionable lifestyle of vapid change, vanity, and artifice. Machiavelli's *The Prince* came under similar fire by moralists for its influential anti-virtue stance. Like much advice to successful courtiers, it focused primarily on constructing an appearance of goodness, rather than

---

[36] Ruth DeFord, *Tactus, Mensuration, and Rhythm in Renaissance Music* (Cambridge: Cambridge University Press, 2015), 171–200, and Roger Mathew Grant, *Beating Time and Measuring Music in the Early Modern Era* (New York: Oxford University Press, 2014), 63–90.

[37] See Boni, *Les Quatrains*, ed. Colin, 188; Annie Cœurdevey, "La Notation du rythme ternaire dans les recueils d'*Airs* de Le Roy et Ballard (1552–1598)," *Revue de Musicologie* 96 (2010): 7–33; and Denise Launay, "Les Rapports de tempo entre mesures binaires et mesures ternaires dans la musique française (1600–1650)," *Fontes artis musicae* 12, no. 2–3 (1965): 166–94.

becoming good or doing good. In other words, moralists invested in the Mirror of Princes tradition accused Machiavelli of offering a broken mirror, for he explicitly encouraged the prince to adopt a morality that could not be reflected by or extended to the populace.[38]

Moral collections like Pibrac's and Chandieu's had far deeper ethical roots. Although these collections became associated with the civility training in the social arts outlined by Baldasarre Castiglione's *Book of the Courtier* (1528), this later moral corpus was grounded in the unassailable Stoic notion of virtue that recommended the *telos* of living a life of constancy and temperance over pleasing a fickle, unreasonable crowd. A common refrain confirmed that the most virtuous person (and indeed the happiest) is precisely the opposite of the typical social elite. As Seneca explained in Letter 45.9, such persons take Nature for their teacher, living according to her laws and commands; they stand undevastated by even violent winds of Fortune; and are "unerring in judgment, unshaken, unafraid, . . . moved by force but never moved to distraction."

These Stoic attacks on the pleasure-seeking courtiers, coupled with their frequent admonitions to mistrust and despise worldly goods, have led to a misunderstanding of the Stoics as promoting asceticism. While Zeno, the founder of the Stoa, did train under Diogenes the Cynic—which accounts for a prominent strain of ascetic language in the school—he deliberately moved away from his teacher's doctrine of chosen poverty and ultimately found a middle ground between asceticism and hedonism.[39] As Guillaume Du Vair explained in his *Philosophie morale des Stoiques*: all external goods and worldly benefits are "indifferents, which are rendered good or evil according to the minds of those who use them."[40] The Stoic theory of indifferents was one of their most original and distinctive teachings, and it offered a crucial counterpoint to their doctrine of the radical singularity of virtue. Not only did the Stoics allow a place for worldly riches, comforts, and delights, but they also acknowledged their short-term value and recognized that they could be rationally "preferred" when available. The key to virtue and

---

[38] See Lines, Introduction to *Rethinking Virtue*, 3; Pauline Smith, *The Anti-Courtier Trend in Sixteenth Century French Literature* (Geneva: Droz, 1966); and Susannah Carson, "'Ils se veut faire voir': The Modern Courtier in Castiglione and Montaigne," in *Religion, Ethics, and History in the French Long Seventeenth Century*, ed. William Brooks and Rainer Zaiser (Oxford: P. Lang, 2007), 117–30.

[39] A. A. Long, "Zeno of Citium: Cynic Founder of the Stoic Tradition," in Diogenes Laertius, *Lives of the Eminent Philosophers*, trans. Mensch, 603–10.

[40] Du Vair, *La Philosophie morale des Stoiques*, 5–6; in *Traictez philosophiques*, ed. Tarête, 60.

lasting happiness, however, was to hold these indifferents with an open hand, recognizing their ephemerality and remaining ready to release them without emotional devastation when they are taken away by Fortune's turning wheel.

This nuanced Stoic position on material benefits was carefully retained in the moral collections central to this study. Pibrac's Quatrain 69, *Plus n'embrasser*, for example, strikes this critical balance, advising in the final couplet to "Use goods and not desire them / Neither wish for death, nor fear it" (*User des biens, et ne les desirer; / Ne souhaitter la mort, et ne la craindre*). Boni's setting offers this moral contradiction in his setting of this critical line of text as he builds desire for closure by delaying the arrival of a cadence.[41] Mathieu's Tablette II.75 also affirms this necessity of using worldly goods for virtuous aims: "Goods are great trouble to those who mishandle them: The miser hoards them, the prodigal loses them." (*Les biens sont de grands maux à celuy qui n'en use, / L'espargant les acquiert, le prodigue les pert.*) Mathieu makes the point even more directly in Tablette II.97. Here he critiques equally the deliberately impoverished position of Diogenes the Cynic (who dressed in rags and famously rejected even a simple drinking cup as an excess) and the indulgence of Marcus Gavius Apicius (the iconic Roman gourmet who lived during the time of Tiberius): "I blame Apicius and Diogenes equally," the poet explains, "one for loving too much and the other too little."[42]

Chandieu's Octonaire on this theme first critiques the Aristotelian view of wealth and health as goods, and then offers the flexible Stoic position of wealth as an indifferent, which can be used by the wise for good or evil:

> Antiquité, pourquoy as-tu donné
> Le nom de biens aux richesses mondaines,
> Puis qu'il n'y a que maux, ennuis et peines,
> Pour l'homme vain, qui y est adonné?
> Mais toy, Mondain, pourquoy abuses-tu
> De ce qui est instrument de vertu?
> Les biens font mal à qui des biens abusent.
> Les biens font bien aux bons qui bien en usent.

---

[41] Boni, *Les Quatrains*, ed. Colin, 134–35, mm. 15–16.

[42] "Je blame esgallement Apice et Diogene, / L'un pour aymer le trop et l'autre le trop peu." On Diogenes throwing away the cup, see Diogenes Laertius, *Lives* 6.37.

[Antiquity, why have you given / The name of goods to worldly riches, / Since they are only evil, trouble, and pain / For the vain person, who devotes themselves to these things? / But you, Worldly One, why do you abuse / What is an instrument of virtue? / Goods create evil in those who abuse them. / Goods create goodness in the good people who use them well.]

L'Estocart's four-voice setting for *Antiquité, pourquoy as tu donné* (I.13) exemplifies his willingness to use discordant harmonies in the service of text painting. [Web 4.10] Note the harsh dissonance between the tenor and superius going into the cadence on "worldly riches" (mm. 36–37). The subsequent collapse of the upper three voices on a D octave at "maux," at the caesura of the third line (m. 41), turns "bad" as the bass enters early on A and bungles the sense of reprieve. Even worse, as the verse continues with "annoyances and pains" (*ennuis et peines*), the singers get into real trouble as the signed B♮ in the tenor clashes with the simultaneous B♭ in the contratenor (m. 45). Henry Expert understandably presumed that this natural was a printing error and corrected it in his modern edition. However, the specific word placement of this impossible dissonance at "worry/trouble," which is expressively extended in the dramatic augmented-sixth lead into the D cadence at "pain" (mm. 47–49), lends strength to the possibility of the diminished octave as a deliberately expressive move. James Haar's work on similarly chromatic sixteenth-century repertoire cautions editors against suppressing these piquant dissonances; and Jacques Chailley and Marc Honegger have argued the point specifically for L'Estocart's *Octonaires*, noting that these shocking moments correspond to equally vivid illustrations in the text.[43] An augmented octave troubles L'Estocart's Octonaire I.8 (*Jamais n'avoir et tousjours desirer*) at the warning of the damaging "effects" of the one who loves and lusts after the world; and another augmented octave in I.9 (*Quand le mondain travaille*) constructs a similarly disastrous sonority at "he builds his ruin." Regardless of whether one accepts these dissonances as strategy or fortuitous error, these events as printed in the partbooks would have certainly led singers into performance conflicts, forcing them to choose a safe resolution or let the sonic discomfort remain unchallenged.

Returning to L'Estocart's *Antiquité, pourquoy as tu donné*, we encounter another evocative moment in lines 5 and 6, when he switches to a ternary

---

[43] L'Estocart, *Second livre des Octonaires*, ed. Chailley and Honneger, xi, and James Haar, "False Relations and Chromaticism in Sixteenth-Century Music," *JAMS* 30 (1977): 415.

Table 4.1. Stoic *pathē* vs. *eupatheiai*

Pathē (unhealthy passions to be eliminated)	Eupatheiai (healthy states of feeling to be cultivated)
DISTRESS (*lupē, aegritudo*) = irrational suffering based on a judgment of present evil	n/a
PLEASURE (*hēdonē, laetitia*) = irrational delight in that which has no lasting value or causes harm	JOY (*khara*) = rational delight over that which is worth choosing
FEAR (*phobos, metus*) = irrational anxiety over something incorrectly perceived as bad or harmful	CAUTION (*eulabeia*) = rational avoidance and aversion for that which is truly harmful
DESIRE (*epithumia, libido, appetitus, cupiditas*) = irrational longing for that which is incorrectly valued	WISHING (*boulēsis*) = rational desire for virtue and things worth choosing

passage with a signed 3 to underscore the salient change in address to the worldly *Mondain* ("Mais toy, mondain, pourquoy abuses tu, / De ce qui est instrument de vertu?") in contrast to the more distant critique directed at the past (*Antiquité*) in the surrounding lines. Concluding the setting, L'Estocart reaffirms the potential benefits of using worldly goods for virtue ("Les biens font bien aux bons qui bien en usent") as he unleashes a series of theatrical suspensions that are expertly used for the pleasure of the singers.

The Stoics framed the passions as a balanced set of opposing emotional states. In Cicero's account in *Tusculan Disputations* 4.14—which was probably modeled after Chrysippus—the four unhealthy passions (*pathē*) that had to be eliminated were distress, pleasure, fear, and appetite.[44] The definitions of these passions, however, reveals a crucial caveat for understanding the Stoic view of the emotions, for we can see that each unhealthy passion is defined as an inappropriate or mistaken judgment, whereas the positive "good" emotions (*eupatheiai*) are the rationally appropriate counterpart to these destructive states (see Table 4.1). By this logic, the Stoics defined the passion of Fear as an irrational anxiety over something mistakenly perceived to be harmful, whereas caution is the rationally guided emotional response to a present danger. Pleasure is thus far more restricted than our normal sense of the word, for it is defined as an irrational delight in something that

---

[44] See Sellars, *Stoicism*, 114–20; and Sorabji, *Emotion and Peace of Mind*, 29–47.

is worthless or even harmful. Joy, by contrast, is the appropriate delight in something that is rationally worth choosing. In other words, much of the Stoic and Neostoic dismissal of pleasure refers to what we would now call at worst pathological (such as an addiction to a harmful drug) or at best a guilty pleasure (such as the irrational enjoyment of fast food, which is harmful to the body long-term, lacks nutrition, and whose de-localized chain model damages communities). This contrasts with the rational and "wise" delight in experiences deemed to be good for both the individual and society at large, such as the pleasure of a farm-to-table meal that can be savored in the moment with no long-term harm to self or others, provided that the experience is held without obsession or fear of its loss.

The Stoic warnings against addiction to pleasure were thus a critical counterpart to their paradox of virtue as the only good, and their efforts to cultivate the resilient tranquility of the sage. Indeed, worldly riches and pleasures often lead for a craving for more, or to a fear of losing them, and thus undermine whatever ephemeral happiness they might offer in the moment. Although the Stoics never fully subscribed to the Platonic/Pythagorean view of the body as a contamination that must be divorced from the mind, they remained deeply concerned with the immersive power of pleasurable sensory experiences to suppress reason entirely, leave false opinions unchallenged, and give free rein to the destructive passions. Their concern to restrain this sort of experience was not rooted in a hatred of sensual enjoyment: it was born out of their acute observation that a life centered on pleasure might very well achieve less of it. In a passage harnessing similar language to the closing lines of Chandieu's Antiquité, pourquoy as-tu donné, Mornay's Excellent discours warns of this "false hunger," where, "full of water, they are dying of thirst, or on a pile of wheat cry famine. They have goods, but lack the will to use them ("Ils ont des biens, et n'en osent user")."[45] Mathieu's Tablette I.23 likewise warns of "this pleasure that exhausts but never gives you your fill" (Ce plaisir qui te lasse, et jamais ne te saoule). This Stoic dismissal and "despising" of worldly goods was thus predicated on one of the Stoics' core paradoxical doctrines—that an attachment to "false goods" (faux biens) leads not to security and comfort, but rather to greater dissatisfaction and discontent. As Pibrac put it in Quatrain 114: "Man is the enemy of his own contentment. The more he has the more he still desires."[46] In Quatrain

---

[45] Duplessis-Mornay, Excellent discours, 26–27.
[46] "L'homme ennemy de son contentement, / Plus a et plus pour avoir se tourmente." Pibrac, Les Quatrains, ed. Petris, 84.

69, however, he offers the critical Stoic nuance of the indifferent, closing the final couplet with "User des biens, et ne les desirer: / Ne souhaiter la mort, et ne la craindre." Use goods, but do not long for them. Wish not for death, but do not fear it, either.

Therapeutics of Contradiction

Reflecting the padoxical unity of their approach to both the emotions and worldly goods, Chandieu's *Octonaires* displayed a concerted interest in contradiction as a therapeutic device for treating the problems of desire and pleasure. We see this in *Qu'as-tu? Povre amoureux*, which harnesses the rhetoric of contradiction to remind the "half-dead" (*demy-morte*) lover of the world that her happiness is entirely in her control. "Blame nothing but yourself" (*N'accuse rien que toy*), the poetic sage whispers, for "Your problem is your desire; and what you are complaining about is your own pleasure" (*Ton mal est ton desir, / Et ce dont tu te plains, est ton propre plaisir*). Following this same Stoic logic, Chandieu's sage describes pleasure as a "sweet-bitter" (*doux-amer*) beverage that leaves the person who indulges drunk but not satisfied, for pleasure and sorrow are paradoxically bound together as "painful pleasure" and "pleasing pain" (*Ton plaisir douloureux et ta douleur plaisante*). The poetic deployment of even more concise compound words such as "birthing-dying" (*naissant-mourant*) and "alive-dead" (*vifve-morte*)—boils down the Stoic rhetoric of brevity and contradiction into its most potent, crystalized form.

Scholars have long attributed Chandieu's rhetorical contradictions in the *Octonaires* to the influence of Petrarch, who is well known to have developed the paradox as an innovative poetic device.[47] While late sixteenth-century French poets certainly recognized the Petrarchan lineage of these stylistic paradoxes, they were equally aware of Petrarch's work as a purveyor of Stoic therapy—a system that, as we have seen, was built upon brevity, paradox, and contradiction. In addition to Petrarch's celebrated fondness for the *Paradoxa Stoicorum*, the grand humanist was known for his devotion to Seneca. Petrarch's Stoic credentials were well established in the sixteenth century, in part due to Erasmus's influential editions of Seneca's works (1515, expanded 1529), which include an introductory essay (*Vita Senecae*) that inscribes

---

[47] See L'Estocart, *Second livre des Octonaires*; ed. Chailley and Honegger, ix.

Petrarch into the Stoic lineage along with Boccaccio and St. Jerome.[48] Goulart followed this model by calling upon the authority of Petrarch in his address to the reader for his later French translation of the works of Seneca, as Petrarch "confessed that none of the Greeks was comparable to Seneca in moral philosophy."[49]

In his *Remedies for Fortune Fair and Foul*, Petrarch experimented with verbal techniques for treating the problem of Fortune's inconstancy. He clearly understood a core point of Stoic therapy—that the "treatments" were not to be applied only after a tragic event. Rather, these rhetorical-moral exercises were appropriate and necessary for all people, regardless of where they were located on Fortune's moving wheel. Petrarch thus sculpted an enduring template for how Stoic therapeutics could be aestheticized and tasted through poetic devices as "verbal medicines" (*medicamenta verborum*). As Petrarch explained, paraphrasing Stoic teachings, "Invisible diseases of the mind require invisible cures."[50] Thus, Petrarchan contradiction as a poetic and stylistic device inevitably pointed to a deeper moral underpinning rooted in Stoic philosophy and its therapy of desire.

Chandieu's *Tu me seras tesmoin*, which L'Estocart placed second in his first collection of *Octonaires*, stages the problem of inconstancy through rhetorical contradiction:

> Tu me seras tesmoin, ô inconstante France,
> Qu'au monde n'y a rien qu'une vaine inconstance,
> Car ta paix est ta guerre et ta guerre est ta paix,
> Ton plaisir te desplaist et ton soulas t'ennuye.
> Tu crois qu'en te tuant tu sauveras ta vie,
> Flotant sur l'incertain de contraires effects.
> Il n'y a chose en toy qui ferme se maintiene,
> Et n'as rien de constant que l'inconstance tiene.

[48] Seneca, *Joannes Frobenius Verae Philosophiae Studiosis S. D. En tibi lector optime, Lucii Annaei Senecae sanctissimi philosophi lucubrationes omnes: additis etiam no[n]nullis Erasmi Roterodami cura* . . . (Basel: [Johann Froben], 1515), 7. See also Ross Dealy, *The Stoic Origins of Erasmus' Philosophy of Christ* (Toronto: University of Toronto Press, 2017), 48–100.

[49] Seneca, *Œuvres morales et meslées de Senecque*, trans. Goulart, vol. 1, fol. iiir.

[50] Letizia Panizza, "Stoic Psychotherapy in the Middle Ages and Renaissance: Petrarch's *De remediis*," in *Atoms, Pneuma, and Tranquillity*, ed. Osler, 39–66. Among the numerous editions circulating in the period, see Francesco Petrarca, *De remediis utriusque fortunae* (Lyon: Clementem Baudin, 1577), 15.

[You will be my witness, O inconstant France, / That in the world there is only a vain inconstancy, / Because your peace is your war and your war is your peace, / Your pleasure displeases you and your relief irritates you. / You believe that in killing yourself you will save your life, / Floating on uncertain and contrary effects. / There is nothing in you so firm remaining, / And nothing as constant as your inconstancy.]

Chandieu's text, Étienne Delaune's accompanying emblem, and L'Estocart's musical setting all harness this rich lineage of paradox to illuminate a moral tension that offers no simple resolution. Delaune's emblem emphasizes the opposition between philosophical tranquility and worldly instability. The image portrays France as the crowned figure of Fortuna, balancing precariously on a ball in the turbulent waves and holding a dagger to her own throat, while the town behind her engages in battle. The sage, by contrast, stands on firm ground near a peaceful copse of trees, offering a promise of relief from this scene of chaos. [Web 4.11]

L'Estocart's musical setting for *Tu me seras tesmoin* constructs similar oppositions through harmony, rhythm, and gesture. [Web 4.12 and 4.13] In his sonic portrayal of the pull between opposing forces, L'Estocart fully exploits the chromatic alterations conventional for G Dorian, beginning with a series of block G chords, with a signed B-natural, that pivots to an expansive C minor sonority in measure 3. The appearance of a signed E-flat in this modal area was a standard alteration for G Dorian, justified melodically as a way to reinforce the upper boundary of the crucial G–D diapente. Lacking the normal melodic ascent that establishes the modal octave, however, L'Estocart's application of the flattened sixth degree in measures 2–3 generates a sense of wonder through the cross-relations produced by the move from B-natural in the superius to the E-flat in the tenor, with its implied need for a harmonizing B-flat. True to its fundamental variability, the line denies the satisfaction of the sweeter B-flat and closes with a return to an unexpectedly harsh B-natural signed into the superius part (m. 9). After another aptly unpredictable cadence at "inconstance" (mm. 16–17), L'Estocart musically develops the moral point of the text by exposing the link between violence and instability. For instance, the stabbing motive in line 5 that strikes out through the texture is answered in the next line by the swirling, rising eighth notes that sweep across line 6 (mm. 51–53), like flotsam on agitated water. Even more powerfully, L'Estocart undermines the solidity of the entire setting by strategically denying a satisfying cadence at each opportunity suggested by the divisions of the text, in some cases through rhythmic evasion (as seen in mm. 22, 27, 30, 36, 51, 59, 70, 75, 81, and 86), or through harmonic destabilization (in mm. 69–70).

L'Estocart utilizes similar layers of text expression in his setting for Chandieu's *Mondain, si tu le sçais* (I.3). This Octonaire, which is entirely constructed around a series of relentlessly paradoxical "If... then" questions, reflects Chandieu's documented interest in Stoic logic as a mode of posing hypotheticals to inspire reflection on a moral question that has no easy answer.[51]

> Mondain, si tu le sçais, di moy, quel est le monde?
> S'il est bon, pourquoy donc tant de mal y abonde?
> S'il est mauvais, pourquoy le vas tu tant cerchant?
> S'il est doux, comment donc a il tant d'amertume?
> S'il est amer, comment te va il allechant?
> S'il est amy, pourqouy a il ceste coustume
> De tuer l'homme vain, sous ses pieds abatu?
> Et s'il est ennemi, pourquoy t'y fies tu?

[Worldly One, if you know, tell me, what is the World? / If it is good, why then does so much evil abound? / If it is evil, why do you go seeking after it? / If it is sweet, why therefore has it so much bitterness? / If it is bitter, how do you find it appealing? / If it is a friend, why does it have this custom / Of killing foolish men, crushed under its feet? / And if it is an enemy, why do you trust it?]

Delaune's illustration for this text (see Plate 1) emphasizes these contradictions through the contrast in setting: the ancient sage sits upon a rock in his timeless grove, while the elegant Mondain and his victim are positioned in front of a village that is in the process of being attacked and burned.

L'Estocart's evocative setting for *Mondain, si tu le sçais*, which arrives immediately after *Tu me seras tesmoins* in his first collection of *Octonaires*,

---

[51] Although Chandieu's scholastic treatises are framed in Aristotelian terms, his persistent use of the hypothetical syllogism reveals a direct borrowing from Stoic logic. See van Raalte, *Antoine de Chandieu*, 26.

confirms the capacity of a polyphonic composition to heighten a paradox and deftly unpack its moral potential. [Web 4.14 and 4.15] Note the ascending and descending parallel 6/3 chords in the old *fauxbourdon* style to illustrate the action of going in search of something (mm. 27–32), and the clever pairs of repeating quarter notes to invoke violent blows or stomping feet (mm. 68–73). At a more abstract level, L'Estocart again deploys chromatic alteration for expressive purposes. An initial shock comes at the brief cadence on "know" (m. 4), as the B♮ creates a brilliant, hard hexachord before falling back to B♭ in the next measure. In the second line, as the text questions whether the world is "good" (*bon*), L'Estocart leads the voices through a striking augmented sonority (m. 16) that warns the singer that the answer is not going to be an easy yes. The poignant rhythmic shift to a slow, homophonic texture for "If it is sweet" (m. 35–39) draws out the gentle wonder of the resonant E♭ sonority before breaking the fantasy with a sour, augmented chord at "bitterness" (m. 47) (see Example 4.4). By this point, the singers and listeners should be prepared for the lesson that the supposedly good things of this world can end in harsh regret. This disastrous sonority seems to have been produced as a result of three separate voice-leading choices made according to the logic of each separate line, without taking into account their collective harmonic consequences—an apt musical metaphor for exactly the kind of clash of personal desires that leads to widespread civil conflict and destruction.

Conclusion

Music—and particularly the polyphonic vocal music of this period—resonates well with the Stoic penchant for harmonizing opposites in the interest of achieving balance. This embodied moral lesson is predicated on the relationality and connectedness of the independent vocal lines as they unfold in the imitative polyphonic tools available at the time. One of the most potent aspects of this style is its ability to build up unity from separate, relatively equal melodic lines, each exhibiting its own internal modal logic, but also relating to the other voices, which are brought together through voice leading to unite in moments of vertical, harmonic significance at cadence points. Frequent contrasts in texture further emphasize this opposition between independence and interdependence, as passages of imitative polyphony are offset by arresting moments of homophony, where some or all

Example 4.4 Paschal de L'Estocart, *Mondain, si tu le sçais*, mm. 35–48, in
Premier livre des Octonaires de la vanité du monde (Lyon: Barthélemy Vincent
[Geneva: Jean I de Laon], 1582). Based on the edition by Henry Expert

voices come together in rhythmic unison for a weighted declamation of a significant phrase. When crafted by philosophically minded composers like L'Estocart, these musical procedures could go beyond the facile expression of simple text painting to stage a dynamic, open-ended engagement with the moral poetry through sound.

Powerful—if precarious—musical sound could extensively manipulate emotional responses and intellectual understandings of the world and its attachments. For this reason, the Stoics generally considered music to be a preferred indifferent. Du Vair took this general position in his argument for eloquence, which, "like all the most excellent things of the world, can lead to evil or good, depending on how they are possessed and deployed."[52] He drives home the point that even philosophy and understanding can be used for destructive ends; should we reject them? Protestant leaders, attentive to these Stoic currents, directly borrowed the Stoic concept of the indifferent to church music, to allow the different branches of Protestantism to suspend their disagreements over what music should accompany the liturgy. As *The Praise of Musick* (1586) reported, "this is the resolution of all our late divines, Bucer, Bullinger, Calvin and the rest, which with one consent agree, that it is an indifferent thing, having no hurt, but rather much good in it, if it bee discreetly and soberly used."[53] The concept of the indifferent thus operated practically as a mode of avoiding dogmatism on the use of worldly benefits and pleasures like wealth, sophisticated intellectual knowledge, and skill in the performance and appreciation of the art of music.

Even as music was cultivated and praised in this way—as a mode of training in virtuous sagehood—the Stoic tradition also issued plenty of warnings about the immersive power of musical experience and its social affiliations with status, political power, and wealth. They were clearly opposed to elite and haughty connoisseurship, in which making value judgments on music and art is a form of status-building designed to flaunt how little satisfaction one takes in commonplace or amateur musical practices. They also cautioned against an obsessive or unhealthy attachment to music that positioned it as essential for happiness. What if you lost your hearing? This was a point raised by Marie Le Gendre in her contribution to the Neostoic discourse.[54] Or, indeed, what if you injured your hand so that you could no longer play your

---

[52] Du Vair, *De l'eloquence*, fol. 17r; ed. Radouant, 146.

[53] *The Praise of Musick, 1586*, ed. Kim, 145.

[54] Le Gendre, *L'Exercice de l'âme vertueuse*, ed. Winn, 72.

lute? What if you experienced a change in fortune and lost your treasured musical instruments and costly partbooks? It was through this nuanced line of thinking about worldly goods and skilled crafts as preferred indifferents that the Stoics made space for the full range of artistic experience, from the simplest expressions all the way to the most cultivated artistic genres and practices. Here was evidence of human rationality at its most mature: the ability to choose and appreciate excellent things, for as long as Fortune made them available.

Plate 1 Étienne Delaune, Emblem D, *Mondain, si tu le sçais*. F-Pneph, Ed. 4.a. Rés, in-folio. Photo: author. Courtesy of the BnF

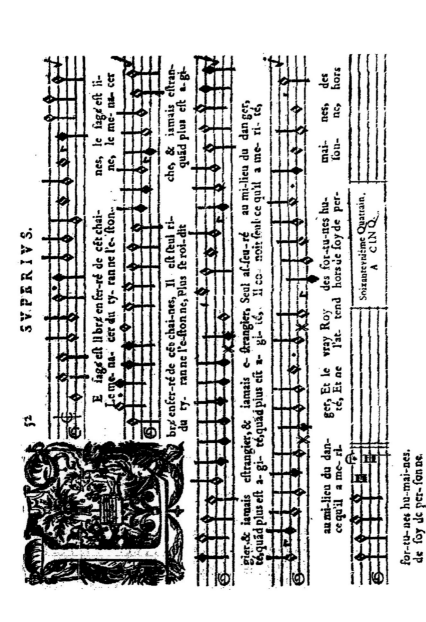

Plate 2 Paschal de L'Estocart, *Cent vingt et six quatrains du Sieur de Pibrac* (Lyon: Barthélemy Vincent [Geneva: Jean I de Laon], 1582), Quatrains 59–60, Superius, 52. Biblioteca Nazionale Universitaria di Torino. Photo: IMSLP/Public Domain

Plate 3 Werner van den Valckert, *An Allegory of Music* (1625), oil on panel. Private collection. Photo: © Lawrence Steigrad Fine Arts, New York/Bridgeman Images

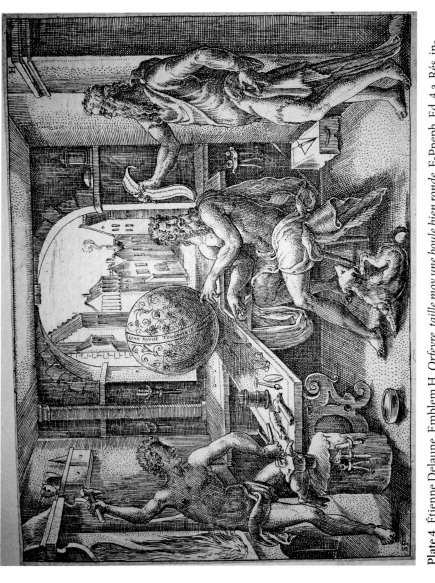

Plate 4 Étienne Delaune, Emblem H, *Orfevre, taille moy une boule bien ronde.* F-Pneph, Ed. 4.a. Rés, in-folio. Photo: author. Courtesy of the BnF

Plate 5 Detail of Étienne Delaune, Emblem H, *Orfevre, taille moy une boule bien ronde*

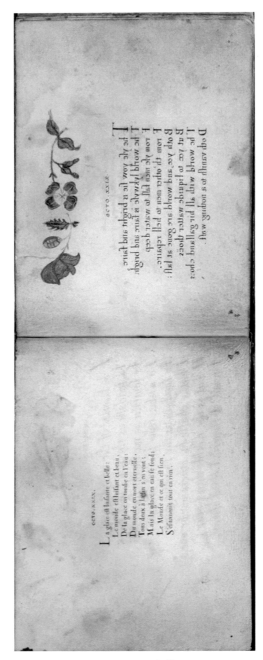

Plate 6 Esther Inglis, *La glace est luisante et belle*, in *Octonaries upon the Vanitie and Inconstancie of the World* (1600), fols. 29v–30r. US-Ws, MS V.a.91. Photo: Courtesy of the Folger Digital Image Collection

Plate 7 Étienne Delaune, Emblem I, *La glace est luisante et belle*. F-Pneph, Ed. 4.a. Rés, in-folio. Photo: author. Courtesy of the BnF

Omnia percipiunt Senfus animoq; miniftrant
Externa externj qualiacunq; fient.

HE. fnuent

Quicquid habet tellus, quicquid mare, quicquid et æther,
Quinq; his aftra, aer², Lunaq;, folq; patent.

Plate 8 Hendrick Goltzius, *Les Cinq Senses* (1588). Photo: Courtesy of the BnF, Gallica

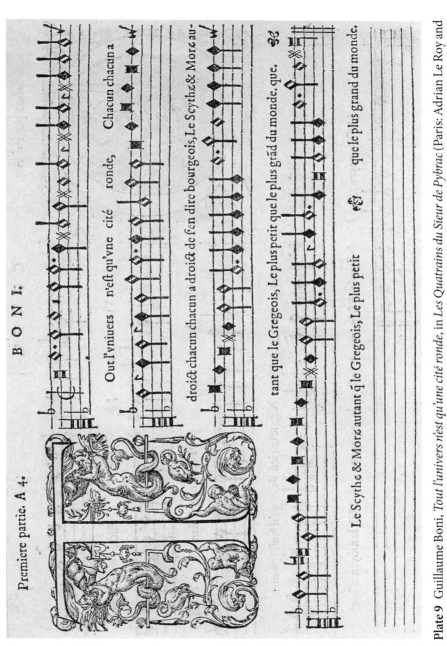

Plate 9 Guillaume Boni, *Tout l'univers n'est qu'une cité ronde*, in *Les Quatrains du Sieur de Pybrac* (Paris: Adrian Le Roy and Robert Ballard, 1582), Contratenor, fol. 5v. Photo: Courtesy of the BnF

Plate 10 Carstian Luyckx, *Vanitas Still Life with Skull, Music Book, Violin and Shells* (mid-17th c.), oil on canvas. Musée des beaux-arts de Marseille. Photo: © Jimlop Collection / Alamy Stock Photo

Plate 11 David Bailly, *Self-Portrait with Vanitas Symbols* (1651), oil on wood. Stedelijk Museum De Lakenhal, Leiden. Photo: © Archivah / Alamy Stock Photo

Plate 12 Simon Renard de Saint-André, *Vanitas Still-Life* (17th c.), oil on canvas. Private collection. Photo: © The Picture Art Collection / Alamy Stock Photo

Plate 13 Étienne Delaune, Emblem K, *L'estranger estonné regarde*. F-Pneph, Ed. 4.a. Rés, in-folio.
Photo: author. Courtesy of the BnF

Plate 14 Marin Le Roy de Gomberville, *Philosopher c'est apprendre à mourir,* in *Doctrine des mœurs, tirée de la philosophie des Stoiques* (Paris: [Louys Sevestre] Pierre Daret, 1646), fol. 92r–v. Photo: Courtesy of the BnF

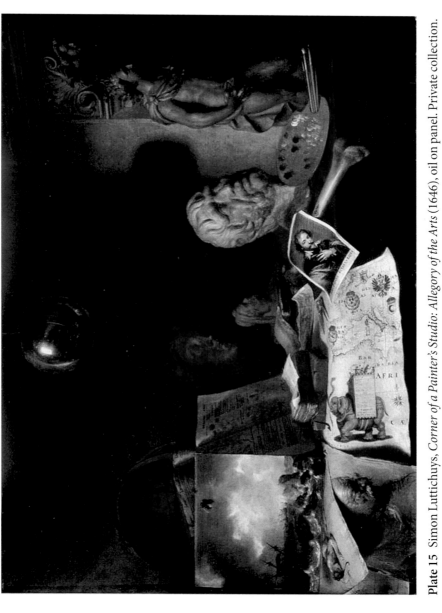

Plate 15 Simon Luttichuys, *Corner of a Painter's Studio: Allegory of the Arts* (1646), oil on panel. Private collection. Photo: © Art Collection 2 / Alamy Stock Photo

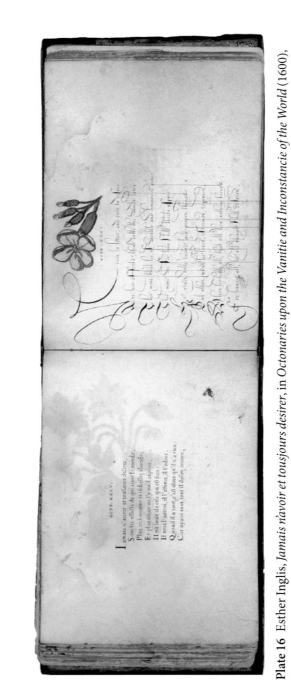

Plate 16 Esther Inglis, *Jamais n'avoir et tousjours desirer*, in *Octonaries upon the Vanitie and Inconstancie of the World* (1600), fols. 35v–36r. US-Ws, MS V.a.91 Photo: Courtesy of the Folger Digital Image Collection

5

Sensing Beauty

He called Beauty the flower of voice,
or as others report it:
Voice the flower of beauty.[1]

The use of song in projects of moral education on both sides of the confessional divide is well documented, and the ethical and didactic aims of singing moral song collections like the *Quatrains de Pibrac* were certainly of prime importance. However, the degree to which beauty and pleasure played a role in the production, purchase, and practice of the moral song repertoire requires a more nuanced investigation, due to a complex cultural ambivalence about these positive experiences that came down, in part, through the anti-rhetorical posturing of the Stoic tradition. The tendency of moral poets to warn against the lure of external beauty and pleasure could cause these collections to be misperceived as subscribing to a narrow didacticism that morally straitjacketed the aesthetic potential of the poetry and musical settings. Indeed, the overwhelming success of the *Quatrains de Pibrac* in its broad poetic and musical printing history could be seen as a triumph of the rationalization of poetry and music, which was aimed at building the knowledge foundation essential for collective moral reasoning. If this rationality were purely an abstract intellectual enterprise, then the pervasive drive toward rational understanding would seem to leave little room for appreciating sound, feeling, and affect—those most powerful and praiseworthy aspects of music that were generally thought to operate upon the emotional or sensual pathways of human experience. Critically, however, Stoic rationality was deeply embodied in and relied upon a robust approach to sensory stimuli that not only accommodated an aesthetic appreciation of artistic forms like

---

[1] Goulart, *Apophthegmes de Zenon* [Sayings of Zeno] No. 18, in Seneca, *Œuvres morales et meslées de Senecque*, trans. Goulart, 3:298. Cited after Diogenes Laertius, *Lives* 7.23.

The Voice of Virtue. Melinda Latour, Oxford University Press. © Oxford University Press 2023.
DOI: 10.1093/oso/9780197529744.003.0006

poetry and music, but also saw these encounters with beauty as an essential marker of the divine *logos*.

In Guillaume Du Vair's opening address to Parlement in 1601, he narrates the powerful story of the Stoic Zeno, known as "one who held contempt for the pleasures and luxuries of the world," who was so moved by the song of a lyre player that he marveled to his followers, "see how even the guts of beasts bring forth an admirable consonance and melody when they are touched justly by proportion."[2] Beauty, for the Stoics, was a state of virtuous proportion consistent with virtue and equivalent to it through its goodness. As Diogenes Laertius explained of the Stoic position: "it is beautiful because it is good; and it is beautiful; therefore it is good."[3]

Even as they displayed a significant interest in this link between beauty and morality, the Stoics recognized a deeper problem, for the experience of beauty was bound up with both pleasure and desire—the foremost provokers of the passions. Although Stoic writers warned against these potentially destructive encounters between beauty, pleasure, and desire, a sensitive consideration of their philosophy reveals that they embraced these risks through their intricate philosophy of mind and moral psychology, which prioritized sense perception of the natural world as the foundation for proper rational judgments.

This chapter focuses on the *Octonaires de la vanité et inconstance du monde*, which offer some of the most creative poetic, visual, and musical responses to Neostoicism. These *Octonaires* are thus better suited to uncover the full range of music's expressive and aesthetic potential than simpler settings of Stoic texts. In contrast to the generally cautious tone of L'Estocart's *Quatrains* preface, a full-blown emphasis on musical beauty and its pleasures as a worthy moral aim takes shape in Paschal de L'Estocart's two polyphonic collections of *Octonaires*. The colorful imagery of the poetry served as a fertile source with which composers explored techniques of text expression that enhanced the moral content through multiple layers of musical representation and sensory recognition. In other words, these settings demand a consideration of the flip side of the ethical-aesthetic hierarchy, for Stoic moral progress was inexorably tied to aesthetic concerns—to a way of feeling, experiencing, and

---

[2] Du Vair, *Œuvres*, 184. See also Seneca, *Œuvres morales et meslées de Senecque*, trans. Goulart, 3:298. Shakespeare, a known Stoic enthusiast, rendered these words of Zeno in *Much Ado about Nothing*: "Now divine aire, now is his soule ravisht, / is it not strange that sheepes guts / should hale soules out of mens bodies?"

[3] *Lives* 7.101; trans. Mensch, 348. See Aiste Celkyte, "The Stoic Definition of Beauty as *summetria*," *Classical Quarterly* 67 (2017): 88–105.

appreciating the world around us that could be harmonized in counterpoint with reason. Thus, the multi-sensory forms of the *Octonaires* corpus found a way to reconcile the presence of beauty and pleasure in music, poetry, and art by addressing the dangers of unmoderated hedonism while valorizing the importance of aestheticized sense impressions for moral understanding.

Serious and Sweet

The rich liminal materials gracing these volumes, composed by L'Estocart's tight-knit circle of Reformed poets, pastors, and scholars, offered a model listening experience that could serve as a script for use by a broader market of singers and musicians who would purchase and perform these prints.[4] Particularly considering that the Calvinist branch of Protestantism has long been characterized as a community hostile to musical aesthetics—probably due to a misunderstanding of its Stoic borrowings—the laudatory verses for L'Estocart's *Octonaires* collections provide an important window into a Protestant justification of the pleasure of musical beauty as morally useful in virtue formation.[5] Although peppered with the expected allusions to Orpheus and Amphion, these liminal verses are not hollow echoes of the *laus musicae* tradition, parroting well-worn tropes of music's ethical power gathered piecemeal from earlier music tutors and treatises. My research on the identities of L'Estocart's laudatory contributors suggests that these poetic references to the *laus musicae* tradition were a serious philosophical engagement, created by a group of professors, scholars, and students at the University of Basel and the Academy of Geneva with documented Neostoic credentials who were immersed in the breadth of Greek and Latin sources driving these musico-ethical concerns.[6] Thus, even though the poetic mode

---

[4] On the ethical work of liminal materials, see Katherine Butler, "In Praise of Music: Motets, Inscriptions and Musical Philosophy in Robert Dow's Partbooks," *Early Music* 45 (2017): 89–101.

[5] For a counter to this negative historiography, see Daniel Trocmé-Latter, "The Psalms as a Mark of Protestantism: The Introduction of Liturgical Psalm-singing in Geneva," *Plainsong and Medieval Music* 20 (2011): 145–63.

[6] Latour, "The Performance of Friendship," 424–34. In addition to Goulart and La Faye, introduced earlier, their fellow pastor-scholars Theodore Beza and Jean Jaquemot also recorded an interest in Stoicism. For example, Jaquemot published poetic paraphrases of Seneca's Letters and Latin renditions of Chandieu's *Octonaires*, works that were ultimately bound together with a Stoicized original work by Beza in Simon Goulart's edition. *Sententiae quaedam ex Senecae epistolis excerptae et singulis tetrastichis expressae a Ioanne Iacomoto Barrensi. Quatrains tirez des Epistres de Senecque traduits du Latin de Jean Jaquemot de Bar le Duc, par S. G. S. Ausquels a este adjousté le Censeur Chrestien imité du Latin de M. TH. D. B. par ledit S. G. S.* (Geneva: Fran. Le Fevre, 1608).

of delivery was "informal," the philosophical content was grounded in the highest level of academic study available in the Protestant world.

The commendatory verses printed in L'Estocart's two polyphonic collections of *Octonaires de la vanité du monde* offer unabashed enthusiasm for their beauty, directly praising the musical settings as "beautiful" (*belle*) and "sweet/pleasing" (*doux*), and noting the power of these settings to delight both singers and listeners, while reinforcing music's ethical capacity. For example, Jean Jaquemot further praises L'Estocart, "the sweetest of musicians," for his beautiful and daring harmonies, "which are so sweet and, with varying harmonies, so chaste."[7] L'Estocart's first collection of *Octonaires* opens with a Latin epigram by Theodore Beza. In contrast to those who would divorce musical pleasure from its ethical function, L'Estocart's musical setting perfectly unites moral utility with musical pleasure (e.g., line 8, "Dulci maritans utile"). Other contributions in these prefaces also directly reference this Horatian dyad, praising L'Estocart's music for its powerful marriage between aesthetic and ethical concerns, which they frequently condense into a joyfully salient compound word (*doux-utile*), rendering the aesthetic form inseparable from moral engagement.

Arguably the most influential formulation of this delicate relationship between moral and stylistic concerns came from a famous passage in Horace's *Ars poetica* (333–37): "Poets aim either to benefit, or to amuse, or to utter words at once both pleasing and helpful to life." Although Stoicism was certainly not the dominant orientation of Horace's work, the *Ars poetica* borrows directly from certain key aspects of Stoic artistic theory, including appeals for brevity, simplicity, and integrity as stylistic and ethical priorities. While scholars generally recognize the *utile dulci* as having been shaped through Aristotelianism, Diogenes Laertius reported that this union was also an integral feature of Stoicism: "Nature, they hold, aims both at utility and at pleasure, as is clear from the analogy of human craftsmanship."[8] The Stoic analogy of human craftsmanship referenced here relied of course on musical practice as a key example. The Stoic geographer Strabo was another influential source of these ideas in Neostoic circles. In his *Geography*, in setting up his defense of the philosophical and moral value of Homer's poetry, he argues that "Eratosthenes is wrong in his contention that the aim of every poet is to

---

[7] "Macte noua virtute, chori, Paschalis, alumne / Castalidum, citharae quae docuere modos / Tam dulces, varijs concentibus, atque pudicos." L'Estocart, *Premier livre des Octonaires*.

[8] *Lives* 7.149.

entertain, not to instruct; indeed the wisest of the writers on poetry say, on the contrary, that poetry is a kind of elementary philosophy."[9] He goes on to develop the point of the wise person as both poet and musician because the practice of these arts tends to discipline and correct character.[10]

Early moderns frequently praised Stoic writings in similar terms that linked their project to the ethical-aesthetic balance of the Horatian *utile dulci,* a dyad that became Stoicized as a union of gravity and sweetness. Du Vair's *On Eloquence* praises the Stoic union of ethics and aesthetics along these lines, describing their "graves et sages sentences" as a flow of "Attic honey," whose sweetness can be tasted and seen as the shining illustration of a well-crafted discourse of reason.[11] Likewise, L'Estocart describes his compositional style in these Stoicized terms in his preface to the first collection of *Octonaires*. In a passage where he details his humanist aim to create musical settings that are well suited to the words, he also clarifies his ethical-aesthetic aims: "to present a gravely-pleasing [*grave-douce*] music, well accommodated to the letter." This claim to a serious musical style suited for morally edifying texts, yet also sweet and pleasing to sing, resonated with L'Estocart's circle of laudatory contributors, whose verses repeatedly reference L'Estocart's arresting merger of this paradoxical dyad.

Illustrating Inconstancy

This tension between the *grave* and the *doux*, between moral content and aesthetic experience, begins with the texts themselves. Following their Stoic models, the *Octonaires* poets treat beauty and pleasure critically across the corpus—as problematically linked to instability of the world. However, the poetic experience of reading these lovely, evocative texts generates an acute sense of resistance to the severe moral message, through the metrical variety and vivid patchwork of natural images illustrating the Stoic themes of human mortality and the endless cycle of worldly change. We see this creative emphasis on inconstancy modeled in *L'eau va viste en s'ecoulant*, L'Estocart's opening setting for his first collection of *Octonaires*. The text, by Chandieu, features a series of natural warnings against the ephemerality of the world and its pleasures:

[9] *Geography* I.I, 7.10.
[10] *Geography* I.I,16.3.
[11] Du Vair, *De l'eloquence*, fol. 16r; ed. Radouant, 145.

> L'eau va viste en s'escoulant,
> Plus viste le traict volant,
> Et plus viste encore passe
> Le vent qui les nues chasse.
> Mais de la joye mondaine
> La course est si tressoudaine,
> Qu'elle passe encor devant
> L'eau et le traict et le vent.

[Water flows quickly / Even faster the flying arrow, / And faster still passes / The wind which chases the clouds / But of worldly joy / Its course is so sudden that it passes even before the water, the arrow, and the wind.]

The inconstancy of water was a favorite moral image for Stoics like Seneca and Marcus Aurelius, for it offered profound aesthetic and ethical significance in its constant flow and variability. I have already cited relevant passages on this theme from Seneca's *On the Brevity of Life* in Chapter 2, but several entries in Marcus Aurelius's *Meditations* rehearse the same guided moral imagery:

> Some things are rushing into existence, others out of it. Some of what now exists is already gone. Change and flux constantly remake the world, just as the incessant progression of time remakes eternity.
> We find ourselves in a river. Which of the things around us should we value when none of them can offer a firm foothold?[12]

L'Estocart's lovely setting for *L'eau va viste* (I.1) picks up on this quality of motion, which is central to the moral analogy and poetic cadence of the Octonaire, offering a cascading rhythmic diminution that picks up speed with each example of quick passing. [Web 5.1 and 5.2] The escalating momentum sets up a dramatic shift to ternary groupings on "worldly joy" with a charming shift to lilting homophony that moves the body in an alluring dance-like rhythm that is gone as quickly as it came. Just as it impossible to stop the flow of water with a single hand, we cannot hold onto our material benefits in this world or to any of its comforts and securities.

Chandieu's *Le beau du monde s'efface* explores this imagery further:

---

[12] *Meditations* 6.15; trans. Hays, 71.

> Le beau du monde s'efface
> Soudain comme un vent qui passe:
> Soudain comme on void la fleur
> Sans sa premiere couleur:
> Soudain comme une onde fuit
> Devant l'autre qui la suit.
> Qu'est-ce doncques de ce monde?
> Un vent, une fleur, une onde.

[The beauty of the world fades away / Suddenly like a passing wind, / Suddenly as we see the flower / After its first blush, / Suddenly as a wave flees / Before another that follows. / What then is this world? / A wind, a flower, a wave.]

Taken at face value, Chandieu's text seems to offer a perfectly straightforward Stoic warning against worldly beauty, which, like the wind, flower, and wave, fades away as part of the transience of all things. However, though the content paints beauty and pleasure in cautionary terms, this exquisite example of *vers rapporté* works in a sophisticated tension with this serious lesson, and perhaps even contradicts it. The lovely cadence, escalation of repeated words and sounds, and delicacy of the poetic imagery offer a heightened poignancy in experiencing—and even treasuring—this fleeting beauty.

L'Estocart's high-voice trio setting of *Le beau du monde s'efface* (I.4) only strengthens this contradictory pull between a detachment from and simultaneous experience of the fragile worldly beauty modeled in Chandieu's poetry. [Web 5.3.] L'Estocart takes advantage of opportunities for simple text/music correspondence, such as the running ascending eighth notes that arrive in imitation on the text ("as a wave flees") (*comme une onde fuit*, mm. 15–16) or the rhythmic flourish that decorates each flower (*fleur*) (mm. 26–29). He also unpacks the moral lesson more subtly: The opening measures begin in a homophonic ternary passage that immediately links "worldly beauty" to the fleeting "worldly joy" from L'Estocart's first setting of the collection (I.1 *L'eau va viste*). In the case of *Le beau du monde s'efface*, the unequal proportion of the ternary passage oddly places less important words/syllables (*le, du, -de*) on long note values, while key words/syllables (*beau, Mon-*) arrive on weaker parts of the unequal pairs. At the end of the line, the setting shifts abruptly back to the standard duple (m. 4). The second line remains in duple meter but imitates the unusual rhythmic effect of the opening in triple by ending the phrase with two quarter notes at the beginning of measure 7. These unexpected short note values at the end of the first and second lines, with their appropriately weak endings (*se face, passe*), drift away quickly, elegantly adding texture to the basic association of the world with ternary passages. Harmonically, a similar fading effect appears throughout the settings as full-voiced sonorities (*Le beau*, m. 1) lose their fifth or third, leaving only an oddly bereft interval in their wake (mm. 2–3, 5, 7, etc.). These compositional strategies leave the singers and listeners with an almost palpable sensation of loss and decay (see Example 5.1).

A fascinating contradiction thus lies at the heart of the *Octonaires*, for even as the serious moral content of the texts warns against the danger of attachment to worldly beauty, the artistic pleasure of the poetic and musical illustrations directly challenges this detachment by offering an aesthetic experience of inconstancy that proves both immersive and compelling. The *Octonaires* poetry paints vivid depictions of the natural world, borrowing some of the favorite images of the Roman Stoics for the inconstancy and vanity of the world. Across the *Octonaires*, the fragile world and its vain pleasures are compared to ocean waves, the wind, smoke, a soap bubble, a wilting flower, an arrow, falling leaves, fruit, dust, a ship in a storm, the planetary bodies, and the four elements—to name only a few.

The vivid images of nature populating the *Octonaires* corpus in its many modalities reflect the central Stoic concern with contemplating the beauty of the natural world as a mirror of moral understanding. According to Diogenes Laertius, "This is why Zeno, in his work *On Human Nature*, said that the goal is to live in harmony with nature, which means to live according to virtue, for nature leads us to virtue."[13] Du Vair's *Philosophie morale des Stoiques* followed by defining the good, by this criteria, as "nothing other than living and acting according to nature."[14] Barthélemy Aneau's *Imagination poétique* (1552) cited this Stoic precept in the commentary for the emblem *Rien ne fault sans bon conseil entreprendre*: "When taking on any project, follow this example: let Nature be your guide, which is (according to the Stoic saying), the Providence of the eternal God."[15]

[13] *Lives* 7.87; trans. Mensch, 344.

[14] Du Vair, *La Philosophie morale des Stoiques*, 3; ed. Tarrête, 58–59.

[15] "Et puy apres la Nature libere / Soit conduisant à ce qu'on delibere. / Qui est (selon la Stoique sentence) / Du tresgrand Dieu l'Eterne providence." Barthélemy Aneau, *Imagination poétique* (Lyon: Macé Bonhomme, 1552), 60.

Example 5.1 Paschal de L'Estocart, *Le beau du monde s'efface*, in *Premier livre des Octonaires de la vanité du monde* (Lyon: Barthélemy Vincent [Geneva: Jean I de Laon], 1582). Based on the edition by Henry Expert

Example 5.1 Continued

Late sixteenth-century Protestants, clearly influenced by this Stoic call to follow nature, began to describe the world of God's creation as a mirror of moral understanding, a "second Bible," which should be imitated as a pattern book for appropriately understanding our place and function during our life on earth.[16] Chandieu's *Lors que la feuille va mourant* describes this moral viewing of nature's life cycle in directly aesthetic terms: "The beautiful face of the year: / There is a mirror of your life" (*Le beau visage de l'année: / C'est là un miroir de ta vie*).

The Stoic call to follow nature demanded a direct sensory experience of the physical world. It was for this reason that the Stoics valorized the bodily senses as the first and primary portal to all knowledge.[17] However, as we will discover further in the next chapter, they exercised some of the caution promoted by their competing Hellenistic school the Skeptics, for the senses were subject to the fragility of human imperfection and could therefore be deceived. The *Octonaires* poets modeled this approach by consistently foregrounding sensory experience. They offer colorful descriptions of the natural world ("la montagne colorée," "d'une lumiere dorée," "sa verte couleur," etc.). Furthermore, they systematically address all five senses and frequently identify them in the act of perception—e.g., Octonaire 44, "I saw, I saw that the World is a dream" and Octonaire 47, "Listen, hear the voice of Virtue")—all while cautioning against an attachment to their delights. While all the senses are addressed, it is sight and hearing that are invoked the most frequently.

In light of the rich natural imagery, metaphors, and allegorical figures woven throughout the *Octonaires*, scholars have suggested that Chandieu's style was influenced by the emblem literature that had been popular among both Protestants and Catholics since the founding of the genre.[18] It thus seems fitting that the first known printed source for the *Octonaires* (Strasbourg, 1580) was illustrated, including eighteen engraved emblems by Étienne Delaune. The texts first appear in their entirety, with each Octonaire introduced by a letter—A, B, C, etc.—that serves as a key to the corresponding emblems found in the second half of the print (see Plate 1). Given

---

[16] Weststeijn, *The Visible World*, 123–70.

[17] Håvard Løkke, "The Stoics on Sense Perception," in *Theories of Perception in Medieval and Early Modern Philosophy*, ed. Simo Knuuttila and Pekka Kärkkäinen (Dordrecht: Springer, 2008), 42–45.

[18] Bonali-Fiquet, *Engagement spirituel et procédés stylistiques*, 25–26, and Cave, *Devotional Poetry in France*, 150–55.

that these emblems also circulated in the form of individual sheets, these subtly presented letters offer an important visual clue for matching up image and text.

L'Estocart may have been familiar with the Strasbourg *Octonaires* print featuring Delaune's emblems as he was working on his musical arrangements of Chandieu's poetry. He uses the identical order for the first four Octonaire settings in his collection (corresponding to emblems B, C, D, and E in the print and in free circulation), beginning with *L'eau va viste*, an ordering that differs both from the earlier extant manuscripts and from the arrangement of the first complete poetic edition of all fifty of Chandieu's *Octonaires* appended to the *Meditations sur le Psalme XXXII* (1583), which established the standard ordering of the collection. Emblem books like Alciato's and Montenay's had long occupied a popular corner of wisdom literature. In addition, L'Estocart's closest friends and collaborators who had a hand in his collections had, themselves, been recently involved in Protestant emblem production. The Jean I de Laon—the Genevan printer who did the presswork for all of L'Estocart's extant prints—was best known for his fine work as a printer of emblems. Immediately before taking the job for L'Estocart's collections, he had printed Theodore Beza's *Icones* (1580) and Goulart's French edition of the work, *Vrais Pourtraits* (1581), borrowing the decorative frames from these previous emblem prints for L'Estocart's portrait at the head of his music prints.[19] After the series of portraits and biographies of venerable figures in the Christian faith, the *Icones* and *Vrais Pourtraits* offered forty-four "Christian emblems" that acknowledge their debt to Georgette de Montenay's enduringly popular emblem book. Beza's and Goulart's emblems, while primarily expressed in Christian terms, often reflect a subtle Stoic accent in their framing of ethical questions, and in some cases offer imagery that may have been directly inspired by the *Octonaires* already in circulation. With all this in mind, it would have been highly improbable that L'Estocart was not personally familiar with emblem literature. However, the more important issue is that whether or not L'Estocart had any specific emblems in mind when composing his highly visual musical settings, it is likely that users of these music prints would have

---

[19] Theodore Beza, *Icones* . . . (Geneva: Jean I de Laon, 1580). Beza, *Les Vrais Pourtraits des hommes illustres. . . plus, Quarante Quatre Emblemes chrestiens*, trans. and ed. Simon Goulart (Geneva: Jean I de Laon, 1581). See Kirk M. Summers, *Morality after Calvin: Theodore Beza's Christian Censor and Reformed Ethics* (Oxford: Oxford University Press, 2017), 53–54; and Alison Adams, *Webs of Allusion: French Protestant Emblem Books of the Sixteenth Century* (Geneva: Droz, 2003), 119–53.

been familiar with the corresponding Octonaires emblems in circulation and would have read these creative illustrations against one another.

A Moral in Color

Emblems as a moral-visual form confronted the same tension between the *grave* and the *doux* that we have found in discussions of moral poetry and music, provoking a similar mode of ethical contemplation that relied (at least in part) upon the pleasure of an overtly sensory process. In Beza's Epistle to the reader of his *Icones*, he addresses critics who might accuse him of hypocrisy for appealing to the senses when his sect was so harsh in its exclusion of sensory religious elements (such as icons, incense, and elaborate liturgical music), stating that artistic crafts have abundant good uses and should not be automatically condemned for their ability to powerfully move people and touch their hearts. Henry Estienne's *L'Art de faire les devises* (1645) later testified that the emblem delivers serious rational content by striking the senses:

> The Emblem is properly a pleasing and moral [*doux et morale*] Symbol, which consists in the painting and words by which one declares a serious [*grave*] sentence . . . The principle aim of the Emblem is to teach by touching our sight through illustrations, and in striking our spirit by their meaning: it is necessary therefore that they be slightly hidden, subtle, joyful, and meaningful.[20]

François Ménestrier, another important theorist of emblems, described the genre along similar lines in his *L'Art des emblemes* (1662): "Emblems are a silent discourse, an eloquence of the eyes, a Moral in colors, and things that signify and express our thoughts."[21] Ménestrier thus emphasized that the popularity of emblems should be attributed to their unique use of the sensory pleasure of visual illustration in the work of moral edification.

In a similar vein, the prefatory material for L'Estocart's three moral collections makes it clear that musically representing the moral text

---

[20] Henry Estienne, sieur des Fossez, *L'Art de faire les devises, où il est traicté des hieroglyphiques, symboles, emblèmes* (Paris: J. Paslé, 1645), sig. B2v–3r.
[21] François Ménestrier, *L'Art des emblemes* (Lyon: Benoist Coral, 1662), 15.

was central to the ethics of beauty proposed by the composer and his circle of friends. References abound throughout these prefaces to music as animating (*animer*) the poetic text. In the bassus part of L'Estocart's first collection of *Octonaires*—in a poem that may have been penned by Beza himself—L'Estocart is lauded for his ability to unite text and music, highlighting the ethical effects possible from a brief, carefully crafted compositional form.[22] In the first stanza of the opening octave, the author suggests that an important aspect of L'Estocart's success was the tightly constructed relationship between text and musical setting (line 3, "bien animer un vers"), which enhances the experience and understanding of the moral lesson (line 4, "Et dans l'ame loger la Musique gentile"; line 8 "Qui revere joyeux ton travail doux-utile"). In the tenor part of the same collection, the esteemed Neo-Latin scholar Dominique Baudier, who had close ties to Lipsius's Neostoic circle at the University of Leiden, lauds L'Estocart in similar terms: "Paschal, you who have been added as a glory among the Aonian bards, who are at hand to animate words with nectar-like rhythms (*modis*)"[23] To describe music as "animating" a text serves a double function: it vividly calls to mind music's capacity to illustrate textual content while also offering an ethical accent. The entry for "animer" given in Cotgrave's 1611 dictionary defines the word as follows: "to quicken, give life unto; inspire breath, infuse a spirit into." Thus, the musical animation of a text was a mode of giving it breath and infusing it with a spirit—language that had long signaled the influence of the Stoic conception of the soul—translated into Latin as *animus* in Cicero's *Tusculan Disputations*— as a hot, fiery breath that infuses all physical bodies.[24]

The Stoics described the human soul as a corporeal breath that infuses the human body and sends the messages of the sense impressions to the *hegimonikon* (the ruling part of the soul). In contrast to Plato's notion of an incorporeal soul, the Stoic soul was a physical body, just as the flesh and blood that we normally call by that name, though different in substance. According to Diogenes Laertius, the Stoic soul was an inborn breath called *pneuma*, which they defined as "nature capable of sense perception." In addition, "Zeno of Citium and Antipater, in their works On the Soul, and Posidonius hold that the soul is a warm breath; through it we live, and by it

---

[22] On "Th. D. S" (Th. de Sautement) as a possible pseudonym for Beza, see Latour, "The Performance of Friendship," 433–34.

[23] "PASCHALI, Aonios inter decus addite vates, / Praesens nectareis verba animare modis."

[24] Levi, *French Moralists*, 13; and Sorabji, *Emotion and Peace of Mind*, 31.

we move."[25] This *pneuma* connected through this shared breath to all other living creatures as part of the divinely ordered, providential, and imperishable World Soul (*anima mundi*). The Stoics further described this *pneuma* that comprises the soul as possessing a kind of tension that vibrates like a string, relying on a metaphor rooted in sensory musical phenomena.[26]

Scholars of Neoplatonism and sixteenth-century musical humanism have recognized that Marsilio Ficino's approach to musical therapeutics in his *De Triplici Vita* was influenced by the Stoic notion of the world soul, whose *pneuma* flows throughout the entire universe and thus brings all levels of the cosmos into an intelligible sympathetic and causal relationship.[27] Ficino's human *spiritus*, like the world soul, had a spherical shape, and its appropriate movements traced this circular form. Guy Le Fèvre de la Boderie, who was the Secretary for François, duke of Anjou and his interpreter of foreign languages, offered Ficino's work in French translation: *Trois livres de la vie* (1581). In the final book, Ficino describes the substance of song in corporeal terms—as "warm air, even breathing, and in a measure living, made up of articulated limbs, like an animal, not only bearing movement and emotion, but even signification, like a mind, so that it can be said to be, as it were, a kind of aerial and rational animal."[28] This material view of song as a body was a conspicuous feature of Stoicism, in contrast to the Platonic and Aristotelian understanding of song as incorporeal.

The Stoics placed particular emphasis on the voice as a trigger of cognition, initiated in the presentation of sense impressions. Diogenes Laertius described voice as a "striking of the air" that is "the proper object of the sense of hearing." His account explains that "according to the Stoics, voice is a body . . . For everything that acts is a body; and voice acts when it reaches those who hear it from those who utter it."[29] The fact that the Stoics viewed both soul and song as bodies presents certain ethical implications. With their view of human beings as "psychosomatic wholes," to borrow Anthony Long's description, the Stoics could

---

[25] *Lives* 7.156; trans. Mensch, 366.

[26] Long, *Stoic Studies*, 212.

[27] Walker, *Music, Spirit and Language*, 139–47; Prins, *Echoes of an Invisible World*, 173; and Tomlinson, *Music in Renaissance Magic*, 101–21.

[28] Marsilio Ficino, *Trois livres de la vie*, trans. Guy Le Fevre de la Boderie (Paris: Abel l'Angelier, 1581), 166–67.

[29] Diogenes Laertius, *Lives* 7.55; trans. Mensch, 334. These Stoic views were outlined faithfully in Goulart, *Ample discours sur la doctrine des Stoiques*, in Seneca, *Œuvres morales et meslées de Senecque*, trans. Goulart, 3:356–57; and François de La Mothe Le Vayer, *Petit discours chrestien . . . et un Discours sceptique sur la musique*. 2nd ed. (Paris: [s.n.], 1640), 98.

understand mind/body, song, and soul as physical forces operating on a shared plane of existence with causal and natural links between them.[30] In this way, Stoicism offered a route toward understanding, in practical terms, just how musical sound and compositional practices might therapeutically influence and shape human souls—bringing lofty doctrines of cosmic harmony down into the realm of human ethics through their robust theory of sense perception.

The Stoics valorized sense perception as the foundation of knowledge (or, the acquisition of "notions of things"). Cicero summarized Zeno's novel contributions to notions of sense-perceptions "regarding them as compounded out of a sort of blow provided from outside (this he called an impression)," adding that Zeno viewed "these impressions received as it were by the senses the mind's assent, which he took to be located within us and voluntary."[31]

It is in the context of explaining the Stoic elements of dialectic—including poetry and music—that Diogenes Laertius brings up the notion of imprinting the soul as an illustration for sense impressions in the Stoic chain of cognition: "An impression is an imprint on the soul, its name appropriately borrowed from the imprints made in wax by a seal ring," adding that "the comprehending impression, which they say is the criterion of reality, is that which arises from an existing object and is imprinted and stamped in accordance with it."[32]

Pseudo-Plutarch's *On the Doctrines of the Philosophers* describes the Stoics' model of imprinting as a mode of explaining how the young build experience in the world in the pursuit of practical wisdom.

The Stoics say when a human being is born, the leading part of his soul is like a sheet of paper in good condition for being written on. On this he inscribes each and every one of his conceptions. The first manner of writing on it is through the senses. For when one perceives something, white, for example, one retains a memory after it goes away. When there are many

[30] Long, *Greek Models of Mind and Self*, 22–37.
[31] Cicero, *Academica* I.40–42; trans. in A. A. Long and D. N. Sedley, eds. *The Hellenistic Philosophers* (Cambridge: Cambridge University Press, 1987), 1:242. See Løkke, "The Stoics on Sense Perception," 35–42.
[32] Diogenes Laertius, *Lives* 7.46; trans. Mensch, 330. See further, Graver, *Stoicism and Emotion*, 24–25.

memories similar in kind, then we say one has experience. For experience is the plurality of presentations similar in kind.[33]

What these impressions offered was not a fixed truth, but a conceptual image triggering a process of critical reflection. Guillaume du Vair brings up Zeno's image of the seal imprinting in wax in his *On Constancy and Consolation* to make this point for therapeutic reasons: "The senses, truly the sentinels of the soul, disposed on the outside to observe all that presents itself, are as a wax seal on which is imprinted, not the true and interior nature, but only the face and external form of things. They carry these images to the soul, with a witness and recommendation of favor, and almost with a prejudgment of their quality."[34] This initial sense impression, shaped by our preexisting value system, ideally moves through the stages of rational assent and judgment. Thus, the Stoic corporeal view of both the soul and song underscores a pragmatic causal relationship for musico-affective illustrations working at the juncture of sensory impression and comprehension.

Sixteenth-century values of text expression, and the more specific techniques of text painting, were informed by this richly embodied and representational view of song. The laudatory verse for L'Estocart's *Quatrains* cited in the preface to this book borrows the imagery associated with the process of forming mental impressions. The author opens in praise of the moral force of L'Estocart's musical settings—"on this paper, I see virtue painted"—before going on to suggest the collection's capacity to remain "imprinted" on the singer's disposition through verse and sound. L'Estocart's musical choices and prefaces reveal a similar recognition of the role of sense impressions in moral understanding, productively linking sight and sound, mind and body through critical musical representation. Scholars have long explained musical figuralisms as a device at the intersection of the intellectual and affective spheres. This most basic level of music/text correspondence thus offers a sensory impression via sound and sometimes sight (*eye music*) that invites comprehension of a corresponding object. In its more sophisticated representations, text painting could invoke complex ideas and abstract

---

[33] Aëtius 4.11.1–2 (Ps.-Plutarch, *On the Doctrines of the Philosophers* 900a–b); trans. Brad Inwood and Lloyd P. Gerson, in *The Stoics Reader: Selected Writings and Testimonia* (Indianapolis, IN: Hackett, 2008), 48.

[34] Du Vair, *De la constance et consolation*, 15–17; in *Traictez philosophiques*, ed. Tarête, 172–73. See Sorabji, *Emotion and Peace of Mind*, 41–45.

concepts that could then be reasonably evaluated and absorbed through attentive melodic and harmonic processes.[35]

As we have seen in settings like *Le beau du monde s'efface*, L'Estocart deploys a stunning array of techniques to paint the text musically. At the most basic level, he uses easily recognizable correspondences between an object, or action, and a musical figure. At a more abstract level, beyond simple word figuralism, L'Estocart musically invokes actions (disappearing, fighting, searching), emotions (desire, pleasure, fear, wonder), colors and visual effects (silver, gold, shimmering, glistening), tastes (bitterness, sweetness), and judgments (good, evil, true, false) through unusual harmonic or rhythmic strategies. He also uses daring chromaticism—such as diminished and augmented sonorities—as a way to express key images in the text. An important feature of L'Estocart's musical illustrations is that they often work at the level of the phrase, rather than a single word, and sometimes strange moments do not come into focus until one considers the meaning of the phrase as it unfolds. Even more significantly, L'Estocart reuses key expressive effects in different settings, opening up intertextual interpretive possibilities across the collections. The musical settings thus offer a more nuanced experience of these texts, inciting provocative readings that go beyond simplistic moralizing and invite a richer and more open-ended contemplation of the ethical questions seeded throughout the poetry.

Worldly Art or Artifice

L'Estocart's strategic use of ternary and/or black notation as a form of text painting offers one affective through line with exceptionally nuanced interpretive possibilities that builds up both a shape and a sonic body across the composer's double volume of *Octonaires*. In contrast to his more formulaic deployment of ternary groupings in his *Quatrains*, which he often uses merely to emphasize an important line of text (rather than illustrating or critically interpreting it), L'Estocart develops a sophisticated deployment of ternary passages in his *Octonaires* that builds moral significance across his collections as a sonic representation of the inconstancy of the

---

[35] See Jean-Pierre Ouvrard, "Les Jeux du mètre et du sens dans la chanson polyphonique française du XVIe siècle (1528–1550)," *Revue de Musicologie* 67, no. 1 (1981): 5–34; and Annie Cœurdevey, "Clément Janequin et l'essor du figuralisme," in *Clément Janequin, un musicien au milieu des poètes*, ed. Olivier Halévy et al. (Paris: Société Française de Musicologie, 2010), 151–203.

worldly sphere. As we have seen, the composer began to establish the moral salience of triple groupings from the start of the collection, with the metrical shift to "worldly joy" in *L'eau va viste* (I.1) that reappears to open *Le beau du monde s'efface* (I.4) in a lilting homophonic passage describing "the beauty of the world." These passages simultaneously offer a dance-like joy and deliver a warning to an attentive listener, who knows that this triple feeling will not last and must soon return to a more stable duple constancy.

L'Estocart continues to enrich the moral salience of this rhythmic shift in his setting for Chandieu's *Orfevre, taille moy une boule bien ronde* (I.8), a text that brings both the metaphor of the round globe and its artistic construction into clear focus:

> Orfevre, taille-moy une boule bien ronde,
> Creuse et pleine de vent, l'image de ce Monde;
> Et qu'une grand' beauté la vienne revestir,
> Autant que ton burin peut tromper et mentir,
> En y representant des fruicts de toute guise,
> Et puis tout à l'entour escri ceste devise:
> Ainsi roule tousjours ce Monde decevant
> Qui n'a fruicts qu'en peinture et fondez sur le vent.

[Goldsmith, craft me a ball well rounded, / Hollow, and full of wind, the image of the World. / With great beauty adorn it / As much as your chisel can deceive and lie, / In representing its fruits of all types, / And then all around this ball incise this device: / Thus rolls always this deceptive World / Whose fruits are only painted and founded on wind.]

This text, with its explicit focus on the earthly sphere and the artistic process of creating it, recalls the Stoics' notion of God as the "craftsman of the universe," or "the craftsman of the world's orderly arrangement." Closely resembling the Platonic Demiurge—but conceived as internal to the universe, rather than transcendent—the Stoic world artisan is a physical force, not merely an intellectual mind.[36] Humans, along with all physical matter, were direct "offshoots" of this natural and divine causal force. Thus, the

---

[36] Diogenes Laertius, *Lives* 7.137 and 7.147; trans. Mensch, 360 and 364. See Long, *Greek Models of Mind and Self*, 175–77.

beauty and artistry of the earth was in the first place a positive reflection of the divine perfection out of which flows the diversity and order of the natural world. The fourth line of the Octonaire, however, brings up the attendant problem of this human connection to God/Nature: the fragility of human artistic activity, whose tools can offer worldly deceptions and disappointment along with their many benefits. Josuah Sylvester offers a particularly effective paraphrase of this Octonaire:

> Friend *Faber*, cast mee a round hollow Ball
> Blown ful of Wind (for Emblem of this All):
> Adorn it fair, and flourish every part
> With Flowrs and Fruits, with Brooks, Beasts, Fish and Fowl;
> With rarest Cunning of thy curious Art:
> And grave in Gold, about my silver Bowl,
> *Thus roules the World (the idol of Mankinde)*
> *Whose Fruit is Fiction; whose Foundation, Winde.*

Étienne Delaune's emblem for *Orfevre, taille moy une boule bien ronde* brings us directly to the master artisan's workshop, where he aptly emphasizes some of his most detailed etching (see Plate 4). Rather than portraying the world as a simple iron ball—in the style generally seen in earlier emblem books like Montenay's—Delaune's emblem portrays a beautifully engraved globe, elaborately decorated with swirling flowers and vines, across which is an incised band of text: "Ainsi Roule Tousjours" (see Plate 5).

L'Estocart's four-voice setting for *Orfevre, taille moy une boule bien ronde* (I.7) reveals his interest in unpacking this tension around artistic craft by musically representing the round shape of worldly inconstancy through a variety of compositional techniques. [Web 5.4] Opening in his standard duple with a signed cut C, L'Estocart launches into the first phrase with points of imitation that curve downward from the superius to the bassus in the shape of the ball requested from the goldsmith's shop. The end of the first line lands on a bold diminished harmony at the start of the cadence on "ronde"—a dissonance that, as we have already seen in L'Estocart's settings, casts harmonic doubt on the supposed perfection of the image of the world (compare, for example, I.3 *Mondain, si tu le scait*). This is confirmed in the following lines of text outlining the beautiful but deceptive qualities of this artistic product. The climax of the setting arrives in the metrical shift at the penultimate line, when L'Estocart offers a vivid ternary passage at measures 63–68 ("Ainsi roule tousjours") that musically incises this phrase onto the rhythmic instability of the rolling ball—mirroring the inscribed ball in Delaune's emblem. This is the problem of artistic craft, embodied in painting and musical expression: the artistic device that could promote understanding could also obscure it through artifice and dissimulation.

Joseph Du Chesne penned an Octonaire highlighting the moral contrast in these shapes, forged at the boundary of worldly perfection and imperfection:

> Peintre, si tu tires le Monde,
> Ne le peins pas de forme ronde.
> Car ce qui en rond est pourtrait
> Est estimé du tout parfait
> Et le Monde ne le peut être,
> Où défaut le souverain bien,
> Et où tant seulement le rien
> Et l'inconstance prennent être.

[Painter, if you draw the World, / Do not paint it in a round form. / Because what is portrayed round / Is esteemed as perfect / And the World cannot be, / Where falling short of the sovereign good, / And where only emptiness / and inconstancy come into being.]

Du Chesne's text recalls that roundness was once a symbol of divine perfection and eternity. It had long been associated with the number three, idealized in the Trinity as an unbroken circle among the members of the Christian Godhead. The spiritual implications of number and meter were clearly exploited throughout the medieval European tradition, with triple meter holding an exalted position as the perfect mode of organizing musical time (*tempus perfectus*) and represented by a complete circle. The shift to a normative duple meter—with triple as exceptional and seen as rooted in a fundamental inequality—was already a matter of controversy in the fourteenth century. By the sixteenth century, duple had accrued positive significance as the shape of constancy, as already witnessed in L'Estocart's and Boni's settings of Pibrac's *La verité d'un Cube*.[37] Squared-off and stable, duple rhythms represented a newly idealized cube, which remained firm and

---

[37] Grant, *Beating Time*, 63–64.

unmoving under pressure. We see this in Beza's emblem, *This circle which you see holding this square*, which reveals a cube within a circle to emphasize a productive ethical relationship between these contrasting moral shapes. The circle symbolizes the circular elegance of following the divinely appointed path, while the enclosed cube illustrates the call to live a steady and constant life that is appropriate to that station.[38]

L'Estocart's five-voice setting for *Peintre, si tu tires le Monde* (Octonaire II.20), elaborates on the dual significance of these musical forms. [Web 5.5] In a clear reference back to his setting for *Orfevre, taille moy une boule bien ronde* (I.7), he returns to the theme of an artist creating an image of the world—this time a painter, who is advised not to map the perfection of the circle onto the imperfect world. After setting the opening two lines in imitative polyphony (mm. 1–38), L'Estocart shifts to a sharp triple homophony in the third line of text when explaining that what is round should be a portrait of perfection. Unusually, the setting continues in this stark ternary homophony, enduring throughout the setting as a sonic model of inconstant constancy (mm. 39–65).

The circle's older association of divinity became increasingly undermined in sixteenth-century moral culture, as rhythmic shifts to triple slid toward a sonic representation of the inconstancy of the terrestrial sphere and the fragility of human nature. Largely due to the dance-like physicality they evoke, ternary groupings map easily onto the body and the senses. When duple becomes the stable and rational norm, the shift to triple reads as a transgressive, as sensual excess. The split moral analogy of the circle was also rooted in its physical properties: the geometric perfection of the unbroken sphere represented eternity and divine perfection, while the inherent mobility and instability of this shape represented terrestrial fragility and the ongoing circular motions of the natural world, from the rotation of the stars and planets to the life cycle of the seasons, all the way down to the birth, growth, and death of a single flower, whose fleeting existence traces the shape of the inevitable life cycle of all living things. Jean Jacques Boissard's *Il y a Vicissitude, et Variation en toutes choses* [*The Vicissitude* and Variation *of All Things*] (1584/ 1588) explores the moral significance of nature's brittle beauty, vulnerable to the ravages of time. The *pictura* depicts the circular life of a rose onto the

---

[38] Beza, *Icones*, fol. 4v; Goulart, *Les Vrais Pourtraits*, 243.

wheel of fortune, mapping its early bud and flowering all the way to its inevitable decay.[39] [Web 5.6]

Chandieu's Octonaire *Le monde est un jardin* likewise draws a moral analogy from the life cycle of flowers:

> Le monde est un jardin, ses plaisirs sont ses fleurs:
> De belles y en a, et y en a plusieurs.
> Le lis espanouy sa blancheur y presente,
> L'oeillet y flaire bon, le thim veut qu'on le sente,
> Et la fleur du soulci y est fort avancée,
> La violette y croist, et la pensee aussi.
> Mais la mort est l'hiver, qui rend soudain transi
> Lis, oeillet, thim, soulci, violette et pensee.

Josuah Sylvester poetically rendered the text as follows:

> The World's a Garden; Pleasures are the Flowers;
> Of fairest hues, in form and number many:
> The Lilly (first) pure-whitest Flowr of any,
> Rose sweetest rare, with Pinked-Gillie-Flowrs:
> The Violet, and double Mari-Gold,
> And Pansie too: but, after all Mischances,
> Death's Winter coms; and kils, with sudden Cold,
> Rose, Lilly, Violet, Mari-Gold, Pink, Panses.[40]

L'Estocart's high-voice trio for *Le monde est un jardin* (I.11) details this floral life cycle through an interwining of the three equal voices and their overlapping registers. [Web 5.7] As usual, the setting establishes a standard duple pulse, with a shift to ternary arriving at the pivotal point in the Octonaire, in the penultimate line where the text brings up the winter that will provoke the death of the flower and prove its transience (mm. 55–60). Up to this point, the poetry and music seem to be about beauty and the static description of the flowers; however, the move to ternary for the passage on

---

[39] Jean Jacques Boissard, *Emblemata cum tetrastichis latinis* (Metz: Jean Aubry, 1584), with illustrations by Théodore de Bry; Boissard's expanded dual language edition was published as *Emblematum liber / Emblemes latins . . . avec l'interpretation françoise du I. Pierre Joly* (Metz: Jean Aubry and Abraham Faber, 1588), 28–29. See Adams, *Webs of Allusion*, 155–291.
[40] Sylvester, *Works*, 1183.

winter's death brings back the image of the round life cycle and the instability of all worldly human affairs.

Delaune's emblem for *Le monde est un jardin* picks up on several of the most important threads across the collection. [Web 5.8] His emblem portrays the toga-clad sage in his typical copse of trees, gesturing to a garden below. The buildings taking up the background of the image are more elaborate than is normal in Delaune's series. The long archway bordering the garden is covered in swirling decorations reminiscent of the ornamentation that Delaune engraved on his globe in the *Orfevre* emblem. In the dark storm cloud above, a skeleton with his scythe appears ready to descend and steal all life and beauty. It is significant that these engraved representations of floral beauty appear both on the incised ball in Delaune's goldsmith's workshop in *Orfevre* and here on the solidly forged structure next to the garden in *Le monde est un jardin*. The engravings are obviously more permanent than their floral counterparts in the natural world; they are not subject to a quick fading or death like the flora depicted so delicately on the ball.

Virtuous Virtuosity

These questions of the role of ornament and artistry were heightened in Esther Inglis's lavishly ornamented manuscripts of the *Octonaires*, offering a graphic link to the emblematic and musical portrayals of these moral texts already in circulation. As a calligrapher, Inglis was unmatched in her time: she had mastered the most elaborate decorative scripts in various sizes, including (but not limited to) *lettera mancina* (mirror writing), *lettera rognosa* (a trembling hand), *lettera tagliata* (writing broken by a strikethrough), and *lettere piacevolle* (featuring curling extensions to ascenders and descenders). In one manuscript alone, she might display around forty different hands. Inglis was also a gifted illustrator, illuminating her texts with decorative borders or images of nature, including flowers, birds, insects, and plants in vibrant, jewel-based colors. Another virtuosic skill was her ability to create astonishingly small manuscripts in perfect detail, illustrating that the moral value of control could be represented powerfully in the disciplined minutiae of a handmade book.[41]

---

[41] See Scott-Elliot and Yeo, "Calligraphic Manuscripts of Esther Inglis," 10–86; and Georgianna Ziegler, "'More Than Feminine Boldness': The Gift Books of Esther Inglis," in *Women, Writing, and*

Inglis was born around 1570 to French Huguenot refugees who wisely fled the mounting persecution of their sect shortly before the St. Bartholomew's Day Massacre. Her father, Nicolas Langlois, was headmaster of the French school in Edinburgh by autumn 1574. She apparently learned the art of calligraphy from her mother. Around 1596, Inglis married Bartholomew Kello, a fellow scrivener who supported his wife's work in a variety of practical and business roles. Already connected to the court of James VI in Scotland, Inglis moved to England and found admirers in the Sidney circle and the household of Prince Henry, as she offered her manuscripts as gifts to an elite clientele known to be interested in the Neostoic philosophy developing in French and Britannic lands.[42] Her use of the full range of her rich craft in copies of her two most gifted collections, the *Octonaires* and the *Quatrains,* reveals a nuanced appreciation of the fundamental paradoxes of Stoic philosophy that were already in play in the poetry, the visual illustrations, and the musical settings. The work of Inglis's virtuosic hand transformed these moral collections into elaborately ornamented luxury objects fit for the collections of the wealthiest and most powerful. In one copy of the *Octonaires,* she provided the French text in plain lettering on the verso, and on the facing recto, wrote her own Anglo-Scots paraphrase, rendered in diverse scripts, decorated with a different, fully-colored floral illustration heading each recto page. The moral symbolism of flowers and plants in the *Octonaires* are thus brought into decorative relief across the entire collection, drawing attention to the divine beauty of the natural world while recalling the metaphorical function of flora throughout the poetry as a moral illustration of vanity, fragility, and transience.

Inglis followed this valorization of the visual sensorium in her luxurious presentation manuscripts for the *Octonaires.* In addition to her jeweled embroidery and brightly painted decorative illustrations, she deployed virtuosic handwriting scripts that open up an interpretive space between the text and the writing style. In several copies of her *Octonaires,* she used her trembling script (*lettera rognosa*) for a pair of texts (25 and 26 in her collection): *L'eau va vite,* which evokes the instability of water, and *Tu me seras tesmoins,* which, we recall, was portrayed in Delaune's emblem as a woman standing on a ball in the water.[43] [Web 5.9 and 5.10] These complex scripts, which draw the eye

the *Reproduction of Culture in Tudor and Stuart Britain,* ed. Mary E. Burke et al. (Syracuse: Syracuse University Press, 2000), 19–37.

[42] See James Reid Baxter, "Esther Inglis: a Franco-Scottish Jacobean writer and her *Octonaries upon the Vanitie and Inconstancie of the World," Studies in Scottish Literature,* 48.2 (Fall 2022): 71–78.

[43] Esther Inglis, *Octonaries upon the Vanity and Inconstancy of the World,* US-Ws, MS V.a.91, fols. 25v–27r, and MS V.a.92, fols. 30r–31r (Scott-Elliot and Yeo, Nos. 12 and 33).

to the unusual shape and form of the letters before the meaning of the writing can be deciphered as words, thus crucially separate two aspects of reading that are often merged. In one of her *Quatrains* manuscripts, presented in 1607, Inglis strategically used her mirror hand (*lettera mancina*) for Quatrains 59–60 (*Le sage est libre*, fol. 37) and (*Le menasser*, fol. 38), linking the two texts on the constancy of the sage through handwriting that evokes the mirror of princes.[44] It is also significant that in linking these two texts through her choice of script, she mirrored L'Estocart's musical collection, which had bound these two texts together through one of L'Estocart's rare repeated musical settings.

In other words, Inglis created a sort of emblematic impression through her handwriting script that underscores the well-rehearsed notion of the mirror of nature as a mode of self-knowledge. For, as the reader quickly discovers, her mirror script is extraordinarily difficult to read. Typically, in reading a text, the mind understands the content with little to no attention paid to the preliminary visual process of seeing the form of the letters themselves. In Inglis's manuscripts, the unusual and diverse scripts used in the collections create a space between the textual content and the artistic craft that brings that content to the mind through an exposed aesthetic process of seeing that only with focus and effort is harmonized with an understanding of the textual meaning. Thus, even as Inglis offers a handcrafted mirror that appeals to the sight, she poses an artistic enigma that must be decoded through attention both to the poetic contents and their intertextual moral connections.

Inglis also used her mirror hand to join another pair of linked texts in her *Octonaires*, underscoring the moral illustration embedded in Octonaire 29 (*La glace est luisante et belle*) and Octonaire 30 (*Orfevre, taille-moy*), which represent the shiny reflection of the ice or the goldsmith's round ball as the mirror of the transient world (see Plate 6). Chandieu's poetry for *La glace est luisante et belle* generated this sensory warning against trusting in the glittering beauty of the world, a warning that likewise opens up a space between thinking and feeling a moral question:

> La glace est luisante et belle:
> Le monde est luisant et beau.
> De la glace on tombe en l'eau,
> Du monde en mort eternelle.

---

[44] Newberry Library, Wing MS ZW 645.K292, fols. 37–38 (Scott-Elliot and Yeo, No. 31).

> Tous deux à la fin s'en vont.
> Mais la glace en eau se fond,
> Le monde et ce qui est sien,
> S'esvanouit tout en rien.

[The ice is glistening and beautiful; / The world is glistening and beautiful. / From the ice we fall into water, / From the world into eternal death. / Both of them in the end go away. / But the ice melts into water; / The world and what is its own, vanishes into nothing.]

Beza's *Icones* and Goulart's translation, *Les Vrais Pourtraits*, circulated an emblem that may have been directly inspired by this Octonaire penned by their friend and fellow pastor Chandieu.[45] The simple image delivers its warning against worldly attachment through its strong feeling of physical movement as it portrays a man in the dramatic physical act of slipping on ice. [Web 5.11] Étienne Delaune's corresponding emblem for *La glace est luisante est belle* offers a more complex image that highlights the tension between the roles of sensory pleasure—music in particular—as moral guide and worldly seducer (see Plate 7). The background shows a frozen pond with people falling into the icy water. A noble couple and their attendants take up the central focus in the foreground. Turning away from the sage's warning gesture, the couple gazes into each other's eyes, moving, like a dancing pair of lovers, to the mocking strains of the fool who fiddles them toward the yawning pit of death waiting to consume them.

L'Estocart's musical setting of *La glace est luisante et belle* (I.5) strategically leads the singer to a vivid experience of this moral lesson through creative musical choices at the level of harmony and rhythm. [Web 5.12] He creates an unusual harmonic shimmer in the second line at "luisant et beau," where the raised C flashes an unexpected brilliance as part of an augmented sixth leading to the cadence on D (mm. 8–9) (see Example 5.2). The musical painting of the dangerously quick slip from the ice into the water in the third line finds rhythmic and melodic illustration in measures 11–13, as the homorhythmic dotted figure that falls in all voices but the tenor descends as if into the water, where we are denied a satisfying cadence. The musical reflection of the fall from the world into

---

[45] Beza, *Icones*, Emblem XIX; *Les Vrais Pourtraits*, trans. Goulart, 259.

Example 5.2 Paschal de L'Estocart, *La glace est luisante et belle*, in *Premier livre des Octonaires de la vanité du monde* (Lyon: Barthélemy Vincent [Geneva: Jean I de Laon], 1582). Based on the edition by Henry Expert

Example 5.2 Continued

eternal death that develops throughout the rest of the text comes on more subtly, emphasizing that, unlike the slip from the ice (perceived in an instant), the descent to death is long but inevitable. The final line of verse caps off this exquisite setting with a charming return to homophony. A brief dotted-quarter and sixteenth-note declamation of "s'esvanouit" in measure 32 leads to four quarter notes that quickly vanish as the piece ends abruptly on the fourth beat, followed (shockingly, for the music of the period) by a rest in all parts. This rhythmic effect thus snatches away the singer's awaited closing formula, leaving a desolately empty final measure in its place.

L'Estocart's setting of the Octonaire *Toy qui plonges ton coeur* (I.22) by Chandieu offers one of the most visual and sensual musical settings of his collection, unfolding like a sequence of sonic portraits.

> Toy qui plonges ton cœur au profond de ce Monde,
> Sais tu ce que tu es? le sapin temeraire
> Qui saute sur le dos de la furieuse onde,
> Eslancé par les coups d'un tourbillon contraire.
> Raison, ton gouvernail est pieça cheut au fond.
> Tu erres vagabond où le vent variable
> De tes plaisirs t'emporte, et qui en fin, il te rompt
> Contre le roc cruel d'une mort miserable.

[You who plunge your heart into the depths of this world, / Do you know what you are? The reckless ship / That jumps onto the back of the furious wave, / Dashed apart by the opposing blows of the vortex. / Reason, your rudder fell to the depths long ago. / You wander errantly wherever the wind / Of your pleasures carries you, and which in the end, breaks you / Against the cruel rock of a miserable death.]

Chandieu's text centers on the metaphor of a ship in the storm, a central Stoic image, used to illustrate the paradox of virtue as the only good not subject to the whims of Fortune. The crashing waves model the instability of worldly goods and the attendant danger of being swept away by such fickle pleasures. As Marcus Aurelius put it in his *Meditations*, "be grateful that on this raging sea you have a mind to guide you. And if the storm should carry you away, let it carry off flesh, breath and all the rest, but not the mind. Which can't be swept away."[46] Du Vair's *On Eloquence* uses similar imagery in characterizing the discourse of reason as "the rudder of souls" (*le gouvernail des ames*), which moves morals and affections like musical tones, tempered and arranged in melodious harmony. Du Vair later clarifies that this softening and sensual power of artistry operates like putting iron into the fire before submerging it in the cold water of reason.[47]

L'Estocart's *Toy qui plonges ton cœur* matches the episodic flavor of Chandieu's dramatic tale. [Web 5.13 and 5.14] For example, in the third line, where the poetry describes a reckless ship that gets caught in the current of a turbulent wave, L'Estocart shifts to rapid lines that roll up and down the texture (mm. 48–51). Reason, the rudder of the ship, emerges as a heroine in the fifth line, with triumphant leaps that echo across the texture (mm. 69–71). This hopeful stability is short-lived, however, as the lower voices then plunge down to the bottom of the range for each voice part (mm. 80–87): the rudder of reason has fallen to the depths of the ocean. When the sixth line of text speaks of the wind that blows the worldly person off the path of virtue, L'Estocart writes an unexpectedly syncopated rhythm that would probably sweep all but the most confident singers off course (mm. 90–96). More pointedly, he sets the seventh line's warning of the dangers in store for the worldly person who is carried away by pleasure with a long descending chain of suspensions rubbing between the upper two voices that is particularly striking in the context of a compositional idiom that rarely utilizes such devices. At the arrival of each dissonance, the singer and listener accustomed to this idiom would feel the arousal of desire for resolution that becomes satisfied through an erotic stepwise slide into consonance. The clear effect of this figuralism is that at the precise moment where the poetry warns against the danger of being carried away by pleasure, L'Estocart indulges his singers and listeners with one of his most exquisite moments of musical pleasuring (mm. 96–101) (see Example 5.3). The composer quickly restrains this excess, of course, by immediately restoring a disciplined, uniform quarter-note homophony to close the phrase in measures 102–3.

These alluring sensory representations of the moral text in music, which could tempt as well as teach, dramatize the dilemma of using a sensual musical setting and visual form to promote worldly detachment. Indeed,

---

[46] *Meditations* 12.14; trans. Hays, 164.
[47] Du Vair, *De l'eloquence*, fol. 17r; ed. Radouant, 142–46.

Example 5.3 Paschal de L'Estocart, *Toy qui plonge ton cœur*, mm. 94–102, in *Premier livre des Octonaires de la vanité du monde* (Lyon: Barthélemy Vincent [Geneva: Jean I de Laon], 1582). Based on the edition by Henry Expert

the *Octonaires* warns against exactly the kinds of powerfully immersive experiences of worldly beauty and desire that are on full, glorious display in the imperfect charm of the heterometric poetry, the enigma of the artistic emblem, and the sonic allure of the musical setting. Although all these moral lessons can be contemplated with the intellect, they are experienced most powerfully by singing, seeing, and hearing them—a point that appears throughout L'Estocart's prefaces. Thus, these prints emphasize an embodied philosophical engagement that places artistic experience at the forefront of moral reasoning. This illustration of beauty in moral poetry, music, and image demands a mode of ethical reflection that follows the Stoic refusal to divorce ethical epistemology from the body and its faculties. In exploring the fullness of sensory experience, this musical engagement appreciates mundanity, even as it gestures toward transcendence. It is a reflection on the ephemeral experience of beauty, made even more precious as it vanishes so quickly.

6

Sound Judgment

To live according to nature is to remain
unperturbed by the passions, and to comport oneself
toward all things that present themselves according to right reason.[1]

Andrea Alciato's emblem *Intelligence matters, not beauty* depicts a fox who
enters the workshop of a theatrical producer and finds an actor's mask
that is so beautifully crafted as to seem almost alive. [Web 6.1] Handling
and admiring this perfect representation of a human head, the fox "found
nothing to say, seeing a work so beautiful, where nothing was missing but
voice." The fox exclaimed, "What a beautiful head, but it doesn't have a brain."
The commentary closes by citing the Stoic Cleanthes as saying "that the igno-
rant differ from the beasts in appearance alone."[2]

The Stoic valorization of sense perception as the foundation of wisdom, or
of following nature as a mirror of self-knowledge and understanding, offered
clear moral opportunities for musical and visual expression, as we began to
see in previous chapters. The artistic appeal to the senses remained problematic, however, particularly with reference to the precarious relationship
between sensory experience, intellectual knowledge, and practical wisdom.
In these concerns over the deceptions and delusions made possible by sensory processes, the Stoics developed a point of shared interest with their
Hellenistic adversaries the Skeptics. One of the most fruitful areas of overlap
was in their exploration of the sense–knowledge paradigm, which interested
early moderns attempting to navigate the complexities of moral musical
practices.

Rob Wegman has shown that a "crisis of music" had been underway since
the fifteenth century, provoked by anxieties about music's role as a transmitter

---

[1] Du Vair, *La Philosophie morale des Stoiques*, ed. Tarêtte, 63.
[2] Alciato, *Emblemata / Les emblemes* (1584), fol. 260r–v.

The Voice of Virtue. Melinda Latour, Oxford University Press. © Oxford University Press 2023.
DOI: 10.1093/oso/9780197529744.003.0007

of knowledge, as a way of thinking, and as a mirror of human understanding.[3] These philosophical themes sprang from the Platonic fount and developed in distinctive ways through the Stoic and Skeptic traditions. The Skeptic school was another direct descendant of the Platonic tradition and a philosophical cousin of Stoicism. It is thus no coincidence that many prominent figures at the heart of the late sixteenth-century Neostoic resurgence—such as Michel de Montaigne and Pierre Charron—were also significant figures in the parallel revival of Skepticism. Just as Stoicism played a critical role in shaping Hellenistic and early modern discussions of the emotions, Skepticism played a crucial role in the long conversation concerning epistemology and the senses. Thus, it is difficult to understand the Stoic and Neostoic approach to moral psychology and their therapeutic exercises without an understanding of their relationship to the Skeptic tradition.

Two sixteenth-century Skeptic philosophers summed up the early modern response to these concerns in their mottos—Montaigne, with his famous "What do I know?" (*Que sçay-je?*), and Francisco Sánchez, with his question, "What?" (*Quid?*), which he mounted like an obelisk at the end of his treatises. Together, these mottos embody the relentless quest for truth and knowledge that left no assumption or authority unchallenged. The purpose of this chapter is to illuminate how music evolved as a way of knowing that exploited this tension between intellectual knowledge and embodied experience—often discussed as wisdom. Music proved to be a perfect example of the problem of knowledge in these debates, as it was clear that human musical practices modeled a complex interplay of physical skill and mechanics, sense perception and understanding, and it had the power to elicit a powerful emotional response that could either cement knowledge or bypass cognitive processes altogether.

As the epistemological stakes continued to rise, it is no wonder that the musical conversation ranged from the theoretical and philosophical to the prescriptive and speculative. How should music properly engage the soul/ mind and senses? And how would a proper use of music's rational and sensory potential affect compositional style and musical performance? The reactions to these issues in the sixteenth and seventeenth centuries were diverse and led to more doubts than conclusions. This chapter will trace the musical ways of knowing depicted in folly literature, rehearsed in the moral

---

[3] Rob Wegman, *The Crisis of Music in Early Modern Europe, 1470–1530* (London: Routledge, 2005), 3–19.

song repertoire, and visualized in iconography, reading them through the Stoic and Skeptical debates of the time. It will conclude with the surprising transformation of these debates over knowledge in the age of encounter, as Europe's traditions and ideas were brought into counterpoint and conflict with those from cultures beyond its frontiers. Over time, the instability of the sixteenth-century Skeptical turn gave rise to various musical and philosophical strategies for establishing a secure basis of knowledge through observation and applied experimental practice, arriving at a moderated Skepticism that allowed for the value of critical and cautious judgments based on sensory experience—a pragmatic position, which had been advocated by the Stoics all along.

A Theme Song for Fools

Sebastian Brant's best-selling wisdom print, *The Ship of Fools* (1494), opens with a series of woodcuts, attributed to Albrecht Dürer, that depict raucous scenes of fools taking a journey to the nonsense land of Narragonia.[4] [Web 6.2] After traveling by horse-drawn cart in the upper scene of the first woodcut, the fools get on a boat in increasingly aural illustrations of boisterous revelry. The iconic costume of the fool, with his double-horned cap and jangling bells, already signals that noise was a baseline marker of folly. The two shipboard scenes take this sonic foolishness even further by foregrounding the musicality of the ship of fools. Some fools are shaking rattles or clanging handbells, some are playing flutes, and the open mouths of the banner-waving fools gesturing to the musical flag flown proudly on both ships invites us to hear song. This musical banner clearly displays the opening neumes of the Introit chant *Gaudeamus omnes* ("Let us all rejoice"). It was an established custom by this point to cite the *Gaudeamus omnes* in non-religious contexts—as a cry of common joy, as parody, and even for blasphemous purposes. The sacred call to rejoice in God's glory thus doubled as a carnivalesque call to worship human folly through bacchic pleasure.[5] The musical banner of *Gaudeamus omnes* shrewdly accommodates this paradox, serving as the theme song for the land of fools while simultaneously

---

[4] Sebastian Brant, *Dass Narren schyff* [Basel: Johann Bergmann von Olpe, 1494].

[5] See Bernhold Schmid, "Das 'Gaudeamus omnes' - Zitat in Lassos Motette *Nunc gaudere licet* und sein Kontext - Aspekte der geistlichen Parodie bei Orlando di Lasso," *Journal of the Alamire Foundation* 5, no. 2 (2013): 237–59; and Paromita Chakravarti, "Natural Fools and the Historiography of Renaissance Folly," *Renaissance Studies* 25 (2011): 208–27.

proposing a musical passage to redemption. Brandt's ship portrays music as an object and action that falls on both sides of the wisdom/folly binary: for music embodies the ridiculous warblings of the dissolute fool and also offers the ideal art of the sage, who knows how to handle the dangerous potential of musical sensation.

The musical jester featured in several of Étienne Delaune's emblems for Antoine de Chandieu's *Octonaires* continues this tradition of linking musical sound to folly. Appearing with his fiddle in the emblem for *La glace est luisante et belle* that was discussed in the previous chapter, the fool leads the dancing couple to their destruction (see Plate 7). This prancing fool appears again with his cap, bells, and bauble in Delaune's emblem for Chandieu's *Plustost on pourra faire*, another image that evokes noisy musical sound. [Web 6.3] The text plays upon the well-rehearsed trope of the upside-down world (*Plustost que . . .*), with classic juxtapositions of the opposites of day and night, God and the world, and wisdom and folly.[6] Delaune's emblem heightens these contradictions visually. The sage stands on the high ground (if a bit precariously), his left arm looped around a tree for support as he clutches his book. With his free hand, he gestures down toward the noisy group of carousing townsmen whose musical activities are directed by the iconic horned-cap-wearing fool. Far from simplifying the relationship between music and knowledge, these singing fools laid their own subversive claim to wisdom across the folly tradition. Nurtured by fideistic and Skeptical challenges to religious and disciplinary authority positioning all human knowledge as mere foolishness to God, these subversive musical references rely on a universal delight in turning the tables on those in positions of power, justifying on religious and intellectual grounds their themes of a topsy-turvy world wherein the weak shame the strong and the humble outwit the learned.[7]

Not only music, but philosophy itself was subject to this fool's treatment, as we see in Delaune's emblem for Chandieu's *Celuy qui pense pouvoir*, a text warning against seeking assurance and stability in the world. [Web 6.4] The emblem features Delaune's normal teaching sage standing on solid ground in his timeless grove, offering a firm path toward the secure and gated tower in the background. As the foil to this philosopher, Delaune avoids a depiction of

---

[6] See Vincent Robert-Nicoud, *The World Upside Down in 16th-Century French Literature and Visual Culture* (Leiden: Brill, 2018).

[7] For a more detailed account of the musical consequences of Skepticism, see Melinda Latour, "Philosophies: The Crisis of Musical Knowledge," in *A Cultural History of Music in the Renaissance Age*, ed. Jeanice Brooks and Richard Freedman (London: Bloomsbury, forthcoming).

Lady Fortune standing on her ball in the ocean, his standard representation of worldly instability. His choice of contrasting figure, unusually, is another philosopher: a mirror image of the teaching sage who sits on a large ball in the water. His garb and teaching hand gesture to what lies beyond the em- blem, serving a reminder that even the knowledge of the sage, if experienced in this earthly realm, should not be trusted as a firm foundation.

The Art of Doubting

Two streams of ancient Skepticism enriched these discussions of musical wisdom and folly. The Academic stream developed in the Platonic Academy in the third century BCE and later known primarily through Cicero's *Academica* concluded that no knowledge is actually possible. In Socrates' words, "All I know is that I know nothing." The Greek stream—known as Pyrrhonism—went a step further than their Academic counterparts in eschewing all knowledge claims—even the claim to know nothing, which they viewed as a form of negative dogmatism. The only surviving texts from the Pyrrhonist stream come from Sextus Empiricus's second-century BCE treatises *Outlines of Pyrrhonism* and *Against the Professors*, which began to recirculate in numerous manuscript versions in the sixteenth century in Italy and later beyond the Alps and were printed in translation for the first time in Henri Estienne's important 1562 Latin edition.[8] *Against the Professors* offered a systematic challenge to the learned disciplines of the day, with the entirety of the sixth book (*Against the Musicians*) devoted to refuting all the dogmatic claims of experts regarding musical knowledge. Considering that music was widely valued as a practice for promoting mental health (both in ancient discussions of the ethics of music and in later revivals), these Skeptic attacks turned the tables by suggesting that the "not knowing" of music might be a truer route to peace.

The endpoint of both streams of Skepticism was the suspension of judg- ment, which was thought to lead to a desirable state of mental tranquility. This aim to free the mind from all disturbances was something that the Skeptics shared with the Stoics and was rooted in a therapeutic view of phi- losophy inherited from the Platonic tradition. However, their methods

[8] Richard Popkin, *The History of Scepticism: From Savonarola to Bayle* (New York: Oxford University Press, 2003), xvii–xx.

for achieving it differed. Whereas Stoic *apatheia* (freedom from passions) desired to eliminate extreme emotional states that were the result of false value judgments, the Skeptic goal of *ataraxia* (tranquility) demanded the elimination of judgments altogether.

Although the standard Stoic position on knowledge did not go to this Skeptic extreme of denouncing all disciplinary expertise as ignorance, we have already noted similar moralizing against empty instruction. Remember that Pibrac highlighted the Stoic mode of moral progress as rooted not only in intellectual learning but also in lived experience, such that one could become not merely educated, but, more importantly, wise. Duplessis-Mornay's *Excellent discours* outlines a version of the Stoic attack on disciplinary knowledge for being pointless if not accompanied by a corresponding moral capacity to work out this learning in the art of living. For example, he critiques those who have learned to divide the smallest fractions through arithmetic but have not learned how to share a penny with their brother; or the one who has learned geometry to measure a field but cannot measure herself. In critiquing these learned disciplines, Duplessis-Mornay arrives at music: "The musician tunes voices, sounds, and tones together, and yet has nothing in his heart but discord." His conclusion: that when divorced of moral action, "these sciences work the mind endlessly and don't satisfy it. The more that one knows, the more one wishes to know. They don't appease the discord that people feel in themselves. They don't heal the sicknesses of the spirit, they make men learned, but not good, knowledgeable [*savant*] but not wise [*sage*]."[9] Virtue, like music, thus required an embodied mode of practice that could turn the building blocks of disciplinary skill into lived wisdom.

Pibrac frames his *Quatrains* within this contradictory paradigm. His collection of maxims—largely guided by the Stoic pursuit of self-knowledge, self-mastery, and radical self-reliance—concludes with two final poems (Quatrains 125 and 126) that harness a Skeptic maneuver for undermining the solidity of his route toward wisdom:

> Cil qui se pense et se dit estre sage
> Tien le pour fol, et celuy qui sçavant
> Se fait nommer, sonde le bien avant,
> Tu trouveras que ce n'est que langage.
> Plus on est docte, et plus on se deffie

---

[9] Duplessis-Mornay, *Excellent discours*, 48–49.

> D'estre sçavant: et l'homme vertueux
> Jamais n'est veu estre presumptueux.
> Voila des fruicts de ma Philosophie.

Josuah Sylvester rendered this pair of texts lucidly:

> He that esteems and vaunts himself for wise,
> Think him a foole: And Him that doth assume
> The name of Learned, whoso soundly tries,
> Shall finde him nothing but bare words and fume.
>
> The better Learned, learn the more their want,
> And more to doubt their owne sufficiencie:
> And Vertuous men are never Arrogant.
> These are the Fruits of my Philosophy.[10]

Ever since Augustine's uncharitable critique of Stoic virtue in *City of God*, those interested in Stoicism remained on the defensive against charges that the self-reliance of the sage equated to pride and arrogance.[11] Skepticism offered Neostoics a useful corrective to the perceived dangers of the classical Stoa; for even as the Stoics were venerated for their austerity and gravity, the Skeptics were specifically admired by early moderns for their humility in recognizing the limits of human knowledge. Of course, Skepticism had its own dilemma: once the limit of human knowledge is recognized, how does one believe *anything*, make *any* judgment, or commit to *any* course of action? In its ruthless attack on all dogmatic positions, Skepticism ultimately leads to its own self-destruction. As Luciano Floridi strikingly puts it, "It is not an easy attitude, and the Skeptic is usually a negative hero, a Samson who dies with all the Philistines when he makes the temple of certainties collapse."[12] Stoicism offered a critical sense theory that shared some of the foundational concerns of the Skeptics, but found a way out of their inevitable

---

[10] Sylvester, *Works*, 584.

[11] Augustine, *De civitate Dei* 19.25. See Christopher Brooke, *Philosophic Pride: Stoicism and Political Thought from Lipsius to Rousseau* (Princeton, NJ: Princeton University Press, 2012), 1–11.

[12] Luciano Floridi, *Sextus Empiricus: The Transmission and Recovery of Pyrrhonism* (Oxford: Oxford University Press, 2002), 32.

paralysis or self-destruction. Taken together, therefore, Stoicism and Skepticism tempered each other's most extreme failings.

Although Skeptics and Stoics came to their musical conclusions by different routes, they shared a practical interest in moving away from the complexity and so-called artifice of most learned musical practice in favor of compositional clarity and comprehensibility that prioritized a new intimacy between text and music. Singers making their way through Pierre Mathieu's predominantly Stoic *Tablettes* would have the opportunity to engage with the core Skeptic argument challenging the authority of traditional disciplinary knowledge in Tablette I.29:

> De l'homme le sçavoir n'est que pure ignorance,
> On voit le plus sçavant bien lourdement broncher:
> On veut renouveller des doutes la science,
> Et l'on perdra le vray pour trop le rechercher.

> [The knowedge of man is only pure ignorance, / The most learned person appears heavily perturbed: / Science extends doubts, / And one loses the truth by seeking it too much.]

Artus Aux-Cousteaux's trio setting for this text, first published in his 1636 *Quatrains de Mr Mathieu*, offers an instructive approach to the problem of musical knowledge. Arriving in Aux-Cousteaux's eighth mode (Hypolydian), the setting confronts the inherent difficulty of the F modes with their structurally problematic B♮. Aux-Cousteaux allows the B to remain in its hard form, a sonic marker of an elite knowledge of the declining modal system, which by this point in an increasingly tonal landscape of the early seventeenth century could just as easily be heard as musical ignorance. The uncharacteristic melismas that break free in the first and third lines of text as expressions of ignorance and doubt gesture back to the association of musical ornamentation with irrational, unknowable sound, in contrast to the clarity of knowledge offered by the easily comprehended syllabic texture governing the rest of the setting. To read the setting at all, the singer would require at least some musical education; but to truly grasp the nuance of the moral setting, a singer would require enough expertise to understand the musical conventions both guiding and undermining the poet's warning about disciplinary knowledge.

(Un)Reasonable Sounds

It was music's unique position as both *scientia* (an abstract body of knowledge passed down by expert authorities) and *ars* (embodied musical practices and skills) that posed an enduring problem as well as valuable opportunities for those who sought to understand music's role in the acquisition of wisdom or folly. In the same way, music flummoxed related binaries of the period—rational/non-rational, mind/body, masculine/feminine, virtue/vice. The lack of clarity about whether music maps onto folly or wisdom was clearly most problematic when the musicking body was feminine. A survey of the many illustrations of the parable of the Wise and Foolish Virgins from the gospel of Matthew reveals just how unsure early moderns were about what moral stand to take regarding music. Two examples from around 1600 illustrate opposite views of music's relationship to wisdom and foolishness. In Suzanne de Court's plate (after a design by Hieronymus Wierix), music appears as an activity of the wise virgins, who are all depicted as industriously engaging in the traditional artistic and scientific disciplines, while the foolish group lounges barefoot in a lazy, sensual stupor. [Web 6.5] In Hieronymus Francken the Younger's painting of this scene, however, it is the foolish virgins who are playing musical instruments, while the wise virgins are silent, busy with their pious domestic work. [Web 6.6] One reading of this contradiction is that the illustrations of the wise virgins with music on their side represent the more theoretical, learned side of music (as we see in Wierix's version), where music is being "studied" as a formal discipline. (None of the wise virgins are shown in the act of playing the instruments or reading from the partbooks that lie in their midst.) In pointed contrast, Francken's depiction of the foolish virgins emphasizes making music as a practice, and like numerous similar representations of the foolish virgins from this period, it pairs a sonically vibrant scene of musicking with dancing, drinking, games, and other rowdy pastimes.

Considering the extremes to which feminine virtue was scrutinized, it is not surprising to find an intense concern to regulate the ways girls and women practiced and performed music. Even more alarming, however, was the supposed power of the female body to deprive the masculine mind of its reason through a sensual and eroticized vocal assault.[13] Song was

---

[13] See Chiara Bertoglio, *Reforming Music: Music and the Religious Reformations of the Sixteenth Century* (Berlin: de Gruyter, 2017), 123–31; and Linda Phyllis Austern, "'Alluring the Auditorie to

understandably the most powerful site for confronting these concerns, for the union of sound, harmony, time, and semantic substance offered a prime site for exploring the mind–body relationship.[14] For Augustine, Calvin, and numerous other church leaders across the ages, concerns about the seductive voice involved warnings against the "effeminizing" and sensual effects of musical hearing as a direct onslaught on a presumably masculine rational ideal.

Pibrac and Mathieu likewise offered repeated warnings against beauty, pleasure, and uncritical trust in the senses—a discourse that maps the corporeal view of musical sound onto a woman's fleshly body, which was seen as luxurious, excessive, decorative, and frivolous, and thus threatening to the cultivation of reason. These concerns over hearing underline the feminization of the senses and underscore a seductiveness of sonic beauty that was also feminized. L'Estocart's use of interspersed ternary passages in his setting for Pibrac's *Fuy jeune et vieil de Circe le bruvage* (Quatrain 91) warns youthful ears against Circe's potent sonic charms. In contrast to his more formulaic use of ternary elsewhere in the collection, the composer shifts into triple at the most sensory moments, opening in triple for line 1 ("Flee young and old from Circe's drink") and remaining in this meter through the warning to "not listen" (*n'escoute*) at the start of line 2, before shifting to duple meter and luscious melismas in each voice part for the sirens' song. The setting shifts back to triple again in line 3 for this sonic sorcery ("Car, enchanté"), driving home the association of triple with sense deception. Of course, these devices are an extension of the traditional device of using black notation for references to blindness. L'Estocart and Boni both use this figuralism in their settings for Pibrac's Quatrain 37 (*Ne mets ton pied*), shifting to blackened notes for the phrase "Du pauvre aveugle."

L'Estocart further develops the moral implications of using black notation as "eye music" in his trio setting for Chandieu's *J'ay veu, j'ay veu que le Monde est un songe*:

> J'ay veu, j'ay veu que le Monde est un songe
> Lors que la voix de Dieu m'a resveillé.
> Car il n'y a au Monde que mensonge:
> L'œil y est clos, et l'esprit travaillé.

Effeminacie': Music and the Idea of the Feminine in Early Modern England," *Music and Letters* 74, no. 3 (1993): 343–54.
[14] See Austern, *Both from the Ears and Mind*, 98–114.

> Tout y est nuict, l'homme y est hors de l'homme,
> Se repaissant de vaine opinion
> Et ne sentant sa propre passion,
> Ne voudroit pas qu'on luy rompist son somme.

[I saw, I saw that the World is only a dream / When the voice of God woke me up. / Because there is nothing in the World but lies: / There the eye is closed, and the spirit troubled. / Everything there is night; man is outside of himself, / Nourished by vain opinion / And not sensing his own passion, / Would rather not have his sleep broken.]

Chandieu's text recalls the foundational Platonic imagery for dreams versus reality (*Republic* IX), as well as the Stoics' development of this distinction, which Diogenes Laertius described as the difference between a sense impression grounded in reality and a figment of the imagination that creates a dream-like illusion.[15] As Marcus Aurelius reminded himself, "Awaken; return to yourself. Now, no longer asleep, knowing they were only dreams, clear-headed again, treat everything around you as a dream."[16] Chandieu's text offers a sensitive Neostoic take on this question of dream versus reality, guided by the voice of God—the divine *logos*—as he stages a process of critical sense reflection, first emphasizing sight and then reflecting critically on its potential delusions.

L'Estocart's setting for *J'ay veu, j'ay veu que le Monde est un songe* (I.24) continues his pattern of depicting irrationality through ternary groupings. [Web 6.7] In this case, the entire Octonaire progresses in triple, offering a clear reference to his rare triple-meter setting for the inconstancy of courtesans in his *Quatrains* and recalling his occasional shifts to triple earlier in his first collection of *Octonaires* when depicting the sensory pleasures of the round globe. L'Estocart's *J'ay veu, j'ay veu* drives home the moral salience of these associations even further in this triple-meter setting by visually blackening the notes at "lies / The eye is closed" (*mensonge / L'œil y est clos*, mm. 18–24), and again in the phrase "all is night, man is outside of himself" (*Tout y est nuict, l'homme y est hors de l'homme*, mm. 28–33).

---

[15] *Lives* 7.50.
[16] *Meditations* 6.31; trans. Hays, 76.

Picking up this same musical imagery, Claude Le Jeune's four-voice setting for Joseph Du Chesne's *Quelle est cette beauté* (XI.2) sonically unpacks the danger of a feminized sensory experience of this fragile world, outlining suggestively the beauty of a woman's body as it strikes the various senses:

> Quelle est cette beauté que je vois tant extrême,
> Qui avec ses cheveux, et sa voix et ses yeux,
> D'un lien et d'un charme, et d'un trait amoureux,
> Et s'enchaîne et s'enchante, et s'aveugle soi-même?
> C'est le Monde, changé en courtisane infâme,
> Qui se va déguisant de mille fards le corps.
> Mais c'est une beauté seulement du dehors,
> Qui ne peut effacer les laideurs de son âme.

[What is this beauty so extreme that I see, / Who with her hair, her voice, and her eyes, / With a rope and a spell and an amorous arrow, / Enchains and enchants and blinds herself? / It is the World, transformed into an infamous courtesan, / Who disguises her body with a thousand paints and creams. / But it is a beauty only on the outside, / That cannot hide the ugliness of her soul.]

After beginning in imitative polyphony, Le Jeune shifts toward homophony at the caesura in line 1, which introduces the intense allure of this beautiful sight, continuing in a lightly decorated homophony that exposes the woman's hair, voice, and eyes to view.[17] [Web 6.8 and 6.9] The moral danger arrives in the third and fourth lines, as the stricter syncopated homophony binds reason to the senses and ultimately overcomes it through sensory enchantment. All is then revealed in the climactic fifth line, where the revelation that the woman is an allegory for the world is marked by a shift to triple meter and black notation in the upper voices, heightening the irrationality, blindness, and feminine excess plaguing the previous lines.

Early modern misreadings of Plato were cited in support of this gendered split, which first established the superiority of the mind over the body, and then explicitly mapped men and women onto this moral divide. Women were not only argued to be imperfect, or deformed men (as Aristotle had

---

[17] Claude Le Jeune, *Octonaires de la vanité et inconstance du monde (IX–XII)*, ed. Henry Expert (Paris: Senart, 1928), 27–30.

it) but were denied access to growth in rationality and wisdom.[18] Erasmus's *Praise of Folly* narrates this view of women (distorted from *Timaeus* 91A–D) as the embodiment of extreme folly. Even those women seeking wisdom "are doubly foolish in my opinion attempting to achieve wisdom against the express will of Nature." The account goes on to cite the proverb that says a monkey will still be a monkey even when gowned in purple, and coming to the damning conclusion that "A woman is always a woman, that is to say foolish, no matter the appearance that she disguises herself with."[19] Some Neostoic materials use language infected with this gendered notion of wisdom, as we see in Goulart's praise of Stoic eloquence in his *Ample discours* as "quite male and courageous," or in Henri Estienne's emphasis on manliness and virility in his opening remarks for his *Introduction to the Reading of Seneca*.[20] Their sexist language substantiates recent critiques of the modern-day revival of Stoicism as promoting stereotypically gendered traits of rationality, heroism, courage, fortitude, and mastery of emotion, bolstered by a heavy admiration for the Spartans—all coded as masculinist cultural values.

This hyper-masculine vision of the Stoic tradition, however, is certainly not the full picture, as the famous story of ancient musical ethos related to Sparta suggests: It was said that to quell the rising unrest in their city, the Spartans brought in the singer Terpander from Lesbos, whose music was able to restore the city to a harmonious order.[21] Even more important than their admiration of the Spartan sensitivity to musical sound, the Stoics proposed radical views on gender. As we recall, the Stoics argued that women had the same rational capacity and connection to the divine *logos* as men. Their approach to gender is just one way that the Stoics both worked within existing structures and systems and pushed beyond them, reinventing them.[22] Based on their fundamental cosmology and anthropology, the Stoics argued that it was a woman's nature and her calling—as much as for her male counterparts—to engage and cultivate her mind by studying philosophy and reaching her full human potential

---

[18] See Desmond Clark, *French Philosophy, 1572–1675* (Oxford: Oxford University Press, 2016), 220–48; and Rebecca Wilkin, "The *Querelle des femmes*," in *The Cambridge History of French Thought*, ed. Michael Moriarty and Jeremy Ralph Jennings (Cambridge: Cambridge University Press, 2019), 190–97.

[19] Erasmus, *La Louange de la sotise*, trans. Hélie Poirier (La Haye: Theodore Maire, 1642), 45–46.

[20] Seneca, *Œuvres morales et meslées de Senecque*, trans. Goulart, 3:335–36; and Estienne, *Introduction à la lecture de Sénèque (1586)*, ed. Carabin, 40–43.

[21] On the sources and circulation of this tale, see M. L. West, *Ancient Greek Music* (Oxford: Clarendon Press, 1992), 31.

[22] See Reydams-Schils, *The Roman Stoics*, 6–13.

in both reason and wisdom.[23] As François Poulain de la Barre famously articulated the Stoic view in *De l'égalité des deux sexes* (1673), "the mind has no sex."[24] Early modern women, such as Marie Le Jars de Gournay, Madeleine de l'Aubespine, and Mary Sidney, displayed a clear interest and involvement in the Stoic revival, perhaps recognizing this greater inclusivity and expanded view of human rationality advocated by the school.

Even undergirded, theoretically, by Stoic support for women's full rationality and access to virtue, women intellectuals of the period nonetheless struggled to undermine these strong cultural assumptions of female irrationality, for as Linda Phyllis Austern has demonstrated, abundant early modern materials continued to reinforce an alignment between the female body, irrationality, falsehood, animal sensation, and the fragility of human nature.[25] Barthélemy Aneau's emblem *Retour de bestise, a raison* represents the base nature of mankind with a depiction of a beastly half-woman, half-ox inspired by Ovid's *Metamorphoses*.[26] [Web 6.10] Even Montenay offered an emblem in this tradition, with her *Crass Ignorance* depicting a woman with donkey ears pouring excrement from a chamber pot over the round ball symbolizing the world.[27] [Web 6.11] Gilles Corrozet's emblem *Feminine Nature* illustrates inconstancy with a naked woman, topped with a housewife's headdress, compared to a flighty flock of birds.[28] [Web 6.12] Courtesans were attacked in other ways, being portrayed either as frivolous women or as "effeminized" men with double tongues who have become enslaved by luxury.[29] And, of course—as the example *par excellence* for this study—we have Lady Fortune, whose popularized image on her slippery ball in the passionate waves represented every danger of irrational sensual attachment to the unstable world.[30]

Sara Matthews Grieco has demonstrated that Montenay's *Emblemes, ou Devises chrestiennes* often reference the tropes and images from earlier

---

[23] See Musonius Rufus, "That women too should do philosophy," transmitted through the Stobaeus anthology, in *The Stoics Reader*, ed. Inwood and Gerson, 177.

[24] François Poulain de la Barre, *De l'égalité des deux sexes, De l'éducation des dames, De l'excellence des hommes*, ed. Marie-Frédérique Pellegrin (Paris: Vrin, 2011), 99.

[25] See Linda Phyllis Austern, "The Siren, the Muse, and the God of Love: Music and Gender in Seventeenth-Century English Emblem Books," *Journal of Musicological Research* 18 no. 2 (1999): 95–138.

[26] Aneau, *Imagination poétique*, 149.

[27] Montenay, *Emblemes, ou Devises chrestiennes*, fol. 22r.

[28] Corrozet, *Hécatomgraphie*, sig. L7v–8r.

[29] See Alciato's emblem *Contre les Courtisans* in the 1536, 1549, 1584, and 1615 editions of his *Emblemata*; and La Perrière, *Le Theatre des bons engins*, Emblem 104.

[30] See Chapter 4 of this volume (Web 4.7 and 4.8).

emblem literature, but frequently subvert their sexist imagery, inscribing her work within the long tradition of Christine de Pisan, carving out as it does a more equal opportunity for women as voices of knowledge, reason, and wisdom.[31] A landmark collection in numerous respects, Montenay's collection was not only the first emblem book created by a woman, but it was also the first to reframe the philosophical themes endemic to the emblem genre within an overtly Protestant Christian framework. A further innovation of the book was its eschewing of woodcut in favor of copperplate engraving (by fellow Protestant Pierre Woeiriot), which would became the standard, followed by later emblemists like Delaune. Although it was more typical for emblem books to rely upon stock images already in the corpus or in the printer's shop, Montenay's unique illustrations for her *Emblemes, ou Devises chrestiennes*, and their non-traditional approach to gender, stand out in the emblem literature (as opposed to the entirely conventional work done by Woeiriot elsewhere), lending support to Montenay's authorship of both text and image. Her emblem *Keep Watch* depicts a woman holding candles representing the light of truth against ignorance, which she has portrayed as a man hiding with the beasts in the shadows.[32] [Web 6.13] Another notable example is her emblem *For Virtue There is Everywhere a Way*, where Lady Virtue stands on a rock and holding a pillar (the symbol of constancy and strength), while a man dressed in ancient military garb is the one tossed about by the inconstancy of the storm and struggling to make progress toward a radically feminized ideal of stability.[33] [Web 6.14] In one sense, this aligns virtue with faith, and critiques classical pagan philosophies as themselves formed of unreliable opinion—an image that upends the traditionally-gendered assignment of inconstancy to women and wisdom/reason to men.

Though Montenay's emblems were widely influential in the Reformed world, Matthews Grieco has traced how her unique gender correctives were lost as these images returned to masculine control. Jean Jacques Boissard's *Emblemata* offers an illuminating example. A reputed scholar of antiquity and devout member of the Reformed faith, Boissard, like Beza and Goulart, was a deep admirer of Montenay's work, and many of his emblems from his 1584/1588 editions are directly modeled after her book. Boissard, however, relies on more conventional representations of women. His version of

---

[31] Sara Matthews Grieco, "Georgette de Montenay: A Different Voice in Sixteenth-Century Emblematics," *Renaissance Quarterly* 47, no. 4 (1994): 793–822.

[32] Montenay, *Emblemes, ou Devises chrestiennes*, fol. 51r.

[33] Ibid., fol. 60r.

the emblem *Mille douleurs ensuyvent volupté* [A Thousand Sorrows Follow Pleasure] features a female monster beside a trap, offering commentary by Pierre Joly that confirms the link between its womanly body, beauty, and inconstancy: "Its face is beautiful; yet shameless / Its appearance is proud, inconstant, and flighty" (*Le visage en est beau; toutesfois eshonté: / L'allure en est superbe, inconstante, et legere.*).[34] [Web 6.15] This emblem mirrors the sonic strategy already noted in Le Jeune's setting of Du Chesne's *Quelle est cette beauté*, with its collapse of triple-meter groupings onto a feminized, sensual irrationality.

Echoes and Deceptions

The alluring creature depicted in Boissard's emblem was part-woman, part-lion, and part-bird, drawing on deep wells of cultural knowledge warning against the danger monstrous women posed to the eyes, but also the precarity of hearing her voice. Homer's tale of Ulysses and the Sirens in book 12 of the *Odyssey* spawned the most vivid images of this sensory danger, easily mapped onto the presumed conflict between feminine sensuality and masculine rationality. Often pictured as either half-bird or half-fish, the womanly Sirens possessed magical singing voices that so enchanted the ear that passing sailors would lose their will and reason entirely and be dashed upon the rocks. The tale of the Sirens served a continual reminder that music was caught in a sticky web of questions and doubts regarding the relationship between rational faculties and the sensory experience that feeds and informs our mind.[35]

In one major interpretive tradition, the Sirens offered excessive carnal pleasure through their song, and the antidote to this sensual assault was the power of knowledge. In the commentary for numerous editions of Alciato's emblem of the Sirens, these beautiful monsters were calling to the irrational aspect of the men via his most vulnerable sensory portal of the ear; thus, "the best remedy against them that is available is study of the arts and sciences, and travel."[36] [Web 6.16] Knowledge, however, was not always the hero of

---

[34] Boissard, *Emblematum liber / Emblemes latins* (1588), 84–85.

[35] For early modern interpretations of the sirens, see Elena Calogero, *Ideas and Images of Music in English and Continental Emblem Books, 1550–1700* (Baden: Koerner, 2009), 96–122.

[36] Alciato, *Emblemes* (1549), 142–43. See also Alciato, *Emblemata / Les emblemes* (1584), fols. 160r–161r.

this story. Cicero's *De finibus bonorum et malorum* (5.49) suggested that what these singing monsters really offered their listeners was the lure of greater understanding and perfect knowledge, rather than vapid carnal desire. "Apparently it was not the sweetness of their voices or the novelty and diversity of their songs, but their professions of knowledge that used to attract the passing voyagers; it was the passion for learning that kept men rooted to the Sirens' rocky shores."[37]

Early modern Skeptics picked up on this line of critique, for was not the temptation of perfect knowledge the original sin, used to tempt Eve and Adam in the garden? Worse yet, were not dogmatic claims regarding religious knowledge the root of the violence and divisions plaguing the European continent and destroying the peace? It seemed clear that the Scholastic framework backing the authoritative knowledge paradigm had fallen into exactly this dangerous trap: they had recycled the confident platitudes of their logic and sense theories without taking into adequate account the utter fallibility of the human faculties that were integral to these processes.

The tale of the Sirens symbolizes the moral and epistemological precarity of hearing as both a site of potential edification and of deception. Although from Aristotle onward, sight had retained the position of first sense, followed by hearing, early modern discussions of the senses devoted increased attention to the power of hearing.[38] For some, hearing even became the primary sense. Jacques Amyot's French translation of Plutarch's *On Listening to Lectures* (Comment il fault ouir) circulated an argument for the moral primacy of hearing over all the other senses. Hearing, he explains, has been held by some authorities as the most emotional faculty, for no other sense causes "such great troubles, nor such grand fears, as that which enters the soul by means of noise, sound, and voice which come to strike the ear."[39] Plutarch's essay points out its greater rationality, asserting that hearing has even more capacity to stimulate reason. His conclusion is that "there are several places and parts of the body, which give to the vices entrance in order to pour into the soul, but virtue has only one single entrance into young people, that is the

[37] Stephen Buhler, "The Sirens, the Epicurean Boat, and the Poetry of Praise," in *Music of the Sirens*, ed. Linda Phyllis Austern and Inna Naroditskaya (Bloomington, Ill.: Indiana University Press, 2006), 176–93; and Harry Vredeveld, "'Deaf as Ulysses to the Siren's Song': The Story of a Forgotten Topos," *Renaissance Quarterly* 54, no. 3 (2001): 846–82.

[38] See Kate van Orden, "An Erotic Metaphysics of Hearing in Early Modern France," *The Musical Quarterly* 82 (1998): 678–91.

[39] Plutarch, *Œuvres morales et meslées de Plutarque*, trans. Jacques Amyot (Paris: Michel de Vascosan, 1572), fols. 24v–25r.

ears." These well-established moral and intellectual benefits of hearing served as music's strongest claim to wisdom; consequently, musical hearing merited special attention in the effort to shore up strong critical defenses against its own sensory limitations.

Concerns about the fragility of hearing came down through multiple branches of the Socratic tradition, citing the acoustic decay of sound and the natural echo as their main lines of attack. Erasmus, for example, had voiced his discomfort with the impermanence of musical sound: "a ringing of voices that strikes the ears and soothes with trifling pleasures that die away instantly."[40] Leonardo da Vinci's well-known argument for privileging sight over hearing is similar: harmony, when heard through the ears, "dies as soon as it is born, and dies as fast as it was born." In his account, music "begins to waste away the very moment it comes into being."[41] In a more detailed account, Matthaeus Herbenus's *On the Nature of Song and the Miracles of the Voice* (1496) argues against polyphony on the grounds of sensory fallibility, wedged at the intersection of acoustic ephemerality and the limits of human hearing. Herbenus, a Dutch scholar who was connected to both Erasmus and the Italian Neoplatonists, located his arguments against elaborate polyphony in exactly the sort of "catalogue of the senses" deployed in later Skeptical writings. After discussing the problem of vision in the case of iridescence, which does not allow the mind to form a judgment of it before it changes, he comes to hearing: "In those songs, therefore, which fly past the ears so swiftly that they vanish before there could be a judgment of them, the capacity to judge is overwhelmed."[42]

Skeptics argued that because these sense faculties are the sole portal to knowledge, and because they are corruptible or imperfect in their transmission, human reason cannot escape error. Montaigne most famously articulated the Skeptic arguments against traditional theories of knowledge in his *Apologie de Raymond Sebond* (1580), where he thoroughly proves the utter fallibility of human reason. Charron's *Sagesse* (1601) follows in this Skeptical vein, detailing the numerous factors that could cause the senses to be deceived, mistaken, or confused, including illness, old age, strong emotions, distance, natural phenomena, and preexisting biases.[43]

---

[40] Desiderius Erasmus, *Annotations on the New Testament: Acts – Romans – I and II Corinthians*, ed. Anne Reeve and Michael Andrew Screech (Leiden: Brill, 1990), 507.

[41] Cited in Wegman, *The Crisis of Music*, 38.

[42] Matthaeus Herbenus, *De natura cantus ac miraculis vocis*, ed. Joseph Smits van Waesberghe (Cologne: Arno Volk, 1957), 59. See Wegman, *The Crisis of Music*, 175–77.

[43] Charron, *De la sagesse*, I.12, 104–5.

Both Montaigne and Charron were influenced by Guy de Brués's *Dialogues* (1557, reprinted 1587), which offers a similar interrogation of sensory knowledge.[44] The *Dialogues* stage a fictional debate between four esteemed interlocutors connected to the Pléiade, several of whom were participants with Le Jeune in the Academy of Poetry and Music—namely, Pierre Ronsard, Jean-Antoine de Baïf, Jean Nicot de Villemain, and Guillaume Aubert.[45] Brués presents the dialogue as a defense of traditional Aristotelian and Stoic sensory theories against the Skeptical position, which is framed as a threat to religion. As Jean-Claude Carron has pointed out, however, the winner of the debates is in no way settled in these fascinating dialogues.[46] Based primarily on Cicero's *Academica*, the *Dialogues* present Baïf and Aubert arguing the Skeptic position and its deep concerns with sensory deception. Ronsard and Nicot counter as the protagonists confirming an accepted Christian position based primarily on the traditional Aristotelian and Stoic sensory tradition and natural law in support of the possibility of arriving at some workable and practical route toward human knowledge.

Deeply intertwined with the Aristotelian sensory tradition, the Stoic approach to the senses resolutely prized sensory experience as the portal to knowledge; however, they also gave considerable credence to Skeptic concerns over the problem of sensory fragility and deception.[47] Guillaume Du Vair's *Philosophie morale des Stoiques* rehearsed the argument for the importance of sense impressions that came down through Aristotle and Epictetus, agreeing that they are "the sentinels of the body, keeping watch for its conservation." He further praises the senses as "the messengers and couriers of understanding, and a sovereign part of the soul, and serve as ministers and instruments of discourse and of reason."[48] He goes on to explain the critical point that they must be governed by reason because they have

---

[44] Guy de Brués, *Les Dialogues de Guy de Brués, contre les nouveaux Academiciens, que tout ne consiste point en opinion* (Paris: Guillaume Cavellat, 1557; and Paris: Hierosme de Marnef, et la Veufve Guillaume Cavellat, 1587). Montaigne clearly used Brués's *Dialogues* as a resource for his Skeptical ideas, as he cites the work multiple times.

[45] Panos Paul Morphos, *The Dialogues of Guy de Brués: A Critical Edition with a Study in Renaissance Scepticism and Relativism* (Baltimore, Md.: The Johns Hopkins Press, 1953), 19–25.

[46] Jean-Claude Carron, "Dialogical Argument: Scripting Rhetoric (The Case of Guy De Brués's *Dialogues*)," *South Central Review* 10, no. 2 (1993): 20–22.

[47] Stoicism had been used to shore up the ambiguities in Aristotle's sensory theory by the influential Arabic commentators Al-Kindi and Averroes. On the influence of Stoicism in reading Aristotle and shaping the new science in this period, see Ulrich Langer, "Moral Theories: Aristotelianism and Neo-Stoicism," in *The Cambridge History of French Thought*, ed. Moriarty and Jennings, 59–61; and Dennis Sepper, *Descartes's Imagination: Proportion, Images, and the Activity of Thinking* (Berkeley, CA: University of California Press, 1996), 14–30.

[48] Du Vair, *La Philosophie morale des Stoiques*, 15–16; ed. Tarrête, 66.

an inherent fragility that allows them to be deceived often by appearances ("souvent trompez par l'apparence") when accepted uncritically. With this attention to sense deception and decay prominent in their tradition, the Stoics focused far more attention on the critical reflection phase, before the mind either "assents" to the initial impression as a rationally sound judgment or rejects it as a false appearance.[49]

This brings us back to the Stoic interpretation of the Sirens and their dangerous songs. The musical consequences of this flexible Stoic position on the senses, offering a deeply critical yet embodied route toward cognition and empirical knowledge, formed the theoretical underpinning of the equally nuanced Stoic positions on music, poetry, and the arts in education.

The Ciceronian account of Homer's Sirens expressed this bold Stoic approach to sensory and specifically musical knowledge, reading the Sirens' song as offering Ulysses a chance at sonic edification as well as posing an incomparable danger to the proper functioning of his cognitive process. A critical aspect of this version of the Siren's tale is that Ulysses both recognized the danger of song and found a way to benefit prudently from its ravishing power. This hero, therefore, showed both courage and cunning in demanding that his men bind him to the mast so that he could remain open to hearing—and thus grow wise from—the Sirens' potent harmonic instruction, while his sailors with wax in their ears rowed to safety completely deaf and unchanged by these sounds. This interpretation of the Siren's harmonic instruction was also widely transmitted through Plutarch's *On how the young person should listen to poetry* (15d), which, as mentioned earlier, was modeled on Chrysippus's treatise bearing the same title. The key difference was that the dangerous sonic wisdom offered by the Sirens was not only for the hero:

> Shall we, then, stopping up young people's ears with a hard and unyielding wax, as the ears of the Ithacans were stopped, force them to put to sea in the Epicurean boat, and to avoid poetry and steer their course clear of it? Or shall we instead, standing them up against some upright standard of reason, and binding them there securely, straighten and watch over their judgment, so that it will not be carried away by pleasure toward that which will harm them?[50]

[49] Reydams-Schils, *The Roman Stoics*, 26.
[50] Cited in Nussbaum, "Poetry and the Passions," 131.

The Stoics' built-in safeguard of the binding power of this "upright standard of reason" allowed them to follow Ulysses in resolutely keeping their sensory pathways fully open and fully attuned to the sense impressions coming from the world around them, such that they could profit from the harmonious edification of these encounters without being swept away by harmful or addictive pleasures or held captive by false opinions.

This exceptionally nuanced Stoic and Neostoic position, falling somewhere between Aristotle and the Skeptics, led early moderns to align the Stoics in some cases with the Aristotelian tradition (as we see in Brués's account, which cites Stoic writings on numerous occasions as an extention of the older Aristotelian view). At other times, the Stoic position was read as much closer to their Hellenistic antagonists the Skeptics (as we see in Pierre de La Primaudaye's account of the senses).[51] This position has been unfortunately misread in recent musicological work. Kate van Orden's recent work on the musical settings of Pibrac's *Quatrains* has offered a distorted picture of the Stoic approach to the senses, based on a misreading of La Primaudaye's *Suite de l'Académie françoise*. Van Orden claims that "The *Suite* begins with an important argument against Stoic philosophy and its rejection of sensual experience as a foundation for knowledge."[52] In her supporting note, she offers the citation from La Primaudaye's *Suite* (fol. 27v), adding the bracketed clarification as follows: "Eusebe disputant au contraire [against the Stoics] monstre que les sens servent grandement à acquerir sapience." (Eusebius argued on the contrary [against the Stoics] showing that the senses serve greatly in acquiring wisdom.) However, a look at the full passage that Van Orden cites from the *Suite* reveals that the sentence immediately prior explicitly states that La Primaudaye's critique is aimed at Plato—who was indeed famous for his denigration of the physical sensorium.[53] La Primaudaye even offers a helpful note in the margins that cites Plato's *Timaeus* as his source of this problematic anti-sensory view. What probably provoked Van Orden's misunderstanding is that La Primaudaye had lumped the Stoics and

---

[51] See for example, Pierre de La Primaudaye, *Suite de l'Académie françoise, en laquelle il est traicté de l'homme* (Paris: Guillaume Chaudière, 1580), Ch. 10 "Des sens," fol. 27v.

[52] Van Orden, *Materialities*, 241.

[53] "Platon a escrit en plusieurs lieux, qu'il falloit seulement croire à l'intelligence, qui voit ce qui est simple et uniforme, et tel qu'il est: Et qu'il n'y avoit science, sinon en ces raisons et discours que l'ame faisoit quand elle n'est troublées des empeschmens corporels: comme de la veuë, et de l'ouye, de douleur et de volupté. Eusebe disputant au contraire, monstre que les sens servent grandement à acquerir sapience: et quand ils demeurent en leur droite habitude naturelle, qu'ils ne deçoivent jamais l'esprit bien attentif. Or poursuyvans nos discours des instrumens des sens, nous cognoistrons amplement de leur utilité." La Primaudaye, *Suite de l'Académie françoise*, fol. 27v.

Skeptics together at the beginning of the passage, as schools concerned with the problem of sense deception and decay.

Resonating with much of La Primaudaye's Christian synthesis—and at times overtly shaping it—Stoic sensory theory recognized the fragility of the senses but argued for their essential value in wisdom-cultivation as a fundamental technology of natural law (another extremely important Neostoic contribution to the period).[54] When approached critically through the stages of assent and judgment, this sensory fallibility did not pose an insurmountable obstacle to the Stoic pursuit of scientific or moral knowledge. The senses *did* need the governance of reason, however, as a check against sense deception or indulgence. Although the Stoics shared a basic recognition of the physical fragility of the worldly sensorium with their Platonic and Skeptic interlocutors, they developed these natural phenomena as a warning against the moral fragility of sense perception, which was particularly vulnerable to deception and loss of rational powers when overwhelmed by the passions of pleasure, desire, fear, or grief, or when guided by an inappropriate attachment to the world.

This broad moralizing approach to the fragility of all five senses, including musical hearing, found poetic expression in Chandieu's twelfth Octonaire:

> La beauté soudain passe, et eschappe à tes yeux:
> Tu ois, puis tu n'ois plus le son melodieux:
> Le vent t'oste l'odeur qui ton flairer contente:
> Le plaisir du toucher a sa peine presente:
> Et le goust favoureux n'a de long que trois doigts:
> Est-ce donc sans raison, Mondain, que je t'accuse?
> Ce que tu sens est vain, et ne sens toutesfois
> Ceste grande vanité qui tous tes sens abuse.

In this catalogue of the senses, Chandieu addresses hearing second and uses a musical analogy ("You hear, then you hear no longer the melodious sound"), cited here in Josuah Sylvester's liberal English paraphrase.

> How swift is Beauty vanisht from thine Ey!
> How sudden Musick drowned in thine Ear!

---

[54] On the Neostoicism of La Primaudaye's work, see Carabin, *Les Idées stoïciennes*, 104; and Dana Jalobeanu, "Francis Bacon's Natural History and the Senecan Natural Histories of Early Modern Europe," *Early Science and Medicine* 17, nos. 1–2 (2012): 202–3.

How soon doo Odours from thy Nostrils fly!
How short, touch-Pleasures (tipt with Pain and Fear)!
How sowre, Taste-sweetest, in small time's expense-is!
Then, Epicure, well may wee blame thee, since,
All under Sense thus vain, Thou hast no sense
Of Vanity, which so besots thy Senses.[55]

In the visual realm, Hendrick Goltzius offered a similar portrayal in *Les Cinq Senses* [The Five Senses] (1588), depicting them as a group of women with luminous flesh—a particular talent of the artist, even when working in pen (see Plate 8). Based out of Haarlem, Goltzius was a leading artist of Dutch Mannerism. His diverse oeuvre displays a persistent interest in classical philosophy, an interest that he shared with the younger Antwerp painter Peter Paul Rubens, whose ties to Justus Lipsius and Neostoicism have been well documented.[56] Goltzius and Rubens developed a close relationship, both personally and artistically, and together they influenced a generation of philosophically driven artistic practices. *The Five Senses*, engraved by Goltzius's stepson and pupil Jacob Matham, portrays all five senses together in a narrow valley, in a vividly sensual reimagining of these figures that warns of the moral dangers lurking at the boundaries of sense perception. While Smell enjoys the scent of a cut (i.e., already dying) flower, Taste, pictured in the lower foreground, eats an apple, in a clear reminder of Eve's original sin. Sight lies above them, looking in a mirror while touching her nipple, and Touch flies above them while being bitten by the snake coiled around her arm. Hearing occupies a visually dominant position in the lower left foreground, with her beautifully sculpted nude back presented to the viewer as she draws her bow across the strings of her bass instrument. Pointed toward the cavernous valley, her music will certainly produce the echo so frequently mentioned as the prime example of aural deception.

Like iridescence in the visual domain, the echo offered a natural sense deception through its double and distorted effect on hearing and served as a clear reminder to critically evaluate impressions gained by the senses. Chandieu's Octonaire 14 offers the echo as a symbol of the fragility of sense

---

[55] Sylvester, *Works*, 1178.
[56] See F. Vermeylin and K. De Clippel, "Rubens and Goltzius in Dialogue: Artistic Exchanges between Antwerp and Haarlem during the Revolt," *De Zeventiende Eeuw: Cultuur in de Nederlanden in interdisciplinair perspectief* 28, no. 2 (2012): 149; and Morford, *Stoics and Neostoics*, 3–13.

perception, framed here as a moral and epistemological consequence of the feminized inconstancy of the world:

Ce n'est rien qu'une Echo tout cest immonde Monde,
Sortant d'un bois, d'un roc, et d'une profonde onde,
Un son naissant-mourrant, une voix vifve-morte,
Un air rejaillissant, qu'un vent leger emporte,
Un parler contrefaict, qui est esvanoui
Si tost qu'il a trompé celuy qui l'a oui.
Tais-toy, fuy loin de moin, Echo, fuy, Monde immonde,
Demeure au bois, au roc, et en l'onde profonde.

In Sylvester's English rendering:

What is the World, but a vain *Eccho's* Sounding,
From Woods, and Caves, and hollow Rocks rebounding
A new No-noise, a dead-live Voice, to summon
Deluded Ears to listen to a Dumb-one:
A speaking Fiction of a mocking Faëry:
A formall Answer, in Effect but aiëry
      Hence, hence, vain *Eccho*, with thine idle Mocks:
      Keep in thy Woods, sleep in thy Caves and Rocks.[57]

Oddly enough, neither L'Estocart nor Claude Le Jeune chose to include settings for these texts in their *Octonaires* collections, perhaps wisely choosing to keep the dangerous echo in her cave.

The echo, in all its messy musical and philosophical glory, became an object of fascination across Europe during this time, inspired by the popularity of Ovid's account of Echo and Narcissus in his *Metamorphoses* (I, 380–392) and no doubt propelled by the fomenting concerns over the precarity of hearing. The repertoire associated with the *concerto delle dame*—a virtuoso trio of ladies who were sponsored by the court of Alfonso II d'Este, duke of Ferrara in the late sixteenth century—includes numerous Echo texts. Two collections by Lodovico Agostini, *The Echo, and Musical Enigma* (1581) and *The New Echo* (1583), reveal how these broader concerns about the nature of hearing and the possibility of distortion/deception through "artifice" could

---

[57] Sylvester, *Works*, 1179.

be negotiated by skilled female voices. The centerpiece of Agostini's second collection—the "Odi, Ninfa de gl'antri hor come io godo"—features several echo passages, in which the leading voice is followed closely by cascading echoes. The printed music for these settings invites improvisation and a display of creative vocal virtuosity by the echo voices—in effect, beautifully distorting the leading (original) voice in a way that would have confirmed every fear that the sense of hearing could delightfully mislead the listener.[58]

Claude Le Jeune's final setting of his *Mélange* offers his own instructive take on the echo effect in his ten-voice, double-choir arrangement of the text *Quae celebrat thermas*. Announced in the collection simply as "Echo," the setting unfolds as a dialogue between a nymph and her own echo. Unique in its genre, the setting is almost entirely homophonic, with syllables afforded a minim or a breve. What is fascinating here is that Le Jeune's echo exactly repeats the nymph's initial phrase melodically and harmonically, but it alters the rhythm, in what turns out to be a correction of the prosody, according to the new rules of *musique mesurée* codified in Baïf's Académie.[59] Within these multi-pronged debates over musical knowing, we can understand the wider philosophical implications of the experiments in *musique mesurée* as resonating with the broader humanist fascination with sensory knowledge, crucially popularized in Brués's fictional *Dialogues* account (and voiced by none other than Baïf and his colleagues). The echo serves as a useful mirror that, while still feminized, offers a viable route to wisdom after all.

Knowledge in Transit

The massive global exploration launched between the fifteenth and seventeenth centuries raised the political and philosophical stakes for interrogating the validity of these sense–knowledge paradigms; it also revealed debates about human rationality that were not only musically feminized but also deeply racialized. As European explorers and colonizers roamed the world, they documented an unexpected diversity in human physiognomy, language, religions, laws, and morals that exacerbated concerns that all knowledge is

---

[58] Lodovico Agostini, *L'Echo, et Enigmi musicali a sei voci* (Venice: Alessandro Gardano, 1581); and *Il nuovo Echo* (Ferrara: Baldini, 1583). See Laurie Stras, *Women and Music in Sixteenth-Century Ferrara* (Cambridge: Cambridge University Press, 2018), 256.

[59] Claude Le Jeune, *Livre de mélanges (1585)*, ed. Isabelle His (Turnhout: Brepols, 2003). See Isabelle His, "Claude Le Jeune et le rythme prosodique: La mutation des années 1570," *Revue de Musicologie* 79, no. 2 (1993): 220.

really just opinion (and based on extremely limited knowledge, at that). On the other hand, these new explorations produced an abundance of fresh data regarding the world's geography and peoples that, it was hoped, could be used to build a storehouse of reliable human knowledge. Music proved to be one of the most fascinating of human universals, although it quickly became evident that it was an example of radical local particularity, for music was not performed, understood, or appreciated in any degree of uniformity across the globe.

Some travel writers made the effort to document unfamiliar music traditions by including transcriptions of indigenous songs. Most famously, Jean de Léry notated five South American Tupinamba chants in his *History of a Voyage Made in the Land of Brazil* (1578), and Marc Lescarbot included transcriptions of three Mi'kmaq songs in his *History of New France* (1609).[60] Gabriel Sagard borrowed these transcriptions by Léry and Lescarbot for his expanded 1636 *History of Canada*. In a radical act of colonial translation, Sagard printed four of these chants in short homophonic settings for four voices. The original chant was in the superius and was supported in the lower voices by a plain syllabic texture, resembling the simple polyphony of French Protestant and Catholic devotional music popular in the late sixteenth century. In this way, the colonizing effort led to a complete reversal of the relationship between polyphony and knowledge. Whereas monophonic song had served as the rational ideal in the arguments against church polyphony in the early sixteenth century, the colonial landscape transformed polyphony —at least to some ears—into a powerful symbol of European rationality and civilization.[61] Thus, although florid polyphony was still not the ideal vehicle for ensuring the comprehension and cognition of texts, its symbolic value as a marker of European learning and religious authority made it the perfect cultural agent to promote colonial hegemony.

Sagard's polyphonic transformations of indigenous song are an early example of what eventually became a more widespread colonial phenomenon: musically binding cultural "others" into an unequal relationship that served European aesthetic and ideological interests at home and abroad. The travel literature and the strange musical translations thus co-opted

[60] Olivia Bloechl, "The Pedagogy of Polyphony in Gabriel Sagard's 'Histoire du Canada,'" *Journal of Musicology* 22, no. 3 (2005): 366–7.

[61] See David Irving, *Colonial Counterpoint: Music in Early Modern Manila* (Oxford: Oxford University Press, 2010), 2–6; and Vanessa Agnew, *Enlightenment Orpheus: The Power of Music in Other Worlds* (New York: Oxford University Press, 2008), 75–119.

foreign sounds and musical values into culturally recognizable and accept-able frameworks, made legible through the experience of wonder. As Olivia Bloechl explains: "The suspension of judgement that wonder induced in travelers and their readers was a momentary recognition of the limits of European knowledge and experience, yet it also provided an impetus for Europeans' subsequent knowledge, interpretation, and other forms of empowered action in the colonial sphere."[62] These colonial music projects thus harnessed wonderment to achieve precisely the intellectual benefits most desired in the post-Skeptical era: a recognition of the limits of human knowledge and a route to empirical knowledge-building, both leading to the calm—and, perhaps, smug—suspension of judgment.

Within this context of expansion, the question of both the nature of human difference and its attendant obligations escalated in urgency, as the idea of the world city (*civis mundi*) became the seventeenth-century mark of expanding geographical horizons.[63] In the preface to the court geographer Nicolas de Nicolay's *Quatre premiers livres de Navigations et Pérégrinations* (1567), dedicated to Charles IX, the author justifies the expansionary impulse, arguing that the earthly globe is so immense, beautiful, and ornate that it must be a (European) human duty to explore and inhabit it.[64] Claiming support from Socrates on this point, Nicolay cites the notion of the "cosmopolite," or cit-izen of the world, as a justification for European rights of colonization and global sovereignty.

Crucially, however, the ancient Stoic notion of the world city was linked to their concept of universal harmony and was harnessed by Neostoics as a direct challenge to rising interests in human cultural subjugation and the expansion of empire. Cicero's *Dream of Scipio* was rightly interpreted throughout the Stoic tradition as a reminder of the vanity of empire-building and war, for when the entire earth is viewed "from above," it is possible to see how ridiculously pointless and arrogant these projects of national and cul-tural glorification prove to be. They will all, without exception, end in ruins. Framed by the broader concerns over sensory knowledge dominating the earlier sections, Brués shifts his third *Dialogue* to focus on these geographical implications. His speaker, Aubert, upholds the Stoic position on the futility of dividing up the earth, arguing that according to nature, all things should

---

[62] Bloechl, "The Pedagogy of Polyphony," 406.

[63] Pibrac, *Les Quatrains*, ed. Petris, 148n9.

[64] Nicolas de Nicolay, *Quatre premiers livres de Navigations et Pérégrinations* (Lyon: G. Rouille, 1567), 2.

be held in common, for God created humans "all from the same material." He continues in the vein of paradoxical argument that we have already discussed in previous chapters of this book in claiming that this form of ambition and greed never satisfies. He offers the classic Neostoic example of the greedy person so intent on eating more than his share of the food that he vomits it up without any true gain for his selfishness. He then calls upon Seneca to assert that "the republic will attain happiness when the words *Mine and Yours* are no longer heard."[65] Next, he turns the tables on European notions of superiority by citing an example from the Stoic Strabo, whose *Geography* (Bk. 7) held up the nomadic Eurasian Scythians for their model of communal living that not only allowed them great prosperity, but also, according to Hesiod, rendered them invincible.

The Scythians, and even more so the darker Moors originating from Africa, were commonly depicted in the period as irrational or threatening others who were exoticized and grouped with women as examples of a base, more sensual strata of humanity.[66] In this cultural context, it is particularly striking that Pibrac's Quatrain 9 challenges these negative portrayals in his account of the Stoic world city—naming both the Scythian and the Moor as models of an equal human rationality, virtue, and right of citizenship that every person on earth shares through their connection to the divine *logos*:

> Tout l'univers n'est qu'une cité ronde,
> Chacun a droict de s'en dire bourgeois,
> Le Scythe et More autant que le Gregeois,
> Le plus petit que le plus grand du monde.

[The entire universe is only a round city, / Each one has a right to citizenship, / The Scythe and Moor as much as the Greek, / The smallest as much as the greatest of the world.]

Pibrac's expression of Stoic universalism offered a radical challenge to the established Augustinian link limiting the rights of citizenship to members of the *corpus christianum* ("cives sumus, in quantum Christiani sumus").[67] As

---

[65] Seneca, *De beneficiis* VII, 6.; and Brués, *Dialogues*, III, 274.

[66] Ralph Locke, *Music and the Exotic from the Renaissance to Mozart* (Cambridge: Cambridge University Press, 2015), 48–49.

[67] Augustine, *Enarratio in Psalmum* LXXXVI, 1.

Loris Petris explains, during and after the Wars of Religion, this Stoic idea of the community of sages was radically extended to religious and confessional differences as well as to geographic and racialized differences.[68]

Other writers influenced by Stoicism followed this more inclusive view of human difference. Montaigne's ethnography of the Tupi songs in his "Des cannibals," for example, acknowledges their cultural practices as a valid mode of civilization rather than as evidence of inferiority. His *Apologie de Raymond Sebond*, moreover, offers a relativistic approach to his own Christian religion, recognizing that it is received and believed just like other world religions, based on one's geographic and cultural upbringing rather than by access to some universal truth: "We happen to have been born in a country where it was in practice. . . . Another region, other witnesses, similar promises and threats, might imprint upon us in the same way a contrary belief."[69] In other words, cultural, geographic, or religious difference is not an indicator of superiority or inferiority, but should be understood as representative of the diversity of human experience.

Even with these clear challenges to the growing politics of Eurocentrism and white sovereignty marshaled from Stoic corners, we can see that the informal modes of disseminating these arguments often relied on modes of illustration that reinforced these inequalities and were bolstered by rising economic motivations for asserting racial hierarchies as a justification for greater involvement in the global slave trade. As we already have seen with regard to women, the modes of illustration at the disposal of artists, intellectuals, and composers linked to the Stoic tradition still frequently drew upon problematic cultural tropes that reinforced gendered and colonial hierarchies by mapping bestial ignorance and irrationality onto feminized and racialized bodies. For example, in their settings for Pibrac's *Tout l'univers n'est qu'une cité ronde*, Boni (1582), Planson (1583), and Bournonville (1622) each rely on the same stock madrigalism of blackened notation as a visual trope that illustrates the darker skin tone of the Scythian and Moor (for Boni, see Plate 9; for Planson and Bournonville, see Web 6.17 and 6.18).[70]

---

[68] L'Hospital made this point in January 1562 ("Et plusieurs peuvent estre *Cives, qui non erunt Christiani*. Mesmes un excommunié ne laisse pas d'estre citoyen."). Cited in Pibrac, *Les Quatrains*, ed. Petris, 149n10.

[69] Montaigne, *Apology for Raymond Sebond*, II.12; Michel de Montaigne, *The Complete Works: Essays, Travel Journal, Letters*, trans. Donald Frame (New York: A. A. Knopf, 2003), 394. See William Hamlin, "On Continuities between Skepticism and Early Ethnography: Or, Montaigne's Providential Diversity," *Sixteenth Century Journal* 31 (2000): 361–80.

[70] Boni, *Les Quatrains* I.7, mm. 10–12 and 18–19; Planson, *Les Quatrains*, 5. Line 3 is black notes; Bournonville, *Cinquante Quatrains*, 7.

Thus, even as the quatrain explicitly announces the Stoic doctrine of equal global citizenship for these diverse groups, the musical experience of that message undermines its morally transformative power. Not only does the madrigalism exoticize these groups as racial others, but worse yet, the shift to blackened ternary visually and sonically imprints their skin color onto the blindness, ignorance, and irrationality that these black-note groupings so frequently represent throughout the moral song corpus.

This problematic allegorization of racialized blackness as a moral illustration for night or darkness can be seen in Golztius's intricate chiaroscuro woodcut *Nox* (1588–90) and another Golztius design that was engraved by Jan Harmensz. Muller, *The First Day (Dies I)* from *The Creation of the World: The Separation of Light from Darkness* (1589). [Web 6.19 and 6.20] This allegorical link between dark skin and moral corruption or ignorance as a contrast to the white-skinned representation of light, knowledge, and truth proved exceptionally harmful and far-reaching, as Kim Hall's landmark study of premodern critical race studies has demonstrated.[71] Not only did these allegories justify exploitative relations with geographically distant peoples, but they also lubricated the evolving racialization of the Black African population living in Europe, many of whom had musical careers. Recent scholarship on Black musicians in early modern Europe has demanded a greater recognition of their social integration and agency, while also noting the damaging effects of this moralized color symbolism on their social, legal, and professional pathways.[72]

The ancient biblical traditions, writing from warmer climates, had access to a positive analogy for darkness, as a healing and protective shade from the brutal assault of the sun.[73] However, this affirming metaphor of blackness did not gain traction in the pre-modern European tradition. What *was* passed down and circulated widely was the Prophet Jeremiah's analogy—can the Ethiopian change his skin, or the leopard his spots?—echoed in ancient

[71] Kim Hall, *Things of Darkness: Economies of Race and Gender in Early Modern England* (Ithaca, NY: Cornell University Press, 1995), 69.
[72] Emily Wilbourne, "Little Black Giovanni's Dream: Black Authorship and the 'Turks, and Dwarves, the Bad Christians' of the Medici Court," in *Acoustemologies in Contact: Sounding Subjects and Modes of Listening in Early Modernity*, ed. Emily Wilbourne and Suzanne G. Cusick (Cambridge: Open Book Publishers, 2021), 135–66; Arne Spohr, "'Mohr und Trompeter': Blackness and Social Status in Early Modern Germany," *JAMS* 72, no. 3 (2019): 613–29; and Kate Lowe, "The Stereotyping of Black Africans in Renaissance Europe," in *Black Africans in Renaissance Europe*, ed. T. F. Earle and Kate Lowe (Cambridge: Cambridge University Press, 2010), 17–40.
[73] I am grateful to Esther Brownsmith for this observation.

Greek sources such as Aesop's *Fables*.[74] Rousson's preface to his *Recueil de chansons spirituelles* (1621), which included monophonic arrangements for Mathieu's *Tablettes*, also deployed this illustration in warning against forming bad habits for they are as impossible to change "as whitening the skin of a Moor."[75] Emblem books were among the many early modern sources to illustrate this violent and racist tradition. An influential example was Alciato's *Impossible*, which circulated various depictions of a Black man being forcefully restrained and washed by two white figures in a vain effort to lighten his skin.[76] [Web 6.21] The moral lesson, to not attempt an impossible task—which resonated with Epictetus' advice on the importance of understanding what is within and what is outside of human control—thus linked otherwise neutral and practical advice to a persistently racist mode of early modern viewing.

L'Estocart's setting for Pibrac's *Tout l'univers n'est qu'une cité ronde* stands apart from the rest of this racialized artistic corpus. Set in the composer's most comfortable exposition of G Dorian, the opening offers his recognizable move toward wonder at the size of the universe: "tout l'univers" expands from the initial G sonority into his wondrous E♭ sonority and its more expansive sense of the universe. Each of the next two lines repeats a version of this move to E♭, although in these later cases the move is by leap, rather than the normal procedure justifying the flatted 6th degree that is approached by step from the fifth degree and returns to it immediately after (as he models at the opening). His text painting is most interesting in the climactic fourth line that deals with the equal rights of all classes to global citizenship, as it breaks away from the rather repetitive first three phrases into a joyful dotted motive at the "le plus petit," which spreads through the texture and "populates" his setting with the masses of ordinary people. It is notable, considering L'Estocart's general eagerness to utilize black notes as an expressive device, that he is the only *Quatrains* composer to avoid this racialized trope for the Scythian and Moor in line 3. Perhaps he understood the Stoic point of the quatrain best, for the underlying doctrine was about the fundamentally shared humanity and equality of all people, regardless of geographical

---

[74] Jeremiah 13:23; Aesop's *Fable* 361; *Apostolius* 1.71. See Anu Korhonen, "Washing the Ethiopian White: Conceptualising Black Skin in Renaissance England," in *Black Africans in Renaissance Europe*, ed. Earle and Lowe, 94–112.

[75] "C'est un Prophete qui le dit pour nous en advertir, qu'il est autant dificile d'oster une mauvaise accoustumance comme de faire blanchir la peau d'un More." Rousson, *Recueil de chansons spirituelles*, unpaginated preface.

[76] Alciato, *Emblemata / Les emblemes* (1584), fols. 86r–86v.

location, culture, or religion—all endowed with *logos*, and thus full citizens of the world city.

In the visual realm, Werner van den Valckert's *An Allegory of Music* (1625) offers an even more sensitive illustration of the resonant composition of the world city, reflecting a thoughtful engagement with the flourishing of Neostoicism in the Dutch Republic at the time and the exceptionally close relationship between art and philosophy (see Plate 3). Although very little is known about Valckert, scholars agree that he was a student of Goltzius and that his style was influenced by both his teacher and by Rubens.[77] The four singers in the image—all reading from partbooks—are strategically presented with no background context to root them in a particular place. The focal point of the image is the princely Moor, wearing a feathered turban and exotic pearl earrings, whose thoughtful gaze arrests the viewer. Beside him is a bare-breasted woman in the guise of a Muse wearing crystal drop earrings and a vivid flowered garland on her head. The two figures in the foreground represent the contrasts of age, with a curly-headed youth singing cherubically from one side balanced by an old man on the other side of the human lifespan, wearing glasses and struggling to see the pages. This image is striking in the absence of any traditional European figure of virtue: each of these four singers falls outside the long-standing Renaissance ideal of *virtù* as theorized by Machiavelli, due to age, gender, or racialized representation (which could also signal religious difference). Although Valckert heightens the physical and cultural contrasts so often used to stereotype this diverse cast of singers, the artistic genius of the portrait is in the visual harmony and unity that he achieves through these differences, as each singer adds their unique voice—a rational spark of the divine *logos*—to the polyphonic fabric of an interconnected and sympathetic world city.

77 See "Werner van den Valckert, *An Allegory of Music*." http://www.steigrad.com/van-der.

7

Moral Ordering

What follows coheres with what went before.
Not like a random catalogue whose order is
imposed upon it arbitrarily, but logically connected.
And just as what exists is ordered and harmonious, what comes into
being betrays an order too.
Not a mere sequence, but an astonishing concordance.[1]

In 1598, the same year that Henri IV brought a measure of peace to the kingdom with the Edict of Nantes, Claude Le Jeune published his renowned work, the *Dodecacorde, contenant douze Pseaumes de David, mis en musique selon les douze modes*.[2] His dedication to the Duke of Bouillon opens with a vivid expression of hope in music's power to restore harmony after a long period of conflict: "I have thought it appropriate, in a time when so many discords have been resolved, to give the French something to unify tones like thoughts, voices as well as hearts." The preface then goes into some detail about how this unity might be worked out through musical sound, through attention to the ethos of certain modes that can provoke divergent affections:

> If this music is heavy and serious, I supposed that we should be tired of our
> flighty modulations and mutations. It pleases God to use the Dorian Mode
> to extinguish the fury that the Phrygian has aroused, and to be as powerful
> in the effects of my harmony, as Posidonius claims Damon Milezien to have
> been. Other more energetic movements are also necessary, to calm the
> Phrygian furies of the French.[3]

[1] Marcus Aurelius, *Meditations* 4.45; trans. Hays, 47.
[2] Claude Le Jeune, *Dodecacorde, contenant douze Pseaumes de David, mis en musique selon les douze modes* (La Rochelle: Hierosme Haultin, 1598).
[3] For the full text and translation of the preface, see Claude Le Jeune, *Dodecacorde: Comprising Twelve Psalms of David Set to Music According to the Twelve Modes*, ed. Anne Heider (Madison, WI: A-R Editions, 1988), xvi–xvii.

The Voice of Virtue. Melinda Latour, Oxford University Press. © Oxford University Press 2023.
DOI: 10.1093/oso/9780197529744.003.0008

This interest in modal ethos—the notion that the proportions or ratios embedded in different musical octave species could be assigned ethical power—had come down through the Platonic tradition, with numerous theorists commenting upon the moderate nature of Dorian in contrast to the war-like enthusiasm of Phrygian.[4] What is striking in the *Dodecacorde* prefatory discussion is that the ancient authority cited was not the expected Plato, but the Stoic philosopher Posidonius, who studied under Panaetius and was an influential figure in Middle Stoicism during the first century BCE.

Although none of Posidonius' works survive, he was well known to early moderns through direct and indirect citations of his writings in editions of Cicero, Galen, the Stobaeus collection of Stoic writings, Strabo's *Geography*, and Diogenes Laertius' *Lives*. Galen cites Posidonius quite extensively in books IV and V of his *On the Doctrines of Hippocrates and Plato*, where he narrates the tale of Damon and the moderating power of the *aulos* player as part of a larger critique of music's ethical power in light of the classical Stoic theory of the unified, rational soul.[5] As Galen's account makes clear, Posidonius' views came closest to the Platonic position on music and its influence on the soul by framing the ethical force of music as involving both rational and non-rational habituation. The passage from Galen, with its vigorous debate on music's affective and therapeutic powers, suggests the controversial possibility of an embedded ethos specific to certain musical modes that could be exploited to alter the emotional state of a listener. For Stoics like Posidonius, however, music's ethical power was not limited to magical essences or disembodied thought, but, as we will see, could be approached through corporeal, practical, and psychological methods, consistent with the radically interconnected approach of the philosophical system as a whole.[6]

Resonating with these debates, Le Jeune's *Dodecacorde* preface directs the therapeutic possibilities of the modal system toward a social and political notion of harmony and the possibility of concord after discord. Le Jeune's

---

[4] In a particularly famous passage in *Republic* (III, 398c–403c), Plato discusses the Dorian and Phrygian modes for their role in instilling courage, moderation, and self-control. What he meant by these modal terms remains ambiguous. See *Strunk's Source Readings in Music History*, vol. 1, ed. Thomas Mathiesen (New York: W. W. Norton, 1998), 9–19; and Andrew Barker, *Greek Musical Writings*, vol. 1 (Cambridge: Cambridge University Press, 1984), 64n42.

[5] Galen, *De placitis Hippocratis et Platonis*, V 6.16–43; ed. Phillip De Lacy (Berlin: Akademie-Verlag, 1984), 331–35. See Christopher Gill, "Galen and the Stoics: Mortal Enemies or Blood Brothers?" *Phronesis* 52, no. 1 (2007), 88–120.

[6] Sorabji, *Emotion and Peace of Mind*, 95–132; Nussbaum, "Poetry and the Passions," 97–149; and A. G. Long, "Plato, Chrysippus and Posidonius's Theory of Affective Movements," in *From Stoicism to Platonism: The Development of Philosophy, 100 BCE–100 CE*, ed. Troels Engberg-Pedersen (Cambridge: Cambridge University Press, 2017), 27–46.

preface goes on to use tellingly Stoic vocabulary and concepts, characterizing his work as a "music of serious arguments, tones, and measures" and emphasizing the collection's political and moral aim: "that a constant harmony is established in our hearts, and that peace founded on our constancy is a longlasting tranquility."[7] The preface thus not only proposes music as a remedy, but also does so with an explicitly Stoic accent reflective of the dominant interests of Le Jeune's cross-confessional circle.

Le Jeune was closely connected to the high-ranking intellectuals who shaped the Neostoic interests of Henri IV's court. His closest circle of protectors and friends included Agrippa d'Aubigné, the Protestant captain, author of the *Tragiques*, and confirmed Stoic enthusiast, who evidently penned Le Jeune's *Dodecacorde* dedication.[8] Le Jeune was also closely connected to the powerful La Noue family. The Huguenot leader François de La Noue was one of Le Jeune's early protectors, and his son Odet de La Noue, the author of the Stoic-inflected *Paradoxe, que les adversitez sont plus necessaires que les prosperitez* (1588), became one of Le Jeune's closest friends and supporters.

Another of Le Jeune's direct connections to Neostoicism came from his close connection to Guillaume Du Vair, for they were both in service to François, duke d'Anjou in the early 1580s (following their prince to the Low Countries and London during these years). Upon the untimely death of their patron in the debacle of Anvers in 1584, both Le Jeune and Du Vair made their way back to the French court, where they were both prominent figures during the reigns of Henri III and then Henri IV. Lending further credence to a personal connection between the two men, we know that Du Vair was familiar with the musical gatherings hosted by Jean-Antoine de Baïf, where Le Jeune was a participant and collaborator, because Du Vair makes mention of "La Musique de Baïf" in his *De la saincte philosophie*, which was penned before 1585.[9] In explaining the Stoic doctrine that true happiness lies not in pursuing temporary pleasures but in following nature and recovering our right reason, Du Vair cites the example of a deaf person "pushing to gain entrance into Baïf's musical gathering." According to Jean Vignes, this remark suggests that Baïf's musical gatherings were continuing as a private enterprise

---

[7] Le Jeune, *Dodecacorde*, ed. Heider, xvi–xvii.

[8] See His, *Claude Le Jeune*, 67; and Jacques Bailbé, "Agrippa d'Aubigné et le stoïcisme," in *Agrippa d'Aubigné*, ed. Robert Aulotte et al. (Paris: H. Champion, 1995), 3–19.

[9] Du Vair, *Œuvres* (1619), 643.

in the early 1580s, no longer under the official support and regulations of the Académie, which was probably defunct by 1576.[10]

Le Jeune's *Dodecacorde* preface suggests a sensitivity to the rationalizing tendencies guided by Neostoicism, tinged, unsurprisingly, with Skepticism. After bringing up the issue of modal ethos, Le Jeune wisely evades the contentious question of modal nomenclature, in the first place to do away with confusing and ostentatious jargon, and second, because of the "dissension of the ancients and their diversity of opinions": Le Jeune held that he "would rather be their disciple than their judge."[11] Thus, the preface overtly suspends judgment on these speculative questions, suggesting that his detailed discussion of mode was directed toward the larger moral power of modal organization as a symbolic and practical tool, rather than treating modes as fixed essences that could mystically influence human behavior. Richard Freedman has recognized the significance of this shift away from fixed modal essences and toward therapy. In his account, Le Jeune's modal organization offers a means of "spiritual exercise," and Freedman concludes that Le Jeune's "framing system of modality was not so much a set of intrinsic, emotional states as a kind of musical 'grid' on which humanity itself might be oriented."[12] In other words, Le Jeune's mature interest in mode moves away from an enchanted approach to modal ethos and toward a more rational and systematic appreciation of the power of modal ordering as a praxis for the therapeutic cultivation of personal and civic harmony.

The Stoicism accenting Le Jeune's dedication for the *Dodecacorde* offers clear philosophical backing for Freedman's spiritual interpretation. The reference to Posidonius is particularly illuminating considering the stated aim of an alignment between musical and social concord. Based on Strabo's influential account, Posidonius was known as the champion of universal sympathy (*sympatheia*), and was credited with the scientific observation of a sympathetic relationship between the moon and the tides based on this theory.[13] Le Jeune's prefatory comments of an invisible connection between

---

[10] Jean Vignes, "Henri III et Jean-Antoine de Baïf: Mécénat rêvé, mécénat réel," in *Henri III mécène: Des arts, des sciences et des lettres*, ed. Jean-François Maillard and Guy Poirier (Paris: PUPS, 2006), 152–53.

[11] Le Jeune, *Dodecacorde*, ed. Heider, xxivn57.

[12] Richard Freedman, "Le Jeune's *Dodecacorde* as a Site for Spiritual Meanings," *Revue de Musicologie* 89, no. 2 (2003): 305.

[13] Leo Spitzer, *Classical and Christian Ideas of World Harmony: Prolegomena to an Interpretation of the Word "Stimmung"* (Baltimore, MD: The Johns Hopkins Press, 1963), 10; Karl Reinhardt, *Kosmos und Sympathie* (Munich: Beck, 1926), 54; and Bernard Joly, "Stoic Influences on Sixteenth and Seventeenth-Century Theories of Tides," *Revue d'histoire des sciences* 61, no. 2 (2008): 287–311.

voices and hearts that could model a peaceful reharmonization of the French populace thus gain therapeutic specificity through an understanding of the powerful notion of universal sympathy at the core of the harmonious Stoic cosmos. After outlining the legacy of universal sympathy, in this chapter I examine Le Jeune's final collection, the *Octonaires*, through this therapeutic lens. Featuring the same modal organization that he used for his polyphonic Psalms in the *Dodecacorde*, Le Jeune's *Octonaires* take these musical techniques into explicitly philosophical terrain that work out a mode of spiritual exercise resonant with the Stoic connections between a cosmic universal sympathy and a musical mode of self-guided therapy.

Sympathetic Resonance

The Stoics viewed the cosmos as governed by laws that establish a mutual sympathy among all things—described in Diogenes Laertius' account of Stoicism as a universe formed by "the cohesive breath and tension that bind together things in heaven and on earth."[14] As Marcus Aurelius summarized it in *Meditations* 6.38, "Keep reminding yourself of the way things are connected, of their relatedness. All things are implicated in one another and in sympathy with each other. This event is the consequence of some other one. Things push and pull on each other, and breathe together, and are one."[15] He continues on this theme in *Meditations* 7.9:

> Everything is interwoven, and the web is holy; none of its parts are unconnected. They are composed harmoniously, and together they compose the world.
> One world, made up of all things.
> One divinity, present in them all.
> One substance and one law—the logos that all rational beings share.
> And one truth . . .
> If this is indeed the culmination of one process, beings who share the same birth, the same logos.[16]

---

[14] *Lives* 7.140; trans. Mensch, 361.
[15] *Meditations* 6.38; trans. Hays, 77.
[16] *Meditations* 7.9; trans. Hays, 86.

Marcus Aurelius deems this sympathetic interconnection of the cosmos the core substance of universal harmony—a doctrine that for the Stoics bridged physics (how to understand the nature of the cosmos) with ethics (which seeks to understand how to live in harmony with that cosmic principle and at the same time live in a proper relationship with other humans). This notion of Stoic universal sympathy was embedded in the broader notion of universal harmony grounded in the Platonic/Pythagorean lineage and narrated in Cicero's *Dream of Scipio*. The Stoic dictum of living in harmony with nature, as A. A. Long and Paul Scade have amply demonstrated, was based on this musical analogy—fundamentally rooted in a musical language of ratio and proportions and the sonic relationship of an individual musical part that is well tuned to the whole.[17]

The Stoic notion of universal sympathy, like the related notions of harmony and concord, also tapped into the metaphorical riches of commonplace musical experience, in this case through reference to sympathetic resonance, a scientifically demonstrated phenomenon based in nature. Sympathetic resonance is heard when the vibrations of one sounding object set another object into vibration, such as wine glasses that might dance, hum, or even explode when a certain pitch is sounded at the right frequency. The ethical implications of this harmonic phenomenon became a point of interest in the emblem literature of the period.[18] Although the classic example today is of two tuning forks, the most common illustration of sympathetic resonance for early moderns was a pair of stringed instruments, with the passive instrument vibrating in response to the nearby instrument that is being played. Jacob Cats, a Protestant jurist and known friend of Neostoicism, produced a trilingual emblem book, *Silenus Alcibiadis* (1618), that became a beloved example of the genre. The *pictura* for his emblem *What does Love not Sense* featured the sympathetic resonance of a pair of lutes, one being tuned by a man seated at a table and another resting on the table.[19] [Web 7.1] Other examples, such as Camillo Camilli's *Imprese Illustri di Diversi* (Venice, 1586), offered an emblem with the motto *Aliis pulsis resonabunt* [As others are struck, they will resound] appearing in rippling waves over two liras da braccio. The instrument on the right has a bow touching the strings, while

---

[17] A. A. Long, *Stoic Studies*, 202–21; and Paul Scade, "Music and the Soul in Stoicism," 197–218.

[18] Calogero, *Ideas and Images of Music*, 150–68; and María Paz López-Peláez Casellas, "'No la una sin las dos': Sympathetic Vibration in Emblem Treatises," *Music in Art* 35 (2010): 145–56.

[19] Jacob Cats, *Silenus Alcibiadis, sive Proteus, vitae humanae ideam, emblemate trifariàm variato, oculis subijciens* (Middleburg: Johannis Hellenii, 1618), 84–85.

the one on the left is responding "due to sympathy, which acts in a marvelous way over things."[20] The image of these instruments added richness and possibility to the moral and spiritual image because each lira da braccio appeared to have its own internal sympathetic possibilities through the auxiliary string built into the instrument. Through the same principle of sympathetic vibration, the auxiliary strings added to various types of viols could sound without needing to be touched, an effect that could only be produced through proper tuning between the primary and resonating strings, as Michael Praetorius was careful to remind his readers in the *Syntagma musicum*.[21]

The rich implications of tuning as a sensorial and moral process became a point of focus in emblems dedicated to the five senses created throughout the sixteenth and seventeenth centuries and under explicit scrutiny in the debates over sense perception and knowledge discussed in the previous chapter. In the standard iconographic formula, each sense (sight, hearing, taste, smell, touch) was personified by a woman and a representative animal. The series produced by Cornelis Cort (1561) after designs by Frans Floris portrays Hearing (*Auditus*) as a woman playing the lute, surrounded by numerous other instruments and several open music books. [Web 7.2] Beside her is a deer, which was associated with the virtue of prudence because of its extraordinary sense of hearing. The deer's head is turned toward the woman, its ears perked attentively as she tunes her lute. This careful act of tuning, which demanded both skill and finesse, beautifully mirrors the contemplative process of tuning the inner soul, understood in both the Platonic and Aristotelian traditions as a harmonizing of the rational and irrational faculties.

Stoics and Neostoics also harnessed this metaphor of tuning as the process of harmonizing the leading part of the soul according to the just proportions of reason. Connected to their notion of the soul as a breath (*pneuma*), the Stoics described the soul in varying degrees of vibrating tension that could be tuned like the strings of a musical instrument. Chrysippus called this proper tension in the soul *eutonia*, which the Stoic Hierocles defined as the mark of a "well-tempered" person.[22] A sentence attributed to Diogenes and included in abundant collections of *Apophthegmata* from the period (including editions

---

[20] Camillo Camilli, *Imprese illustri di diversi* (Venice: Francesco Ziletti, 1586). Cited and translated in Casellas, "'No la una sin las dos': Sympathetic Vibration," 152.

[21] Michael Praetorius, *The Syntagma Musicum*, ed. H. Blumenfeld (New York: Da Capo, 1980), 47–48.

[22] Stobaeus IV, 672; cited in A. A. Long, *Stoic Studies*, 212.

by Erasmus and Jean Luis Vives, for example) circulated the Stoic position. As one French version explained this Stoic sentence, "It is a great folly of those who tune the notes of a wooden psaltery, and yet do not tune their mind, which in this moral body is to live according to reason."[23] Mornay's *Excellent discours* used this metaphor in his distinction between head knowledge and embodied wisdom, deploying the sensory act of tuning the voice, sounds, and tones with the internal work of harmonizing the passions through an aurality governed by reason.

These analogies of tuning a single instrument were thus embedded within the more complex analogy of sympathetic resonance, where each instrument generates its own sympathetic possibilities. The work of tuning and the possibilities of resonant concord and harmony operated through multiple ethical vectors. At its most personal, this careful tuning and consequent sympathy aligned the individual as a psychosomatic unity, honoring and fulfilling the logic of the divine *logos*. However, these musical metaphors were also extended externally to model the proper relationships of individuals with each other, as a properly tuned, just, and harmonious human community—as we see in emblems like Alciato's *Alliances*, where the properly tuned strings of the lute represent political concord and harmony.[24] [Web 7.3] Ménestrier's *L'Art des emblemes* (1652) puts the sympathetic resonance of the lute to this ethical use: "A lute player, who in plucking one string, sounds another that is on the neighboring table," offers a physical exemplar of a person who takes into consideration the interests of her friend.[25] Hans Holbein the Younger's extraordinary painting, *The Ambassadors* (1533) relies upon this fundamental image of the lute as social concord. [Web 7.4] An artist living in Basel and connected to Erasmus during the period of his editing Seneca, Holbein's painting displays distinctly Stoic overtones that will be explored further in the following chapter. The visually distorted skull at the foot of the painting—a *memento mori* symbol that only comes into clarity with a shift of perspective—draws acute attention to the problem of visual sense deception. Calling up the related problem of sonic decay, the broken string offers a reminder of the fragility and vanity of diplomacy, and when read against the globe with Africa prominently displayed, casts doubt on the legitimacy of empire-building.

---

[23] Charles Fontaine, *Les Dicts des sept sages* (Lyon: Jean Citoys, 1557), 38.
[24] Alciato, *Emblemata / Les emblemes* (1584), fols. 15v–16r; and Zecher, *Sounding Objects*, 94–103.
[25] Ménestrier, *L'Art des emblemes*, 123.

For the Stoics, the images and concepts of harmony and sympathy linked physics directly to ethics, for their rigorous doctrine of personal self-reliance was always held in a delicate tension with the reminder of the unbreakable links connecting every individual across the world city. The language of sympathy was both an appeal to the fabric of the universe and a reminder that humans were social beings, made for a mutually beneficial relationship, which implied a duty to seek justice and avoid harming ourselves or others. Marcus Aurelius clarified this connection in *Meditations* 9.1: "Injustice is impiety. For in that the Nature of the Universe has fashioned rational creatures for the sake of one another." Sympathy, symphonia, and concord were thus complementary ways of musically illuminating the relationship between distinctive individuals within a cohesive whole—a philosophical vision that we have already seen portrayed exquisitely in the harmonious diversity of singers cast in Valckert's *An Allegory of Music* (1625) (see Plate 3).

Modal Ordering

The growing sixteenth-century impulse toward modal organization likewise resonates with these philosophical concerns, foregrounding the musical relationships of parts to wholes via a systematic progression through all possible octave species.[26] Polyphonic collections like Le Jeune's *Dodecacorde*, which paired self-conscious modal organization with an interest in moral repair, offers compelling ground for probing the possibilities of modal organization as a site of spiritual meaning and mode of self-guided therapeutic exercise. Before delving into Le Jeune's mature work, it is crucial to sketch briefly the problematic historiography of applying modal theory to the polyphonic repertoire.

The medieval 8-mode system had developed as a practical tool for organizing plainchant; thus the application of modal categories to the multiple lines of polyphonic music posed abundant problems that

[26] On the editorial penchant for modal organization, see, for example, Howard Mayer Brown, "Theory and Practice in the Sixteenth Century: Preliminary Notes on Attaingnant's Modally Ordered Chansonniers," in *Essays in Musicology: A Tribute to Alvin Johnson*, ed. Lewis Lockwood and Edward Roesner, 75–100 (Philadelphia: American Musicological Society, 1990); Stanley Boorman, *Studies in the Printing, Publishing and Performance of Music in the 16th Century* (Aldershot: Ashgate, 2005), 426; and Jane Bernstein, *Print Culture and Music in Sixteenth-Century Venice* (New York: Oxford University Press, 2001), 152.

sixteenth-century theorists sought to solve.[27] Pietro Aaron's treatise *Trattato della natura et cognitione di tutti gli tuoni di canto figurato* (1525) represented a novel effort to reconcile the framework of traditional 8-mode theory with contemporary polyphonic composition, for he was the first theorist to attempt to apply modal categories to the existing polyphonic repertoire. Heinrich Glarean's *Dodecachordon* (Basel, 1547) took Aaron's work further, offering a novel attempt to rationalize the problematic aspects of the modal system by appealing to the universal, logical principles founded in nature and embedded in the ratios of Pythagorean mathematics. Glarean's explicitly humanist project was inflected with a clear Stoic bent, no doubt shaped by his deep friendship with Erasmus in Basel and encouraged by his reliance on music theorists like Ptolemy, whose *Harmonics* is laced with Stoicism.[28] Ptolemy influenced Boethius, another prominent early music theorist who borrowed extensively from the Stoic tradition (a borrowing primarily felt in his *Consolation of Philosophy* but also had echoes in his *De musica*).[29] Although grounded in Pythagorean and Platonic cosmologies, Ptolemy and his followers reveal their Stoic influences in their stress on the importance of critical sense perception, their assertion of the interconnected rational universe (which is radically knowable and thus, crucially, capable of being studied and experienced empirically and scientifically), and their use of vocabulary and concepts borrowed from Stoic cognition and moral psychology.

Guided by this nascent systematizing impulse already present in music treatises, Glarean's project further rationalized modal theory by expanding the system to include twelve modes, thus transforming the misbehaving irregular finals A and C into proper modal subjects within a newly recognized 12-mode system. Importantly, Glarean's scientific and critical approach was not pure theory; rather, he sought to demonstrate that the fundamental principles of his rational organizational system were drawn from antiquity and were already in use in the existing polyphonic repertoire—a move that strategically recognized church authority by citing actual polyphonic music prints and classifying them according to his new modal system.[30] After the

---

[27] Cristle Collins Judd, *Reading Renaissance Music Theory: Hearing with the Eyes* (Cambridge: Cambridge University Press, 2000), 37–73.

[28] A. A. Long, *Stoic Studies*, 219; and Andrew Barker, *Greek Musical Writings*, vol. 2 (Cambridge: Cambridge University Press, 1989), 375. See also Iain Fenlon and Inga Mai Groote, eds., *Heinrich Glarean's Books: The Intellectual World of a Sixteenth-Century Musical Humanist* (Cambridge: Cambridge University Press, 2013).

[29] Colish, *The Stoic Tradition*, 2:280–90.

[30] Judd, *Reading Renaissance Music Theory*, 120–88; and Sarah Fuller, "Defending the *Dodecachordon*: Ideological Currents in Glarean's Modal Theory," *JAMS* 49, no. 2 (1996): 194–204.

publication of Gioseffo Zarlino's *Istitutioni harmoniche* (1558), composers and editors had another humanist 12-mode system at their disposal, one that built upon Glarean's model but altered the order in the revised and expanded 1573 edition to begin on the C modes.

Even as these theoretical publications offered new expressive guidelines recommending mode as a coherent compositional strategy, the degree to which modal theory actually drove the pitch organization of music in the later sixteenth century must be ascertained on a case-by-case basis, for mode was not the only organizing framework in the compositional toolbox. The modal organization of Boni's collections, for example, makes more sense when viewed in light of the looser categorization by tonal types (grouped by the system, cleffing, and final of the piece) as a way to structure a large-scale collection for practical use.[31] In the "Avertissement" for Boni's *Quatrains*, the publisher Adrian Le Roy boasts of the collection's elaborate modal organization, carefully explaining the system of groupings according to mode and vocal scoring as a pragmatic system designed to make the collection easier to use for singers. Boni's interest in modal organization was not limited to practical concerns—as his *Quatrains* might suggest. Jeanice Brooks has revealed that Boni's interest in modal organization was not only a longer pursuit, spanning several publishers (Du Chemin and Le Roy et Ballard) and multiple large-scale collections, but that, like Antoine de Bertrand, he was interested in using modal organization to support a textual narrative.[32] Even so, Boni's inconsistent approach to modal criteria at the level of individual settings suggests that his internal compositional choices were probably directed by older contrapuntal processes, rather than based on the newer systematic modal composition outlined by the theorists.

L'Estocart, by contrast, showed little interest in modal theory or its large-scale organizing potential. Almost half of his settings were composed within the basic parameters of G Dorian—the most commonplace and straightforward of the modes—and, as such, corresponded largely by default to the theoretical criteria agreed upon for that mode. However, when L'Estocart does

[31] See Harold Powers, "Tonal Types and Modal Categories in Renaissance Polyphony," *JAMS* 34 (1981): 435–39; and Harold Powers, "Is Mode Real? Pietro Aron, the Octenary System, and Polyphony," in *Musical Theory in the Renaissance*, ed. Cristle Collins Judd (Farnham, UK: Ashgate, 2013), 9–52.

[32] Brooks, "Music and Devotion in Renaissance Toulouse," 17–32; cf. Van Orden, *Materialities*, 250–55. For Bertrand's modal ordering, see Jeanice Brooks, "'Ses amours et les miennes tout ensemble': La structure cyclique du Premier Livre d'Anthoine de Bertrand," *Revue de Musicologie* 74, no. 2 (1988): 201–20.

diverge from this comfort zone of G Dorian, his writing rarely maps clearly onto other modal categories. Several of his *Octonaires* settings (e.g., II.1 and II.9) seem to be composed entirely outside the modal system, in a similar vein as Cipriano de Rore's later, non-modal madrigals analyzed by Jessie Anne Owens.[33] Overall, L'Estocart's style can best be understood as the result of both traditional and experimental contrapuntal and harmonic procedures, founded on basic modal assumptions, yet beginning to display an interest in long-range techniques of tonal expectation, as Megan Kaes Long illuminates, in the related homophonic repertoires gaining traction across Europe in these decades around 1600.[34]

By the end of the sixteenth century, however, there was growing evidence that more composers had begun to explicitly experiment with either the new 12-mode system advocated by Glarean, or with the traditional 8-mode system—not only composing cycles externally organized by modal criteria at the outset, but also internally composed and featuring the unique possibilities and problems inherent in each mode.[35] Although Le Jeune's posthumous *Airs* (1608) suggests a case of modal organization that was more likely a post-compositional editorial decision, his two finest collections, the *Dodecacorde* and the *Octonaires*, both offer solid evidence that the composer used modal theory as a compositional guide in crafting an internally coherent exposition of each of the twelve modes encountered systematically through the collection.

Although the title for the *Dodecacorde* certainly aligns the work with Glarean's project, Le Jeune's choice to begin his modal collection with the transposed C modes (Ionian) reveals that Zarlino's 1573 *Istitutioni* was his most direct model.[36] Le Jeune generally follows Zarlino quite clearly, as seen in his choices of octave species, final, ambitus, and cadences for each of

---

[33] Jessie Anne Owens, "Mode in the Madrigals of Cipriano di Rore," in *Essays on Italian Music in the Cinquecento*, ed. Richard Charteris (Sydney: Frederick May Foundation for Italian Studies, University of Sydney, 1990), 1–15.

[34] On linear versus vertical modes of composition, see Jessie Ann Owens, *Composers at Work: The Craft of Musical Composition 1450–1600* (New York: Oxford University Press, 1997); and Megan Kaes Long, *Hearing Homophony: Tonal Expectation at the Turn of the Seventeenth Century* (New York: Oxford University Press, 2020), 3–17.

[35] This later repertoire offers the strongest justification for the kind of modal analysis undertaken by Susan McClary in *Modal Subjectivities: Self-fashioning in the Italian Madrigal* (Berkeley, CA: University of California Press, 2004), 194–200, an approach spearheaded by Bernhard Meier's landmark study, *The Modes of Classical Polyphony*, trans. Ellen S. Beebe (New York: Broude Brothers, 1988).

[36] Le Jeune, *Dodecacorde*, ed. Heider, xiv–xvi; and Jessica Herdman, "Zarlinian Modality in Claude Le Jeune's Dodecacorde," *Musicological Explorations* 10 (2009): 33–71.

Zarlino's modes. Furthermore, in his *Dodecacorde*, Le Jeune displays an effort to match Psalm texts to their corresponding modal ethos, as he discusses in his dedication. His choice of Psalter tune further reveals his interest in matching the text to the ethos of a particular mode. Zarlino advocated the idea of modal ethos and described the E modes as fitting for laments or sorrowful texts. Out of the five possible Psalter tunes in the fifth mode, Le Jeune chose the only text that conforms to Zarlino's recommendation. Even more importantly, Le Jeune revised the fourth and fifth phrases of the Psalter tune for Psalm 102—an unprecedented move in the large body of monophonic and polyphonic Psalm settings in the sixteenth century—to illustrate better Zarlino's profile of Phrygian.[37] He altered the Psalm tune from an ambitus of E–C (with most cadence points on A) to a perfect authentic ambitus of E–E (with cadential tones that support cadences on E and G). In other words, Le Jeune brought the rationalizing project of Glarean to its musical conclusion, with a composer crafting a collection according to the ordered logic of the extended modal system. Mode, in Le Jeune's case, was not only "real," but also pragmatic, rational, and scientific, and we will see that his approach to modal affect was grounded in the fundamental musical structures and harmonic implications posed by each octave species.

Modality in Le Jeune's *Octonaires*

Le Jeune's polyphonic collection of *Octonaires* contains thirty-six settings of texts by Chandieu, Goulart, and Du Chesne, organized according to the same modal plan as his earlier *Dodecacorde*. Le Jeune based this system on Zarlino's but used transposed versions of the first four modes, beginning from F Ionian and F Hypoionian and working his way to the eleventh and twelfth A modes of Aeolian and Hypoaeolian. Le Jeune set three pieces for each authentic and plagal mode. The first two settings in each group were scored for four voices, with the third setting always scored for three voices. This strategy of closing each group with a reduction in voices goes against the more typical pattern of moving from smaller to more elaborate, larger scorings, and it suggests the philosophical culture of preferring a rhetorical process of concision and condensation over one of accumulation.

Because Le Jeune passed away before publishing his *Octonaires*, we have no additional prefatory writings that might have further explained

---

[37] Freedman, "Le Jeune's Dodecacorde," 300.

his interest in Stoic music therapeutics. His choice of texts and his organizational and compositional choices, however, reveal a growing experimentation with the philosophical potential of modal theory and its exploration of physical, human, and musical relationships within larger ordered wholes. Continuing the pattern begun in his *Dodecacorde*, Le Jeune's *Octonaires* reveal modal theory as the driving logic in the composition and organization of the settings. A significant difference between these two late collections was that Le Jeune's *Octonaires* incorporated no preexisting musical material. The Geneva Psalm tunes that he had used as slow-moving cantus firmi in the *Dodecacorde* anchored the collection in a certain metrical and modal continuity. The *Octonaires* had no such grounding, and thus allowed Le Jeune greater freedom to experiment with rhythm, texture, and mode.

Le Jeune does not follow any of the prior orderings for Chandieu's *Octonaires*, although there had long been a standard ordering by that point. He also intermingles texts by Goulart and Du Chesne throughout the collection, rather than bracketing them off as a discrete group, as L'Estocart's multiauthored second collection had modeled (see Appendix 2, Tables A2.1 and A2.3). In her pioneering monograph on the composer, Isabelle His proposed that Le Jeune's *Octonaires* do not attempt to organize the texts according to the "ethos" of each mode. In her view, although the moral groupings establish a musical relationship among the poems included in each mode, each setting should be viewed as independent and the groupings as arbitrary. Freedman has also viewed the *Octonaires* texts as topically homogenous, and thus unable to support a reading of modal ethos based on different emotional characteristics communicated by individual texts.[38]

My analysis of the modal organization in Le Jeune's *Octonaires* through the remainder of this chapter diverges from these earlier views on several key points. Although I agree that the *Octonaires* offers a topically cohesive collection of *vanitas* texts, Le Jeune's modal groupings reveal a deeper understanding of the distinct philosophical concepts and imagery underpinning the poetry, guided at least in part by Stoicism. This more nuanced appreciation of the diversity of moral and illustrative content embedded in these texts also opens a related point of divergence from earlier scholarship on the *Octonaires*, for there is evidence of Le Jeune's continued interest in modal ethos, at least to the same limited degree that we saw in the *Dodecacorde*,

---

[38] His, *Claude Le Jeune*, 98; and Freedman, "Le Jeune's *Dodecacorde*," 305.

where again it is mostly visible in the texts chosen for the unstable and conflicted Phrygian mode.

Recognizing this innovative arrangement of the collection strengthens Freedman's notion of the modal system offering singers a form of spiritual exercise—particularly when read in light of the Neostoicism of Le Jeune's circle. Le Jeune's selection and organization of *Octonaires* texts guide the singer through a loose philosophical sweep in the shape of a large U that charts a course through the three interconnected fields of Stoic philosophy (logic, physics, and ethics). The rational and systematic modal organization of the collection as a whole represents the domain of logic and the foundational importance of the harmonic system as a model of the ordered proportions of the universe. The oft-cited Stoic metaphor of harmony possessing "all the numbers of virtue," as well as numerous references to principles of music theory (and the internal relationships of the diapason), resonates particularly well with the post-Glarean, rationalized twelve-mode system, which progressively works its way through all of the possible combinations of octave species, with their unique internal species of fourth and fifth, known to set up different types of harmonic possibilities, ambiguities, and tensions. The content of the collection, however, engages predominantly with Stoic physics and ethics. Modes 1–3 (Physics) begin the collection in the cosmos, building up a picture of the divine universe, the elements, and God. The central modes, 4–10 (Ethics), move the focus downward to earth, focusing on the constant inconstancy of the natural and human world. The final modes, 11–12 synthesize the major themes of the collection and slowly return the focus again to a bird's-eye perspective of the universe, closing modes 11 and 12 with prayers to God for assistance in living a life of constancy.

The subtle arc of this collection, moving from a view of the cosmos down to a consideration of the gritty conflicts of human endeavors and activities, and finally back up to the heavens, offers the singer a dual philosophical benefit. In the first place, Le Jeune's insightful organization leads the singer logically through the major doctrines and problems of Neostoicism highlighted in scattered form across the broader textual corpus. Even more importantly, Le Jeune's ordering of the collection—both philosophically and modally—leads singers through the gradual shifting of perspective of the "view from above."[39] Such changes in perspective—both zooming out to view the

---

[39] For an introduction to this Stoic exercise, see Chapters 1 and 2 of this volume; Hadot, *Philosophy as a Way of Life*, 238–50; and Robertson, *The Philosophy of Cognitive-Behavioural Therapy*, 210–18.

cosmos and then looking back down to earth—are a way to gain critical understanding of the value, nature, and significance of all earthly goals, problems, and legacies. Built upon the Platonic foundation of the harmony of the spheres, this Stoic exercise ultimately offers a rational mechanism for treating destructive passions through the power of an altered perspective that progressively undermines the ambition, avarice, and excess that are the sources of internal and external conflict.

Modes 1–3: Physics

Le Jeune's first mode, F Ionian, establishes a vision of the cosmos that begins with *Quand on arrestera* (I.1), describing the relentless inconstancy of the universe as a site of moral contemplation. [Web 7.5] This first setting reveals why Le Jeune's collection became a textbook of modal composition, for it crafts a melodic contour that perfectly outlines the octave species for F Ionian (F–C–F), with the high voice outlining the F–C diapente in the opening measures by first skipping downward through the fifth and then filling it in to clarify the species of fifth, followed by a leap contouring the C–F diatessaron, which then is filled in (see Example 7.1).[40] In addition to landing on the appropriate final of F at the close of the setting, the internal cadences fall on the expected resting points of F and C. After this extremely stable approach to mode in the first setting, Le Jeune takes advantage of the broader possibilities of F Ionian in *Qui ne s'esbahira* (I.2). [Web 7.6] While the initial melodic contours still carve out the expected species of fifth and fourth in the top voice, the entrance of the two lower voices in homophony with F-sharps signed into the opening phrase complicates the modal profile at the outset and prepares a fuller set of possible cadence points for this mode, including A and D as well as C and F.[41] This text stresses the act of lifting one's eyes to the cosmos ("levant en haut ses yeux") and seeing the constant inconstancy of the path of the stars ("voyant l'ordre . . . ") as a way to properly understand the course of life on this earth. Le Jeune emphasizes this relationship between

---

[40] Claude Le Jeune, *Octonaires de la vanité et inconstance du monde (I–VIII)*, ed. Henry Expert (Paris: Senart, 1924), 1–5.

[41] Le Jeune, *Octonaires (I–VIII)*, ed. Expert, 6–10. Although the D cadences would be irregular according to Zarlino, some theorists, like Pietro Cerone and Johannes Andreas Herbst, included A as a possible cadence point for a transposed Ionian mode. See Ann Smith, *The Performance of 16th-Century Music: Learning from the Theorists* (New York: Oxford University Press, 2011), 223.

Example 7.1 Claude Le Jeune, *Quand on arrestera*, mm. 1–4, in *Octonaires de la vanité et inconstance du monde* (Paris: Pierre Ballard, 1606). Based on the edition by Henry Expert

restriction and expansion musically by using cycle-of-fifths motion at "inconstant" and "sans repos" to explore more chromatic territory—an effect that is particularly remarkable when encountered after the narrow modal exposition given in the opening setting (see Example 7.2).

Although the first two settings retain the ordering standardized in the 1583 edition, Le Jeune inserts *Plustost on pourra faire*, which was number 29 in the 1583 edition, into the third position to round off this modal group. Like the first two texts, *Plustost on pourra faire* addresses questions of physics, which, importantly, include both the working of nature and theological questions of God.[42] [Web 7.7] Chandieu's text uses elemental contrasts—between day and night, between fire and water—to reject the notion that God could be joined with the world in the closing phrase ("Que de conjoindre Dieu / Avec le monde"). This text, playing on the folly trope of the world upside-down (*Plustost que . . .*), offers an important critique of classical Stoic physics that was widely asserted in treatises by Neostoics defending themselves against the potentially heretical aspects of Stoicism. The closing couplet of Le Jeune's previous Octonaire, *Qui ne s'esbahira* (I.2), had asserted a belief in a better life after death, and this third text confronts the other most important point rehearsed by Neostoics: the explicit denial of pantheism that the Stoic slippage between God, Nature, Fate, and Reason might suggest.

---

[42] Le Jeune, *Octonaires (I–VIII)*, ed. Expert, 11–13.

Example 7.2 Claude Le Jeune, *Qui ne s'esbahira*, mm. 27–38, in *Octonaires de la vanité et inconstance du monde* (Paris: Pierre Ballard, 1606). Based on the edition by Henry Expert

Importantly, as we will discuss below, Stoic theology is not pantheistic in the way most people would define it today. Their theology was quite ambiguous and is best understood as falling somewhere between a pantheistic and a Christian position on God and nature. Diogenes Laertius' account of Stoic physics reveals the potential confusion (and opportunity). After defining the cosmos as God himself, he explains "that the cosmos is a living being, rational, endowed with a soul, and intelligent. . . . And it is endowed with a soul, as is clear from the fact that each of our souls is a fragment of it." The passage continues on to describe the Stoic view of God in personal terms that bear a striking resemblance to the Judeo-Christian notion of deity: "God is a living being, immortal, rational, perfect in happiness, immune to anything bad, exercising forethought for the cosmos and all it contains. But he is not of human shape. He is the craftsman of the universe and, as it were, the father of all things."[43] Of course, the account becomes problematic for a Christian audience again when noting that God "pervades everything." Bringing these later readers back to safer ground, Diogenes clarifies that the Stoics considered God to be one being—although called by many names (such as Zeus, Athena, Hera, Poseidon, etc.)—an interesting nod toward monotheism, considering that traditional Greek mythology portrayed all these deities as fully independent entities.

The second modal group, F Hypoionian, continues the focus on physics, this time with a consideration of the elements, beginning with Chandieu's *Le feu, l'air, l'eau, la terre.*

> Le Feu, l'Air, l'Eau, la Terre ont tousjours changement,
> Tournant et retournant l'un à l'autre element.
> L'Eternel a voulu ce bas Monde ainsi faire
> Par l'accordant discord de l'element contraire,
> Pour monstrer que tu dois ta felicité querre
> Ailleurs qu'au Feu, qu'en l'Air, qu'en l'Eau et qu'en la Terre
> Et que le vray repos est un plus haut lieu
> Que la Terre, que l'Eau, qu l'Air et que le Feu.

[Fire, Air, Water, and Earth are always changing, / Turning and returning from one to another element. / The Eternal wanted this base World to do

---

[43] *Lives* 7.142–7; trans. Mensch, 363–64.

so, / By the accordant discord of contrary elements, / To show that you must
seek your happiness / Elsewhere than in Fire, Air, Water, and on Earth, /
And that true repose is found in a higher place / Than Earth, Water, Air,
and Fire.]

Although these themes of cosmic inconstancy and changeability
circulated influentially in Platonism, they go back even further to the
pre-Socratic Heraclitus, who proposed the continuous transformation
among all four elements (as opposed to Plato's view that only three of
the elements change, while the earth remains stable). The Stoics drew
their fundamental cosmology from Heraclitus in framing their interest
in inconstancy and quad-elemental transformation. In fact, Chandieu's
text could have been drawn directly from Diogenes Laertius' detailed
account of Stoic physics in *Lives* 7.142. The Stoics say, "the cosmos is
created when the substance is transformed from fire through air into
moisture, and then the dense part of the moisture congeals and becomes
earth, while the fine part becomes air, which, when further rarefied,
generates fire."[44]

Le Jeune's *Le feu, l'air, l'eau, la terre* (II.1) offers a delightful musical view of
the transformation of the elements.[45] [Web 7.8] Again, this first setting in the
mode offers a very clear modal exposition of F Hypoionian. Opening with
the top voice singing "le feu" on a solo C, this voice is then joined by the next
lower voice, which adds an F (quickly carving out the F–C upper diapente,
harmonically) before adding the next lower voice at "l'eau" and then adding
the bottom voice for a full homophonic statement of "la terre." This downward trajectory is then immediately reversed as the elements are described as
always changing ("ont toujours changement"). As is the norm for Le Jeune,
the tenor and soprano are the clearest mode-bearing voices, both marking
out the C–F–C octave species at the outset and generally providing the
strong, stepwise descent through the fifth or fourth in one of these voices
moving toward final cadence. These melodic contours set up predictable cadence points arriving on C and F, and in most cases clearly mark the breaks
in the poetic line. This balanced phrasing allows the image of the downward
and upward trajectories of the elemental transformations to stand out in the
homophonic texture. The final repeat of the closing line suggests a change

---

[44] *Lives* 7.142, trans. Mensch, 362.
[45] Le Jeune, *Octonaires (I–VIII)*, ed. Expert, 14–18.

in directionality as Chandieu's text inverts the order of the elements—from the ground up: from earth, to water, to air, to fire. Le Jeune picks up this contrast at the structural level, closing the final phrase with a similar treatment as his opening, but this time moving in all voices upward until the final arrival on fire. At the center of these contrary transformations, the most memorable moment of Le Jeune's setting arrives with the vivid text painting of "accordant discord," where he offers a chain of first-inversion triads in the old fauxbourdon style of the fifteenth century, which by this point was heard as a strangely harsh harmonization.

This musical description of the cosmos as built upon a harmony of discordant elements was cited critically in Plato's *Symposium* 187: "perhaps Heraclitus intends as much by those perplexing words, 'The One at variance with itself is drawn together, like harmony of bow or lyre.' Now it is perfectly absurd to speak of a harmony at variance, or as formed from things still varying." The singers and hearers of the *Octonaires* would probably have also known Diogenes Laertius' summary of Heraclitus' philosophy in *Lives* 9.8–9, which ties his foundational concept of the harmony of opposites together with his elemental transformation theory.

The Stoics, who, as we have seen, fully embraced contradiction and paradox as a productive tension, borrowed extensively from Heraclitus, including this notion of accordant discord. Cleanthes' famous *Hymn to Zeus*, known to early moderns through the Stobaeus anthology, also famously framed this harmony of opposites: "You [Zeus] know how to make the crooked straight, to give order to the disorderly . . . for thus you have harmonised everything into one, good with bad, so that a single everlasting *logos* of everything is achieved."[46] What Cleanthes is doing seems more figurative (evaluative) than an actual quantitative order, and communicates a vision of a balanced and proportional cosmos. Again, we can see how the Stoics framed much of their philosophy with contradictory dualities; however, the two parts are not severed; rather, they are always held together as a unified tension, as disparate elements that form a harmonious whole.

This fundamental Heraclitean union—found in the changing elements, the harmony of opposites, and the constantly inconstant movement of water—offered a stream of moral imagery borrowed extensively across the Stoic tradition. The next two settings in Le Jeune's second mode—*Y a il rien si*

---

[46] Cited in A. A. Long, *Stoic Studies*, 207.

fort (II.2) and *Le beau du monde s'efface* (II.3)—continue the focus on three of the elements: water ("le flot de la mer" II.2, "une onde fuit" II.3); air ("les vens tourmenté" II.2; "le vent qui passe" II.3); and earth ("le sable aresté" II.2; "la fleur" II.3). The elements here provoke a comparison of earthly natural forces as visions of transience and as warnings against the force of human desire and uncontrolled passions. Flowing out of these images, water becomes the binding image of Le Jeune's third mode, G Dorian, the most commonplace mode of the period, and a case where the transposed mode was used more frequently than the original. The opening setting of this group, Chandieu's *Comme de l'Aigle* (III.1), begins in the air, but follows the eagle swooping down to earth on the air currents to view the ship on the water, carried along by the wind. The following two texts, also by Chandieu, *L'eau va viste* (III.2) and *Vous fleuves et ruisseaux* (III.3), further develop the water analogy as a warning against looking for happiness in unpredictable and fleeting worldly joys, which can disappear without a trace.

Modes 4–8: Ethics

In Mode 4, G Hypodorian, the texts dive down, away from physics and the cosmos, to plunge into the grittier, ethical topics of human greed, ambition, folly, and the intoxication of the senses that comes from an attachment to the world. In a clear exposition of Stoic ethics, the texts here—all by Chandieu—demonstrate the principle that our desires are at the root of our troubles, and that pleasure and pain, sweetness and bitterness are always tied together. This was the progression of the *Dream of Scipio*, in which, after looking at the cosmos and hearing the stunning harmony of the spheres, Scipio Africanus directs his grandson to consider the folly of human ambition and the incessant fighting from high above, with earth seen as a mere point in space. That discussion leads to an important "Where are they now" passage, and a strong warning against the futility of empire-building and glory—because, after all, everything ends in ruins, dust, and smoke.

It is here in the "ruins" texts, set in the fifth mode (E Phrygian), that we see the clearest indication that Le Jeune was still interested in modal ethos in his choice of texts for each mode, for this group of texts—the outer two by Simon Goulart and one by Chandieu—warn against the pride of human achievement and the ambition of empire-building, the root causes of war and strife. As Goulart's text *Mon ame, où sont les grand discours* (V.1), set as the opener for this modal group, puts it, "Where are the magnificent courts / Of Kings who waged war against heaven?" (*Ou sont les magnifiques cours / Des Rois qui au ciel ont fait guerre?*) This text thus offers appropriate material for the war-like Phrygian mode, especially considering its obvious reference to the recent French conflict. Le Jeune's third text in this mode, Goulart's *Le rocher orgueilleux* (V.3), builds up a picture of human ambition that personalizes the forces of nature and time in a way designed to appeal to his Christian audience. It is the force of God's hands that not only has the power to break down natural elements (rocks, storms, lightning bolts) but also tears down the "proudest humains" from their elevated places.

I will come back to this theme of ruin and decay in the context of "rehearsing death" in the following chapter. For the moment, I wish to point out that Le Jeune's strategic use of Phrygian for these texts on empire-building and war not only reinforces that he was still interested in modal ethos, but also that he recognized the affective possibilities of Phrygian as rooted in the inherent qualities of the E–E octave species. It was not magic, but it was no less powerful. In contrast to consistent modes like Dorian, the Phrygian mode possessed a natural instability and ambiguity due to its problematic arrangement of semitones, as the second degree is only a half-step above the final. Thus, the mode cannot access the cadential procedures that easily harmonize the fifth degree and set up a strong arrival to the final.[47] Le Jeune's exposition of this mode retains his general pattern of beginning with a textbook iteration of the modal profile according to Zarlino, but then pushing it to its expressive limits by the third setting of the mode. Le Jeune's *Mon ame, où sont les grans discours* thus allows the problematic semitone to remain and destabilize the E–B relationship throughout the entire setting, leading to an ambiguity with Aolian that is common in Phrygian, and that is reinforced here through signed G-sharps.[48] [Web 7.9] Neither mode feels conclusive, however, and although the cadence points return to the E final to close lines 1, 2, 3, and 8, the persistently weak cadential motion disintegrates these foolish efforts like a scattering of dust in the wind.

In the second setting of Mode 5, *Quand le jour, fils du Soleil* (V.2), Le Jeune introduces an F♯, which would be necessary to set up a cadence on the third degree, G.[49] [Web 7.10] He botches it, however, and instead of shoring up the

---

[47] McClary, *Modal Subjectivities*, 208.
[48] Le Jeune, *Octonaires (I–VIII)*, ed. Expert, 52–55.
[49] Ibid., 56–59.

fifth degree, the F♯ creates a wildly discordant "wake-up call" (*resveil*) in the form of an augmented monstrosity that resolves sweetly into a cadence on G to conclude the second line. He tries again in the sixth line, significantly at "Le beau," and finally succeeds in using his F♯ as a harmonization for the fifth degree in two half-cadences closing line 7 that offer an un-Phrygian stability that seems justified by the more peaceful and contemplative tenor of the text. By the third setting of the mode, *Le rocher orgueilleux*, Le Jeune's play with the conflicted semitone bears even more fruit.[50] [Web 7.11] After opening with an outline of the E–B–E octave, the voices join their ambitions in the F♯ at "pride" (*orgueilleux*) that creates what would be the strongest cadential movement of the entire modal group were it not rhythmically undermined by its position in the middle of a phrase. By this point in the modal exposition, we can viscerally feel just how dangerous this desire for the forbidden security turns out to be—and how futile. Mode 6 (Hypophrygian) continues to develop the allegoric importance of Phrygian as a musical model of inherent instability that is in conflict with human efforts to establish an unshakable security.

Modes 7 (Lydian) and 8 (Hypolydian) focus on the three Stoic vices: ambition, luxury, and avarice. Cicero's *Tusculan Disputations* 4.10–13 offered a famous account of this trio as "diseases of the mind," and Seneca also offered several important discussions of this vicious trio, particularly in his Letters 47 and 69, emphasizing that the unexpected consequence of giving free rein to ambition, sensual indulgence, and avarice is not fulfillment, but slavery. A range of emblems, such as Alciato's *Contre les courtisans*, circulated this warning through the image of the courtesan who is pictured in lavish dress but in the stocks or some other position of bondage, and supported by a reference to Seneca's enduring analogy of "golden handcuffs."[51] [Web 7.12]

Read through the Stoic notion of the soul as a properly tuned string, we can see that these three vices all missed the mark of an appropriately balanced, rational soul-tension. Each vice represents too much tension or too little—either a manic overstriving to store up wealth (avarice) or glory (ambition), or an indolence born out of sensual excess (luxury). Le Jeune's choice of these texts for the Lydian modes bears emphasizing, as the internal relationships of the two versions of that octave species were historically problematic in terms of its internal tensions—its troubling tritone and the pivotal

---

[50] Ibid., 59–61.
[51] Alciato, *Les Emblemes* [Part One] (1615), 163–64.

question of whether to leave the B in its hard hexachord or to soften it with a signed flat.[52] The choice of B♮ led to an overly harsh result; while the more relaxed and softer B♭ produced a musical allure that, according to Bonnie J. Blackburn, had long teetered on the edge of the erotically lascivious.[53] In keeping with his rigorous attention to the modal progression through the collection, Le Jeune generally opts for the pure form of the Lydian modes, although he gradually slides toward the pleasurable flat side as he works through Mode 8. In his setting of Chandieu's *J'ay de l'Avare et de l'Ambitieux* (VIII.2), Le Jeune drives home this moral play between the harsh brilliance of effort against the softness of relaxation with a long double-voice melisma at "extreme sorrow" (*extremes douleurs*) that feels like a sweet release of tears.[54] [Web 7.13]

Modes 9–12: Summary

For Modes 9 (Mixolydian) and 10 (Hypomixolydian), Le Jeune returns to nature, and the more stable modal terrain that he had chosen for his earlier natural texts. This time, he offers a series of texts on the four seasons and the moral lessons to be drawn from these cyclical changes. In Modes 11 (Aolian) and 12 (Hypoaolian), Le Jeune gradually shifts the perspective outward to a bigger picture, through allegorical representation of his earlier themes. *Ambition, Volupté, Avarice* (XII.1), Le Jeune's first setting in Hypoaolian, returns to the trio of Stoic vices and warns against the long-term cost of these desires.[55]

> Ambition, Volupté, Avarice,
> Trois Dames sont à qui on faict service,
> Et les Mondains se travaillent sans cesse,
> Pour en avoir Honneur, Plaisir, Richesse.
> Tous sont payez. Le vain Ambitieux,

[52] Ptolemy's *Harmonics* I.12, I.16 discusses the "tenser" genera as those in which the inner tones of the tetrachord are relatively high, thus the "hard" hexachord, which can be compared to Plato's criticism of the "relaxed" Ionian and Lydian modes (*Republic* III 398e10). See A. A. Long, *Stoic Studies*, 213; and McClary, *Modal Subjectivities*, 211–13.

[53] Bonnie J. Blackburn, "The Lascivious Career of B-flat," in *Eroticism in Early Modern Music*, ed. Bonnie J. Blackburn and Laurie Stras (Farnham, UK: Ashgate, 2015), 26.

[54] Le Jeune, *Octonaires (I–VIII)*, ed. Expert, 89.

[55] Ibid., 34–38.

N'a que du vent. Le fol Voluptuex,

Un repentir. L'Avare, un peu de terre,

Et moins en a, d'autant plus qu'il en serre.

[Ambition, Pleasure, Greed, / They are three ladies whom one serves /
And the Worldly Ones work themselves without ceasing / To have honor,
pleasure, and riches. / All are paid. The vain Amibitious / Has only wind.
The mad Voluptuous, / Repentance. The Greedy, a little earth / And he has
less of it by dint of seeking ever harder to hold on to it.]

Considering the close relationship between Phrygian and Aolian mentioned
earlier, we can see a thoughtful intertextuality between Le Jeune's earliest
Phrygian texts (warning against human ambition) and this concluding allegorical text. [Web 7.14] He charmingly introduces the three vicious ladies in
homophonic duos while outlining the lower A–E diapente for Hypoaolian.
Before reaching the first satisfying cadence on C at the end of the second
line, the note values augment in a fitting illustration of the long service that
these vices demand from their subjects. This payment is expressed even
more overtly in the following phrase, where the Mondains "work themselves
without ceasing" (*se travaillent sans cesse*) in overlapping, repeated lines that
extend several times beyond the expected closure. The strain of this fruit-
less labor can be felt particularly in the superius and tenor, whose parts leap
into their challenging upper range. The most evocative moment in the setting, however, comes in the following line at "pleasure," whose long, luxurious melismas offer a glorious warning against the allure of sensual excess
(see Example 7.3). In this, one of Le Jeune's most fabulous settings, the message remains clear: that all of these vices must be paid for, and they result in
nothing but wind, regret, and increased desire.

Conclusion: Neostoic Prayers

Although Le Jeune offered a novel approach to his ordering of the
Octonaires overall, his choice of texts for his final two modes, 11
(Aolian) and 12 (Hypoaolian), was probably influenced by his knowledge of the prior editions—both print and musical—which typically
closed with an Octonaire whose final lines took the form of a prayer,
describing God in Stoic terms as the only example of wisdom and

Example 7.3 Claude Le Jeune, *Ambition, Volupté, Avarice*, mm. 25–34, in *Octonaires de la vanité et inconstance du monde* (Paris: Pierre Ballard, 1606). Based on the edition by Henry Expert

constancy (and implied sagehood), and beseeching his divine aid in living out these values on earth. L'Estocart's collections offered a direct musical model for these punctuating prayers, for Le Jeune's closing text for Mode 11 (*C'est folie et vanité*, by Chandieu) was the final setting of L'Estocart's first collection of *Octonaires*, and the close of Mode 12 (*Ce Monde est un pelerinage*, by Du Chesne) was the closing setting of L'Estocart's second collection.

> C'est folie et vanité
> D'estre en ce Monde arresté,
> Le plaisir de ceste vie
> N'est qu'ennuy et fascherie.
> O Dieu, seul sage et constant,
> Fay moy, pour vivre content,
> Recevoir de ta largesse,
> Ma fermeté et sagesse.

[It is folly and vanity / To be attached to this World, / The pleasure of this life / Is only annoyance and trouble. / O God, alone wise and constant, / Help me to live happily, / And receive from your generosity / My steadfastness and wisdom.]

> Ce Monde est un pelerinage
> Les meschans forcenez de rage,
> Y sont les devots pelerins
> Qui fourvoyés des drois chemins,
> Tombent en la fosse profonde
> De la mort.
> Mais, ô toy mon Dieu,
> Guidant mes pas en autre lieu
> Tire moy du chemin du Monde.

[This World is a pilgrimage. / Bad people deranged by rage / Are devout pilgrims there, / Who led astray from straight paths / Fall into the profound pit / Of death. / But you, O my God, / Guiding my steps toward another place, / Draw me from the path of the World.]

The analogy of life as a pilgrimage was frequently mentioned in Stoic and Neostoic sources, including Seneca and Epictetus. As Du Vair summarized it in his *Philosophie morale des Stoiques*, if our reason is guiding us appropriately, we are invulnerable to misfortune, for all the earth is the country of the sage. "His country is heaven where he aspires, passing here below only as by a pilgrimage, and stopping at towns and provinces as in hostels."[56] Le Jeune's setting of *Ce monde est un pelerinage* (XII.3) draws out this schism between the world's promises and its realities through shifts between imitative polyphony and brief passages of *musique mesurée*.[57] The imitative opening for the first line of text ("This World is a pilgrimage") evokes a feeling of journey and motion through the overlapping entrances of the three voices as they outline the E–A–E octave species for Hypoaolian. This loping motion is brought into the strictly controlled accents of homophonic *musique mesurée* for the next two lines of text, "Bad people deranged by rage / Are devout pilgrims there" (see Example 7.4). This rhythmic effect perfectly represents the fundamental Stoic paradox at the heart of these lines of text—that being controlled by destructive passions like anger results in mental bondage. Another significant moment is the repetition of the fifth and sixth lines— "Fall into the profound pit / Of death" (*Tombent en la fosse profonde / De la mort*)—first felt through the traditional note values of *musique mesurée*, but then visually dramatized for the singers by a move to black notation for that mortal slide. [Web 7.15] Le Jeune marks the beginning of the prayer in line 6 with a lofty ascent back to imitative, melismatic polyphony. This expansive appeal then abruptly returns to more practical terrain in the request for divine assistance driven through downward chains of homophonic *musique mesurée*—a rhythmic effect that takes on positive meaning here as a path toward divine freedom through earthly restraint.

The prayers that close *C'est folie et vanité* and *Ce monde est un pelerinage* may seem at first glance to be a strictly Christian element that supports the occasional reference to Christ, eternal life, or hell scattered across the *Octonaires* corpus—a religiosity inserted onto the philosophical content. It is critical to understand, however, that these prayers to God for aid in living a life of constancy and fortitude were a core element of the Stoic tradition.

---

[56] Du Vair, *La Philosophie morale des Stoiques*, 54; ed. Tarrête, 90.
[57] Le Jeune, *Octonaires (IX–XII)*, ed. Expert, 46–49.

Example 7.4 Claude Le Jeune, *Ce Monde est un pelerinage*, mm. 5–14, in *Octonaires de la vanité et inconstance du monde* (Paris: Pierre Ballard, 1606). Based on the edition by Henry Expert

Seneca cited a prayer of Cleanthes in his Letter 107 that begins, "Lead me, O Master of the lofty heavens, / My Father, whithersoever thou shalt wish."[58] Epictetus offered another important version of this same Stoic prayer, closing his *Handbook* with the following appeal:

> Guide me, O Zeus, and thou, O Destiny,
> To wheresoever you have assigned me;
> I'll follow unwaveringly, or if my will fails,
> Base though I be, I'll follow nonetheless.
> Whoever rightly yields to necessity
> We accord wise and learned in things divine.[59]

---

[58] Seneca, *Epistles* 107.11. The original prayer is found in Cleanthes, Frag. 527 von Arnim. St. Augustine (*Civ. Dei*, v. 8) also circulated this Stoic prayer, but misattributes it to Seneca.
[59] Epictetus, *Handbook* 53; in *Discourses, Fragments, Handbook*, trans. Hard, 304.

Many early modern editions left these Stoic prayers unaltered, presenting them in their Greek or Latin versions to Zeus and Jupiter. Angelo Poliziano's milestone Latin translation of Epictetus's *Handbook* offered a faithful rendition of this prayer in both languages.[60] However, early French translators of Epictetus, such as Antoine Du Moulin, display clear concern about translating a pagan prayer and merely summarize it.[61] That said, another Protestant, André de Rivaudeau, who, like Le Jeune, was connected to the La Noue family, published a French edition with supplemental commentary on Epictetus' *Manual* entitled *La Doctrine d'Epictete stoicien* (1567), in which he preserved the original Stoic prayer in its pagan nomenclature ("Guide moy Jupiter et toy ma destinée").[62] Guillaume Du Vair's French translation renders the Stoic prayer faithfully, though substituting the generic French word for God ("Mon Dieu conduisez-moy par la voye ordonnée"), which would have made the prayer theologically acceptable for a Christian.[63]

Contrary to the occasional accusation that their sect supported atheism, the Stoics were both pious and religious. As we have already begun to see, some Roman Stoic writings discuss God in ways that were so resonant with the Judeo-Christian tradition as to be easily mistaken for Christian texts. Epictetus was the most overt of the Stoics in talking about God in a way that infused a more personal and caring element into the providential cosmos.[64] Seneca's writings frequently communicate a relational and personal God in ways that fed into the long-standing idea that Seneca, for example, was a converted Christian. The musical implications of this turn out to be significant, as we see in Epictetus's *Discourses*:

> If I were a nightingale, I would perform the work of a nightingale, and if I were a swan, that of a swan. But as it is, I am a rational being, and I must sing the praise of God. . . . and I invite all of you to join me in this same song.[65]

---

[60] Angelo Poliziano, *Omnia opera Angeli Politiani, et alia quædam lectu digna, quorum nomina in sequenti indice uidere licet* (Venice: Aldo Manuzio, 1498). The important Geneva edition, *Thesaurus philosophiae moralis . . .* ([Geneva] Lyon: Jean II de Tournes, 1589) also offered a faithful Greek/Latin edition of Epictetus's *Handbook* along with other works.

[61] *Le Manuel d'Epictete . . . Les sentences des philosophes de Grece*, trans. Antoine du Moulin, 2nd ed. (Lyon: Jean de Tournes, 1544), 59.

[62] *La Doctrine d'Epictete stoicien*, trans. André de Rivaudeau (Poitiers: E. de Marnef, 1567), 32.

[63] Epictetus, *Le Manuel d'Epictete* [*Les Responces d'Epictete aux demandes de l'empereur Adrian*], trans. Guillaume Du Vair (Paris: A. Langelier, 1591), 68; in *Traictez philosophiques*, ed. Tarrête, 140.

[64] A. A. Long, *Epictetus*, 147.

[65] *Discourses* 1.16.20–21; in *Discourses, Fragments, Handbook*, trans. Hard, 38.

Singing was a fundamental mode of connecting to the divine, which, as we will recall, was founded on harmony. Or, in Marcus Aurelius' words in *Meditations* 4.23, "All that is in tune with thee, O Universe, is in tune with me!" The concordant relationships forged among a group of singers only furthered the analogy of the sympathetic relationship between a humble yet courageous individual voice sung in harmony with the universal whole.

Chandieu's poetic contributions to the Neostoic contemplative tradition may have inspired the opening words of Thierri Gautier's 10-line epitaph published in honor of Chandieu's death, printed at the head of his translation of Jean de L'Espine's *On the Tranquility of the Soul* (1591): "Alas, we who do not carry the iron hearts of Stoics, to us, alas it is permitted to lament, though moderately." The closing line of the epitaph calls out to God, "Moerori Omnipotens, ah moderare meo!"[66] The well-known musical refrain, "O Mater dei memento mei" (O Mother of God, remember me), has transformed into a fully Stoicized prayer that is no less musically resonant: "Oh God, moderate me!"

[66] Jean de L'Espine, *De tranquillitate animi, libri VII*, trans. Thierri Gautier ([Geneva]: Jacob Stoer, 1591), sig. b3r f. Translation from van Raalte, *Antoine de Chandieu*, 11.

8

Rehearsing Death

> Bear in mind that everything that exists is already fraying at the edges,
> and in transition, subject to fragmentation and to rot.
> Or that everything was born to die.[1]

"Rehearse for death." "Practice death." "Study death." This constant refrain
punctuates the writings of the Roman Stoics, who argued, paradoxically, that
lasting happiness could be best secured through the daily exercise of negative visualization of misfortune, strategic denial of pleasure, and persistent
contemplation of worldly transience. This entirely counterintuitive approach
to happiness drew scorn, but as Epictetus pointed out in *Discourses* 1.25–26,
many more difficult truths are easily accepted as facts of life:

> "The philosophers talk paradoxes," you say. But are there not paradoxes in
> the other arts? And what is more paradoxical than to lance a man in the eye
> in order that he may see? If anyone said this to a man who was inexperi-
> enced in the art of surgery, would he not laugh at the speaker? What is there
> to be surprised at, then, if in philosophy also many things which are true
> appear paradoxical to the inexperienced?

This pointed analogy was probably the inspiration for the emblem *Healing
the soul is the most necessary*, printed in Marin Le Roy Gomberville's *Doctrine
des mœurs, tirée de la philosophie des Stoiques* (1646). The *pictura* shows a
man in the process of eye surgery, while Death hovers near and Virtue offers
the patient a small book that could very well be a wisdom print. Like most
worldly people, the man foolishly resists the book and its difficult remedies.[2]
[Web 8.1]

---

[1] Marcus Aurelius, *Meditations* 10.18; trans. Hays, 137.
[2] Gomberville, *Doctrine des mœurs*, fols. 14v–15r.

The Voice of Virtue. Melinda Latour, Oxford University Press. © Oxford University Press 2023.
DOI: 10.1093/oso/9780197529744.003.0009

Throughout this book, we have seen abundant evidence that both Stoics and Neostoics harnessed a full range of artistic applications of these initiatives to learn to die in order to learn to live. These initiatives were worked out through visual illustration and music as partners in an open-ended therapeutic experience of moral contemplation that, it was hoped, would aesthetically shape feelings about death to better correspond to the rational judgment that death is natural and not to be feared. The introduction to this volume introduced several key works in this lineage, such as Paschal de L'Estocart's pair of settings on learning to die in his 1582 *Sacred Songs*, which invite singers into an occasionally uncomfortable rehearsal of death through illustrative musical experiences of harmony and duration that unpack the counterintuitive lesson. As noted already, attentive singers familiar with the Neostoic corpus would probably have recognized not only that these maxims had Senecan origins, but also that L'Estocart's source for his French version of the maxim, *Pour mourir bien heureux*, was featured on the title page of Duplessis-Mornay's widely-circulated *Excellent discours de la vie et de la mort*, where they would have found both the author's original Neostoic treatise and a large selection of Seneca's writings on death. These writings circulated the core allegorical images that guided people in achieving the moral aims undergirding the *vanitas* and *memento mori* genres across their artistic, poetic, and musical expressions.

Seneca's imaginative descriptions of the brevity of human life—as a shining candle that flickers in the wind and is suddenly extinguished, leaving only a trail of smoke in its wake; as a theatrical farce whose act may come to a sudden close; as a stay in a hostel on a journey far from home; as a river that rushes by as quickly as time; as a slippery and uncertain surface—served as symbolic and allegorical anchors of the rich and varied corpus of *memento mori* and *vanitas* poetry, music, and art that flourished in the period of Neostoicism. Appearing in conjunction with artistic representations of a human skull, the hourglass, dying flowers, and musical instruments (sometimes equipped suggestively with a broken string or two), these sensory markers of transience in moral poetry, polyphonic musical settings, and still-life paintings harnessed the fragile properties of sight and sound as a precarious invitation to contemplate mortality and the paradox of time and duration.

One example from this prodigious artistic corpus came from the brush of Carstian Luyckx (active 1640–58), an Antwerp painter who is believed to have worked in France in the 1650s and had such a profound influence on the court painter Simon Renard de Saint-André that several of Luyckx's *vanitas* paintings have long been misattributed to him.[3] Like many of his contemporaries, Luyckx displayed a concerted interest in bringing artistic experiences of sight and sound into philosophical tension. One of his numerous *vanitas* paintings features a gleaming human skull with the remnants of a laurel wreath resting on top of an open music book (see Plate 10). Leaning on the skull is a dance-master's pochette fiddle and bow, ready to play the lively Allemand shown in the open score. In the left foreground, a pair of shells—exotic collector's items—graces the table, while a lit candle flickers and an hourglass in the upper right background—shiny with a reflection of the windows on the other side of the room—underscores the moral value of perception and perspective.

In the previous chapters, I have drawn attention to the early modern interest in sense perception, focusing on the contributions of the Skeptic and Stoic traditions to this discourse. Abundant still lifes and emblems in the *vanitas* tradition feature musical instruments and partbooks, in some cases portrayed alongside other artistic tools, such as painting knives or palettes. Positioned frequently among coins, jewelry and other displays of wealth, these musical and artistic status symbols certainly warned against luxury. However, an alternate explanation for their appearance comes from their association with the senses: they may have warned of the dangers of sense decay and sense deception. Likewise, the poetry and musical settings of the *Octonaires* and *Tablettes* corpus offered detailed sensory exposure to this overarching effort to eliminate false views of death that cause fear and immoderate desire. Musically, these philosophical problems were expressed through harmonic and rhythmic strategies that both relied upon established genre conventions of the time and deliberately subverted these conventions for expressive purposes. In the visual realm, the "stillness" of the inanimate objects depicted in the painted genre belies the subtle dynamism that animates these deceptively simple works. In fact, their energy and lifelike realism productively expose the intimacy between death and life, and show an acute beauty and aliveness witnessed in the detailed exposure to decay.

In each artistic modality, the play of sensory and moral perspective developed at the rich intersection between these practices was confronted and bridged in philosophically provocative ways: through poetry that paints

---

[3] Fred G. Meijer at the Netherlands Institute for Art History, The Hague has confirmed the attribution. https://rkd.nl/explore/images/21494.

a picture (*picta poesis*), through visual emblems and paintings that offer a silent eloquence (*peinture parlante*), and through musical settings that engage the fragile portals of the mouth, eyes, and ears. In this chapter, I consider musical, poetic, and visual practices forged by this Stoic call to rehearse death. After progressing through the *vanitas* symbols of bubbles and ruins in the multi-sensory corpus of *Octonaires*, I conclude with the Stoic musical portraits composed by Artus Aux-Cousteaux several decades later and linked to the artistic and literary circle of Christian Stoics in mid-seventeenth-century Paris.

Homo Bulla Est

Hendrik Goltzius's 1594 emblem *Homo bulla* ("Man is a bubble") [Web 8.2] depicts a cherubic *putto* blowing soap bubbles, reclining on a skull in front of an open grave. Smoke rises in the background while wilting flowers point to the gravestone, which warns, "Who will escape?" (*Quis Evadet?*). The Latin *inscriptio*, penned by Franco Estius, delivers a clear Stoic message: "The fresh silvery flower, fragrant with the breath of spring, withers instantly as its beauty wanes. So the life of man, already ebbing in the newborn child, disappears like a bubble or like fleeting smoke."[4] The *Homo bulla* inspired an abundance of iconography stretching back through the Middle Ages, but gained heightened popularity during the Neostoic revival, where the popular childhood pastime of bubble-blowing was often framed by moralizing inscriptions on learning to die.[5]

Simon Goulart's *J'apperceus un enfant*, included in L'Estocart's second collection of *Octonaires*, offers a poetic exploration of this playfully serious theme:

> J'apperceus un enfant, qui d'un tuyau de paille
> Trempé dans le savon, avecques eau meslé,
> Des ampoules souffloit encontre une muraille,
> Dont l'œil de maint passant estoit esmerveillé.
> Riches elles sembloyent, fermes, de forme ronde.
> Mais les voyant crever en leur lustre plus beau,

---

[4] Translation cited after Horst Woldemar Janson, *16 Studies* (New York: H. N. Abrams, 1973), 25.
[5] Ingvar Bergström, "Homo Bulla: La boule transparente dans la peinture hollandaise à la fin du XVIe siècle au XVIIe siècle," in *Les Vanités dans la peinture au XVIIe siècle*, ed. Tapié, 49–54.

Voir soudain, soudainement, voila, dis-je, un tableau
De la fresle splendeur et vanité du Monde.

[I saw a child with a straw tube, / Soaked in soap and mixed with water, /
Blowing bubbles against a wall, / Amazing many passing by. / They seem
rich, firm, and round in form. / But seeing them burst in their most beautiful luster, / Seeing this unexpectedly, all of a sudden, I said, there is a portrait / Of the frail splendor and vanity of the World.]

L'Estocart's four-voice musical setting for *J'apperceus un enfant* (II.6)
emphasizes the act of visual perception in the opening "I saw," which is
repeated in each voice as it falls through all voices in points of imitation.
[Web 8.3 and 8.4] The repeated calling out of this action of seeing across
the voice ranges—a total of twenty times in just the first thirteen measures of the setting—brings to the forefront the moral question of sight
perception, emphasizing its jointly individual and collective experience.
After witnessing the child with the straw tube dipped in the soapy water,
a scene that unfolds sedately in a series of clear homophonic passages
marking out the F-Ionian octave species, the third line launches into
a buoyant and playful passage of imitative polyphony that evokes the
lift of the soap bubbles blown by the child. In this passage, L'Estocart
mirrors the roundness of the bubbles, shaping each melodic line with a
dotted figure that blows outward in descending points of imitation (mm.
26–36) and then floating them up the texture with rising puffs of breath
at "souffloit" (mm. 30–33). The texture returns abruptly to a slow homophony in the next line, which again calls attention to sight, as the
"eye," engaging the passing bubbles, becomes fixated on a sustained harmony at measure 40 before gently coming to cadence on F. L'Estocart
paints the line of text that follows ("Riches elles sembloyent"), expressing
the illusory spectacle of the soap bubbles with a shift to ternary (mm.
45–46).

By this point in L'Estocart's second collection, a brief ternary passage such
as this recalls several layers of significance, tying the round form of the bubble
(and its attendant inconstancy) to the aesthetic richness of worldly sense
deception. The bubble elicits appreciation and wonder from those viewing
it, and it seems both rich and firm in its round shape—a point reinforced
harmonically by the unexpected F♯ on "riches," which recalls the gleam of

the shiny ice from L'Estocart's *La glace est luisante et belle* (I.5) discussed in Chapter 5. L'Estocart's ternary shift in the fifth line of *J'apperceus un enfant* more deliberately plays with the relationship between sight and sound, as he expresses the unstable bubble in progressively more elaborate and extended forms that play with the relationship between duple and triple, simplicity and artifice. Immediately following the ternary passage, L'Estocart shifts back to his cut C, but he sets the firm illusion of the bubble in a two-note, isolated homophonic rendering bracketed by rests on either side, whose unequal relationship (whole note to half note) would sound to anyone not looking at the partbook as though it was still a continuation of the ternary passage. The first rendering of "de forme ronde" (mm. 50–52) in a clear three-voice homophony again uses the condensed, dotted figure to signify shape and aesthetic beauty, whereas the second and third iterations stretch out the phrase length and distort the shape through the introduction of polyphony that culminates in the luxurious cadential ornament that brings the phrase to a powerful arrival on C (mm. 53–62). The sixth line of text, which describes the act of seeing the bursting of the bubble in its beautiful luster, again recalls *La glace est luisante et belle*, as the superius leaps upward in shimmering solitude at the peak of the phrase, with the lower voices rejoining in rich homophony as the harmony shifts toward an irregular arrival on G (mm. 63–69). For the penultimate line of Goulart's text, L'Estocart illustrates the call to "see, sudden, suddenly" the bursting bubble with appropriately quick note values that gain speed in the bassus part, like the text, before shifting back to stately homophony as Goulart signals his own voice ("voila, dis-je") and his creation of a moral picture ("un tableau") of the vanity of the world. L'Estocart's overarching cadential structure, marked by chains of rising fifths across the setting (F–C–G–D), adds a sense of buoyant harmonic lift across the first seven lines of text. The glorious final line of the setting (mm. 74–90), though deflating the harmonic focus back to F, rises in frail splendor through the imitative texture and is punctuated by the poignant return of the dotted figure, first presented in its most condensed form in measure 77, and then elongated in the final measures as a musical relic of the vanity of the world.

This hollow yet resonant experience of perception, which glistens and bursts throughout L'Estocart's setting of Goulart's *J'apperceus un enfant*, recalls Stoic lessons in temporality and perspective. As Marcus Aurelius's *Meditations* 8.20 clarified: "Nature has looked to each thing's ending no less than its beginning and its course in between . . . What good is there for the bubble in being blown or harm for it in being burst? And the same is true of a lamp."[6] Seneca's extensive commentary on the unity of living and dying in Letter 24 invited people to focus on the process of human aging and living well across the entire life cycle, serving the crucial reminder that, from the moment of our birth, we are dying every day. Mathieu's Tablette II.6 poetically rendered Seneca's words:

On meurt le mesme jour que l'on commence à naistre,
On s'oblige au naufrage entrant en ce bateau:
Naître et mourir n'est qu'un, l'estre n'est qu'un non-estre,
Il n'y a qu'un soûpir de la table au tombeau.

[Death begins the same day as birth, / We must inevitably shipwreck upon boarding this boat / Birth and death are one and the same, being is the same as non-being, / There is but a sigh from the birthing table to the tomb.]

The breath that blows the soap bubble through the child's straw tube offers the connective life force in Mathieu's portrait of aging. The painter David Bailly, working in the Neostoic milieu of seventeenth-century Leiden, plumbed the connections between these philosophical concerns.[7] In his *Self-Portrait with Vanitas Symbols* (1651), which he painted near the end of his life, the artist depicts himself twice—as an old man in the self-portrait "within" the painting, and four decades younger in the life-like portrayal of himself (see Plate 11). The floating bubbles, the recently extinguished candle, the skull, and a wealth of subtler Stoic symbols frame the commentary on aging as a simultaneous exploration of the fictive and the real, mastered in the mature artist's technique. Bailly foregrounds the aurality of this critical sense perception in the image of the lute player (one of his earlier works) tacked onto the wall as well as in the recorder on the table. Through a trick of perspective, the instrument seems to be extended out to viewers, inviting them to pick up the instrument and make a sound that must eventually fade.

[6] *Meditations* 8.20; trans. Robin Hard, with an introduction and notes by Christopher Gill (Oxford: Oxford World Classics), 73.

[7] Bailly studied with Adriaen Verburgh, the brother-in-law of Jacques de Gheyn II, whose portraits and vanitas still lifes clearly influenced Bailly's work. See Walter Liedtke, *Dutch Paintings in The Metropolitan Museum of Art I* (New York: The Metropolitan Museum of Art; New Haven: Yale University Press, 2007), 14.

Art historians have consistently noted the importance of perception in the *vanitas* genre, and the overt way artists represent their craft in morally ambiguous terms that both valorize and warn against the power of the artist to present both the real and the fictive.[8] What has gone largely unnoted is that this artistic concern with perspective and the development of trompe l'œil had an evident philosophical underpinning in Stoic philosophy, with its multivalent discourse on the power of perspective that links both the symbols and the techniques of *vanitas* paintings to an entire complex of questions related to ethics, art, deception, and pleasure. In fact, in Bailly's painting, close attention leads the eye to a discreet etching on the other corner of the wall, where a woman's face appears beyond the glass beaker. Her eye, quite literally, "sees through the glass, though dimly," recalling one of St. Paul's most Stoicized statements.[9]

This emphasis on perception and moral foresight takes center stage in a series of emblems included in the final section of Gomberville's *Doctrine des mœurs, tirée de la philosophie des Stoiques*, which aimed to cultivate the perspective necessary for correctly accounting for the inevitability of human mortality. The commentary for the emblem *Tout se pert avec le temps* [All perishes with time] identifies the Stoic roots of this exercise in moral perception: "But the Stoic, that is to say the perfect and consummate sage, ponders where old age leads; and as with eyeglasses familiarizes himself early with death. He remembers that it is said a thousand times that the great Zeno said that the life of the philosopher, must only be a continuous meditation of death."[10] [Web 8.5]

Gomberville's metaphor of the magnifying power of spectacles that the wise person will use to gain insight into the distant (or not so distant) endpoint of death became an important *vanitas* image. It was no coincidence that Josuah Sylvester chose *Spectacles* as the title of his English version of Chandieu's *Octonaires*, since their meditation on the transience of all things underlines the moral aim of the collection.[11] His edition further enriches the significance of this alternate title, for underneath the word *Spectacles*,

---

[8] See Alan Chong and Wouter Kloek, *Still-life Paintings from the Netherlands, 1550–1720* (Zwolle: Waanders Publishers, 1999), 30–31; and Marc Fumaroli, "Still Life, Nature morta, Vanitas and Trompe l'œil," in *Art and Illusions: Masterpieces of Trompe l'œil from Antiquity to the Present Day*, ed. Anna Maria Giusti (Florence: Mandragora, 2009), 47–63.

[9] I Corinthians 13:12. On the influence of Stoicism on St. Paul's ethical language, see Thorsteinsson, *Roman Christianity and Roman Stoicism*, 137–206.

[10] Gomberville, *Doctrine des mœurs*, fol. 91v.

[11] Sylvester, *Works*, 1176.

Sylvester offers an illustration of a pair of eyeglasses, with the words "New-New-Polished" printed on the bridge, "Perspective, Spectacles of Especial Use" on the left glass, and "To discern the Worlds Vanitie, Levitie, and Brevitie" on the right. Below the glasses is printed, "These Glasses in indifferent Lights Serve Old, and yong, and midle Sights."[12]

The presence of spectacles in *vanitas* paintings points to this moral question of sight and perspective. For instance, the elderly singer in Valckert's *An Allegory of Music* (see Plate 3), who is straining to see the music through his spectacles, evokes the moral discourse of both sense perception and wisdom in the fullness of the human life span, especially when he is partnered with the fresh innocence of the youth singing opposite him in the ensemble. The Parisian still-life painter Simon Renard de Saint-André, who was *peintre ordinaire de la Reine* in 1646 and was later received into the Académie des beaux-arts, delivers this contemplation of mortality through all five senses in his *Vanitas Still-Life*, doubling the moral warning that sensory pleasure fades quickly, like human life (see Plate 12).[13] Alongside a human skull, he offers notated music, a vase of cut flowers in various stages of blooming and decline, an hourglass, coins, dice, diplomatic correspondance, an open book (which can be identified as Jean Puget de La Serre's *Le Tombeau des delices* [1630] turned to the chapter on smell), and a pair of spectacles.[14] Like most *vanitas* symbols, the spectacles presented here have multiple layers of significance that could serve doubly as admonition and inspiration. Duplessis-Mornay referenced the imagery of eyeglasses in his *Excellent discours* in a warning against sense deception and the danger of bookish knowledge unmoored from wisdom. Spectacles also symbolize old age, and perhaps tied to this association of age with wisdom, serve more positively as an index of perspective, attentiveness, and moral foresight, as we see in the mode of magnified examination proposed in Gomberville's emblem.[15]

---

[12] Duplessis-Mornay also used the imagery of eyeglasses, in a warning against potential sense deception, and as a lure of knowledge that is ultimately fragile and potentially deceptive. Duplessis-Mornay, *Excellent discours*, 61.

[13] See Nicole Lallement, "La Musique dans les vanités de Simon Renard de Saint-André," *Musique-images-instruments* 5 (2003): 166–74; and Michel Faré, *Le Grand Siècle de la nature morte en France, le XVIIᵉ siècle* (Fribourg: Office du livre, 1974), 168–79.

[14] Jean Puget de La Serre's *Le Tombeau des delices du monde* (Paris: Philippe Gaultier, 1630), Ch. 4, "Le Tombeau des plaisirs de l'odorat." La Serre later published French poetic paraphrases of Seneca's teachings in *L'Esprit de Sénèque, ou les plus belles pensées de ce grand philosophe* (Paris: André Soubron, 1657).

[15] Duplessis-Mornay, *Excellent discours*, 61.

The problem of changing one's perspective—discussed in the overlap between the Stoic and Skeptic concerns with sense deception and the fragility of sound—played a role in the meditations on death illustrated in a variety of artistic modalities, including musical settings, emblems, and paintings. The motif of the spectacles, however, also points to the problem of human sensory failure, which becomes far more common in old age. Although the Stoics were consistent in recommending the rehearsal of death and the contemplation of mortality for all stages of life, learning how to die was obviously a more pressing concern for those who knew themselves to be living in their final years. Cicero's *On Old Age* was an important fictional dialogue set in the past between two generations of revered Stoics. It portrayed Cato the Elder bestowing Stoic teachings on aging upon his younger admirers, Scipio Aemilianus and his friend Gaius Laelius. Plutarch made his own contribution to the literature on aging, giving advice largely based on Cicero's account.[16] Simon Goulart followed in their footsteps by penning his own treatise on death and aging, *Le Sage Vieillard* (1606), which treats some of the Stoic themes of his earlier *Octonaires*. Goulart's treatise, though largely Christian in its approach, directly acknowledges his borrowing of the Stoics' timeless advice on aging.[17] For example, in Chapter 13, dedicated to illuminating the profit that the aging sage can draw from pagan philosophy, he cites the value of the "beautiful remedies" of ancient writers like Cicero and Seneca, who "so courageously disdained death [*mesprisé la mort*]."[18] Goulart explains the core Stoic argument of consolation—useful for the young but essential for the aging—that there is no death more dreadful than the fear of death. As Mathieu's *Tablettes* III.73 expressed it:

> Des frayeurs de la mort le sage se delivre
> Car il sçait qu'en tous lieux il la peut encourir
> Avant que viellir il faut apprendre à vivre,
> Et vieillissant il faut apprendre à bien mourir.

---

[16] See Tim Parkin, *Old Age in the Roman World: A Cultural and Social History* (Baltimore, MD: Johns Hopkins University Press, 2004), 57–89.

[17] Simon Goulart, *Le Sage Vieillard descrit de divers authers* (Lyon: Antoine de Harsy, 1606).

[18] Ibid., 302–3.

[The sage delivers himself from the fear of death, / Because he knows that it could occur anywhere. / While young, it is necessary to learn to live; / And growing old it is necessary to learn how to die well.]

Learning to die is thus important for the young but essential for the aging, and it demands a critical process of confronting and eliminating the framework of values that generates these false anxieties.

Monsters and Masks

Epictetus boiled down Stoic consolation to this fundamental point: "It is not things themselves that trouble people, but their opinions about things. Death, for instance, is nothing terrible (otherwise, it would have appeared that way to Socrates as well), but the terrible thing is the opinion that death is terrible. So whenever we are frustrated, or troubled, or pained, let us never hold anyone responsible except ourselves, meaning our own opinions."[19] Thus, our negative emotional responses to mortality and loss are grounded in our beliefs and choices—which can be shaped and altered through daily exercise in preparation for life's changing fortunes. Madeleine de l'Aubespine offered an important recommendation to practice this premeditation of misfortune in her *Cabinet des saines affections*, which she explains will change this underlying value system and allow practitioners to experience the onset of tragic loss with a reduction of negative emotion. "Such foresight" she explains "marvellously softens the impact of misfortune."[20]

The engraver and still-life painter Jacques de Gheyn II explored this premeditation on misfortune and death through critical visual techniques foregrounding the moral salience of perspective. Born into a family of artists, Jacques de Gheyn II studied and collaborated with the influential engraver Hendrik Goltzius, whose engraving of the five senses was discussed in Chapter 6. De Gheyn eventually settled in Leiden between 1596 and 1602 and worked closely with the famed Neostoic legal scholar Hugo Grotius, who created inscriptions for De Gheyn's engravings.[21]

[19] Epictetus, *Handbook* 5; in *How To Be Free: An Ancient Guide to the Stoic Life. Epictetus, Encheiridion and Selections from Discourses*, trans. A. A. Long (Princeton, NJ: Princeton University Press, 2018), 11–13.

[20] L'Aubespine, *Cabinet des saines affections*, Discourse III, ed. Winn, 45.

[21] Susan Kuretsky, *Time and Transformation in Seventeenth-Century Dutch Art* (Poughkeepsie, NY: Frances Lehman Loeb Art Center, Vassar College, 2005), 152.

De Gheyn's *Vanitas Still Life* (1603), introduced in Chapter 4 [Web 4.5], marks an early exploration of the therapeutic possibilities of linking *memento mori* symbolism (cut flower, smoking urn, bubble, human skull) with artistic techniques heightening an awareness of visual perception (trompe-l'œil). Set within an arched recess, a large bubble that floats above the skull serves as the panel's focal point and therapeutic hinge. The laughing Democritus and weeping Heraclitus carved into the arch gesture downward, linking their cries of emotional aurality to the visual dynamism of the fragile bubble, on the verge of bursting. At first glance, the bubble symbolizes human transience. Closer attention reveals an added moral dimension, crafted through De Gheyn's virtuosic technique that creates a small reflection on the surface of the bubble. The reflected objects (a wheel and leper's rattle), mirror items located across the room from the arched recess. They also serve as a contemplative mirror, suggesting the futility of clinging to the wealth and status represented in the coins and medals on the ledge below the skull, and recalling the Stoic call to regularly meditate on the impending possibility of misfortune and loss as a core exercise in their program of emotional regulation.

The practice of looking ahead to prepare for misfortune and death was essential for the success of the exercise, for the Stoics agreed that applying the arguments of consolation to fresh tragedy could do more harm than good. They did not seek to repress or deny the presence of emotion; rather, they sought to reshape the surrounding framework of value judgments that sustains these psychological states. As Richard Sorabji explains in the introduction to his in-depth study of Stoic emotion: "Stoicism can be very helpful in dealing with counter-productive emotion. But it is not a matter of gritting your teeth. It is about seeing things differently, so that you do not need to grit your teeth."[22] In other words, the process of reducing or eliminating destructive emotion was ultimately a matter of perception and perspective.

Not all strong emotion was unwanted or unhelpful, as the Stoics and Neostoics were careful to remember. Stoic consolation was thus a psychological process tied to the sense-perception/judgment process, in that external stimuli for anxiety, fear, and other strong emotions were subjected to critical reflection. According to Sorabji, the Stoic process of critical sense perception acknowledged what we now describe as an initial "fight or flight" response in the amygdala when confronted with a possible threat.

---

[22] Sorabji, *Emotion and Peace of Mind*, 1.

This instinctive response could then be evaluated rationally (relying on the critical ability of the prefrontal cortex), to choose a course of action based on a determination of the real or illusory danger posed by the initial impression. Epictetus explains this critical evaluation in his *Discourses* 2.1, describing the impression of fear when confronted with death as merely a childhood monster, what Socrates had called a "bugbear," which we should bring out from under the bed to prove its impotence: "What is death? A bugbear. Turn it about and learn what it is; see, it does not bite."

Chandieu's Octonaire *Quel monstre vois-je la*, which is one of the most imaginative in his collection, depicts a hideous beast with multiple heads, eyes, and ears that could very well be Socrates' bugbear or the "monster of many shapes" described by Seneca in his *On Constancy* 2.2.[23]

> Quel monstre voy-je là, qui tant de testes porte,
> Tant d'oreilles, tant d'yeux, de differente sorte:
> Dont l'habit par devant, est semé de verdure,
> Et par derriere n'a qu'une noirceur obscure,
> Dont les pieds vont glissant sur une boule ronde,
> Roulant, roulant, roulant avec le temps, qui l'emporte en courant
> Et la mort court apres, ses flesches luy tirant?
> Je le voy, je l'ay veu. Qu'estoit ce donc? le Monde.

[What monster do I see there, who has so many heads, / So many ears and eyes of different sorts? / Whose garment in front is spread with greenery / And behind has only an obscure darkness, / Whose feet go sliding on a round ball, / Rolling, rolling, rolling with time, which carries it off / With death following behind, his arrows drawn to him? / I see it; I have seen it. What then is this? The World.]

Responding to Chandieu's poetic emphasis on the role of human perception in viewing this monster, L'Estocart's four-voice setting of *Quel monstre voy-je là* (I.20) opens in a clear homophony that emphasizes this first-person speech and self-interrogation [Web 8.6 and 8.7]. This transparency, however, is undercut with a modal ambiguity that refuses to confirm either a C Ionian or G Mixolydian orientation, raising both as a mode of self-questioning

---

[23] Seneca's monster in *On Constancy*, however, is human ambition, a vice that was closely related to the problem of fear and death for the Stoics.

(mm. 1–16). The couplet that follows introduces the paradox of perception of this monster, who appears a verdant green in front, but whose back side is completely black. L'Estocart elides the firm cadence on C at measures 16–17, which should have closed his interior monologue, slipping into a jubilantly lush imitative soundscape (mm. 17–30). The following line turns back to homophony, beginning with an upper-voice duo in measures 30–32 that gains support from the lower voices as it moves to the pivot of the text, where the monster's darkness is revealed. Unsurprisingly, L'Estocart shifts to a signed triple here, with blackened square breves and semibreves that paint the "obscure darkness" onto the score (mm. 36–38) and map this blackness onto the triple meter of the rhythm. Rather than shifting immediately back to his standard duple and white notation, L'Estocart extends the impact of this notational shadow throughout the next line of text ("Whose feet go sliding on a round ball"), which accelerates along the way—rolling into triple groupings that hint at the creature's hidden identity (mm. 39–43). The shift back to duple in measure 44 does nothing to slow down the momentum of time in the setting of lines 6 and 7, with voices chasing after one another and death not far behind (mm. 44–59). The entry into the final line of the Octonaire is again obscured rhythmically, but L'Estocart capitalizes on the interesting implications of Chandieu's text, repeating the act of sight first in the present ("Je le voy") and again in the past ("Je l'ay veu"), with the offset voices resounding with different perspectives that are finally brought into unity by the close on C in measures 65–67. However, he turns the tables once more by shifting to triple—this time remaining in white notation, as the text questions its own perceptions: "What is it then?" (mm. 68–69) with a harmonic departure to F. This question is then repeated in a syncopated duple-meter homophony that gives way to a staggered answer—"the World"—supporting this truth with the arrival of an authentic G cadence (clarified as the point of arrival all along). Astute singers and listeners could have predicted the revelation of the monster as the world through L'Estocart's prior worldly associations of triple meter and would have received a musical reward for that correct judgment through the clarity afforded by the final measures.

This highly perceptive musical setting imitates Epictetus' revelation of the monster as merely a mask that frightens a child lacking experience and knowledge. The mask can only be lifted through a process of cognition that arrives at a proper assessment of reality, and the recognition of what should or should not be feared. Du Vair's *Philosophie morale des Stoiques* summarizes Epictetus in describing these fear-inducing "masques de maux" that are able to harm us, stealing the tranquility of the present through our false opinion of them: "O ingenious passion, that draws from an imagined evil a living and real suffering!"[24] Seneca's Letter 24 also harnessed the analogy of the scary mask within a broader Stoic discourse on sense perception and sound judgment by describing the importance of getting to the bottom of things, to see what lies beneath our anxiety about loss and death. Seneca concludes: "We should strip the mask, not only from men, but from things, and restore to each object its own aspect."

Claude Le Jeune's setting for *Quel monstre voy-je là* (VII.1) offers a vibrant take on this question of reality versus illusion that takes advantage of the theoretical instability of F-Lydian outlined in the previous chapter, which Le Jeune further destabilizes through his varied rhythmic vocabulary.[25] [Web 8.8] In contrast to L'Estocart's sober, homophonic opening for this text, Le Jeune launches the setting in a rollicking imitative polyphony, with carefully accentuated overlapping imitative lines that clearly outline the boundaries of the F–C–F octave species while creating a strong sense of momentum and syncopation. Le Jeune finally moves to his signature homophonic *musique mesurée* style for the pivotal couplet of the Octonaire ("Dont l'habit . . ."), where the text exposes the contrasting green and black sides of the many-headed monster. He remains in this heavily syncopated duple meter through to the end of the fourth line, even as the "obscure darkness" at the close of the phrase extends and elongates the rhythms into the cadence. After a bit of fun with the contrast of stable and slow "feet" slipping into quick, rolling lines on "a round ball," Le Jeune moves to a signed triple, with black notes for the following phrase—"Roulant avec le temps"—mapping onto the round world. He stabilizes the triple rhythm in the short–long accentuation that corresponds to this section of the text. However, he intersperses a measure of duple on "l'emporte" that retains the proper accentuation, while also allowing for a bit more time to illustrate the pull of time with the eighth-note ascent in the contralto voice. Le Jeune's setting of the final lines breaks back into a cacophony of imitative voices for the text on sight and its perceptions, present and past, with the answer "le Monde" receiving a brief, understated response that deflates the overblown monster into simple mundanity.

Read through the Stoic corpus, the masks that appear occasionally in emblems, *vanitas* art, and moral poetry accrue a multivalent symbolism that

---

[24] Du Vair, *La Philosophie morale des Stoiques*, 37, ed. Tarrête, 80.
[25] Le Jeune, *Octonaires (I–VIII)*, ed. Expert, 72–76.

could represent death itself (via the custom of making death masks, revived in the Renaissance), theatrical or artistic deception and the problem of beauty, or a warning about false opinions that, like a scary mask, cause unnecessary fear. Such warnings, against representational artifice as the underpinning of false opinion and fear, point to an artistic and musical preference for aesthetic naturalism embedded in the overarching Stoic call to "follow nature." Jacques de Gheyn II himself reportedly shifted from his work as an engraver to painting as he reportedly found the brush "the most adequate to resemble life or nature."[26] Beginning with the association of brevity and truth, this drive toward an unflinching refusal of artifice developed into the astonishing realism in the techniques associated with the Neostoic artistic genres of portraiture, landscape, and still life. We see these themes tied together beautifully in another of De Gheyn's paintings, his *Vanitas Still Life* (1621). [Web 8.9] A triangular composition, the balanced scene offers the characteristic effect of three-dimensional realism. On the shelf above the table with the skull and laurel wreath rest a trio of sculpted heads. Seneca rests on the far right. In the middle is the agonized face of Laocoön's younger son, Thymbraeus, who was killed alongside his family in a serpent attack that was pivotal to the ill-fated Greek acceptance of the Trojan horse. The third head resembles the youthful innocence of the *putto*.[27] A Latin motto tacked to the table on a creased and worn leaf of paper admonishes the viewer in the Stoic directives: "Observe moderation, be mindful of the final goal, and follow nature." Within the context of the *memento mori*, this reminder to follow nature guides a mode of rehabilitation that brings thoughts and feelings about death and suffering into harmony with the ordered principles of the universal *logos*.[28]

[26] De Gheyn's associate, the Dutch mannerist artist and theorist Karel van Mander (1548–1606), made this statement. Cited in David Merrill, "The *Vanitas* of Jacques de Gheyn," *Yale Art Gallery Bulletin* 25, no. 3 (1960): 11. Van Mander's *Schilder-Boek* (1604) remains a critical source of information on northern European and Italian artists and their works in the fifteenth and sixteenth centuries. For these artists and their context, see Gero Seelig, "Dutch Mannerism," in *The Ashgate Research Companion to Dutch Art of the Seventeenth Century*, ed. Wayne Franits (London: Routledge, 2016), 252–64.

[27] The middle head is copied from the Greek (probably Hellenistic era) marble sculpture *The Laocoön and his Two Sons*, held at the Vatican. For the Neostoic interest in the Laocoön as a model of physical and mental suffering, which Rubens drew at least fifteen times, see Lusheck, *Rubens and the Eloquence of Drawing*, 129–38.

[28] See Chong and Kloek, *Still-life Paintings*, 16; and B. A. Heezen-Stoll, "A Vanitas Still Life of 1621 by Jacques de Gheyn II: a Reflection of Neo-Stoic ideas," *Oud Holland - Quarterly for Dutch Art History* 93, no. 4 (1979): 246–50.

Time and Temporality

Le Jeune's *Octonaires* fully explore the moral stakes of "following nature" in musical time. Patched into the background fabric of imitative polyphony, his interspersions of syncopated homophony reveal the extent to which the composer was interested in the dual effects of these uncomfortable passages, which prioritize natural text declamation while also offering a subtle accrual of expressive meaning through rhythmic manipulation. Le Jeune sensitively attends to principles of declamation in crafting his counterpoint throughout the collection. Thus, the intelligibility of the text is retained throughout his more complex passages of imitative polyphony, even as the sense of the musical measure or tactus remains the guiding principle, with the text fitted into these recurring, regular groupings. What sets off Le Jeune's quasi-*musique mesurée* passages from his general attention to text declamation is a clear prioritizing of the textual stress at the expense of a consistent musical meter. The shifts between these contrasting value structures lead to a regular destabilization of the metrical foundation across the collection and pose significant performance challenges for the singers attempting to decode these uncomfortable rhythmic relationships.

Isabelle His, who has published extensively on *musique mesurée*, points out that the style has always existed in an awkward relationship with measured music and its presumably equal bars and neutral tactus. Building upon Paul-Marie Masson's foundational opposition, she explores the interpretive challenges of *musique mesurée* as a conflict between "musiciens" and "métriciens."[29] Because *musique mesurée* prioritizes a strict correlation between the value of the metered syllables and the rhythmic duration, this experimental style of music generally creates a prolonged sense of syncopation, as the text does not remain easily within the normal bounds of equal musical measures. This metrical destabilization produces a gasping or panting effect, although it might also be felt as fluid and energizing.[30]

---

[29] Isabelle His, "Vers mesurés et 'mesure' musical," in *Poésie et musique à la Renaissance*, ed. Olivier Millet and Alice Tacaille (Paris: Presses de l'université Paris-Sorbonne, 2015), 123–40.

[30] D. P. Walker and others have attempted to resolve these metrical difficulties by proposing an "unequal" tactus for *musique mesurée*. However, His's work suggests that Le Jeune's shifts into *musique mesurée* within his polyphonic settings of non-measured poetry (as seen his *Octonaires*) must retain a regular (i.e., equal) tactus. See Walker, *Music, Spirit, and Language*, 151–86; and Isabelle His, "Claude Le Jeune et le rythme prosodique: La mutation des années 1570," *Revue de Musicologie* 79, no. 2 (1993): 201–26.

Le Jeune's shifts between imitative polyphony and *musique mesurée* in his *Dodecacorde* suffer from none of these problems, for the continued presence of the slow-moving Psalm tunes anchor the meter and prevent these passages from achieving the complete homorhythm that is a hallmark of the style.[31] By contrast, Le Jeune's *Octonaires* have no such metrical anchor to smooth over the ruptures of musical time that occur as imitative polyphony gives way to *musique mesurée*. As Brian MacGilvray points out, "The sense of meter is often doubly obscured: by layers of syncopation in the imitative sections and by fleeting interruptions of two-, three-, or four-part homophony, either in triple meter or syncopated duple meter."[32] As MacGilvray's sensitive reading of Le Jeune's settings reveals, the relationship between these destabilizing metrical strategies and the moral texts does not lend itself to predictable or facile interpretations, but ultimately invites highly subversive readings that challenge the moral and epistemological function of *musique mesurée*. The properly accentuated passages no longer symbolize truth (as one would expect from the philosophical aims of the Académie's experiments), for Le Jeune paradoxically applies his most conspicuous moments of homophonic clarity when the text indicates deception or ignorance—such as his use of *musique mesurée* for moral blindness in *Quand la face noire* (VI.1)—thus decoupling the ontological claim of an ethical union of text and music.[33]

It is only by reading Le Jeune's *Octonaires* against L'Estocart's earlier collections that we can understand the reason for the moral slippage. Although the careful prosody of *musique mesurée* offered an intelligible— and even naturalistic—moral ideal vis-à-vis the Académie, the rhythmic similarity of the lopsided alternations of long and short note values became linked to the symbolism of the black-note ternary passages developed so thoroughly in L'Estocart's collections. Le Jeune's setting for Chandieu's *Quand la Terre au Printemps* (IX.1) offers an example of this critical merger, as the imitative polyphony that opens the setting shifts to the homophonic clarity that recalls *musique mesurée* in lines 3 and 4—"Its flowers are the heralds / Of the fruit that we hope for" (*Sa fleur est messagere / Du fruit que l'on espere*) — and then returns to it again in lines 7 and 8 "Your flower that deceives and lies, / Is only a plaything of the wind" (*Ta fleur qui trompe et*

[31] Le Jeune, *Dodecacorde*, ed. Heider, ix.

[32] Brian MacGilvray, "The Subversion of Neoplatonic Theory in Claude Le Jeune's *Octonaires de la vanité et inconstance du monde*." PhD diss., Case Western University, 2017), 25.

[33] Le Jeune, *Octonaires (I–VIII)*, ed. Expert, 64, at "Et d'un aveuglement."

ment, / N'est qu'un joüet du vent), this time in triple meter with black notation that fully exposes the trickery.[34] [Web 8.10]

Le Jeune had long been experimenting with ternary passages. As Isabelle His has amply demonstrated, his frequent use of ternary in the four-voice chansons published in his *Melanges* suggests it as a route to respect the prosody of a text and craft the most natural declamation. Furthermore, His's study reveals that Le Jeune was also experimenting with the use of both quantitative prosody and shifts to ternary as text-painting devices in this earlier repertoire. The composer's five-voice chanson *Helas j'ay sans mercy* offers a salient example, as he shifts to ternary at "de vertu excellent" to illustrate the older notion of triple as the meter of divine perfection.[35]

Le Jeune's *Octonaires* continue to develop the expressive possibilities of ternary and *musique mesurée*, although, following L'Estocart's foundational example, these lilting rhythms come to be most illustrative of the material world and its precarious transience. Like L'Estocart, Le Jeune establishes duple meter as his norm, though he marks his entire collection with a C, a newer sign that was beginning to replace the standard cut C of L'Estocart's day. Both *musique mesurée* and ternary deviated from the strict boundaries of duple time. In some cases, the syncopated effect of these homophonic passages that destabilize a sense of the duple tactus create what His describes as "a ternary in disguise."[36] We can see that Le Jeune exploits the clear relationship between ternary passages and *musique mesurée*, whose syncopations in duple time can indeed feel like a masked triple. Taken in combination with the fact that both the shifts to *musique mesurée* and the black-note/triple passages are homophonic, and that in some cases the shift to triple is a different way of notating an accentual pattern that accomplishes the same quantitative effect as *musique mesurée*, they become linked in their moral possibilities, though they retain their distinctive nuances (audibly, visually, and in terms of potential tempo).

Le Jeune's first setting, *Quand on arrestera* (I.1), introduces this *musique mesurée* effect in the sixth line, "Which runs through the night across the void of the heavens." The second setting, *Qui ne s'esbahira* (I.2), uses the effect at the end of the third line, "firm and stable earth" (*la terre ferme et*

[34] Le Jeune, *Octonaires (IX–XII)*, ed. Expert, 1–4.

[35] His, "Claude Le Jeune et le rythme prosodique," 213–25.

[36] Ibid., 217. See also Launay, "Les Rapports de tempo entre mesures binaires," 166–94; and Cœurdevey, "La Notation du rythme ternaire," 7–33.

stable), with a small reprise linking back to this at the beginning of line 6, "Is deciduous and mortal" (*Est caduc et mortel*). These inconstant constancies of nature set up the more overtly moral imagery in the fifth setting, *Y a-il rien si fort* (II.2), where Le Jeune illustrates the text "wind of your desires" (*vent de tes desirs*) with a marked 3 and the use of black notation. He then develops the association in the next setting, *Le beau du monde s'efface* (II.3), by shifting to 3 for each of the natural illustrations of transience (wind, flower, and wave). The following setting, *Comme de l'Aigle* (III.1), again uses triple, this time arriving in the wake of deceptive or disappointing pleasure ("le plaisir decevant"). The very next setting, *L'eau va vite en s'écoulant* (III.2), shows how this accruing rhythmic significance can pay off.[37] [Web 8.11] Like L'Estocart's setting for the same Octonaire, Le Jeune attends to the rhythmic build embedded in the poetry and in the corresponding passage in Seneca's *On the Brevity of Life*, discussed in Chapters 2 and 5. Opening in imitative polyphony between the upper two voices, the trickling melisma on "quickly" (*vite*) that appears in each voice in the first line returns and gains momentum in the second and third lines "Even faster the flying arrow, / And faster still passes" as more fleeting eighth-notes (and more voices) are swept into the melisma for each new line. In keeping with the constant flow of the imagery, the expected cadences are strategically evaded until the abrupt close on G, marked by the first rest in all voices, which arrives unexpectedly just after "the wind" at the beginning of the fourth line of text (m. 11). At this point, Le Jeune destabilizes the metrical grounding of the setting by immediately shifting to a black-note ternary passage, marked by a cut C and 3, illustrating the wind chasing the clouds (mm. 12–17). All of this rhythmic significance reaches its apex in the fifth line of text ("Mais de la joye mondaine"), where Le Jeune adds a twist to L'Estocart's ternary illustration for this passage (mm. 18–20). Returning to his standard C—but starting on a rest—the homophonic passage accelerates into dance-like triplets at "worldly joy" (see Example 8.1). The setting gains a frenetic energy as the voices return to polyphony and chase each other across the texture in wispy motives that remain always out of reach until the wind suddenly dies away, dropping the voices weakly on the final beat of the measure.

---

[37] Le Jeune, *Octonaires (I–VIII)*, ed. Expert, 31–34.

Example 8.1 Claude Le Jeune, *L'eau va vite*, mm. 8–21, in *Octonaires de la vanité et inconstance du monde* (Paris: Pierre Ballard, 1606). Based on the edition by Henry Expert

Example 8.1 Continued

The Ruins of Time

Questions of time, temporality, and transience were central to the Stoics and united under the rubric of learning to die. The Roman Stoics were famous for their recitals of the "ruins of history"—lists of powerful, wealthy, and accomplished individuals who all shared the same ignoble end in death. Marcus Aurelius used this strategy on several occasions in his *Meditations*. After a recital of deceased figures whose achievements were already lost to time, he continues:

When you look at yourself, see any of the emperors.
And the same with everyone else. Then let it hit you: Where are they now?

Nowhere . . . or wherever.

That way you'll see human life for what it is. Smoke. Nothing. Especially when you recall that once things alter they cease to exist through all the endless years to come.

Then why such turmoil? To live your brief life rightly, isn't that enough?[38]

Neostoic works followed this model of cataloguing the deaths of grand historical figures, including Duplessis-Mornay's *Excellent discours*, which includes a detailed rehearsal of ancient and more recent notables—from Emperor Augustus to Charles V—and their shared end. Following in this tradition, Mathieu's *Tablettes* offer a longwinded list of historical exemplars of famous deaths. Mathieu was the historian for Henri IV, after all, so he took the opportunity modeled by the Stoics to indulge in an extensive narration of all manner of famous and unusual deaths, with the recent murder of Henri IV offering a resonant case in point that all human accomplishments, even those of the "King of Reason," will end in dust and smoke.

An Octonaire penned by Simon Goulart embarks on this therapeutic exercise, following Marcus Aurelius in asking the probing question: "Where are they now?"

> Mon ame, où sont les grands discours
> De ces hautains fils de la terre?
> Ou sont les magnifiques cours
> Des Rois qui au ciel ont fait guerre?
> Je cuide voir, en y pensant,
> Une fume s'amassant,
> Au feu d'un bois sec que l'halaine
> Du vent escarte par la plaine.

[My soul, where are the great speeches / Of these lofty sons of earth? / Where are the magnificent courts / of Kings who have made war against the heavens? / I seem to see, in thinking of them, / An amassing smoke / From a fire of dry wood that the breath / Of the wind carries across the plains.]

---

[38] *Meditations* 10.31; trans. Hays, 139–40. See also *Meditations* 6.47.

The moral illustration of metrical destabilization arrives in full force through Le Jeune's setting for *Mon ame, où sont les grand discours* (V.1). As the lower voices fall to the lure of courtly magnificence, the third line of text fractures into a syncopated homophony that destabilizes the sense of meter. This rhythmic unease continues to build through the references to war and the expressive move to a signed triple and black notes for the hazy perception ("Je cuide voir en y pensant") of amassing smoke.[39] [Web 8.12]

Jacques de Gheyn II's *Allegory on the Equality of all Mankind in Death* (1599) created a more complex version of his teacher Goltzius's *Homo bulla* print, embedding that bubble imagery within a fuller range of Stoic ruin symbolism and supported by Hugo Grotius's Latin inscriptions. [Web 8.13] This pen and brown ink drawing features the same boy blowing bubbles from a straw pipe. The child is seated on a stone dais, with a winged hourglass overhead (symbolizing the fleeting rush of time), while the platform and arch are carved with the key mottos *Homo bulla* and *Quis evadis*. This message on human transience is positioned underneath a canopy with another core Stoic message: "Death makes the scepter and spade equal." Although the peasant and the king are drastically unequal in life, they are equal in death, as represented by the desiccated corpses in front of the boy. Their bodies point in different directions: one directs the viewer's gaze to a smoking urn, and the other to a vase of cut flowers. The opposing circles framing the upper part of the image remind the Christian viewer of the biblical treatment of death, with the Fall of Man on the left side and the Crucifixion on the right. The skull and crossbones that ornament the Fall of Man depiction represent that it was sin that introduced human mortality; and the cherubic ornament gracing the Crucifixion symbolizes the conquering of death through the innocence of Christ. Hanging above the raised dais, a larger image of the Last Judgment signals that living well results in tranquility not only in this life (the Stoic project), but in the next as well (the Christian goal).

It is well known that the sixteenth century developed a fascination with ruins that dovetailed with the turn toward recovering intellectual and cultural artifacts from the ancient past—with notable examples from the visual realm, such as Hieronymus Cock's print collection *View of Roman Ruins* (1551), and from poetry, such as in Joachim Du Bellay's small collection of sonnets, *Les Antiquités de Rome* (1558). The frequent depiction of ruins in *vanitas* paintings formed a moral nexus with the

[39] Le Jeune, *Octonaires (I–VIII)*, ed. Expert, 52–55.

conversation on aging in the Stoic and Neostoic traditions, for the image
of decaying buildings—formerly glorious markers of human accomplishment and power—was a reminder that time and mortality will erode
all things on this earth, from human bodies to trees and stone edifices.
Hendrick Goltzius's engraving *Fame and History*, from the series *The
Roman Heroes* (1586), links these visual and moral themes, featuring the
allegorical flying figure of Fame blowing her trumpet above a landscape
of Roman ruins, a winged hourglass, a skull, and History reading a book.
[Web 8.14] An even more arresting *vanitas* image that ties together the
topic of human and architectural aging is Goltzius's *Young Man Holding
a Skull and a Tulip* (1614). [Web 8.15] An exceptionally subtle example
of the genre, this drawing depicts a handsome youth wearing an elegant
doublet and plumed beret, beneath which appears his soft, cherubic face.
With full lips and with eyes gazing to the side, the youth's fresh humanity
dominates the scene. Behind him, in the shadows, is an hourglass set
within the niche of a ruined wall that bears the inscription "Quis evadet?"
(Who escapes?). Beneath it, the answer: "nemo" (no one). In his left hand,
the boy holds a skull, whose hard, empty eye sockets point in the same
direction as the boy's soft gaze, drawing a clear contrast between life and
death. In the boy's right hand is a tulip whose stem looks like a writing instrument, or "burin," for engraving the skull. Following the tulip's shapely
stem upward, the viewer's eye falls upon more ruins, this one bearing the
artist's monogram and the date.

Numerous *Octonaires* were penned in this poetic "ruins" tradition, no-
tably Chandieu's *L'estranger estonné regarde*:

> L'estranger estonné regarde, et se pourmeine
> Par les antiquitez de la gloire romaine.
> Il void les arcs rompus et les marbres luisans
> Mutilez, massacrez par la fureur des ans.
> Il void pendante en l'air une moussuë pierre,
> Qui arme ses costez des longs bras du lierre.
> Et qui est-ce, dit-il, qui ce bas, bas se fonde:
> Puis que le temps vainqueur triomphe de ce Monde.

[The foreigner looks amazed, walking / by the antiquities of Roman glory.
/ He sees broken arches and shining marble / mutilated, massacred by the
fury of years. / He sees hanging in the air a mossy stone, / its sides embraced

by long arms of ivy. / And who is it, said he, that settles themselves here: / since victorious time triumphs over this World.]

Delaune's emblem for Chandieu's *L'estranger estonné regarde* humorously confirms the identity of the teaching figure as an ancient sage by portraying him as a marble statue whose right arm has been broken off (see Plate 13). The witty visual also serves a reminder—which would have been agreeable to both the Skeptics and the Stoics—that even sages and their philosophies are subject to the brutal ravages of time.

Situated in the middle of L'Estocart's first collection of *Octonaires*, *L'estranger estonné regarde* (I.12) opens a trio of "ruins texts" composed by Chandieu. The second text in the group, *Antiquité, pourquoy as-tu donné* (I.13), was already discussed in Chapter 4 as a critique of the Aristotelian view of worldly goods, though credited, importantly, as a general fault of ancient times and their hollow material ambitions. This is followed by another of Chandieu's texts on antiquity, *Le Babylonien à rengé sous ses loix* (I.14). L'Estocart's settings for these three *Octonaires*, all in four voices, build sonic images of physical ruins through a strategic use of dissonance and shifts in texture that seem to expose the inner musical parts, much like a structure whose composition of beams, joints, and change in surface texture becomes more visible as it undergoes the process of decay. After a slow polyphonic build that frames the outlines of G Dorian and suggests an expansive sight of Roman ruins on view, L'Estocart's *L'estranger estonné regarde* (I.12) begins to break down this seamless fabric. [Web 8.16] Short, homophonic insertions rupture the sonic landscape with broken arches ("il void les arcs rompus," mm. 23–27) and lead to a harmonic shimmer on "les marbres luisans" (mm. 30–31) as the shadowy softness of the E-flat sonority catches a gleam of light in the signed F♯ at the weak D cadence that closes the line. The image supplied by Delaune's emblem—of the marble sage with a broken-off arm—finds musical purchase in L'Estocart's setting of this third line of text, where the soprano juts out from the otherwise homophonic texture, breaking off in a downward third at "mutilated" and "massacred" (mm. 31–34). L'Estocart continues this provocative use of dissonance and texture in *Le Babylonien a rengé sous ses loix* (I.14), witnessed in his preliminary cross-relation between the C♯ in the tenor and C♮ in the soprano in measure 29 that escalates into a simultaneous clash between these same tones as Persia is "vanquished" by time (m. 49). [Web 8.17] The final phrase setting "fallen monarchs" (*Les Monarques tombez*) again breaks down these ancient empires through a slow series of falling thirds that move across the four voices before seeming to crack with a harsh dissonance (an F in the soprano against a signed F♯ in the tenor at m. 116). These melodic and harmonic "cracks" mirror the globe depicted in Delaune's emblem for *Le Babylonien a rengé sous ses loix*. [Web 8.18] Although the sphere is often depicted as blank, here Delaune shows an atlas surrounded by representatives of the four empires, inscribed with what might be the contours of the continents, but which look more like cracks that might have come about through age, wear, or the damage of war.

L'Estocart's depiction of the musical beauty of ruins, decay, and aging, and his detailed attention to tone color, vocal texture, and rhythmic entropy foreground the aesthetic power of ruins. What art historians have noted, of course, is that this breakdown of exterior surfaces—represented in such severe and exquisite detail in seventeenth-century artistic ruins—illuminates detailed surface textures and exposes previously hidden structural elements. There is a surprising beauty revealed in the process of decay.[40] The philosophical and artistic reflection on ruins linked the broken-down remains of human accomplishment to the natural aging process that imprints the marks of time on all aspects of the natural world—from trees to human faces to flowers. We see this ethical and aesthetic concern with ruins in Marcus Aurelius' *Meditations*, as his recital of dead notables leads into one of his most stunningly beautiful entries:

> If you've immersed yourself in the principles of truth, the briefest, most random reminder is enough to dispel all fear and pain:
>
> . . . leaves that the wind
>
> Drives earthward; such are the generations of men.[41]
>
> Your children, leaves.
>
> Leaves applauding loyally and heaping praise upon you . . . A glorious reputation handed down by leaves.
>
> All of these "spring up in springtime"—and the wind blows them all away. And the tree puts forth others to replace them.
>
> None of us have much time. And yet you act as if things were eternal—the way you fear and long for them . . .
>
> Before long, darkness. And whoever buries you mourned in their turn.[42]

---

[40] Kuretsky, *Time and Transformation*, 29.
[41] Citation from Homer, *Illiad* 6.147 ff.
[42] *Meditations* 10.34; trans. Hays, 141–42.

Anyone who has witnessed the glorious display of leaves changing in the fall, as autumn bursts into riotous reds, golds, and yellows, can understand this metaphor of human transience as something intensely beautiful and appealing in its urgency. Although the changing leaves mark the imminent arrival of a long and perhaps dismal winter, these brief months of seeing leaves in the splendid process of seasonal decay remind many to stop and appreciate the present season for its impermanent majesty.

Chandieu's tenth Octonaire uses the vision of dying leaves in autumn for a similar moral aim, warning against the futility of any lasting human accomplishment:

> Lors que la feuille va mourant
> Par l'Automne, deshonnorant
> Avec sa laideur bazanée
> Le beau visage de l'année:
> C'est là un miroir de ta vie,
> Ores verte, et ores flestrie,
> Mondain, dont la vie s'enfuit
> Sans laisser ny feuille, ny fruit.

[When the leaf is dying / by Autumn, dishonoring / with its bronzed ugliness / the beautiful face of the year: / There is a mirror of your life, / now green, and now withered, / Worldly One, whose life flees / leaving neither leaf nor fruit.]

Le Jeune's four-voice setting of *Lors que la feuille va mourant* (X.1) rhythmically accomplishes this breakdown of time.[43] [Web 8.19] After a duo opening in his carefully accented prosody, all four voices come together by the middle of the musical phrase in the homorhythm characteristic of *musique mesurée*. Rather than switching back to imitative polyphony (as is the norm for Le Jeune), this setting continues on in *musique mesurée* for the next five lines of text—a surprising move that strips the leaves of the tree down to their most elemental movements. Dutch art theorists following Karel van Mander recognized two types of artistic virtuosity: *net* (a polished technique that obscures the artist's hand) and *rouw* (a rough stroke

---

[43] Le Jeune, *Octonaires (IX–XII)*, ed. Expert, 12–14.

that overtly draws attention to the artist's technique).[44] Le Jeune's brutal rhythmic exposure throughout most of his setting for *Lors que la feuille va mourant* offers a sonic version of the *rouw* touch—subverting the sense of the meter and leaving the singer clinging only to the stark beauty of these jagged musical contours.

Musical Still Lifes

Artus Aux-Cousteaux's one hundred musical settings for Mathieu's *Tablettes*—published in his two collections, *Les Quatrains de Mr Mathieu* (1636/1643) and *Suites de la première partie des Quatrains de Mr Mathieu* (1652)—were likewise inscribed in this philosophical landscape of musical "ruins."[45] Deeply conservative even at the time of their composition, Aux-Cousteaux's *Tablettes* settings offered a musical continuation of the earlier flourishing of polyphonic moral song established in the time of L'Estocart and Le Jeune. Like the poetic and musical collections featuring Pibrac's texts, a subtle framework of musical constancy and order pervades Aux-Cousteaux's settings, from which the composer then occasionally diverges with surprising and subtly provocative illustrative effects.

Mathieu's opening text sets the tone for the entire collection, and places this work within a long line of Neostoic meditations on death:

> Estime qui voudra la Mort espouventable,
> Et la fasse l'horreur de tous les animaux:
> Quant à moy je la tiens pour le poinct desirable,
> Ou commencent nos biens, et finissent nos maux.

[Let those who so wish, think death dreadful, / and make it the horror of all animal life: / For my part, I hold it as the most desirable end, / where our good begins and our troubles end.]

Mathieu's text may have been directly inspired from a passage in Du Vair's *Philosophie morale des Stoiques* where he explains the Stoic argument for

---

[44] Kuretsky, *Time and Transformation*, 30.

[45] Artus Aux-Cousteaux, *Les Quatrains de Mr Mathieu, mis en musique à trois parties, selon l'ordre des douze modes* (Paris: Pierre Ballard, 1636, reprinted 1643); and *Suites de la première partie des Quatrains de Mr Mathieu, mis en musique à trois voix, selon l'ordre des douze modes* (Paris: Robert III Ballard, 1652).

therapeutically reframing our opinions of death, which are the root cause of anxiety, sorrow, and anger. To secure happiness, Du Vair explains, "we must become disposed to not worry about death at all, and to not fear it when it arrives," for death "has nothing dreadful" (*n'a rien d'espouventable*) and is not an evil but rather is the "end of all misfortune" (*la fin de tous maux*).[46]

Aux-Cousteaux's opening musical setting, *Estime qui voudra*, offers an experience of this Stoic consolatory argument (see Example 8.2). Unfolding in sober homophony, the setting of the first line ("Let those who so wish, think death a dreadful thing") sets up a clear modal profile in the announced first mode (C Ionian), with the high voice marking out a perfect melodic profile for C modes with its initial C–G leap and then the slow stepwise descent from A down to C (mm. 4–6), leading into an utterly conventional cadence at the close of the line on the word "dreadful" (*epouvantable*) (mm. 6–7). Considering the evocative text, this musical setting seems remarkably unremarkable. There is no hint of dread or horror at the terrifying reality of death that is the subject of this Tablette; instead, this supremely bland setting retains an unflappable predictability and confirmation of the stated mode through each subsequent melodic phrase, predictable cadence, and signed repeat of the final line. Thus, the setting generates musical assurance, steering the confrontation with death away from disgust, terror, and anxiety and toward a familiar and harmonious acceptance of both death and life, both rooted in natural law and offering "nothing strange, frightening, or imperfect" (Tablette I.2).

Aux-Cousteaux's third arrangement, of Mathieu's *Cette difformité de la Mort n'est que feinte* (I.3), inspired by Stoic discussions of stripping away the fear-inducing mask from the face of death, operates along similar principles of musical assurance:

> Cette difformité de la Mort n'est que feinte,
> Elle porte un beau front sous un masque trompeur:
> Mais le masque levé il n'y a plus de crainte,
> On se rit de l'enfant qui pour un masque [a] peur.

[This ugliness of Death is only a ruse, / she wears a beautiful face under a deceptive mask: / But when the mask is lifted there is no more fear, / We laugh at the child who is afraid of a mask.]

---

[46] Du Vair, *La Philosophie morale des Stoiques*, 59–60, ed. Tarrête, 93–94.

Example 8.2 Artus Aux-Cousteaux, *Estime qui voudra*, mm. 1–17, in *Les Quatrains de Mr Mathieu* (Paris: Pierre Ballard, 1636)

With a modal clarity that mirrors that of the opening setting, Aux-Cousteaux's *Cette difformité de la mort* offers another stately homophonic opening, this time establishing the F Ionian mode. However, the diminished dissonance caused by the tricky F♯ that arrives in the middle voice at "only a ruse" leads to more deception in the next measure, creating a cross-relation with the B♮

in the high voice before resolving into a cadence on C. After describing the mask in line 2, Aux-Cousteaux begins to destabilize its homophonic certainty through a tactile series of suspensions that lift the disguise and show that there is nothing to fear.

Aux-Cousteaux's union of philosophical and modal pedagogy seems to have resonated enough with the Ballard atelier's readership to have justified the 1643 reprint and the companion *Suite* of 1652, which set the second fifty of Mathieu's *Tablettes*, just before Aux-Cousteaux's death. Although the fashion for *basse continue* had become widespread by this point, Aux-Cousteaux's *Tablettes* retain a self-consciously antiquated polyphonic style, which the composer admitted "was no longer in fashion," recalling the illustrious ancients, "Orlande, Claudin le Jeune, du Caurroy, et Bournonville."[47] Outdated musically, but still current philosophically and pedagogically at the time of its composition, Aux-Cousteaux's settings thus forged a sonic link back to the important polyphonic collections produced for Pibrac's *Quatrains* and the *Octonaires* corpus decades earlier. Moreover, they harnessed increased moral force according to the Neostoic logic of naturalizing difficult moral precepts by rendering them familiar and rationalizing them through the recognizable progression of the logically ordered modal settings.

Aux-Cousteaux's dodecacordal approach follows Le Jeune's *Octonaires* in beginning with the C modes. However, Aux-Cousteaux presents a more ambitious modal system, offering both natural and transposed versions of each mode in their "harmonic" and "arithmetic" divisions of the octave species (see Appendix 2, Tables A2.4 and A2.5). The harmonic (authentic) modes suggest a division of the octave species into a fifth, then a fourth, while the arithmetic (plagal) modes begin with a fourth, then a fifth. For Aux-Cousteaux, these differences in octave species go beyond vocal range to indicate his attention to exploring the melodic and harmonic implications of these alternate octave divisions, experimenting with both the hard B♮ and soft B♭ that posed such enduring challenges for modal composition.[48]

Aux-Cousteaux generally retains the order of Mathieu's published *Tablettes*; however, he displayed some interest in shaping the relationship

[47] Aux-Cousteaux, *Suite de la première partie des Quatrains de Mr Mathieu*, "Advertissement au Lecteur."

[48] Marin Mersenne praised Aux-Cousteaux for this in *Harmonie universelle* (Paris: R. Charlemagne et P. Ballard, 1636), VI, 422.

between text and modal assignment by switching the fifteenth and sixteenth texts and varying how many pieces he set in each modal category,
from one to four settings each. Well-suited to the consistent tone of
Mathieu's poetry on death, Aux-Cousteaux's *Tablettes* emphasize the symbolic importance of the modal system as a therapeutic musical exercise
that was explored extensively in Le Jeune's *Octonaires*, a collection that
was still highly regarded within Aux-Cousteaux's elite circle. A laudatory
poem by F. Gougeon for Aux-Cousteaux's *Suite* hints at this underlying
modal therapeutics:

> Aux-Cousteaux, rare esprit, dont la belle methode
> Traite icy doctement les cadences du Mode,
> Tu nous as temperé les aigreurs de la Mort;
> Si bien, que ta douceur tient nostre ame ravie,
> Et personne ne peut, s'il ne se plaint à tort,
> Asseurer que la mort est contraire à la vie.[49]

[Aux-Cousteaux, rare wit, whose lovely method / treats here learnedly
the cadences of the Modes, / You have tempered for us the bitterness of
Death; / So well, that your sweetness holds our souls ravished, / And no
one can, if he does not complain wrongly, / Affirm that death is contrary
to life.]

The success of Aux-Cousteaux's *Tablettes* among artistic elites of his day,
when considered in light of the prevailing concerns of Neostoicism, was
supported by an artistic logic built around the Stoic aesthetics of consolation.
As we have seen so amply demonstrated, Neostoics preferred formats that
were stylistically simple, yet allegorically profound. Aux-Cousteaux's sonic
images of life and death were anchored to the slow progression through the
modal system, a self-guided exercise that suggested a shift in musical perspective for each octave species.

Attention to Aux-Cousteaux's laudatory poets for these collections
reveals that his music found an audience among adherents of philosophical and artistic Neostoicism in Paris in the first half of the seventeenth

---

[49] Aux-Cousteaux, *Suite de la première partie des Quatrains de Mr Mathieu*, fol. iiir. The identity of
F. Gougeon remains unknown.

century. Aux-Cousteaux's music appealed to a highly placed Parisian circle of poets, playwrights, and painters affiliated with the Académie française and the Académie royale, many of whom displayed a documented interest in Neostoicism. One of Aux-Cousteaux's laudatory contributors was the Parisian poet and playwright Hélie Poirier (b. 1600), whose professional affiliations and publications linked him to Neostoic circles.[50] Another of Aux-Cousteaux's admirers was the poet and dramaturg Charles de Beys (1610–59), who offered laudatory contributions for both the *Meslanges* (1644) and *Suites* (1652). Beys also penned his own Stoic poetry. His published *Stances, sur le mespris de la mort* included a clearly Senecan paraphrase: "The one who dies thus every day of his life will never fear dying." (*Celuy qui meurt ainsi tous les jours de sa vie, / Ne craindra jamais de mourir.*)[51]

Nicolas Bellot (c. 1600–72), who was both *peintre ordinaire du Roy* and a syndic for the Académie royale de peinture et de sculpture, also penned laudatory verse for Aux-Cousteaux's first collection of *Tablettes*.[52] Although we have no known record of artistic work by Bellot, he did publish a fascinating treatise at the intersection of art and philosophy titled *Le Stoïque chrestien, ou la victoire de la joye innocente et vertueuse sur la tristesse* (1655).[53] In his Avertissement to the reader, Bellot reveals his desire to offer his friends "some sentiments of Stoic philosophy that can be called an ample and rich shop of intellectual pharmaceuticals, which can remedy by reason all the evils of life." He takes the time to educate his readers on Zeno's foundation of the school under a large porch (*stoa*) in the city of Athens, thus leading the group to be named the Stoics, or in French: *l'école du Portique*. Bellot critiques the older, more extreme form of Stoicism as complete *apatheia*—"too savage in its first fervor"—and reiterates the critique of the sect as effectively creating a statue, not a sage. He

---

[50] After converting to Protestantism, Poirier became affiliated with the Leiden Calvinist circle of André Rivet, and then entered Descartes's circle at the court of Christina of Sweden. Poirier's literary works include a French edition of the Dutch Neostoic Hugo Grotius's *De l'antiquité de la république des hollandois*, published in Poirier, *Deus harangues panégyriques, l'une de la pais l'autre de la concorde* (Amsterdam: Jan Blaeu, 1648). See H. W. van Tricht, "Hélie Poirier, Translator of Erasmus," *Quaerendo* 10 (1980): 153–55.

[51] Charles de Beys, *Œuvres poétiques* (Paris: Quinet Toussaint, 1651), 94.

[52] Christian Michel, *The Académie royale de peinture et de sculpture: The Birth of the French School, 1648–1793*, trans. Chris Miller (Los Angeles, CA: Getty Research Institute, 2018), 7–11. Although Bellot's date of birth remains uncertain, he was married to Marie Leclerc before 1638. There is another, unrelated Nicolas Bellot (b. 1580, Darnieulles, Vosges; d. 1640 in Épinal), who was also a painter.

[53] Bellot, *Le Stoïque chrestien*.

goes on to advocate for a more moderated Stoicism, which he credits to the example of Seneca, allowing that the "Honneste homme" can in fact experience both sadness and joy without disorder. He advocates the pursuit of:

> This praiseworthy mediocrity, that flees equally the extremes of all the passions, and particularly those which carry us to sadness and joy; to prevent the one from degenerating into dissolution, as much as the other in an incurable melancholy. I found remedies against both of these abuses, in reading the works of the Stoics and the beautiful way, of which our century, being quite corrupted, is not so destitute, as to find yet some people capable of rebuilding an excellent Porch on the ancient ruins of Athens.

Bellot then praises the Neostoic work of several of his contemporaries, including the painter Peter Paul Rubens and Marin Le Roy Gomberville, whose *Doctrine des mœurs, tirée de la philosophie des Stoiques* had appeared almost a decade prior. These artists shared an interest in what Bellot describes as "the art of reasoning" (*l'art de raissoner*) through "a truly speaking painting" (*une véritable peinture parlante*)—language long at the heart of emblem theory.[54]

Bellot concludes his Avertissement to *Le Stoïque chrestien* by describing his participation in a gathering of Neostoics:

> the sweet society of honest people, who gather together sometimes under the title of *Stoic Christians*. They are grounded in solid virtue, and their conversation agrees so powerfullly with those who practice it, that several nobles who wish to live without ceremony already use with pleasure the proverb that is common and familiar among them, *in the Stoic fashion* [*à la stoïque*].

Links between Bellot and other contributors of Aux-Cousteaux's laudatory poetry (like Beys) suggest that the composer and his friends may have been among this group of "Stoic Christians," along with influential members of

---

[54] See for example, Claude Mignault's "To the Learned and Honest Reader" for his groundbreaking "Treatise on Symbols" that prefaced his edition of Alciato, *Emblemata* (Antwerp: Christophe Plantin, 1577). "Everyone knows that a picture is a silent poem and a poem is a talking picture, the poem expresses the spirit, the picture the body." Translated in Denis Drysdall's critical edition, available at https://www.emblems.arts.gla.ac.uk/Mignault_letter.html.

the Académie française known to be connected to Bellot's circle (such as Gomberville, Tristan L'Hermite, and Guillaume and François Colletet).[55]

Backed by this prestigious creative network, Bellot makes a strong argument in Le Stoïque chrestien for the importance of music, painting, and poetry as "honnestes recreations"—practices with therapeutic value in their Stoic approach that "contribute much to guide us toward mental tranquility and deliver us from all sorts of sadness."[56] The laudatory poetry prefacing Bellot's work frequently mentions music (along with poetry and painting) as expressions of this beautiful Stoicism, as we see in the opening lines of Étienne Carneau's lengthy poem in praise of Bellot and his work:

> Que j'aime la Stoïcité!
> Que sa maniere est accomplie
> Pour vaincre la melancolie
> En combatant l'adversité!
> Eloigné du terroir Attique,
> BELLOT, tu repeins ce Portique . . .

[How I love Stoicism! / How accomplished a means it is / To vanquish melancholy / Far from the Attic lands, / Bellot, you repaint this Porch . . .]

Carneau went on to admire the success of Stoic music and art, which "imitates the beauty of nature" and inspires a "new Court" that is natural and without artifice, without embellishments, and without malice.

Another laudatory contribution for Bellot, signed by De Montigny, praises Bellot's union of the arts: "Handling pleasantly the paintbrush, the pen, and the lyre" all in "the name of Stoicism, through an air that pleases everyone." (Maniant agreablement / Le pinceau, la plume, et la lyre. . . . Le nom de la Stoïcité / D'un air qui plaist à tout le monde.) The final laudatory sonnet, by Pierre Du Pelletier, calls Bellot's treatise "a sweet charm for my senses" (un doux charme pour mes sens) and praises the way "poetry and

---

[55] Tristan l'Hermite was a pseudonym of François l'Hermite (c. 1601–1655, Paris); he was a dramatist, poet, and one of the founders of French classical drama. His tragedy La Mort de Sénèque (1644) was one of his important works.

[56] Bellot, Le Stoïque chrestien, 136–37.

music here come together in sweet accents" (*La poësie et la Musique / Y composent de doux accens*).[57]

Gomberville's Stoic emblem book, *Doctrine des mœurs*, ellicited praise from Tristan l'Hermite, another member of the Académie française with ties to Bellot and Beys, in similarly potent musical terms:

> Superbe Gallerie, où du grave Stoique
> Les austeres Leçons touchent si bien le sens,
> Tu n'as point de Tableaux qui ne soient ravissans,
> Et n'as point d'ornement qui ne soit magnifique.
> L'ame qui se promene en ta belle fabrique
> Cede sans resistance à tes attraits puissans,
> Où la Philosophie en des tons si pressans
> Nous forme des Vertus un concert harmonique.

[Superb Gallery, where from the grave Stoic / the austere lessons touch the senses so well, / You have no portraits that are not ravishing, / and no ornaments that are not magnificent. / The soul that walks through your beautiful invention / gives way without resistance to these powerful attractions / where Philosophy in compelling tones creates for us a harmonious concert of Virtues.]

These laudatory poems testify to the broader musical interests of these confirmed Stoic enthusiasts. Read together with their social links to Aux-Cousteaux, and Bellot's own role as a contributor of laudatory poetry for Aux-Cousteaux's music, it seems likely that the artistic activities of Bellot's group of Stoic Christians included singing and listening to Aux-Cousteaux's *Tablettes*.

Even as there is clear evidence that this union of philosophy, art, and music generated enthusiasm among at least some elite practitioners, the negative stereotype of Stoicism persisted. Aux-Cousteaux's *Tablettes* may have generated the witty musical riposte in François de La Roche's drinking song (*air à boire*) titled *Amis, qu'un esprit de Stoïque*. It was printed by Robert III

---

[57] "un doux charme pour mes sens"; "La poësie et la Musique / Y composent de doux accens." Liminal verse by Pierre Du Pelletier for Bellot's *Le Stoïque chrestien*.

Ballard in 1658, just a few years after he had published Aux-Cousteaux's final collection.[58] The first *sizain* mockingly sings:

> Amis, qu'un esprit de Stoïque
> Depuis peu me paroist un estrange animal,
> De vouloir establir pour maxime authentique
> Que la mort est un bien sans mal:
> Ce sentiment est faux, je ne puis plus le croire,
> Puisqu'elle nous ravit le doux plaisir de boire.

[My friends, it has recently struck me / That a Stoic spirit is a strange beast, / Wishing to establish as a genuine maxim / that death is a good without evil: / This sentiment is false, I cannot believe it, / since it robs us of the sweet pleasure of drinking.]

Launched from the outside, this satire suggests an awareness of the cultural importance of song in disseminating Stoic and Neostoic philosophy in this period, which offered the unusual focus on morbid contemplation as the sweetest path to human consolation and constancy.

Musically antiquated, Aux-Cousteaux's *Tablettes* offered an easy target for the kind of anti-Stoic mockery regularly launched against devotees of the philosophy. However, serious Stoic practitioners would have been well-situated to appreciate the composer's highly allegorical approach to sound that had defined the earlier corpus of polyphonic moral song. Aux-Cousteaux's setting for Mathieu's moderating text *L'un ayme cette vie, et l'autre la mesprise* (I.8) offers just a hint of these rewards, with an unusual leap and attendant suspension at "cherche l'honneur" and a cascading release of pleasure that begins in the bottom part and is caught by the high voice at "l'aymer les plaisirs." In his setting of *La vie est un flambeau* (I.10), composed according to the Zarlinian criteria for D Dorian, Aux-Cousteaux allows the harsh brilliance of the B♮ and C♯ to flame across his opening phrase (mm. 2–4), before blowing it out with little bursts of melismatic breath (mm. 6–7, 10–11, and 12–13) that puff across the texture until the light is fully extinguished by the beginning of the third line ("La

---

[58] François de La Roche, *V. Livre d'airs à quatre parties* (Paris: Robert Ballard, 1658), fols. 24v–25r.

fait fondre et couler") mm. 16, with the arrival of black notation and a melodic softening of the B♮ to B♭ that dims to darkness (see Example 8.3).

Although offered on an even smaller scale than these earlier settings, Aux-Cousteaux's *Tablettes* settings continued to explore the fundamental questions of time, duration, and transience through shifts to ternary rhythm and metrical subversion as a mode of text expression that built on the moral tropes developed by composers like Boni, L'Estocart, and Le Jeune. In his setting for Mathieu's *Le fruit sur l'arbre prend sa fleur* (I.11), Aux-Coustaux sketches the life cycle of the dying flower that appears in so many *vanitas* paintings—from first bloom to last wilting. One of the most rhythmically-driven settings in the collection, Aux-Cousteaux's *Le fruit sur l'arbre prend sa fleur* accelerates into the climactic third line, where the botanical stages of birth through death are mapped onto the wheel of time ("voila sur quelle roué") in a circular melodic shape reminiscent of Boissard's emblem of the floral life cycle on the wheel of fortune discussed in Chapter 5 [see Web 5.6]. Aux-Cousteaux's setting for Mathieu's Tablette I.51, *Il n'y a point de mort soudaine à l'homme sage* (*Suite* 1) also offers a clever musical surprise that recalls L'Estocart's denial of the final closure as an image of vanishing in his setting for the Octonaire by Chandieu *La glace est luisante et belle*. Aux-Cousteaux underscores the Stoic advice to premeditate on misfortune so as to be unshaken by any accidents or perils of ocean travel. He dramatically closes the setting by leaving the unwary singers stranded at sea, as his final measure releases each voice from the texture in succession, drifting upward to a poignant cessation of sound like the fading wind ("quand il n'a plus de vent") (see Example 8.4). Another salient example is Aux-Cousteaux's setting for Mathieu's *La vie est une table* (I.13), which musically depicts life as a card game with four players. The second line shifts to the metrical and moral salience indicated by black notation when observing that "Time has the upper hand" (*le temps tient le haut bout*). The setting closes as the masterful fourth player, Death, takes all.

Conclusion

Throughout both the ancient Stoic corpus and the corpus of moral song settings, the paradox of time and temporality remained a central point of

Example 8.3 Artus Aux-Cousteaux, *La vie est un flambeau*, mm. 1–20, in *Les Quatrains de Mr Mathieu* (Paris: Pierre Ballard, 1636)

Example 8.4 Artus Aux-Cousteaux, *Il n'y a point de mort soudain*, mm. 29–32, in *Suite de la première partie des Quatrains de Mr Mathieu* (Paris: Robert III Ballard, 1652)

inquiry that brought numerous philosophical threads into creative tension within the *memento mori* tradition. This persistent rehearsal of death, decay, and ruin may seem depressingly morose or perversely macabre; however, as Ryan Holiday reminds his modern-day readers in *The Daily Stoic*: "Meditating on your mortality is only depressing if you miss the point. It is in fact a tool to create priority and meaning. It's a tool that generations have used to create real perspective and urgency. To treat our time as a gift and not waste it on the trivial and vain. Death doesn't make life pointless but rather purposeful. And fortunately, we don't have to nearly die to tap into this. A simple reminder can bring us closer to living the life we want."[59] The Stoic goal, according to Epictetus, is a life of tranquility, fearlessness, and freedom.[60]

Montaigne's essay "That to philosophize is to learn to die" explains that the only way to overcome the havoc wrought by our discomfort with death is through attentive sensory familiarization, which can build over time:

> Let us learn to meet it steadfastly and to combat it. And to begin to strip it of its greatest advantage against us, let us take an entirely different way from the usual one. Let us rid it of its strangeness, come to know it, get used to it.

---

[59] https://dailystoic.com/memento-mori/
[60] Epictetus, *Discourses* 2.1.

Let us have nothing on our minds as often as death. At every moment let us picture it in our imagination in all its aspects.[61]

By this logic, it is not surprising that these severe collections of poetry on death and transience attracted such a range of poetic and musical settings, offering as they did precisely this kind of imaginative contemplation of death in a temporarily flexible modality that could be practiced regularly by a small group of performers and listeners. Gomberville's emblem *That to philosophize is to learn to die* recalls Montaigne's famous essay and subtly draws upon a musical analogy for the progression of Time (see Plate 14).[62] Although Time leads the unwitting into old age in despair or insensibility, it passes with grace and dignity for the attentive sage who listens to the voice of Prudence. Noisy and chaotic, the *pictura* shows a sage seated in a busy scene of sensory distraction. Ignoring the aggressive voices and gestures of the surrounding figures, the sage calmly holds an oblong music partbook in his lap. His hand is lifted in the standard gesture of a descending index finger marking the passing of musical time. According to Jane Hatter, this physical depiction of the tactus, or musical beat, was an important sixteenth-century artistic trope, offering a well-recognized symbol of the passage of time and human aging.[63] The imagery would have been even more salient for late sixteenth- and early seventeenth-century readers with recourse to the rich corpus of moral settings dedicated to the exposition of these musico-philosophical questions. Singers of this polyphonic moral corpus were exposed to the problem of musical (and human) time on numerous levels, as they were brought into harmony only through their universal relation-ship to the anchoring musical tactus. At the same time, they were collectively subject to all of the practical and symbolic ambiguities embedded in mu-sical time. From Le Jeune's rhythmic virtuosity to Aux-Cousteaux's allegor-ical echoes, these settings persistently manipulate temporal expectations for moral transformation.

The *memento mori* exercise was thus not intended to produce or sustain melancholy. Quite the contrary, this meditation on time and transience proposed a remedy for melancholy that was structured to regenerate dra-matically an immersive appreciation of the present. As Marcus Aurelius put

---

[61] Montaigne, *Essais*, I.19, trans. Frame, 72.

[62] Gomberville, *Doctrine des mœurs*, fol. 92r–v.

[63] See Grant, *Beating Time*, 54–59; and Jane Hatter, "'Col Tempo': Musical Time, Aging and Sexuality in 16th-Century Venetian Paintings," *Early Music* 39 (2011): 3.

it: "Give yourself a gift: the present moment."[64] Attention (*prosoche*) was a core Stoic mode of being, one that is quite similar in some ways to modern mindfulness practices.[65] Marcus Aurelius explained the unexpected fruits of this presentism, worth citing at length to conclude this chapter:

> We should remember that even Nature's inadvertence has its own charm, its own attractiveness. The way loaves of bread split open on top in the oven; the ridges are just by-products of the baking, and yet pleasing, somehow: they rouse our appetite without our knowing why.
>
> Or how ripe figs begin to burst.
>
> And olives on the point of falling: the shadow of decay gives them a peculiar beauty. Stalks of wheat bending under their own weight. The furrowed brow of the lion. Flecks of foam on the boar's mouth.
>
> And other things. If you look at them in isolation there's nothing beautiful about them, and yet by supplementing nature they enrich it and draw us in. And anyone with a feeling for nature—a deeper sensitivity—will find it all gives pleasure. Even what seems inadvertent. He'll find the jaws of live animals as beautiful as painted ones or sculptures. He'll look calmly at the distinct beauty of old age in men, women, and at the loveliness of children. And other things like that will call out to him constantly—things unnoticed by others. Things seen only by those at home with Nature and its works.[66]

This attention suggests a dramatic reconceptualization of the aesthetic experience, offering a mode of feeling that moves beyond the appreciation of paintings or musical arrangements. This aesthetic sensitivity reveals the profound beauty that can be experienced in the simplest encounters of everyday life—blooming, singing, and dying in precious chains of temporal precarity.

---

[64] *Meditations* 8.44; trans. Hays, 110.
[65] Hadot, *Philosophy as a Way of Life*, 84.
[66] *Meditations* 3.2; trans. Hays, 27–28.

Conclusion

Suspensions of Desire

> Your trouble is your desire;
> And what you complain about is your own pleasure.[1]

Allegory of the Arts

At first glance, Simon Luttichuys's *Corner of a Painter's Studio: Allegory of the Arts* (1646) presents a scene of chaos, a jumbled collection of tools and objects typical of an artist's workshop: a painter's palette, a human bone, several busts, a globe, a map, a botanical book, and a seascape painting (see Plate 15). A bubble hangs suspended by a thread above the scene, mirroring the shape of the globe below and offering in its reflective surface a self-portrait of the artist, who can be seen working at his easel. In their catalog of still-life paintings from the Netherlands, Alan Chong and Wouter Kloek recognized several markers of Stoicism in this particular still life, including the prominent bust of Seneca, the human bone, and a copy of the Neostoic painter Rubens's self-portrait. Strangely, they immediately disregard the invitation presented by these philosophical signals: the bust of Seneca represents a vague symbol of "the devotion to knowledge and learning"; the globe, map, and botanical book are merely scientific references "upon which the painter depends"; and the drawings "are source materials for the artist."[2] Chong and Kloek go on to interpret the creative juxtapositions throughout the painting as reference points for the power of art. Particularly salient is the seascape painting featured on the left side of the table. They note that Luttichuys was

---

[1] "Ton mal est ton desir, / Et ce dont tu te plains, est ton propre plaisir." Chandieu, *Octonaires*, ed. Bonali-Fiquet, 65.

[2] Chong and Kloek, *Still-Life Paintings from the Netherlands*, 186–88.

The Voice of Virtue. Melinda Latour, Oxford University Press. © Oxford University Press 2023. DOI: 10.1093/oso/9780197529744.003.0010

not a seascape painter and argued that the seascape must therefore have been owned by the painter, rather than created by him. Their account also marks the presence of illusionistic devices: the fly perching on the painting is a common trompe-l'œil trope, as well as the nail in the wall on the upper left. An even craftier visual pun is the drawing of a nude man lying on the ground that is sticking out from beneath the seascape. As Chong and Loek aptly recognize, this position of the nude drawing "humorously suggests that the figure has been shipwrecked, and even crushed, by the scene above."

After this careful exposition of the visual elements of the painting, Chong and Kloek come to the rather anti-climactic conclusion that this scene of chaos held little moral significance, claiming that "Luttichuys's many references to the power of painting make a vanitas interpretation of the painting highly unlikely. Even seventeenth-century viewers of moralistic inclinations could not have naturally associated this reflection of the artist with the ephemerality of the bubble. Even the bone on the table, which some viewers might consider a reminder of death, could be seen by others as a standard prop in any artist's studio."[3] While the artistic practicality of these objects and tools certainly bears mentioning, what these art historians missed by ignoring the Stoicism signaled in the references to Seneca and Rubens is that the references to the power of art were embedded in the discussions of transience and mortality across the Stoic corpus. Certainly, an uninformed viewer might have read the human bone as a stock artist's prop or viewed the dying flower as just a flower. However, any reader of the Stoic and Neostoic philosophical materials produced during this period would have recognized the underlying order signaled in this chaos, a reasoned arrangement that brought into productive moral conversation both the objects and artistic techniques visible in the painting.

Luttichuys was immersed in the Neostoicism flourishing in the Protestant communities that stretched from Britain to the Dutch Republic. Born in London in 1610, into the community of Huguenot refugees who had fled the persecution of the religious wars, his family eventually settled in Amsterdam, establishing close ties to the English reformed community in the Dutch Republic.[4] His work offers a rich visual guide to the Neostoicism shaping his intellectual and artistic circles: *Allegory of the Arts* gathers together in one visual tableau the diverse precepts and problems encountered

---

[3] Ibid., 187.
[4] Bernd Ebert, *Simon und Isaack Luttichuys: Monographie mit kritischem Werkverzeichnis* (Berlin: Deutscher Kunstverlag, 2009), 33–53.

as one journeys through the landscape of moral song collections. The dominant bust of the ancient Stoic Seneca looming over a smaller print of the Neostoic Rubens, who had died six years before this painting (copied from Anthony van Dyck's *Iconography*) was created, brings up the continuity between past and present versions of the school.

The human bone and the floating bubble obviously represent human mortality and transience. The positioning of the Bible next to an illustrated botanical work, resting on a globe, suggests the relationship between Stoic physics (and natural law) and Christianity—and the idea of Nature as a "second Bible" would certainly have occurred to some viewers. Because these are both printed books, this pairing could have also provoked contemplation of the relationship of the divine, universal *logos* (also known as Nature) to the Christian understanding of the creator God. The round shape of the globe also suggests a relationship to the reflective bubble, recalling the concept of following Nature as the mirror of self-understanding. However, its trustworthiness is cast into doubt by its ephemeral form, which can burst at any moment, much as the life of that figure might expire unexpectedly. The map of Europe and the western coast of Africa could lead to reflection on both the geographical and scientific impulses underpinning Stoic empiricism, as well as the moral implications of the concepts of the world city and the community of sages, coupled with the radical assertion that rationality and universal sympathy are embedded in the universal fabric of the world. The perspective that makes these continents seem small underscores another important theme in Stoic ethics: that all human ambitions and attempts to divide up the earth are futile ambitions that will end in mere dust, subject to the same fragility seen in all living things.

The seascape painting with the illusion of the person shipwrecked in front of it would have been easily recognized as a core illustration throughout the Stoic tradition, gamely serving up a reminder that Fortune's winds are always changing and reinforcing the concept of virtue as the only good through the post-shipwreck reminder that "all that is mine I carry with me." The fleshly castaway thrown in front of the seascape, the witty trompe-l'œil of the nail and the fly, and the subtle reflection of the artist at work all underscore the sensory power of art to engage moral understanding, all while warning against art's simultaneous power to deceive—to replace the real world with an almost lifelike copy. What was more problematic for the overarching illustration of transience was that the art object, cherished and protected, was created to endure and carve out a lasting legacy for the artist, and it might signal an inappropriate desire for the luxury, status, and power that this elite art object represents. The artistic question signaled here through the allegorical images and techniques of production—and throughout the *vanitas* corpus more broadly—is about the power of the artistic object to both incite and therapeutically treat desire.

Of all the arts, music offers the most visceral experience of desire. As Susan McClary has compellingly shown, composers working in the decades around 1600, furnished with an abundant toolbox of sonic conventions developed over centuries of polyphonic practice, displayed an acute interest in simulating desire, denial, and fulfillment.[5] Composers of moral song settings turn out to have played an unusually important role in clarifying the stakes of this musical power, as the Neostoic poetry they were setting was filled with explicit warnings against desire and its close accomplice, pleasure—the prime enemies of constancy, tranquility, and freedom. These recurring moral warnings against desire thus offered composers a brilliant opportunity to harness a well-recognized language of musical desire that could serve as a powerful mode of engaging Stoicism.

We have already seen numerous examples throughout this book of the arousal of musical pleasure and immersive sonic desire through a range of expressive devices that create a fleshly musical counterpart that cannot remain within the boundaries of cold austerity. L'Estocart's setting for Chandieu's pent-up *Jamais n'avoir et tousjours desirer* (I.8) drives home the paradoxical expression of desire in the moral corpus:

> Jamais n'avoir et tousjours desirer
> Sont les effects de qui aime le monde.
> Plus en honneur et richesses abonde,
> Et plus encor on l'y void aspirer.
> Il ne jouit de cela qui est sien,
> Il veut l'autrui, il l'estime, il l'adore.
> Quand il a tout, c'est alors qu'il n'a rien,
> Car ayant tout, tout il desire encore.

---

[5] Susan McClary, *Desire and Pleasure in Seventeenth-Century Music* (Berkeley, CA: University of California Press, 2012), 6–8. For the rhetoric of desire in later French airs, see Catherine Gordon-Seifert, *Music and the Language of Love: Seventeenth-Century French Airs* (Bloomington, IN: Indiana University Press, 2011), 237–59.

[Never having but always desiring / are the effects of loving the world. / The more honor and riches abound, / the more one yearns for them. / Enjoying nothing already owned, / he wants other things, esteeming and adoring them. / When he has all, it is then that he has nothing, / Because having all, he desires everything still.]

Esther Inglis rendered her own version of this Octonaire in her most seductive *lettere piacevolle* script, a hand with such lavishly curling terminals and long descenders that it visually drips with desire (see Plate 16). L'Estocart likewise paints sonic desire in his setting of *Jamais n'avoir et tousjours desirer*, beginning with a slow build from the lowest voice to the superius, shoring up the boundaries of the D to G diapente for G Dorian, but initially empty of the normal melodic filling that establishes the mode (mm. 1–3). [Web C.1] The lower voices quickly declaim the second half of the line "toujours desirer," repeating it until the delayed superius part finally voices "desire" at measure 8 with a luxurious melodic flourish that gains tension through a chain of suspensions in the lower voices before achieving fulfillment in the cadence on D at measure 10. As this setting unfolds, L'Estocart continues to create an unadorned texture of almost entirely syllabic imitative polyphony, from which he diverges at heightened moments expressing love, pleasure, and desire. He offers a small taste of what is to come in measure 19: the contralto sings a simple but emotive melisma at the "love" of the world, but then delivers increasingly lush moments of musical desire through both long melismas and the simultaneous friction of suspensions, for the abundance of riches (mm. 32–35) and for the adoration of worldly goods (mm. 62–66). The setting wraps up in a circular syllabic downward sequence of repetitions of "tout il desire," which enchain the singers in a relentless pull toward the final cadence.

L'Estocart's following Octonaire, setting Chandieu's *Quand le mondain travaille et tracasse* (I.9), also simulates mounting desire. [Web C.2] This setting is one of the rare arrangements where L'Estocart diverges from his comfort zone of G Dorian, centering the Octonaire in the modal domain associated with A Phrygian, though left unconfirmed and struggling against the alternative tonal area suggesting D Dorian. The reward for this futile desire is a stark mounting of pleasure, which arrives in the suspension at "Plaisir dessus plaisir" (m. 19), and then a stunning passage of sensory desire with the sliding suspensions stimulating lavish wish fulfillment ("pour combler le souhait") in measures 24–29. The setting closes with the simple response to the question,

"What is the product of all of this desire?": "He builds his own ruin." (*Il bastit sa ruine.*) Arriving as flickers of arousal within an otherwise carefully restrained setting, these sparks of desire could clearly be fanned into a flame that would threaten to burn the whole moral project down. Why then persistently feature this mode of engagement that so clearly traffics in desire when the Stoic project was ostensibly dedicated to therapeutically eradicating it?

The key to this fraught relationship can be found in the mode of allegory itself. Among the ancient schools, the Stoics were famous lovers of allegory and deeply invested in its moral potential. As Ilaria Ramelli argues, allegory was not merely a literary technique; it was "part and parcel of *philosophy* in Stoicism"; in fact, "allegory was *philosophy* for the Stoics."[6] Glenn Most credits the first generation of Stoics for bringing allegorical interpretation to the center of philosophical activity, but claims that it was the Roman Stoics who surpassed the contributions of Neoplatonism and solidified allegory "as a respectable, indeed virtually indispensable way to save both the poets' myths and the philosophers' doctrines."[7] Neostoic poets like Pierre Mathieu signal an appreciation of the moral possibilities inherent in musical allegory, as we see with stunning clarity in Tablette III.53, which allegorizes both the book of music itself and the expressive application of black notation:

> Qui voit la Cour il voit un livre de musique,
> Elle adjouste tousjours les ennuis aux plaisirs,
> Et à la blanche notte une noire elle applique,
> Les deux ont peu de pause et beaucoup de souspirs.

[The one who views the court will see a book of music. / It always adds annoyance to pleasure, / And at the white note, it applies a black one. / The two have little rest and much sighing.]

Not only does Mathieu's text recall the many uses of black notation across the moral song corpus to map triple meter musically onto the instability of the court, irrational excess, and pleasure, but the use of French musical

[6] Ilaria Ramelli, "The Philosophical Stance of Allegory in Stoicism and its Reception in Platonism, Pagan and Christian: Origen in Dialogue with the Stoics and Plato," *International Journal of the Classical Tradition* 18 (2011): 336.

[7] Glenn Most, "Hellenistic Allegory and Early Imperial Rhetoric," in *The Cambridge Companion to Allegory*, ed. Rita Copeland and Peter T. Struck (Cambridge: Cambridge University Press, 2012), 27–38.

terms for rests—*pause* and *soupir*—offers a rhythmic double entendre on the moral sense of pleasure-seeking offering no rest but always seeking more. A later text in Mathieu's collection, Tablette III.65, again points to the power of music, along with other precarious pursuits to transform moral behavior:

> La musique, le vin, et l'amour ont sur l'homme
> Un pouvoir absolu, la voix ravit les cœurs,
> Le vin trouble l'esprit, la volupté l'assomme,
> Les plaisirs innocens n'alterent point les mœurs.

[Music, wine, and love have over a person / An absolute power; the voice ravishes hearts, / Wine muddles the mind, sensual indulgence knocks them out, / Innocent pleasures never distort morals.]

Music was clearly no innocent player in this moral project; it was a force that could be wielded strategically in the service of Stoic therapeutics.

This Stoic enthusiasm for allegory remained evident in the early modern period and is one of the ways in which the sect produced an outsized influence on European culture, far beyond adherence to its doctrines or therapies. Across its long transmission, the Stoics were lauded and lampooned for their delight in drawing allegorical significance from everything around them. A case in point is François Rabelais's *Cinquième livre*, which pushes Stoic allegorizing to deliberately ridiculous proportions.[8] Cleanthes famously used an allegorical approach to interpreting poetry, arguing that poetry and music are particularly fertile sites for this sort of contemplation of hidden realities.[9] By some accounts, this was one of the Stoics' reasons for choosing a path of moral education that did not include the censorship of poetry and the arts. Even in cases where the original material was licentious or rationally problematic, the Stoics argued that one could still find benefit from it through a process of moral contemplation that drew out a deeper truth. The most famous (and scandalous) example was Chrysippus' argument that one could interpret the votive image of Hera fellating Zeus as a metaphor for the genesis of the world, because instead of getting swept away in the eroticism

---

[8] See Dobbins, *Music in Renaissance Lyons*, 36–37; and Jerry Nash, "Rabelais and Stoic Portrayal," *Studies in the Renaissance* 21 (1974): 63–82.

[9] *SVF* 1.486. See Ramelli, "The Philosophical Stance of Allegory," 336.

of the image, one could productively activate a critical faculty that could produce higher contemplation.[10] Marcus Aurelius suggested a similar defensive
technique of analysis as a rational way to keep musical desire in check:

> To acquire indifference to pretty singing, to dancing, to the martial
> arts: Analyze the melody into the notes that form it, and as you hear each
> one, ask yourself whether you're powerless against *that*. That should be
> enough to deter you.
>
> The same with dancing: individual movements and tableaux. . . .
>
> And with everything—except virtue and what springs from it. Look at
> the individual parts and move from analysis to indifference.
>
> Apply this to life as a whole.[11]

Of course, the abundant evidence of Stoic interest in music should lead us to
take this advice in its larger context. Elsewhere, the Stoic emperor had used
a far more positive musical analogy for Stoic exercise in constancy: "When
jarred, unavoidably, by circumstances, revert at once to yourself, and don't
lose the rhythm more than you can help. You'll have a better grasp of the
harmony if you keep on going back to it."[12] As any music scholar will tell
you, analyzing music at the level of its "individual parts" may offer a rational
hedge against the scorching heat of musical pleasure while in the moment
of study, but the increased understanding accrued through this exercise
can generate an even greater and more pleasurable immersive listening and
singing experience in future encounters. Allegory, analysis, and desire prove
to be unexpected bedfellows.

The composers of moral song that I have discussed throughout this book
strategically manipulate musical allegories of desire, whipping up luxurious
melismas, libidinous suspensions, breathtaking metrical tricks, and other
techniques of sonic pleasuring—all justified through their work in exegeting
the texts. Framed by a grid of Stoic musical metaphors of universal sympathy,
harmonic order, and proportion, these well-established musical devices of
desire offer a striking parallel to the Stoic theory and therapy of the passions.
The Stoic view of the passions as errors of judgment demanded attention
to the value-laden environment that shapes and controls how specific external events are experienced internally; and their therapeutic techniques of

---

[10] *SVF* 11.1071–4. See A. A. Long, *Stoic Studies*, 75–76.

[11] *Meditations* 11.2; trans. Hays, 148.

[12] *Meditations* 6.11; trans. Hays, 70.

consolation sought to expose and reframe these problematic opinions, which foster an environment where the most extreme passions will be acutely felt.

Musical structures, whether in the late modal or the early tonal system in play in the decades around 1600, offer keen attention to this basic principle of the relationship between a surrounding value system and the experience of desire. For example, there is nothing essentially or innately desirable, pleasurable, or painful about any particular tone when sounded in isolation. However, the experience of a tone becomes weighted with significance, emotion, desire, or discomfort depending upon its relationships within its surrounding musical value system. A simple suspension, the most foundational device for musical desire in this period, makes this point clearly, as the application of a neighboring dissonance to any note will produce a marked desire for resolution that can be delayed and built up and extended in numerous ways that extend the trajectory of desire to its fulfillment. Stretching, denying, or fulfilling the expectations of closure at cadences offer an even more inescapable allegory of desire. In McClary's account, these "teleological urges" drive the tectonic shifts toward tonal compositional around these decades.[13] Music, as a system, thus offers an incredibly powerful analogy for the Stoic theory of the emotions, which were deeply attuned to the way context, and the relationship between an environment and a field of judgments, produces desire and its immoderate passions.

The modal organization systematically developed by Boni, Le Jeune, and Aux-Cousteaux directs even more attention to the inherent consequences of these subtle shifts, as each octave species in the modal cycle offered a set of inherent relationships, first at the melodic level, and with certain associated consequences in terms of the vertical harmonies produced as a result. The presence of a particular tone, alteration, or cadence point might be perfectly ordinary in one mode, but could be felt as shocking, inappropriate, or marvelous in another. Furthermore, the model of polyphony, with its independent and relatively equal lines, repeatedly calls to mind the critical determination of what is up to the individual singer (in contrast to what is not). In his Letter 84, Seneca developed this idea through the striking musical analogy of a choir of singers, whose individual parts can be brought together in a type of unity and harmony without losing their distinctiveness. Particularly in this period, when substantial performance decisions—such as the application of *ficta*, the interpretation of metrical relationships, and the

---

[13] McClary, *Desire and Pleasure*, 7–8.

reading of text underlay—were still in flux and largely left to the discretion of the singers, the practical consequences of these choices would be acutely felt across the interconnected group.

Coda: Singers and Listeners

The liminal verses included in the prefaces for these collections testify to their success in crafting a philosophically rich musical experience for a first audience of singers and listeners who were well-versed in these ethical and artistic problems. A laudatory contribution for L'Estocart's second volume of *Octonaires* signals a recognition of these Stoic underpinnings, acknowledging that some "censor" might critique his daring compositions as "un petit logis qui a trop grand portique" ("a small lodging that has too large a porch"). Recall that Stoicism was known as the school of the porch (*stoa*), and in French *l'école du Portique*. For those singers and listeners reading this "philosophy of the porch," the moral underpinnings of these poetic and musical collections would have been unmistakable, thanks to the Stoic flavor of the imagery, language, and moral teachings. These Stoic guideposts would have thus invited a richly textured mode of singing and listening—undergirded by the therapeutic program of Stoic and Neostoic philosophy and its call to daily rehearse death as the foundation for living well.

Perhaps the most surprising musical analogy for Stoicism offered by these settings is the idea that through deliberate self-restraint and stylistic constriction, pleasure very well might be enlarged. The devices encountered in the moral corpus that unleash surprising moments of breathtaking pleasure remind us that these musical devices of desire are all the more moving because of their rarity and their contrast to the calm restraint that generally characterizes these collections. Simon Goulart circulated this surprising point in his collection of sayings of Epictetus: "The rarest pleasures give more pleasure" (*Les plus rares plaisirs donnent plus de plaisir*).[14] Du Vair, in his *Philosophie morale des Stoiques*, arrives at the same counterintuitive conclusion for the other dangerous desires as well: "The truest and shortest means of becoming rich is to scorn riches. To become rich, we must not increase our means, but diminish our desires: the one who is content—he is rich."[15] According to the Stoics, less really is more.

[14] Seneca, *Œuvres morales et meslées de Senecque*, trans. Goulart, 3:210.
[15] Du Vair, *La Philosophie morale des Stoiques*, ed. Tarrête, 77.

Simon Goulart—whom we have gotten to know as L'Estocart's friend, a poet of the *Octonaires*, and an author of vernacular Neostoic texts— contributed a series of exceptionally thoughtful poems in praise of L'Estocart's music. As a prolific publisher of Stoic works, Goulart was well positioned to recognize music's paradoxical potential as an enduringly desirable means of freeing ourselves from an attachment to fleeting worldly desires. He makes this point beautifully in a poem printed in the superius part of the second collection of *Octonaires*:

> J'AY pensé, mon PASCHAL, que les honneurs du Monde,
> Ses biens, ses passetemps, passent l'aile du vent,
> Sechent comme une fleur, vont plus viste que l'onde,
> Et sont un songe vain qui nous va decevant.
> Mais je change d'avis tes doux accords oyant:
> Et puis, qu'impossible est que ta Musique meure,
> Je maintien que le Monde, en si beaux airs fuyant,
> Honnorable, plaisant, riche, et ferme demeure.

[I thought, my Paschal, that the honors of the World, / Its goods, its pastimes, pass on the wings of the wind, / Wilt as a flower, they go more quickly than the wave, / and are a vain dream that is going to disappoint us. / But I change my mind on hearing your sweet harmonies: / And since it is impossible that your Music should die, / I maintain that the World, in such beautiful fleeting airs, / honorable, pleasant, rich, and firm will remain.]

Seneca's *On the Brevity of Life* put it even more simply, citing an older aphorism: *Ars longa, vita brevis.*[16] Life is short; art is long. While Seneca credits for this maxim "the greatest of physicians," Hippocrates, early modern sources like Gilles Corrozet's *Propos memorables* (1579) attributed the saying to Zeno: "The Philosopher Zeno said that there is nothing of which we are so impoverished as time. Life is brief, but art is long, and is more than sufficient for healing the sickness of bodies."[17]

[16] Seneca, *De brevitate vitae* I.1; trans. Davie, 140.
[17] Gilles Corrozet, *Propos memorables, des nobles et illustres hommes de la chrestienté: Augmentez de plusieurs graues et excellentes sentences, des anciens Hebrieux, Grecz, et Latins* (Lyon: Benoist Rigaud, 1579), 87.

Even as this fundamental paradox swept across early modern Europe like a virus, a closer look at its Stoic transmission reveals contradiction as a fundamental device of Neostoic therapy that was harnessed at multiple levels. In creating a tension between oppositions, even seemingly dogmatic statements could lead to thoughtful nuance in practice. Not only does strategic denial of pleasure actually lead to a recalibration of the senses that offers greater pleasure in simple things, but this curtailing of the lust for riches and power counterintuitively leads some people to acquire these very things more easily. It is through an illustration of inconstancy that one recognizes constancy; when pleasure is decentered, it might be increased; in rejecting the pull of ambition, a person becomes truly qualified to lead; and through the daily rehearsal of death comes the freedom to live a fully present life. The epidemic of the paradox proved to be the cure.

Musical Settings of Moral Poetry

Table A1.1. Musical settings of the *Quatrains de Pibrac*

MUSICAL SOURCES, PRINTED

DATE	AUTHOR/TITLE	PUBLISHER	CATALOG/LOCATION	COMMENTS
[1580]	*Nouveau recueil et élite de plusieurs belles chansons joyeuses, honnestes, et amoureuses . . . Avec les quatrains du s. de Pibrac aussi en musique*	Rouen: Thomas Mallard	RISM 993122188; USTC 34667; FB 43522	Monophonic setting for Pibrac's *Quatrains*
1581	*Nouveau recueil et élite de plusieurs belles chansons joyeuses, honnestes, et amoureuses . . . Avec les quatrains du s. de Pibrac aussi en musique*	Rouen: Richard l'Allemand	D-W, 5 Musica	Identical setting as above, different format
1582	Paschal de L'Estocart, *Cent vingt et six quatrains du Sieur de Pibrac . . . mis en musique à deux, trois, quatre, cinq et six parties*	Lyon: Barthélemy Vincent [Geneva: Jean I de Laon]	RISM 990037833; Guillo-L 69; GLN-2951	Polyphonic settings for 126 quatrains (some doubled settings)
1582	Guillaume Boni, *Les Quatrains du Sieur de Pybrac mis en musique à 3, 4, 5, et 6*	Paris: Adrian Le Roy et Robert Ballard	RISM 99006218; Lesure 251; USTC 48550 to 48553; FB 43527 to 43530	Polyphonic settings for 126 quatrains
1583	Guillaume Boni, *Les Quatrains du Sieur de Pybrac mis en musique à 3, 4, 5, et 6*	Paris: Adrian Le Roy et Robert Ballard	RISM 990006219; Lesure 259; USTC 48560 to 48565, 23548; FB 43531 to 43534	Reprint of 1582 edition
1583	Jean Planson, *Les Quatrains du Sieur de Pybrac . . . mis en Musique à 3, 4, 5, et 7 parties*	Paris: Adrian Le Roy et Robert Ballard	Lesure 260; USTC 30566; FB 43542	Polyphonic settings for 18 quatrains
1583	Orlande de Lassus, *Vingtdeuxième livre de chansons à quatre et cinq parties, d'Orlande de Lassus et autres*	Paris: Adrian Le Roy et Robert Ballard	Lesure 263; RISM 1583; FB 33047 to 33050	Polyphonic settings for 7 quatrains
1585	Orlande de Lassus, *Vingtdeuxième livre de chansons à quatre et cinq parties, d'Orlande de Lassus et autres*	Paris: Adrian Le Roy et Robert Ballard	RISM 993120759; Lesure 272; FB 33068 to 33071	Reprint of 1583 edition

Year	Title	Place: Publisher	Source	Description
1616	Piat Maulgred, *Airs et chansons a III, V. VI. et VIII. parties, accomodees tant a la voix, qu'aux instrumens*	Douai: Jean Bogard	RISM 990040120	Quatrain 28, *Le sage fils*
1622	Jean de Bournonville, *Cinquante Quatrains du Sieur de Pybrac, mis en musique à 2, 3, et 4 parties*	Paris: Pierre Ballard	RISM 990006521; Guillo-B 1622-B	Polyphonic settings for 50 quatrains
1703	*Chants des Noels, anciens et nouveaux de la grande Bible, notez avec des basses*	Paris: Christophe Ballard	B-Br, Fétis 2.400 A (RP); F-Psg, Rés Vm 161	Setting of the *Quatrains*, air with basso continuo
1704	*Chants des Noels, anciens et nouveaux de la grande Bible, notez avec des basses*	Paris: Christophe Ballard	RISM 1001183943	Reprint of 1703 edition
1705	Simon-Joseph Pellegrin, *Chants des cantiques des noels nouveaux et des chansons spirituelles*	Paris: Christophe Ballard	BnF Tolbiac, YE-11355 (BIS)	Notated timbre, *Quatrains de Pibrac*

MUSICAL SOURCES, MANUSCRIPT

Source		Description
Paston Manuscript, Fitzwilliam Museum, Cambridge, MS 52A 30-32, fols. 25v–26		Orlande de Lassus, Quatrain 34, *Ce que tu peux*, and Quatrain 22, *Heureux qui met*
Manuscript collection, early 17th c., BnF, Musique, Rés Vmd Ms 49		Tenor part for an unknown setting of Quatrain 33, *Ayme l'Honneur*
[s.d.], Simon-Joseph Pellegrin, *Chants des noels anciens*. BnF; Tolbiac, YE-11355 (BIS)		Notated timbre, *Quatrains de Pibrac*

Table A1.2. Musical Settings of the *Octonaires de la vanité et inconstance du monde*

		MUSICAL SOURCES, PRINTED		
DATE	AUTHOR/TITLE	PUBLISHER	CATALOG	COMMENTS
1582	Paschal de L'Estocart, *Premier livre des Octonaires de la vanité du monde, mis en musique a trios, quatre, cinq et six parties*	Lyon: Barthélemy Vincent [Geneva: Jean I de Laon]	RISM 990037831; GLN-2949; USTC 94276; FB 9771	26 polyphonic settings of texts by Chandieu
1582	Paschal de L'Estocart, *Second livre des Octonaires de la vanité du monde, mis en musique a trois, quatre, cinq et six parties*	Lyon: Barthélemy Vincent [Geneva: Jean I de Laon]	RISM 990037832; GLN-6969	24 polyphonic settings of texts by Goulart (12) and Du Chesne (12)
1606	Claude Le Jeune, *Octonaires de la vanité et inconstance du monde mis en musique à 3 et à 4 parties*	Paris: Pierre Ballard	RISM 990037462; Guillo-B 1606-H	36 polyphonic settings of texts by Chandieu (29), Goulart (4), and Du Chesne (3)
1615	Nicolas Vallet, *Secretum musarum*	Amsterdam: Nicolas Vallet	RISM 990065204	Lute transcription of Le Jeune's setting of *Quand on arrestera* (à 4), from his *Octonaires*
c.1611	Claude Le Jeune, *Octonaires de la vanité et inconstance du monde mis en musique à 3 et à 4 parties par Claude Le Jeune*	Paris: Pierre Ballard	Guillo-B1611-C	Reprint of 1606 edition
1631	Claude Le Jeune, *Octonaires de la vanité et inconstance du monde, mis en musique à 3 et à 4 parties par Claude Le Jeune*	Paris: Pierre Ballard	Guillo-B 1631-C	Reprint of 1606 edition
1641	Claude Le Jeune, *Octonaires de la vanité et inconstance du monde, mis en musique à 3 et à 4 parties par Claude Le Jeune*	Paris: Robert III Ballard	RISM 990037463; Guillo-B 1641-D	Reprint of 1606 edition, but with new liminal poetry

Table A1.3. Musical Settings of Pierre Mathieu's *Tablettes ou Quatrains de la vie et de la mort*

MUSICAL SOURCES, PRINTED			
DATE **AUTHOR/TITLE**	**PUBLISHER**	**CATALOGUE**	**COMMENTS**
1621 Jean Rousson, *Recueil de chansons spirituelles, avec les airs nottez sur chacune d'icelles*	La Flèche: Louys Hebert	RISM 990056259	2 monophonic settings, one for each group of 100 quatrains
1636 Artus Aux-Cousteaux, *Les Quatrains de Mr Mathieu, mis en musique à trois parties selon l'ordre des douze modes*	Paris: Pierre Ballard	Guillo-B 1636-C	Polyphonic settings for Mathieu's first 50 quatrains
1643 Artus Aux-Cousteaux, *Les Quatrains de Mr Mathieu, mis en musique à trois parties selon l'ordre des douze modes*	Paris: Pierre Ballard	RISM 990002883; Guillo-B 1643-A	Reprint of 1643 edition
1652 Artus Aux-Cousteaux, *Suite de la première partie des Quatrains de M. Mathieu, mis en musique à trois voix, selon l'ordre des douze modes*	Paris: Robert III Ballard	RISM 990002884; Guillo-B 1652-A	Polyphonic settings for Mathieu's second 50 quatrains

Organization of Moral Song Collections

Table A2.1. Paschal de L'Estocart, *Premier livre des Octonaires de la vanité du monde, mis en musique à trois, quatre, cinq et six parties.* Lyon: Barthélemy Vincent [Geneva: Jean I de Laon], 1582

No.	Incipit	Rasse des Noeux, BNF Ms fr. 22563	Rime françoise, Houghton Ms Fr 337	Strasbourg Emblem ed. [1580]	Position in Chandieu, 1583	Voices	Cleffing	System	Final
	Note: All texts by Chandieu. Emblems V and T not in 1580 edition.								
1	L'eau va viste en s'escoulant		2	B	25	4	G2C2C3F3	♭	G
2	Tu me seras tesmoin		3	C	26	4	G2C2C3F3	♭	G
3	Mondain, si tu le sçais, di moy	1	5	D	27	4	G2C2C3F3	♭	G
4	Le beau du Monde s'efface	2	6	E	28	3	G2C2C3	♭	G
5	La glace est luisante et belle	6	10	I	31	4	G2C2C3F3	♭	G
6	Quand on arrestera	3	7	F	1	4	G2C2C3F3	♭	G
7	Orfevre, taille moy une boule	5	9	H	30	4	G2C2C3F3	♭	G
8	Jamais n'avoir et tousjours desirer	10	14	M	35	4	G2C2C3F3	♭	G
9	Quand le mondain travaille et tracasse	15	19	Q	40	4	G2C2C3F3	♭	A
10	Au langage des cieux une fois j'entendi	11	15	(V)	36	4	G2G2C2C2	♭	G
11	Le Monde est un jardin	9	13	L	34	3	G2G2C3	♭	G
12	L'Estranger estonné regarde	7	11	K	32	4	G2C2C3F3	♭	G

13	Antiquité, pourquoy as-tu donné	12	16	N	37	4	G2C2C3F3	♭	G
14	Le Babylonien a rengé sous ses loix	13	17	O	38	4	G2C2C3F3	♭	G
15	C'est un arbre que le Monde	8	12		33	3	G2C2C3	♭	G
16	Plus tost ou pourra faire	4	8	G	29	5	G2c2c3c3f3	♭	G
17	Je vi un jour le Monde combattant	16	20	R	41	5	G2G2G2C2F3	♭	G
18	Celuy qui pense pouvoir	14	18	P	39	3	C2C3F3	♭	G
19	O qui pourra avoir ce bien				45	4	G2C2C3F3	♮	A
20	Quel monstre voy-je là				46	4	G2C2C3F3	♮	G
21	Quand le jour, fils du Soleil				6	5	G2C2C3C3F3	♮	A
22	Toy qui plonges ton coeur	17	21	(T)	42	4	G2C2C3F3	♮	G
23	Arreste, arreste, atten, ô Mondain				47	4	G2C2C3F3	♮	G
24	J'ay veu, j'ay veu que le Monde				44	3	G2C2C3	♭	G
25	Où est la mort?	19	23		43	6	G2G2C2C3F3F3	♭	A
26	C'est folie et vanité	18	22	S	50	6	G2G2C2C3C3F3	♭	G

Table A2.2. Paschal de L'Estocart, *Second livre des Octonaires de la vanité du monde, mis en musique à trois, quatre, cinq et six parties*. Lyon: Barthélemy Vincent [Geneva: Jean I de Laon], 1582

No.	Incipit	Poet	Other printed sources	Voices	Cleffing	System	Final
1	Le rocher orgueilleux sent tomber	Goulart		4	G2C2C3F3	♭	C
2	Que sont les conseils humains	Goulart		4	G2C2C1F3	♭	F
3	Mon âme, où sont les grands discours	Goulart		4	G2C2C3F3	♭	F
4	Pauvre ver, travaille, tracasse	Goulart		4	G2C2C3F3	♭	F
5	As-tu mis en oubliance	Goulart		3	G2C2C3	♭	F
6	J'aperçus un enfant	Goulart		4	G2C2C3F3	♭	F
7	Quand je lis, quand je contemple	Goulart		4	G2C2C3F3	♭	C
8	Le Monde est outrageux	Goulart		4	G2C2C3F3	♭	F
9	Ce Monde est une galère	Goulart	Poupo 1585, No. 7	3	G2C2C3	♭	D
10	Qu'est-ce du cours et de l'arrêt du Monde?	Goulart	Poupo 1585, No. 8	4	G2C2C3F3	♭	F
11	Des Monarques la grandeur	Goulart	Poupo 1585, No. 13	5	G2C2C3C3F3	♭	F
12	Mais que ferai-je plus au Monde	Goulart		5	G2C2C3C3F3	♭	F
13	Quelle est cette beauté?	Du Chesne	*Morocosmie* 1583, No. 5	4	C1C3C4F4	♭	G
14	Le péché et la mort	Du Chesne		4	C1C3C4F4	♮	E
15	Morte est la mort	Du Chesne		5	C1C3C4C4F4	♮	E

16	Pourquoi mets-tu ton espérance?	Du Chesne	*Morocosmie* 1583, No. 16	3	G2C2C3	♭	G
17	Tout ce Monde est un tabourin	Du Chesne	*Morocosmie* 1583, No. 25	4	G2C2C3F3	♭	G
18	Monde, pourquoi fuis-tu?	Du Chesne	*Morocosmie* 1583, No. 3	4	G2C2C3F3	♭	G
19	Plutôt les yeux du firmament	Du Chesne	*Morocosmie* 1583, No. 30	5	G2C2C3C3F3	♭	G
20	Peintre, si tu tires le Monde	Du Chesne	*Morocosmie* 1583, No. 6	5	G2C2C3C3F3	♭	G
21	Et le Monde et la mort entre eux	Du Chesne	*Morocosmie* 1583, No. 7	4	C1C3C4F4	♭	G
22	Le Monde est un grand parlement	Du Chesne	*Morocosmie* 1583, No. 4	3	G2C2C3	♭	G
23	Vous peuples basanés	Du Chesne		4	G2C2C3F3	♮	G
24	Ce Monde est un pèlerinage	Du Chesne	*Morocosmie* 1583, No. 20	6	G2C2C3C3C2F3	♮	G

Table A2.3. Claude Le Jeune, *Octonaires de la vanité, et inconstance du monde, mis en musique à 3 et 4 parties*. Paris: Pierre Ballard, 1606

No.	Incipit	Poet	Position in L'Estocart, Octonaires 1582	Position in Chandieu, 1583	Voices	Cleffing	System	Final	Mode
1	Quand on arrestera	Chandieu	I.6	1	4	G2C2C3F3	♭	F	1 (Ionian), transposed
2	Qui ne s'esbahira	Chandieu		2	4	G2C2C3F3	♭	F	1 (Ionian), transposed
3	Plustost on pourra faire	Chandieu	I.16	29	3	G2C1C3	♭	F	1 (Ionian), transposed
4	Le feu, l'air, l'eau	Chandieu		3	4	C1C3C4F4	♭	F	2 (Hypoionian), transposed
5	Y a il rien si fort	Chandieu		4	4	C1C3C4F4	♭	F	2 (Hypoionian), transposed
6	Le beau du monde s'éface	Chandieu	I.4	28	3	C1C3C4	♭	F	2 (Hypoionian), transposed
7	Comme de l'Aigle	Chandieu		19	4	G2C2C3F3	♭	G	3 (Dorian), transposed
8	L'eau va vite en s'écoulant	Chandieu	I.1	25	4	G2C2C3F3	♭	D	3 (Dorian), transposed
9	Vous fleuves et ruisseaux	Chandieu		5	3	G2C1C3	♭	G	3 (Dorian), transposed
10	C'est un grand mal que l'extreme	Chandieu		23	4	C1C3C4F4	♭	G	4 (Hypodorian), transposed
11	Qu'as tu? Pauvre amoureux	Chandieu		24	4	C1C3C4F4	♭	G	4 (Hypodorian), transposed
12	C'est un arbre que le monde	Chandieu	I.15	33	3	C1C3F3	♭	G	4 (Hypodorian), transposed

13	Mon ame, ou sont les grans discours	Goulart	II.3		4	C1C3C4F4	♮	E	5 (Phrygian)
14	Quand le jour, fils du Soleil	Chandieu	I.21	6	4	C1C3C4F4	♮	E	5 (Phrygian)
15	Le rocher orgueilleux	Goulart	II.1		3	C1C2C4	♮	E	5 (Phrygian)
16	Quand la face noire des Cieux	Chandieu		7	4	C2C4F3F5	♮	E	6 (Hypophrygian)
17	Mondain, qui vis et meurs	Chandieu		13	4	C2C4F3F5	♮	E	6 (Hypophrygian)
18	As tu mis en oubliance	Goulart	II.5		3	C2C3F3	♮	E	6 (Hypophrygian)
19	Quel Monstre, voy-je là	Chandieu	I.20	46	4	G2C2C3F3	♮	F	7 (Lydian)
20	Areste, atens, ô Mondain	Chandieu	I.23	47	4	G2C2C3F3	♮	F	7 (Lydian)
21	Plustost les yeux du firmament	Du Chesne	II.19		3	G2C2C3	♮	F	7 (Lydian)
22	L'Ambitieux veut toujours	Chandieu		20	4	C1C3C4F4	♮	F	8 (Hypolydian)
23	J'ay de l'avare et de l'ambitieux	Chandieu		21	4	C1C3C4F4	♮	F	8 (Hypolydian)
24	Pauvre ver travaille	Goulart	II.4		3	C1C3C4	♮	F	8 (Hypolydian)
25	Quand la Terre au Printemps	Chandieu		8	4	G2C1C2C3	♮	G	9 (Mixolydian)
26	L'Esté ralumant ses feux	Chandieu		9	4	G2C2C3C4	♮	G	9 (Mixolydian)
27	La glace est luysante et belle	Chandieu	I.5	31	3	G2C1C3	♮	G	9 (Mixolydian)

(continued)

Table A2.3. Continued

No.	Incipit	Poet	Position in L'Estocart, Octonaires 1582	Position in Chandieu, 1583	Voices	Cleffing	System	Final	Mode
28	Lors que la fueille va mourant	Chandieu		10	4	C1C3C4F4	♮	G	10 (Hypomixolydian)
29	Vois-tu l'Hyver accroupi	Chandieu		11	4	C3C4C4F4	♮	G	10 (Hypomixolydian)
30	Celuy qui pense pouvoir	Chandieu	I.18	39	3	C1C3C4	♮	G	10 (Hypomixolydian)
31	Le Mondain se nourrit toujours	Chandieu		16	4	G2C2C3C4	♮	A	11 (Aeolian)
32	Quelle est ceste beauté	Du Chesne	II.13		4	C1C3C4F4	♭	D	11 (Aeolian), transposed
33	C'est folie et vanité	Chandieu	I.26	50	3	G2C1C3	♮	C	11 (Aeolian)
34	Ambition, Volupté, Avarice	Chandieu		18	4	C1C3C4F4	♮	A	12 (Hypoaeolian)
35	Orfévre taille moy	Chandieu	I.7	30	4	C1C3C4F4	♮	A	12 (Hypoaeolian)
36	Ce Monde est un pelerinage	Du Chesne	II.24		3	C1C3C4	♮	A	12 (Hypoaeolian)

Table A2.4. Artus Aux-Cousteaux, *Les Quatrains de Mr Mathieu, mis en musique à trois parties selon l'ordre des douze modes*. Paris: Pierre Ballard, 1636

No.	Incipit	Mode	No. in Mathieu, *Tablettes*	Cleffing	System	Final
1	Estime qui voudra la mort espouvantable	1 (Ionian)	I.1	C1C3C4	♮	C
2	L'homme abhorre la mort	1 (Ionian)	I.2	C1C3C4	♮	C
3	Cette difformité de la mort n'est que feinte	1 (Ionian), transposed	I.3	G2C1C3	♭	F
4	On deguise la mort de postures estranges	1 (Ionian), transposed	I.4	G2C1C3	♭	F
5	A qui craint cette mort, la vie est desja morte	2 (Hypoionian)	I.5	G2C1C3	♮	C
6	Chacun craint cette mort d'une frayeur égale	2 (Hypoionian)	I.6	G2C1C3	♮	C
7	Quel bonheur te promet la vie pour la suivre?	2 (transposed)	I.7	C1C3C4	♭	F
8	L'un ayme cette vie, et l'autre la mesprise	2 (transposed)	I.8	C1C3C4	♭	F
9	La tourmente en la mer couve sous la bonnasse	3 (Dorian)	I.9	C1C2C4	♮	D
10	La vie est un flambeau, un peu d'air qui soupire	3 (Dorian)	I.10	C1C2C4	♮	D
11	Le fruit sur l'arbre prend sa fleur, et puis se nouë	3 (Dorian), transposed	I.11	G2C1C3	♭	G
12	Cette vie est un arbre et les fruits sont les hommes	3 (Dorian), transposed	I.12	G2C1C3	♭	G
13	La vie est une table, où pour joüer ensemble	4 (Hypodorian)	I.13	G2C1C3	♮	D
14	La vie que tu vois n'est qu'une comedie	4 (Hypodorian)	I.14	G2C1C3	♮	D
15	Le monde est une mer, la galere est la vie	4 (Hypodorian)	I.16	G2C1C3	♮	D
16	La vie est une guerre estrangere et civile	4 (Hypodorian), transposed	I.15	C1C3C4	♭	G
17	Volontiers je compare au Parlement le monde	5 (Phrygian)	I.17	C1C3C4	♮	E
18	Le monde est de l'humeur d'une belle maistresse	5 (Phrygian)	I.18	C1C3C4	♮	E
19	La faveur de la vie est la sphere de verre	5 (Phrygian), transposed	I.19	G2C1C3	♭	A

(*continued*)

Table A2.4. Continued

No.	Incipit	Mode	No. in Mathieu, *Tablettes*	Cleffing	System	Final
20	Cet honneur t'alterant d'une soif d'hydropique	5 (Phrygian), transposed	I.20	G2C1C3	♭	A
21	Et cette ambition qui te donne des aisles	6 (Hypophrygian)	I.21	C2C3F3	♮	E
22	Ce plaisir qui l'oreille à la raison estoupe	6 (Hypophrygian)	I.22	C2C3F3	♮	E
23	Ce plaisir qui te lasse et jamais ne te saoule	6 (Hypophrygian)	I.23	C2C3F3	♮	E
24	La beauté qui des Roys ouvre et ferme la bouche	6 (Hypophrygian), transposed	I.24	G2C2C4	♭	A
25	Une beauté sans grace est un vaisseau sans voiles	7 (Lydian)	I.25	G2C1C3	♮	F
26	Quand la beauté du corps rencontre	7 (Lydian)	I.26	G2C1C3	♮	F
27	Cette beauté que l'air, le vent, la fiebvre efface	7 (Lydian), transposed	I.27	C1C3F3	♭	Bb
28	L'or du monde, l'Amour, le Soleil des abismes	7 (Lydian), transposed	I.28	C1C3F3	♭	Bb
29	De l'homme le sçavoir n'est que pure ignorance	8 (Hypolydian)	I.29	C1C3C4	♮	F
30	De ce qu'il n'entend pas l'ignorant se travaille	8 (Hypolydian)	I.30	C1C3C4	♮	F
31	L'Empire d'Assyrie est tout reduit en cendre	8 (Hypolydian), transposed	I.31	G2C1C3	♭	Bb
32	Où sont ces Empereurs, ces foudres de la guerre	8 (Hypolydian), transposed	I.32	G2C1C3	♭	Bb
33	Où sont tant de citez, si grandes, et si fortes?	9 (Mixolydian)	I.33	G2C1C3	♮	G
34	Tous ces grands bastiments, et ces chasteaux	9 (Mixolydian)	I.34	G2C1C3	♮	G
35	Veux tu voir des grands Roys jusqu'où va la ruine?	9 (Mixolydian), transposed	I.35	C1C3F3	♭	C
36	Voy ce Prince escorché du grand Caire à la porte	9 (Mixolydian), transposed	I.36	C1C3F3	♭	C
37	Voy Gordian qui pend à sa propre ceinture	10 (Hypomixolydian)	I.37	C1C3C4	♮	G
38	Voy de foudre accablé l'orgueilleux Salmonée	10 (Hypomixolydian)	I.38	C1C3C4	♮	G

No.	Incipit	Mode	No. in Mathieu, *Tablettes*	Cleffing	System	Final
39	Voy Attale qui n'a pour sa cour qu'une forge	10 (Hypomixolydian), tranposed	I.39	G2C1C3	♭	C
40	Qui n'aura de l'effroy aux frayeurs de la France	10 (Hypomixolydian), tranposed	I.40	G2C1C3	♭	C
41	Cette Reyne qui n'eut qu'un Chasteau pour retraitte	11 (Aeolian)	I.41	G2C2C3	♮	A
42	Ce Roy qui pouvoit voir en ses Estats	11 (Aeolian)	I.42	G2C1C3	♮	A
43	Celuy qui prefera son jardin de Salone	11 (Aeolian)	I.43	G2C1C3	♮	A
44	D'un insensible cours à la mort l'homme tire	11 (Aeolian)	I.44	G2C1C3	♮	A
45	La mort tuë en tout lieu, au bain Aristobule	11 (Aeolian), transposed	I.45	C1C3C4	♭	D
46	Tel se sauve en la mer, qui se perd en un fleuve	12 (Hypoaeolian)	I.46	C1C3C4	♮	A
47	Toute main luy est bonne, Eric meurt par sa mere	12 (Hypoaeolian)	I.47	C1C3C4	♮	A
48	En diverses façons sa face s'apprivoise, Henry	12 (Hypoaeolian)	I.48	C1C3C4	♮	A
49	Elle peut par sa fureur en toute chose espandre	12 (Hypoaeolian), transposed	I.49	G2C1C3	♭	D
50	Aussi-tost un grand Roy qu'un berger elle emporte	12 (Hypoaeolian), transposed	I.50	G2C1C3	♭	D

Table A2.5. Artus Aux-Cousteaux, *Suite de la premiere parte des Quatrains de Mr Mathieu, mis en musique à trois voix, selon l'ordre des Douze Modes.* Paris: Robert III Ballard, 1652

No.	Incipit	Mode	No. in Mathieu, *Tablettes*	Cleffing	System	Final
1	Il n'y a point de mort soudaine à l'homme sage	1 (Ionian)	I.51	C1C3C4	♮	C
2	Puisque tu ne sçais pas où la mort te doit prendre	1 (Ionian)	I.52	C1C3C4	♮	G
3	Si l'enfant sort du monde aussi-tost qu'il y entre	1 (Ionian)	I.53	C1C3C4	♮	C
4	Pourquoy le bon s'en va, et le meschant demeure	1 (Ionian)	I.54	C1C3C4	♮	C
5	Si du cours de tes ans tu retranche le somme	2 (Hypoionian)	I.55	G2C1C3	♮	C
6	Une rage de dents, une fiebvre, une goutte	2 (Hypoionian)	I.56	G2C1C3	♮	E
7	Quand le terme est venu tu veux payer de fuite	2 (Hypoionian)	I.57	G2C1C3	♮	G
8	Ne remets du depart à demain tes affaires	2 (Hypoionian)	I.58	G2C1C3	♮	C
9	Te plaignant de mourir en la fleur de ton aage	3 (Dorian)	I.59	C1C2C4	♮	D
10	Dresse de tes vertus non de tes jours le compte	3 (Dorian)	I.60	C1C3C4	♮	A
11	La vie par l'effet s'estime, et non par l'aage	3 (Dorian)	I.61	C1C3C4	♮	A
12	Les actes longs ne font bonne la comedie	3 (Dorian)	I.62	C1C3C4	♮	D
13	Qui pour n'avoir vescu cent ans avant que naistre	4 (Hypodorian)	I.63	G2C1C3	♮	D

No.	Incipit	Mode	No. in Mathieu, *Tablettes*	Cleffing	System	Final
14	L'homme n'est pas heureux pour longtemps vivre	4 (Hypodorian)	I.64	G2C1C3	♮	D
15	Et si la mort t'attend et ton sejour prolonge	4 (Hypodorian)	I.65	G2C1C3	♮	A
16	Si celuy qui t'a mis du monde en la carriere	4 (Hypodorian)	I.66	G2C1C3	♮	D
17	Il conduit bien son œuvre et cognoist tes caprices	5 (Phrygian)	I.67	C1C2C4	♮	E
18	Comme il ordonne l'œuvre il veut qu'on la luy rende	5 (Phrygian)	I.68	C1C2C4	♮	E
19	Ou premiers ou derniers à tous la piste est faite	5 (Phrygian)	I.69	C1C2C4	♮	E
20	Tant plus dure ton corps, tant plus ton ame endure	5 (Phrygian)	I.70	C1C2C4	♮	E
21	L'esprit dedans ce corps est retenu par force	6 (Hypophrygian)	I.71	C2C3F3	♮	E
22	L'ame se plaint du corps, le corps se plaint de l'ame	6 (Hypophrygian)	I.72	C2C3F3	♮	A
23	Elle affranchit l'esprit du corps qui sert aux vices	6 (Hypophrygian)	I.73	C2C3F3	♮	B
24	L'ame n'est pas ce corps, son etoffe est plus belle	6 (Hypophrygian)	I.74	C2C3F3	♮	E
25	Si cette ame en ce corps tant de fois morfonduë	7 (Lydian)	I.75	G2C2C3	♮	F
26	Tu crains pour la douleur que cette mort ameine	7 (Lydian)	I.76	G2C2C3	♮	F

(*continued*)

Table A2.5. Continued

No.	Incipit	Mode	No. in Mathieu, *Tablettes*	Cleffing	System	Final
27	Quitte ces tremblements dont ta poictrine est pleine	7 (Lydian)	I.77	G2C2C3	♮	F
28	Le cœur te rompt quittant tes enfants tes entrailles	7 (Lydian)	I.78	G2C2C3	♮	F
29	Tu regrettes ta femme, et ton regret t'excuse	8 (Hypolydian)	I.79	C1C3C4	♮	F
30	Tu te plains de quitter la Cour et ses delices	8 (Hypolydian)	I.80	C1C3C4	♮	F
31	Le marinier qui va de naufrage en naufrage	8 (Hypolydian)	I.81	C1C3C4	♮	F
32	La Cour te trompe ainsi que l'ange des tenebres	8 (Hypolydian)	I.82	C3C4F4	♮	F
33	Tu voudrois en mourant exercer ta vengeance	9 (Mixolydian)	I.83	G2C1C3	♮	D
34	Tu voudrois voir meurir les fruicts de ta science	9 (Mixolydian)	I.84	G2C1C3	♮	G
35	Tu marches à tous pas par la pluye et la fange	9 (Mixolydian)	I.85	G2C1C3	♮	G
36	Tu fais autant de pas en la mort qu'en la vie	9 (Mixolydian)	I.86	G2C1C3	♮	G
37	Quand l'homme est embarqué de ce monde au navire	10 (Hypomixolydian)	I.87	C1C3C4	♮	G
38	On regrette celuy qui est content qu'il meure	10 (Hypomixolydian)	I.88	C1C3C4	♮	G
39	Courir à cette mort, c'est desespoir et rage	10 (Hypomixolydian)	I.89	C1C3C4	♮	D

No.	Incipit	Mode	No. in Mathieu, *Tablettes*	Cleffing	System	Final
40	Quand la derniere areine acheve l'horloge	10 (Hypomixolydian)	I.90	C1C3C4	♮	G
41	Il tarde au pelerin d'achever son voyage	10 (Hypomixolydian)	I.91	C1C3C4	♮	G
42	Pour un temps la clarté du soleil est ravie	11 (Aeolian)	I.92	G1C1C3	♮	A
43	Quel tort te fait la mort, dy mondain, je te prie	11 (Aeolian)	I.93	G1C1C3	♮	A
44	Coüard, tu crains passer sur cette estroitte planche	11 (Aeolian)	I.94	G1C1C3	♮	E
45	Au delà tu verras ces plaisantes campagnes	11 (Aeolian)	I.95	G1C1C3	♮	A
46	Que verras-tu de plus pour vivre davantage	11 (Aeolian)	I.96	G1C1C3	♮	A
47	La mort finit les maux, elle est le seul refuge	12 (Hypoaeolian)	I.97	C1C3C4	♮	A
48	A ce dernier départ l'ame rit, le corps pleure	12 (Hypoaeolian)	I.98	C1C3C4	♮	A
49	Comme l'aube, la mort est du jour la fouriere	12 (Hypoaeolian)	I.99	C1C4F4	♮	A
50	D'un eternel repos ta fatigue est suivie	12 (Hypoaeolian)	I.100	C3C4F4	♮	A

Select Bibliography of Printed Primary Sources

Note: The core repertoire of primary musical sources consulted for this study are listed in Appendix 1. All secondary sources have been fully referenced in the notes and can be located in the index.

Alciato, Andrea. *Emblemata / Les emblemes*. Translated by Claude Mignault. Paris: Jean Richer, 1584.

———. *Les Emblemes*. Translated by Jean Lefevre and Jean II de Tournes. Geneva/Cologny: Jean II de Tournes, 1615.

Aneau, Barthélemy. *Imagination poétique*. Lyon: Macé Bonhomme, 1552.

Bellot, Nicolas. *Le Stoïque chrestien, ou la Victoire de la joye innocente et vertueuse sur la tristesse*. Paris: Jean Paslé, 1655.

Beza, Theodore. *Icones, id est verae imagines virorum doctrina simul et pietate illustrium . . . quibus adiectae sunt nonnullae picturae quas Emblemata vocant*. Geneva: Jean I de Laon, 1580.

———. *Les Vrais Pourtraits des hommes illustres . . . plus, Quarante Quatre Emblemes chrestiens*. Translated and edited by Simon Goulart. Geneva: Jean I de Laon, 1581.

Boissard, Jean Jacques. *Emblematum liber / Emblemes latins . . . avec l'interpretation françoise du I. Pierre Joly*. Metz: Jean Aubry and Abraham Faber, 1588.

Brués, Guy de. *Les Dialogues de Guy de Brués, contre les nouveaux Academiciens, que tout ne consiste point en opinion*. Paris: Guillaume Cavellat, 1557.

Chandieu, Antoine de. *Octonaires sur la vanité et inconstance du monde*. Strasbourg: Bernard Jobin, 1580.

———. *Meditations sur le Psalme XXXII . . . Ont esté aussi adjoustez cinquante octonaires sur la vanité du monde. Par A. Zamariel*. Geneva: G. Laimarie, 1583.

Charron, Pierre. *De la sagesse*. Bordeaux: S. Millanges, 1601.

Cicero. *The Booke of Marcus Tullius Cicero entituled Paradoxa Stoicorum. Contayninge a Precise Discourse of Divers Poinctes and Conclusions of Vertue and Phylosophie According the Traditions and Opinions of those Philosophers, which were called Stoikes. Whereunto is also Annexed a Philosophicall Treatyse of the same Authoure called Scipio hys Dream*. London: T. Marshe, 1569.

———. *Œuvres de M. T. Cicéron, père d'éloquence latine*. Paris: [Maurice Menier] Gilles Corrozet, 1552.

———. *Les Offices de M. T. Cicero, avec les traitez de l'Amitié, de Vieillesse, des Paradoxes, du Songe de Scipion*. Paris: G. Buon, 1583.

———. *Traduction des Paradoxes de Cicéron avec des notes*. Translated by Pierre Coustel. Paris: Charles Savreux, 1666.

Colletet, Guillaume. *Traité de la poésie morale et sentencieuse*. Paris: Sommaville et Chamhoudry, 1658.

Corrozet, Gilles. *Hécatomgraphie*. Paris: Denis Janot, 1540.

———. *Propos memorables, des nobles et illustres hommes de la chrestienté: Augmentez de plusieurs graues et excellentes sentences, des anciens Hebrieux, Grecz, et Latins*. Lyon: Benoist Rigaud, 1579.

Du Chesne, Joseph, sieur de La Violette. *La Morocosmie ou De la folie, vanité et inconstance du monde*. Lyon: Jean II de Tournes, 1583.

Duplessis-Mornay, Philippe. *Excellent discours de la vie et de la mort*. [Geneva]: Jean Durant, 1576.

———. *A Discourse of Life and Death. Written in French by Ph. Mornay and Antonius, a Tragœdie written also in French by Ro. Garnier*. Translated by Mary Sidney Herbert, Countess of Pembroke. London, 1592.

Du Vair, Guillaume. *De la constance et consolation ès calamitez publiques*. Paris: [Mamert Patisson] Abel L'Angelier, 1594.

———. *De la saincte philosophie*. Paris: Abel l'Angelier, 1587.

———. *De l'eloquence françoise*. Paris: Abel l'Angelier, 1594.

———. *Œuvres du Sr. Du Vair Garde des Sceaux de France comprises en cinq parties. Derniere edition, reveuë et corrigée*. Paris: Pierre Billaine au Palais, 1619.

———. *La Philosophie morale des Stoiques*. Paris: [Abel l'Angelier], 1585.

Epictetus. *La Doctrine d'Epictete stoicien, comme l'homme se peut rendre vertueus, libre, heureus et sans passion*. Translated by André Rivaudeau. Poitiers: E. de Marnef, 1567.

———. *Le Manuel d'Epictete . . . Les sentences des philosophes de Grece*. Translated by Antoine du Moulin 2nd ed. Lyon: Jean de Tournes, 1544.

———. *Le Manuel d'Epictete [Les Responses d'Epictete aux demandes de l'empereur Adrian.]* Translated by Guillaume Du Vair. Paris: A. Langelier, 1591.

Erasmus, Desiderius. *La Louange de la sotise*. Translated by Hélie Poirier. La Haye: Theodore Maire, 1642.

Estienne, Henri. *L'Art de faire les devises, où il est traicté des hieroglyphiques, symboles, emblèmes*. Paris: J. Paslé, 1645.

Gomberville, Marin le Roy de. *Doctrine des mœurs, tirée de la philosophie des Stoiques*. Paris: [Louys Sevestre] Pierre Daret, 1646.

Goulart, Simon. *Le Sage Vieillard descrit de divers authers*. Lyon: Antoine de Harsy, 1606.

———. *Six paradoxes chrestiens*. [Geneva: Gabriel Cartier]: Jacob Stoer, 1593.

Jaquemot, Jean. *Sententiae quaedam ex Senecae epistolis excerptae et singulis tetrastichis expressae a Ioanne Iacomoto Barrensi. Quatrains tirez des Epistres de Senecque traduits du latin de Jean Jaquemot de Bar le Duc, par S. G. S. Ausquels a este adjousté le Censeur Chrestien imité du latin de M. TH. D. B. par ledit S. G. S*. Geneva: Fran. Le Fevre, 1608.

La Mothe Le Vayer, François de. *Petit discours chrestien de l'immortalité de l'âme, Le même: avec le corollaire et un Discours sceptique sur la musique*. 2nd ed. Paris: [s.n.], 1640.

La Noue, Odet de. *Paradoxe que les adversités sont plus necessaires que les prosperités*. Lyon: Jean II de Tournes, 1588.

La Perrière, Guillaume de. *Le Theatre des bons engins, auquel sont contenus cent emblemes*. [Paris: Denis Janot, 1540].

La Primaudaye, Pierre de. *Académie françoise*. Paris: Guillaume Chaudière, 1577.

———. *Suite de l'Académie françoise, en laquelle il est traicté de l'homme*. Paris: Guillaume Chaudière, 1580.

La Serre, Jean Puget de. *L'Esprit de Sénèque, ou les plus belles pensées de ce grand philosophe*. Paris: André Soubron, 1657.

———. *Le Tombeau des delices du monde*. Paris: Philippe Gaultier, 1630.

L'Aubespine, Madeleine de. *Des saines affections*. [s.l.: s.n.] 1584; [Paris: Abel L'Angelier], 1591.

Le Gendre, Marie. *L'Exercice de l'âme verteuse*. Paris: Jean Le Blanc, 1596.

Le Jeune, Claude. *Dodecacorde contenant douze Pseaumes de David, mis en musique selon les douze modes, approuvez des meilleurs autheurs anciens et modernes à 2.3.4.5.6. et 7. voix*. La Rochelle: Hierosme Haultin, 1598.

L'Espine, Jean de. *De tranquillitate animi, libri VII*. Translated by Thierri Gautier. [Geneva]: Jacob Stoer, 1591.

L'Estocart, Paschal de. *Sacrae cantiones, quatuor, quinque, sex et septem vocum*. Lyon: Barthélemy Vincent, [Geneva: Jean I de Laon], 1582.

Lipsius, Justus. *De constantia libri duo, qui alloquium praecipue continent in publicis malis*. Leiden: Christophe Plantin, 1584.

———. *Deux livres de la constance de Just. Lipsius: Esquels en forme de devis familier est discouru des afflictions, et principalement des publiques, et comme il se faut resoudre à les supporter*. Tours: Jamet Mettayer, 1592.

Maisonfleur, Étienne de. *Les Cantiques du sieur de Maisonfleur*. Paris: A. Chuppin, 1581.

Marcus Aurelius. *Institution de la vie humaine*. Translated by Pardoux Du Prat. Lyon: Vve G. Cotier, 1570.

———. *Pensées morales de Marc Antonin . . . De soy et à soy-mesme, en douze livres*. Translation by Baron Mathias Balbisky. Paris: Vve J. Camusat and P. Le Petit, 1651.

Mathieu, Pierre. *Tablettes de la vie et de la mort*. Lyon: Pierre Rigaud, 1611.

———. *Tablettes ou Quatrains de la vie et de la mort*. Rouen: Jacques Cailloüe, 1628.

Ménestrier, François. *L'Art des emblemes*. Lyon: Benoist Coral, 1662.

Mersenne, Marin. *Harmonie universelle contenant la théorie et la pratique de la musique*. Paris: S. Cramoisy, 1636.

Montaigne, Michel. *Essais*. Bourdeaux: Simon Millanges, 1580.

Montenay, Georgette de. *Emblemes, ou Devises chrestiennes*. Lyon: Jean Marcorelle, 1567/ 1571.

Petrarca, Francesco. *De remediis utriusque fortunae*. Lyon: Clementem Baudin, 1577.

Pibrac, Guy du Faur de. *Cinquante Quatrains, contenans préceptes et enseignemens utiles pour la vie de l'homme, composez à l'imitation de Phocylidees, d'Epicharmus et autres anciens poëtes grécs*. Paris: Gilles Gorbin, 1574.

———. *Les Quatrains du seigneur de Pybrac . . . de nouveau mis en leur ordre, et augmentez par ledict seigneur*. Paris: Frédéric Morel, 1576.

———. *Les Quatrains de Mr de Pybrac changez en sixains, a la maniere dont on parle aujourd'huy. Avec des annotations qui expliquent les entroits les plus difficiles, pour l'instruction des enfans*. Paris: Jacques Langlois, 1687.

———. *Les Quatrains des sieurs Pybrac, Fabre et Mathieu: ensemble les plaisirs de la vie rustique. Enrichis de figures en taille-douce*. Paris: Antoine Robinot, 1640.

———. *Recueil des poincts principaux de la remonstrance faicte en la Cour de Parlement de Paris, à l'ouverture des plaidoiries aprés la feste de Pasques 1569*. s.l., 1570.

Plutarch. *Œuvres morales et meslées de Plutarque*. Translated by Jacques Amyot and edited by Simon Goulart. Geneva: François Estiene, 1581.

Poèmes chrestiens et moraux. [Geneva: Jean II de Tournes], [c. 1600].

Seneca. *De la consolation de la mort*. Translated by Ange Cappel. Paris: Felix le Magnier, 1584.

———. *Epistres de L. Annœe Seneque, philosophe tres-excellent*. Translated by Geoffrey de la Chassaigne, souldan de Pressac. Paris: Guillaume Chaudière, 1582.

———. *Œuvres morales et meslées de Senecque*. Translated by Simon Goulart. 3 vols. Paris: Jean Houzé, 1595; 4th ed. Geneva: Jean Arnaud, 1606.

Sylvester, Josuah. *Du Bartas, His Divine Weekes and Workes, with a Complete Collection of all the other Most Delightfull Workes*. London: Humphray Lownes, 1621.

van Veen, Otto. *Quinti Horatii Flacci emblemata*. Antwerp: Hieronymus Verdussen, 1607; and Antwerp: Philip Lisaert, 1612.

Index

For the benefit of digital users, indexed terms that span two pages (e.g., 52–53) may, on occasion, appear on only one of those pages.

Tables and figures are indicated by *t* and *f* following the page number